道可道，非常道
無名天地之始。
故常無，欲以觀
此兩者同出而異

A TREASURY OF
MYSTIC TERMS

A TREASURY OF
MYSTIC TERMS

PART I
THE PRINCIPLES OF MYSTICISM

VOLUME 4
THE HIERARCHY OF CREATION

JOHN DAVIDSON

SCIENCE OF THE SOUL RESEARCH CENTRE

Published by:
G.P.S. Bhalla, Secretary
Science of the Soul Research Centre
Radha Soami Satsang Beas
Guru Ravi Dass Marg, Pusa Road,
New Delhi 110005, India

First Edition 2003

10 09 08 07 06 05 8 7 6 5 4 3 2 III II I

ISBN 81-901731-0-3

Printed in India

EDITED AND LARGELY WRITTEN BY

JOHN DAVIDSON

WITH THE HELP OF AN INTERNATIONAL TEAM

A Treasury of Mystic Terms has been compiled using the collective skills of an international team of researchers, contributors, assistant editors and readers with a wide variety of religious and cultural backgrounds. All members of the team are spiritual seekers, most of whom have found inspiration and encouragement in the teachings of the mystics of Beas in India. All those involved have given freely to this project, both as a source of inspiration for themselves, and as a way of showing to others the essential unity behind all the apparent variety in religion, philosophy and mysticism.

Everybody has a perspective or a bias – coloured glasses through which they view the world. So although every attempt has been made to handle each entry within its own religious or mystical context, if any particular perspective is detected, it will inevitably be that of the contributors and their perception of mysticism. This does not mean, of course, that the contributors have always been in agreement. The preparation of the *Treasury* has often resulted in healthy debate!

SEE VOLUME 1 FOR THE LIST OF RESEARCHERS AND CONTRIBUTORS

Contents

ACKNOWLEDGEMENTS

THE TRANSLATIONS OF THE BUDDHIST *DHAMMAPADA* are founded mostly upon the work of S. Radhakrishnan and Narada Thera.

Many scholarly translations of Zarathushtra's *Gāthās* into European languages have been made from defective Pahlavi translations. The translations here are from the Avestan, and are based largely on the original work of Dr I.R.S. Taraporewala.

Quotations from the *Ādi Granth* are from the English translation of Manmohan Singh.

Most of the translations of the *Bhagavad Gītā* have drawn upon the earlier translation of Swāmī Tapasyānanda.

The sayings of Heraclitus are found only as fragments, quoted in the works of other writers of antiquity. Various scholarly numbering systems exist for these fragments, the system employed here being that used by Philip Wheelwright in *Heraclitus* (Princeton, 1959).

Most of the translations of Rūmī's *Maśnavī* are based upon the work of R.A. Nicholson.

The indigenous Guaraní of eastern Paraguay, made up of three large subgroups – the Mbyá, the Paí Cayuá and the Avá-Chiripá – are described in books and articles by the most notable experts in this field, Miguel Alberto Bartolomé, León Cádogan, Alfred Métraux and Egon Schaden. Most of the information used for the Guaraní mystical terms derives from these scholars' studies of the Mybá and Avá-Chiripá. If a term is general to all indigenous Guaraní, it is labelled (G); if a term is known only to apply to the Avá-Chiripá subgroup, it is labelled (AC).

The transliteration conventions used for all Avá-Chiripá terms are the same as those used in Miguel Alberto Bartolomé's article, *Shamanism and Religion Among the Avá-Chiripá,* which resulted from his field studies in the northeastern region of Paraguay in 1968 and 1969. Bartolomé explains that since Paraguayan Guaraní has an officially recognized written form, he does not use phonetic symbols except the letter 'y' for the sixth guttural vowel.

Thanks are due to the many scholars and publishers whose work has contributed to this book. We greatly appreciate the publishers, copyright holders and administrators for giving their permission to include excerpts, as below. In all instances, all rights are reserved by the copyright holders. Full bibliographical details can be found in the bibliography. Dates in square brackets ([ ]), where provided, are of first publication. Excerpts from:

The Old Testament Pseudoepigrapha, 2 vols., ed. J.H. Charlesworth, Darton, Longman & Todd (London), Doubleday (New York), 1983; *The Jerusalem Bible,* copyright © 1966 by Doubleday (USA & Canada) and by Darton, Longman & Todd (rest of the world); reprinted by permission of Doubleday (USA & Canada), a division of Random House Inc. and by Darton, Longman & Todd (rest of the world).

The Concise Encyclopedia of Islam, Cyril Glassé, HarperCollins, 1989, copyright © 1989 by Stacey International and Cyril Glassé; reprinted by permission of HarperCollins Publishers Inc. (USA, Canada, Philippines); *The Concise Encyclopaedia of Islam,* Cyril Glassé, Stacey International, 1989, copyright © 1989 by Stacey International and Cyril Glassé; reprinted by permission of Stacey International (rest of the world).

Gabriel's Palace: Jewish Mystical Tales, selected and retold by Howard Schwartz, Oxford University Press, copyright © 1993 by Howard Schwartz; reprinted by permission of Oxford University Press, New York (USA & Canada) and Ellen Levine Literary Agency Inc. (rest of the world).

The Spiritual Heritage of India, Swami Prabhavānanda, 1993 [1962]; reprinted by permission of Sri Ramakrishna Math (India) and the Vedanta Society of Southern California (rest of the world).

The Thousand and Twelve Questions (Alf Trisar Šuialia): A Mandaean Text edited in Transliteration and Translation, E.S. Drower, 1960; reprinted by permission of Akademie-Verlag.

The Books of Jeu and the Untitled Text in the Bruce Codex, tr. Violet MacDermot, 1978; *The Canonical Prayerbook of the Mandaeans,* tr. E.S. Drower, 1959; *Nag Hammadi Studies* XI: *Nag Hammadi Codices V,2–5 and VI,* ed. Douglas M. Parrott, 1979 (*Acts of Peter and the Twelve Apostles,* tr. Douglas M. Parrott and R. McL. Wilson; *Apocalypse of Adam,* tr. George W. MacRae, ed. Douglas M. Parrott; *Apocalypse of Paul,* tr. George W. MacRae and William R. Murdock, ed. Douglas M. Parrott; *Asclepius,* tr. James Brashler, Peter A. Dirkse and Douglas M. Parrott; *Authoritative Teaching,* tr. George W. MacRae, ed. Douglas M. Parrott; *Concept of Our Great Power,* tr. Frederik Wisse, ed. Douglas M. Parrott; *Discourse on the Eighth and Ninth,* tr. James Brashler, Peter A. Dirkse and Douglas M. Parrott; *First Apocalypse of James,* tr. William R. Schoedel, ed. Douglas M. Parrott; *Second Apocalypse of James,* tr. Charles W. Hedrick, ed. Douglas M. Parrott; *Thunder: Perfect Mind,* tr. George W. MacRae, ed. Douglas M. Parrott);

Nag Hammadi Studies XX: *Nag Hammadi Codex II,2–7,* vol. 1, ed. Bentley Layton, 1989 (*Gospel of Philip,* tr. Wesley W. Isenberg; *Gospel of Thomas,* tr. Thomas O. Lambdin; *Hypostasis of the Archons,* tr. Bentley Layton); *Nag Hammadi Studies* XXII: *Nag Hammadi Codex I (the Jung Codex),* vol. 1, ed. Harold W. Attridge, 1985 (*Gospel of Truth,* tr. Harold W. Attridge and George W. MacRae; *Prayer of the Apostle Paul,* tr. Dieter Mueller; *Treatise on the Resurrection,* tr. Malcolm L. Peel; *Tripartite Tractate,* tr. Harold W. Attridge and Dieter Mueller); *Nag Hammadi Studies* XXVII: *Nag Hammadi Codices III,3–4 and V,1, with Papyrus Berolinensis 8502,3 and Oxyrhynchus Papyrus 1081,* ed. Douglas M. Parrott, 1979 (*Eugnostos the Blessed* and *Sophia of Jesus Christ,* tr. Douglas M. Parrott); *Nag Hammadi Studies* XXVIII: *Nag Hammadi Codices XI, XII, XIII,* ed. Charles W. Hedrick, 1990 (*Allogenes,* tr. John D. Turner and Orval S. Wintermute; *Sentences of Sextus,* tr. Frederik Wisse; *Trimorphic Protennoia,* tr. John D. Turner); *Nag Hammadi Studies* XXX: *Nag Hammadi Codex VII, XIII,* ed. Birger A. Pearson, 1996 (*Paraphrase of Shem,* tr. Frederik Wisse; *Second Treatise of the Great Seth,* tr. Roger A. Bullard and Joseph A. Gibbons; *Teachings of Silvanus,* tr. Malcolm L. Peel and Jan Zandee; *Three Steles of Seth,* tr. James M. Robinson); *Nag Hammadi Studies* XXXI: *Nag Hammadi Codex VIII,* ed. John H. Sieber, 1991 (*Zostrianos,* tr. John H. Sieber); *Nag Hammadi Studies* XXXIII: *Synopsis of Nag Hammadi Codices II,1, III,1 and IV,1 with BG 8502,2,* ed. M. Waldstein and Frederik Wisse, 1995 (*Apocryphon of John,* tr. Frederik Wisse); reprinted by permission of E.J. Brill Academic Publishers, Leiden, The Netherlands.

"Lower (Second?) Section of the Manichaean Hymns", tr. Tsui Chi, in *BSOAS* 11 (1943–46); "A Sogdian Fragment of the Manichaean Cosmogony", W.B. Henning, in *BSOAS* 12 (1947–48); reproduced by permission of Cambridge University Press.

The Authorized Version of the Bible (The King James Bible), the rights to which are vested in the Crown, are reproduced by permission of the Crown's Patentee, Cambridge University Press.

Sources of Chinese Tradition, vol. 1, comp. T. de Bary, Wing-tsih Chan and Burton Watson, *et al.,* 1960; *Chuang Tzu: Basic Writings,* tr. Burton Watson, 1968; reprinted by permission of Columbia University Press.

Fools Crow: Wisdom and Power, Thomas E. Mails, copyright © 1991 by Thomas E. Mails; reprinted by permission of Council Oak Books, 1290 Chestnut Street, San Francisco, CA 941109, USA.

Ḥadīth Ṣaḥīḥ al-Bukhārī, tr. M. Muhsin Khan; reprinted by permission of Dar-us-Salam Publications.

Firefly in the Night, Irene Nicholson, 1959; reprinted by permission of Faber and Faber.

Kashf al-Mahjūb: The Oldest Persian Treatise on Sufiism, 'Alī b. 'Uthmān al-Jullābī al-Hujwīrī, ed. & tr. R.A. Nicholson, 1970 [1911, 1936]; *The Mathnawī of Jalālu'ddīn Rūmī,* 8 vols., ed. & tr. with notes & commentary by R.A. Nicholson, 1925–1940; reprinted by permission of the Trustees of the E.J.W. Gibb Memorial Trust.

The Essential Kabbalah: The Heart of Jewish Mysticism, Daniel C. Matt, 1996, copyright © 1995 by Daniel C. Matt; *Gnosis on the Silk Road: Gnostic Texts from Central Asia,* tr. Hans-Joachim Klimkeit, 1993, copyright © 1995 by Hans-J. Klimkeit; reprinted by permission of HarperCollins Publishers Inc.

The Koran Interpreted, 2 vols., tr. A.J. Arberry, 1964 [1955]; reprinted by permission of HarperCollins Publishers Ltd.

Aristotle, vol. III, Loeb Classical Library vol. 400, tr. E.M. Forster and D.J. Furley, Cambridge, Mass., Harvard University Press, 1955; reprinted by permission of the publishers and the Trustees of the Loeb Classical Library. The Loeb Classical Library® is a registered trademark of the President and Fellows of Harvard College.

Tanakh: The Holy Scriptures, 2 vols., 1955, copyright © 1955 by the Jewish Publications Society; reprinted by permission of The Jewish Publication Society.

The Prayer Book: Weekday, Sabbath and Festival, including *Pirkei Avot (Ethics of the Fathers),* tr. Ben Zion Bokser, 1957; reprinted by permission of Mrs. Kallia Bokser.

Sufi Symbolism: The Nurbakhsh Encyclopedia of Sufi Terminology, 15 vols., Javad Nurbakhsh, tr. Terry Graham *et al.,* 1984–2001; reprinted by permission of Khaniqahi-Nimatullahi Publications.

A Manichaean Psalm-Book, Part II, ed. & tr. C.R.C. Allbery, 1938; reprinted by permission of Kohlhammer GmbH.

The Jerusalem Bible, English text rev. & ed. Harold Fisch, 1992; reprinted by permission of Koren Publishers Jerusalem Ltd.

The Wisdom of the Zohar: An Anthology of Texts, 3 vols., arranged by Fischel Lachower and Isaiah Tishby, with extensive introductions & explanations by Isaiah Tishby, tr. David Goldstein, 1989, 1991; reprinted by permission of the Littman Library of Jewish Civilization.

Gītagovinda of Jayadeva: Love Song of the Dark Lord, ed. & tr. Barbara Stoler Miller, 1984; *The Laws of Manu,* tr. G. Buhler, 1964; *The Padma Purāṇa,* 10 vols., tr. Dr N.A. Deshpande, 1988–91; *The Vedic Experience,* Raimundo Panikkar, 1997; reprinted by permission of Motilal Banarsidass.

"Shamanism Among the Avá-Chiripá", Miguel A. Bartolomé, in *Spirits, Shamans, and Stars: Perspectives from South America,* ed. David L. Browman and Ronald A. Schwarz, 1979; reprinted by permission of Mouton de Gruyter.

The Siva Samhita, tr. Rai Bahadur Srisa Chandra Vasu, 1999 [1914–15]; reprinted by permission of Munshiram Manoharlal.

The Apocryphal New Testament, tr. Montague Rhodes James, 1989 [1924]; *The Apocryphal Old Testament,* ed. H.E.D. Sparks, 1984; *The Secret Adam: A Study of Naṣoraean Gnosis,* E.S. Drower, 1960; reprinted by permission of Oxford University Press.

The Complete Dead Sea Scrolls in English, tr. Geza Vermes (Allen Lane, Penguin Press, 1997), copyright © by Geza Vermes, 1962, 1965, 1968, 1975, 1995, 1997; *The Conference of the Birds,* Farid ud-Din Attar, tr. Afkham Darbandi and Dick Davis (Penguin Classics, 1984), copyright © 1984 by Afkham Darbandi and Dick Davis; *The Rig Veda: An Anthology,* tr. & annotated Wendy Doniger O'Flaherty (Penguin Classics, 1981), London, copyright © 1981 by Wendy Doniger O'Flaherty; reproduced by permission of Penguin Books Ltd.

The Upanishads, 4 vols., tr. & commentary Swami Nikhilananda, Ramakrishna-Vivekananda Center, New York, 1990, 1994, copyright © 1949, 1952, 1956, 1959 by Swami Nikhilananda; *Self-Knowledge (Atmabodha),* tr. & commentary Swami Nikhilananda, Ramakrishna-Vivekananda Center, New York, 1989, copyright © 1946 by Swami Nikhilananda; reprinted by permission of the Ramakrishna-Vivekananda Center of New York.

Meditation and the Bible, Aryeh Kaplan, Samuel Weiser, New York, 1978; reproduced by permission of Red Wheel/Weiser.

The Book of Legends (Sefer ha-Aggadah): Legends from the Talmud and Midrash, ed. Hayim Nahmun Bialik and Yehoshua Hana Ravnitzky, tr. William G. Braude, copyright © 1992 by Schocken Books; reproduced by permission of Schocken Books, a division of Random House Inc.

Manichaean Literature, J.P. Asmussen, 1975; reprinted by permission Scholars' Facsimiles & Reprints.

The Manichaean Hymn-Cycles in Parthian, tr. M. Boyce, 1954; reprinted by permission of School of Oriental and African Studies and Professor Mary Boyce.

The Sufi Path of Love: The Spiritual Teachings of Rūmī, William C. Chittick, State University of New York Press, copyright © 1983 by the State University of New York; reprinted by permission of the State University of New York Press.

The Bhagavadgītā, tr. Kees W. Bolle, 1979; reprinted by permission of the University of California Press.

Black Elk Speaks: Being the Life Story of a Holy Man of the Oglala Sioux, John G. Neihardt, copyright © 1932, 1959, 1972 by John G. Neihardt, copyright © 1961 by the John G. Neilhardt Trust; reprinted by permission of the University of Nebraska Press.

"Mesopotamian Elements in Manichaeism", G. Widengren, in *Uppsala Universitets Arsskrift* 3 (1946); reprinted by permission of University Publications from Uppsala.

We have done our best to track down all the relevant copyright holders or administrators for all material for which it appeared copyright permission would be required. In the event of any errors or omissions, please advise us, so that matters may be rectified.

Thanks are also due to Dr John Smith, Faculty of Oriental Studies, Cambridge University, for making specialist character fonts available to us.

Abbreviations

General

cf.	*confero* (L. I compare), compare
e.g.	*exempli gratia* (L. for the sake of example), for example
ff.	following (pages, lines, etc.)
i.e.	*id est* (L. that is), that is (to say), in other words
lit.	literally
p.	page
pp.	pages
viz.	*videlicet,* from the Latin *videre* (to see) + *licet* (it is permissible), used to specify items
▸2	See *A Treasury of Mystic Terms,* Part II

Dates

b.	born
c.	*circa,* about
d.	died
fl.	flourished
AH	*Anno Hegirae,* the Islamic dating system, from 622 CE, the Hegira *(al-Hijrah),* the year of Muḥammad's flight to Madīnah
BCE	Before Common Era
CE	Common Era

Languages

A	Arabic
AC	Avá-Chiripá
Am	Aramaic
Av	Avestan
C	Chinese
G	Guaraní
Gk	Greek
H	Hindi
He	Hebrew
J	Japanese

L	Latin
M	Marathi
Md	Mandaean
P	Persian
Pa	Pali
Pu	Punjabi
Pv	Pahlavi
S	Sanskrit
Su	Sumerian
T	Tibetan
U	Urdu

Sources Cited

See *Bibliography* for full details of published works. Published collections of the writings of Indian Saints have been referred to in source references as below. Other collections published as the *Bānī, Granthāvalī, Padāvalī* or *Shabdāvalī* of various Indian Saints have been similarly abbreviated.

Bullā Sāhib kā Shabd Sār	*Shabd Sār*
Charaṇdās Jī kī Bānī	*Bānī*
Dhanī Dharamdās Jī kī Shabdāvalī	*Shabdāvalī*
Kabīr Sākhī Sangrah	*Sākhī Sangrah*
Keshavdās Jī kī Amīghūnt	*Amīghūnt*
Kullīyāt-i Bulleh Shāh	*Kullīyāt*
Shrī Nāmdev Gāthā	*Gāthā*

Other texts cited are abbreviated as follows:

AAA	*Apocryphal Acts of the Apostles,* vol. 2 (translation), ed. & tr. W.R. Wright.
ABP1–3	*Avesta: The Religious Book of the Parsees, from Professor Spiegel's German translation of the Original Manuscripts,* 3 vols., tr. A.H. Bleek.
AE	*Apocalypse of Elijah,* ed. G. Steindorff.
AH1–2	*Against Heresies,* in *The Writings of Irenaeus,* 2 vols., tr. A. Roberts and W.H. Rambaud.
AHM	*The Avestan Hymn to Mithra,* tr. & commentary Ilya Gershevitch.
AMBF	*Aḥādīś-i Maśnavī,* B. Furūzānfar.
AN	*Asrār-Nāmah,* Shaykh Farīd al-Dīn 'Aṭṭār Nīshābūrī, ed. Sayyid Ṣādiq Gawharīn.
ANP	*Ancient Nahuatl Poetry,* Daniel G. Brinton.
ANT	*The Apocryphal New Testament,* tr. M.R. James. See *Acknowledgements.*

AOT	*The Apocryphal Old Testament,* ed. H.E.D. Sparks. See *Acknowledgements.*
AW	*The Ancient Wisdom: An Outline of Theosophical Teaching,* Annie Besant.
AYA	*The Holy Qur'ān,* tr. & commentary 'Abdullah Yūsuf 'Alī.
BC	*The Books of Jeu and the Untitled Text in the Bruce Codex,* tr. Violet MacDermot. See *Acknowledgements.*
BDC	*The Book of Divine Consolation of the Blessed Angela of Foligno,* tr. M. Steegman.
BE	*Book of Enoch,* tr. R.H. Charles.
BES	*Black Elk Speaks: Being the Life Story of a Holy Man of the Oglala Sioux,* as told through John G. Neihardt. See *Acknowledgements.*
BGB	*The Bhagavadgītā,* tr. Kees Bolle. See *Acknowledgements.*
BGT	*Bhagavad Gītā,* tr. Swāmī Tapasyānanda.
BLBR	*The Book of Legends (Sefer ha-Aggadah): Legends from the Talmud and Midrash,* ed. Hayim Nahmun Bialik and Yehoshua Hana Ravnitzky, tr. W.G. Braude. See *Acknowledgements.*
BM1–2	*Bet ha-Midrash,* 2 vols., A. Jellinek.
BMJ1–6	*Bet ha-Midrash,* 6 vols., A. Jellinek.
BS	*Bulleh Shah: Love-intoxicated Iconoclast,* J.R. Puri and T.R. Shangari.
BSSS	*Bullā Sāhib kā Shabd Sār;* Belvedere Printing Works.
CAG	"Coptic Apocryphal Gospels", tr. F. Robinson.
CBD	*The Conference of the Birds,* Farid ud-Din Attar, tr. Afkham Darbandi and Dick Davis. See *Acknowledgements.*
CDB1–2	*Charaṇdās Jī kī Bānī,* 2 vols.; Belvedere Printing Works.
CDSS	*The Complete Dead Sea Scrolls in English,* Geza Vermes. See *Acknowledgements.*
CEI	*The Concise Encyclop(a)edia of Islam,* Cyril Glassé. See *Acknowledgements.*
CH	*The Clementine Homilies,* tr. Thomas Smith *et al.*
CHO1–2	*Commentarii ad Homeri Odysseam,* 2 vols., Eustathii.
CPM	*The Canonical Prayerbook of the Mandaeans,* tr. E.S. Drower. See *Acknowledgements.*
CTW	*Chuang Tzu: Basic Writings,* tr. Burton Watson. See *Acknowledgements.*
CV	*Call of the Vedas,* A.C. Bose.
DAA	*The Doctrine of Addai the Apostle,* tr. G. Phillips.
DDB1–2	*Dādū Dayāl kī Bānī,* 2 vols.; Belvedere Printing Works.
DDS	*Dhanī Dharamdās Jī kī Shabdāvalī;* Belvedere Printing Works.
DF	*Divine Flashes,* Fakhruddin 'Iraqi, tr. W.C. Chittick and P.L. Wilson.

DG1–2	*Dariyā Granthāvalī,* 2 vols., D.B. Shāstrī.
DH	*A Dictionary of Hinduism: Its Mythology, Folklore and Development,* James and Margaret Stutley.
DHA	*Dīvān-i Khwājah Ḥāfiẓ Shīrāzī,* ed. Sayyid Abū al-Qāsim Anjavī Shīrāzī.
DHM	*Dīvān-i Ḥāfiẓ;* Malik Ghulām Muḥammad & Sons.
DHWC	*The Dīvān-i-Ḥāfiẓ,* 2 vols., Khwāja Shamsu-d-Dīn Muḥammad-i-Ḥāfiẓ-i-Shīrāzī, tr. H. Wilberforce Clarke.
DIH	*Dīvān-i Ḥāfiẓ,* ed. Qāzi Sajjād Ḥusayn.
DL	*Divine Light,* Maharaj Charan Singh.
DMWA	*Dictionary of Modern Written Arabic,* Hans Wehr.
DOI	*A Dictionary of Islam,* T.P. Hughes.
DP1–4	*The Dialogues of Plato,* 4 vols., tr. B. Jowett.
DPB	*Daily Prayer Book,* tr. & annotated Philip Birnbaum.
DRA	*Discourses of Rūmī,* tr. A.J. Arberry.
DSM	*Discourses on Sant Mat,* Hazur Maharaj Sawan Singh.
DSS	*Sahasrānī,* Dariyā Sāhib, Hindi ms., tr. in *Dariya Sahib: Saint of Bihar,* K.N. Upadhyaya.
DSSB	*Dariya Sahib: Saint of Bihar,* K.N. Upadhyaya.
DSZ	*The Divine Songs of Zarathustra,* I.J.S. Taraporewala.
DYD	*Dariyā Yoga Darshan,* Ramman Dās.
EBB	*Early Buddhism and the Bhagavadgītā,* K.N. Upadhyaya.
EJCD	*Encyclopedia Judaica,* CD-ROM.
EKH	*The Essential Kabbalah: The Heart of Jewish Mysticism,* Daniel C. Matt. See *Acknowledgements.*
ESHS1–4	*Sancti Ephraemi Syri Hymni et Sermones,* 4 vols., T.J. Lamy.
ESR	*S. Ephraemi Syri, Rabulae episcopi Edesseni, Balaei aliorumque Opera selecta,* ed. J. Josephus Overbeck.
FCWP	*Fools Crow: Wisdom and Power,* Thomas E. Mails. See *Acknowledgements.*
FFF	*Fragments of a Faith Forgotten,* G.R.S. Mead.
FIN	*Firefly in the Night,* Irene Nicholson. See *Acknowledgements.*
FLI	*Farhang-i Lughāt va-Iṣṭilāḥāt va-Taʻbīrāt-i ʻIrfānī,* Sayyid Jaʻfar Sajjādī.
FMA	*al-Futūḥāt al-Makkīyah,* Ibn ʻArabī; Cairo, 1950.
FNI1–15	*Farhang-i Nūrbakhsh: Iṣṭilāḥāt-i Taṣawwuf,* 15 vols., Javād Nūrbakhsh.
FNT3	*Farhang-i Nūrbakhsh: Iṣṭilāḥāt-i Taṣawwuf,* vol. 3, Javād Nūrbakhsh (1983 edn.).
GD	*Gyān Dīpak,* Dariyā Sāhib, Hindi ms., tr. in *Dariya Sahib: Saint of Bihar,* K.N. Upadhyaya.
GDST	*Bar Guzīdah-'i Dīvān-i Shams Tabrīzī,* compiled by Jaʻfar Maḥjūb.

GGJ	*Gītagovinda of Jayadeva: Love Song of the Dark Lord,* ed. & tr. Barbara Stoler Miller. See *Acknowledgements.*
GGS	*Guzīdah-'i Ghazalīyat-i Shams (Selected Ghazals of Shams),* Jalaluddin of Balkh (Rūmī), selected by M.R.S. Kadkani.
GOSR	*The Gospel of Sri Ramakrishna: Conversations of Sri Ramakrishna with His Disciples,* Sri Ramakrishna Kathamrita, tr. Swami Nikhilananda.
GPJ	*Gabriel's Palace: Jewish Mystical Tales,* selected and retold by Howard Schwartz. See *Acknowledgements.*
GR1–2	*Ghaṭ Rāmāyaṇ,* Tulsī Sāhib, 2 vols.; Belvedere Printing Works.
GS	*The Gnostic Scriptures,* Bentley Layton.
GSR	*Gnosis on the Silk Road: Gnostic Texts from Central Asia,* tr. H-J. Klimkeit. See *Acknowledgements.*
HBE	*The Hebrew Book of Enoch,* tr. H. Odeburg.
HEDA	*The Hymns and Homilies of Ephraim the Syrian and the Demonstrations of Aphrahat the Persian Sage,* tr. J. Gwynn.
HEU	*108 Upanishads,* ed. Acharya Shivram Sharma.
HG	*Hymns to the Goddess: Translated from the Sanskrit,* Arthur & Ellen Avalon.
HQSA	*The Holy Qur'ān: English Translation of the Meaning and Commentary;* Custodian of the Two Holy Mosques.
HR2	*Handschriften-Reste in Estrangelo-Schrift aus Turfan, Chinesisch-Turkistan II,* F.W.K. Müller.
HRV1–2	*The Hymns of the Rgveda,* 2 vols, tr. R.T.H. Griffith.
HSB	*Ḥadīth Ṣaḥīḥ al-Bukhārī,* tr. M. Muhsin Khan; www.islamworld.net/#hadith. See *Acknowledgements.*
HTU	*One Hundred and Twelve Upanishads and Their Philosophy,* A.N. Bhaṭṭāchārya.
HV1–25	*Hindi Vishvakosh,* 25 vols., ed. Nagendranāth Vasu.
HYP	*Hatha Yoga Pradipika,* tr. Pancham Singh.
HZ	*History of Zoroastrianism,* M.N. Dhalla.
IDB	*Iḥyā' 'Ulūm al-Dīn,* Muḥammad ibn Muḥammad al-Ghazālī; Beirut.
IM	*Indian Mythology,* Veronica Ions.
IS	*Iṣṭilāḥāt-i Ṣūfīyah,* Farīd Aḥmad Ṣamdī.
ISJ	*Iṣṭilāḥāt al-Ṣūfīyah,* 'Abd al-Razzāq al-Qāshānī, ed. Muḥammad Kamāl Ibrāhīm Ja'far.
JB	*The Jerusalem Bible* (1966). See *Acknowledgements.*
JCL	*The CD-ROM Judaic Classics Library (The Soncino Talmud, The Soncino Midrash Rabbah, The Soncino Zohar, The Bible);* Institute for Computers in Jewish Life & Davka Corporation.
JM	*Das Johannesbuch der Mandäer,* M. Lidzbarski (German Translation).

JMM	*Das Johannesbuch der Mandäer,* M. Lidzbarski (Mandaean Text).
JPS	*Tanakh: The Holy Scriptures,* 2 vols.; Jewish Publication Society of America. See *Acknowledgements.*
KA1–10	*Kashf al-Asrār va-'Uddat al-Abrār,* 10 vols., Abū al-Fażl Rashīd al-Dīn Maybudī, ed. 'Alī Aṣghar Ḥikmat.
KB	*The Jerusalem Bible,* English text rev. & ed. Harold Fisch; Koren Publishers. See *Acknowledgements.*
KBS	*Kullīyāt-i Bulleh Shāh,* Faqīr Muḥammad.
KDA	*Keshavdās Jī kī Amīghūnt;* Belvedere Printing Works.
KFF	*Kitāb Fīhi mā Fīhi,* Jalāl al-Dīn Rūmī, ed. B. Furūzānfar.
KI	*The Koran Interpreted,* 2 vols., tr. A.J. Arberry. See *Acknowledgements.*
KJV	*The Authorized Version of the Bible (The King James Bible)* [1611]. See *Acknowledgements.*
KM	*Kashf al-Mahjūb: The Oldest Persian Treatise on Sufiism,* 'Alī b. 'Uthmān al-Jullābī al-Hujwīrī, ed. & tr. R.A. Nicholson. See *Acknowledgements.*
KS	*Kīmiyā-yi Sa'ādat,* Imām Muḥammad Ghazālī, ed. Aḥmad Ārām.
KSS	*Kabīr Sākhī Sangrah;* Belvedere Printing Works.
KSS1–4	*Kabīr Sāhib kī Shabdāvalī,* 4 vols.; Belvedere Printing Works.
KTA	*Kitāb al-Ta'rīfāt,* 'Alī ibn Muḥammad al-Jurjānī, ed. Ibrāhīm al-Ābyārī.
LM	*The Laws of Manu,* tr. G. Buhler. See *Acknowledgements.*
LOSM	*Light on Sant Mat,* Maharaj Charan Singh.
LSMH	"Lower (Second?) Section of the Manichaean Hymns", tr. Tsui Chi. See *Acknowledgements.*
LTTN	*Lao Tzu:* Text, Notes and Comments, Ch'en Ku-ying, tr. & adapted Rhett Y.W. Young and Roger T. Ames.
MA	*The Master Answers,* Maharaj Charan Singh.
MAR	*Mashrab al-Arwāḥ,* Shaykh Rūzbihān, ed. Khwājah Naẓīf Muḥarram.
MBAK	*Meditation and the Bible,* Aryeh Kaplan. See *Acknowledgements.*
MBB	*Ein Manichäisches Bet- und Beichtbuch,* W.B. Henning.
MBS	*Mīrābāī kī Shabdāvalī;* Belvedere Printing Works.
MDI	*Mystical Dimensions of Islam,* Annemarie Schimmel.
MDT	*Manichäische Dogmatik aus chinesischen und iranischen Texten,* E. Waldschmidt and W. Lentz.
MEM	"Mesopotamian Elements in Manichaeism", G. Widengren. See *Acknowledgements.*
MGK	*The Meaning of the Glorious Koran,* Marmaduke Pickthall.
MHCP	*The Manichaean Hymn-Cycles in Parthian,* M. Boyce. See *Acknowledgements.*
MHG	*Les mythes d'Homère et la pensée grecque,* Felix Buffière.

MII	*The Mandaeans of Iraq and Iran: Their Cults, Customs, Magic, Legends, and Folklore,* E.S. Drower.
MJR1–8	*The Mathnawī of Jalālu'ddīn Rūmī,* 8 vols., ed. & tr. with notes & commentary R.A. Nicholson. See *Acknowledgements.*
ML	*Manichaean Literature,* J.P. Asmussen. See *Acknowledgements.*
MM1–3	"Mitteliranische Manichaica aus Chinesisch-Turkestan", 3 vols., F.C. Andreas and W.B. Henning.
MMC	*The Mysteries of Mithra,* Franz Cumont, tr. Thomas J. McCormack.
MMS	*Sri Guru Granth Sahib: English and Punjabi Translation,* 8 vols., tr. Manmohan Singh.
MPB	*A Manichaean Psalm-Book,* Part II, ed. & tr. C.R.C. Allbery. See *Acknowledgements.*
MQ	*The Mystic Quest: An Introduction to Jewish Mysticism,* David Ariel.
MSP1–2	*Mysticism: The Spiritual Path,* 2 vols., Lekh Raj Puri.
MTJM	*Major Trends in Jewish Mysticism,* Gershom G. Scholem.
MV	*Message of the Vedas,* Sir Gokul Chand Narang.
NHS11	*Nag Hammadi Studies* XI: *Nag Hammadi Codices V,2–5 and VI,* ed. Douglas M. Parrott. See *Acknowledgements.*
NHS20	*Nag Hammadi Studies* XX: *Nag Hammadi Codex II,2–7,* vol. 1, ed. Bentley Layton. See *Acknowledgements.*
NHS22	*Nag Hammadi Studies* XXII: *Nag Hammadi Codex I (the Jung Codex),* vol. 1, ed. Harold W. Attridge. See *Acknowledgements.*
NHS27	*Nag Hammadi Studies* XXVII: *Nag Hammadi Codices III,3–4 and V,1, with Papyrus Berolinensis 8502,3 and Oxyrhynchus Papyrus 1081, Eugnostos and The Sophia of Jesus Christ,* ed. Douglas M. Parrott. See *Acknowledgements.*
NHS28	*Nag Hammadi Studies* XXVIII: *Nag Hammadi Codices XI, XII, XIII,* ed. Charles W. Hedrick. See *Acknowledgements.*
NHS30	*Nag Hammadi Studies* XXX: *Nag Hammadi Codex VII, XIII,* ed. Birger A. Pearson. See *Acknowledgements.*
NHS31	*Nag Hammadi Studies* XXXI: *Nag Hammadi Codex VIII,* ed. John H. Sieber. See *Acknowledgements.*
NHS33	*Nag Hammadi Studies* XXXIII: *Synopsis of Nag Hammadi Codices II,1, III,1, and IV,1 with BG 8502,2,* ed. M. Waldstein and Frederik Wisse. See *Acknowledgements.*
NLEM	*New Larousse Encyclopedia of Mythology,* intro. Robert Graves.
NR1–2	*The Nestorians and Their Rituals,* 2 vols., G.P. Badger.
OFP	*Origen on First Principles,* tr. G.W. Butterworth.
OG	*The Other Gospels,* ed. R. Cameron.
ONC	*Or Ne'erav,* Moses Cordovero, ed. Yehuda Z. Brandwein.
OTP1–2	*The Old Testament Pseudoepigrapha,* 2 vols., ed. J.H. Charlesworth. See *Acknowledgements.*
P	*Philebus,* Plato, tr. R.A.H. Waterfield.

PAH	"Some Parthian Abecedarian Hymns", M. Boyce.
PB	*The Prayer Book: Weekday, Sabbath and Festival,* including *Pirkei Avot (Ethics of the Fathers),* tr. Ben Zion Bokser. See *Acknowledgements.*
PM1–5	*Philosophy of the Masters,* 5 vols., Huzur Maharaj Sawan Singh.
POM	*The Path of the Masters,* Julian Johnson.
PP	"A Pahlavi Poem", W.B. Henning.
PP1–10	*The Padma Purāṇa,* 10 vols., tr. Dr N.A. Deshpande. See *Acknowledgements.*
PRC	*Pardes Rimmonim (Orchard of Pomegranates),* Moses Cordovero; Mordekai Etyah.
PS	*Pistis Sophia,* tr. Violet MacDermot.
PSB1–3	*Paltū Sāhib kī Bānī,* 3 vols.; Belvedere Printing Works.
PSGG	*Pistis Sophia: A Gnostic Gospel,* G.R.S. Mead.
QAL	*al-Qur'an,* tr. Syed Abdul Latif.
RAA	*Majmū'ah-'i Rasā'il Khwājah 'Abd Allāh Anṣārī,* ed. Muḥammad Shīrvānī.
RHP	*Recueil des hadiths Prophétiques et des sagesses Mahométanes,* al-Sayed Ahmad al-Hachimi, tr. Fawzi Chaaban.
RI	*The Religion of Islām: A Comprehensive Discussion of the Sources, Principles and Practices of Islām,* Maulānā Muḥammad 'Alī.
RM	*Rābi'a the Mystic and her Fellow-Saints in Islām,* Margaret Smith.
RMP	*A Reader in Manichaean Middle Persian and Parthian,* M. Boyce.
RNV1–4	*Rasā'il Shāh Ni'matullāhī Valī,* 4 vols., ed. Javād Nūrbakhsh.
RV	*The Rig Veda: An Anthology,* tr. & annotated Wendy D. O'Flaherty. See *Acknowledgements.*
SA	*The Secret Adam: A Study of Naṣoraean Gnosis,* E.S. Drower. See *Acknowledgements.*
SAC	"Shamanism Among the Avá-Chiripá", Miguel A. Bartolomé. See *Acknowledgements.*
SAE1–5	*Commentary on Maśnavī I,* 5 vols., Ṣārī 'Abdullāh Efendi.
SB	*Sar Bachan,* Soami Ji Maharaj (Swami Shiv Dayal Singh).
SBB	*Sahajobāī kī Bānī;* Belvedere Printing Works.
SBE	*Sultan Bahu,* J.R. Puri and K.S. Khak.
SBEG	*The Secret Books of the Egyptian Gnosis,* J. Doresse.
SBG	*Shrī Bhaktisāgar Granth: Parishishṭ Bhāg Sahit,* Swāmī Charaṇdās, ed. Shivdayālu Gauṛ.
SBP	*Sār Bachan Chhand-Band (Sār Bachan Poetry),* Swāmī Shiv Dayāl Singh.
SBPS	*Shrīmad Bhāgavata Purāṇam with Shrīdharasvāmin's Commentary,* ed. J.L. Shāstrī.

SBS1–2 *Sant Bānī Sangrah,* 2 vols.; Belvedere Printing Works.
SBSU *Sā'īn Bulleh Shāh;* Radha Soami Satsang Beas (Urdu).
SBU *Ḥaẓrat Sulṭān Bāhū;* Radha Soami Satsang Beas (Urdu).
SE *Sefer Eliyahu,* ed. M. Buttenwieser.
SED *A Sanskrit–English Dictionary,* H.H. Wilson.
SFMC "A Sogdian Fragment of the Manichaean Cosmogony", W.B. Henning. See *Acknowledgements.*
SG *Spiritual Gems,* Maharaj Sawan Singh Ji.
SHI *The Spiritual Heritage of India,* Swami Prabhavananda. See *Acknowledgements.*
SKB *Santon kī Bāṇī;* Radha Soami Satsang Beas.
SKS *Self-Knowledge (Atmabodha),* tr. & commentary Swami Nikhilananda. See *Acknowledgements.*
SMIK1–13 *The Sufi Message of Hazrat Inayat Khan,* 13 vols., Hazrat Inayat Khan.
SOL *Sayings of Our Lord: From an Early Greek Papyrus,* B.P. Grenfell and A.S. Hunt.
SOS *Science of the Soul,* Sardar Bahadur Maharaj Jagat Singh.
SPK *The Sufi Path of Knowledge: Ibn al-'Arabi's Metaphysics of Imagination,* William C. Chittick.
SPL *The Sufi Path of Love: The Spiritual Teachings of Rūmī,* William C. Chittick. See *Acknowledgements.*
SROH *Selections from the Rubaiyāt and Odes of Hāfiz,* tr. by a member of the Persia Society of London (F.M. Rundall).
SSE1–15 *Sufi Symbolism: The Nurbakhsh Encyclopedia of Sufi Terminology,* 15 vols., Javad Nurbakhsh, tr. Terry Graham *et al.* See *Acknowledgements.*
SSV *Siva Samhita,* tr. Rai Bahadur Srisa Chandra Vasu. See *Acknowledgements.*
STG *Shrī Tukārām Bāvāñchyā Abhangāñchī Gāthā,* ed. Shrī P.M. Lāḍ.
SUV *Sixty Upanisads of the Veda,* 2 vols., Paul Deussen, tr. from German, V.M. Bedekar and G.B. Palsule.
TAN1–2 *Tadhkirat al-Awliyā',* Shaykh Farīd al-Dīn 'Aṭṭār Nīshābūrī, ed. R.A. Nicholson.
TAT *Taṣawwuf va-Adabīyāt-i Taṣawwuf,* including *Mir'āt-i 'Ushshāq* (an anonymous glossary of Sufi terms), Y.E. Bertels, tr. from Russian into Persian by Sirus Izadi.
TSM *Thus Saith The Master,* Maharaj Charan Singh.
TTQ *The Thousand and Twelve Questions (Alf Trisar Šuialia): A Mandaean Text edited in Transliteration and Translation,* E.S. Drower. See *Acknowledgements.*
TVS *Thousand Ways to the Transcendental: Vishnu Sahasranama,* tr. & commentary Swami Chinmayananda.

U1–4	*The Upanishads,* 4 vols., tr. & commentary Swami Nikhilananda. See *Acknowledgements.*
VE	*The Vedic Experience,* Raimundo Panikkar. See *Acknowledgements.*
VP	*The Vishṇu Purāṇa,* tr. H.H. Wilson.
WBC1–4	*The Works of Bernard of Clairvaux, On the Song of Songs,* 4 vols., tr. K. Walsh and I.M. Edmonds.
WGMI	*With a Great Master in India,* Julian Johnson.
WO1–2	*The Writings of Origen,* 2 vols., tr. F. Crombie.
WTM1–3	*With the Three Masters,* 3 vols., Rai Sahib Munshi Ram.
WZ1–3	*The Wisdom of the Zohar: An Anthology of Texts,* 3 vols., arranged by Fischel Lachower and Isaiah Tishby. See *Acknowledgements.*
ZSS1–5	*The Zohar,* 5 vols., tr. Harry Sperling and Maurice Simon.

THE HIERARCHY OF CREATION

4.1 The Realms of Creation

Mystics have described the Lord's creation as a vast hierarchical system, spanning a multitude of heavens, the lower reflected, projected or emanated from the higher. Within the heart of all, and permeating everything through the divine creative power, lies the eternity of God Himself. At the 'periphery' is the physical world of gross matter, of the mind made physically manifest. Between are realms or heavens of increasing spirituality, where – in the lower heavens – the mind in a subtle form is still prevalent. These are the regions or heavens of the higher or greater mind, the highest point of which has been called the universal mind.

Many mystics, from different times and cultures, have consistently spoken of realms that equate to what in the English language have been called the astral and causal regions. Together with the physical universe, these comprise three worlds, existing within the realm of the greater mind. Within these realms are found the heavens and paradises – as well as the hells and infernal regions – of most of the world's religions.

Some mystics have also spoken of higher spiritual regions beyond the realms of the mind, between the uppermost borders of the greater or higher mind and the eternity of God. Like God Himself, all these worlds lie within. They are realms of being and are travelled – not in space – but in consciousness.

Terms describing this hierarchy of creation are found in this section, including those terms used for hell and some terms used for the physical universe. Some other terms for the physical universe are found in Section 6.2. Terms for the universal mind are in Section 6.1. Terms for eternity or the eternal realm are in Section 2.1.

Key entries: **aṇḍa**, **heavens**, **mānsarovar**, **regions**, **sahans dal kanwal**, **ta'ayyun**.

Abaddon (He) *Lit.* destruction; a rabbinic and Kabbalistic term for that part of *Gehenna* in which unrepentant and wicked souls suffer, without hope of escape. In *Revelations,* the New Testament apocalypse with a pronounced Jewish character, *Abaddon* is the name of the devil: "The angel of the bottomless Pit, whose name in the Hebrew tongue is *Abaddon,* but in the Greek tongue hath his name *Apollyon.*"[1]

See also: **Gehenna**.

1. *Book of Revelation* 9:11, *KJV.*

abyss That which is bottomless; from the Greek *abyssos* – without *(a)* depth *(byssos);* hence, hell; also, the physical universe; often contrasted with the Height, meaning eternity. It is often uncertain whether abyss refers to hell or this world, or both.

Seeming to refer specifically to this world, one of the Manichaean hymns in Parthian speaks of joy at the time of death, of release from the "abyss" of this world of "deception". Being "held captive in every place" refers to transmigration, a common theme in these hymns:

> Be glad of heart on this day of departing,
> for sickness is ended and all your troubles.
> And you shall go forth out of this deception,
> which has made you faint through distress
> and the agony of death.
> You were held back within the abyss,
> where all is turmoil;
> You were held captive in every place.
> *Manichaean Hymns, Angad Rōshnān VIIa:11–13; cf. MHCP pp.166–67*

In one of the Manichaean psalms in Coptic, addressed to "Jesus, my light", the devotee says that through the practice of "Wisdom", the mystic Word, he has been able to see from the highest to the lowest. Here, "abyss" is probably being used in a general sense to include both this world and the hellish regions:

> I have constantly practised your holy Wisdom,
> which has opened the eyes of my soul
> to the light of your glory;
> And made me see those things that are hidden
> and those that are visible:
> The things of the abyss (this world)
> and the things of the Height (God).
> *Manichaean Psalm Book CCLXVIII; cf. MPB p.86*

The gnostic *Trimorphic Protennoia* equates the "darkness" of this world with the "abyss":

And he (the Saviour) revealed himself
  to those who dwell in darkness,
  and he showed himself to those who dwell in the abyss;
And to those who dwell in the hidden treasuries (realms),
  he told ineffable mysteries;
And he taught unrepeatable doctrines
  to all those who became sons of the Light.

Trimorphic Protennoia 37:13–20, NHS28 pp.406–7

In a hymn attributed to the fourth-century Christian father, Ephraim Syrus, he speaks metaphorically of man's estate. He has been cast out of Eden (eternity) by the Adversary (the devil) into the "abyss of the dead" (this world), also referred to here as *Hadēs:*

From the Height of Eden, the Adversary cast me down,
  and into the abyss of the dead,
  he threw me down that he might deride me.
My beautiful garments (of pure spirituality)
  were swallowed up and do not exist.
I was confused and overthrown,
  and hurled down into *Hadēs.*
And behold I am made a nest of worms,
  and moths and tapeworms gnaw at me.

Ephraim Syrus, ESHS4 629:2; cf. MEM p.59

See also: **bihisht-u dūzakh**, **dūzakh**, **Gehenna**, **Hadēs**, **Height** (2.1), **hell**, **jahannam**, **naraka**, **outer darkness**, **Pit**, **Sheol**.

achint dīp, **achint kanwal** (H/Pu) *Lit.* island *(dīp)* or lotus *(kanwal)* without worry *(achint);* the carefree realm; in this context, *dīp* is derived from the Sanskrit, *dvīpa,* meaning 'island', not to be confused with *dīp* meaning an earthenware lamp or a lighthouse.

The expression has been used by Swāmī Shiv Dayāl Singh and Kabīr for a spiritual 'island' or region in *mahā sunn* (great void), a region of intense darkness on the upward approach to *bhanwar guphā* (rotating cave), the realm lying on the threshold of eternity:

In *mahā sunn, achint dīp* is like a vast lawn *(maidān).*

Swāmī Shiv Dayāl Singh, Sār Bachan Poetry 23:1.39, SBP p.198

In fact, Swāmī Shiv Dayāl Singh speaks of two regions in *mahā sunn, achint dīp* and *sahaj dīp:*

> I crossed *jhajhrī* (*lit.* sieve), and saw an opening
> that is mentioned in the writings of the Saints.
> On the right is *achint dīp,*
> on the left, *sahaj dīp* is situated.
> My soul made its way on the central path,
> and reached *bhanwar guphā,*
> where (the sound of) *sohang* was awakened.
> *Swāmī Shiv Dayāl Singh, Sār Bachan Poetry 6:3.27–29, SBP p.52*

In this context, "right" and "left" refer not to a spatial orientation, but to realms at the same level on the inner ascent. It is the "central path" that leads upward. Kabīr similarly describes *achint* as a "twelve-petalled" lotus on the "right" and *sahaj* as a "ten-petalled" lotus on the left.[1]

Swāmī Shiv Dayāl Singh also describes the creation as consisting of twelve centres or lotuses *(kanwals).* Here, he calls *achint dīp, achint kanwal.* According to this description, the first six centres are the six *chakras* or subtle energy centres of the physical universe, which lie within the body. The seventh is the central powerhouse of the astral realm, the thousand-petalled lotus *(sahans dal kanwal);* the eighth is the causal realm *(trikuṭī);* the ninth lies beyond the realms of the mind in *daswān dwār;* and the tenth – *achint kanwal* – is in *mahā sunn:*

> The tenth, *achint kanwal* is found in *mahā sunn.*
> The eleventh is in *bhanwar guphā,* and the twelfth in *sat lok.*
> *Swāmī Shiv Dayāl Singh, Sār Bachan Poetry 38:5.9–10, SBP p.340*

1. Kabīr, *Shabdāvalī* 1, *Bhed Bānī* 22:20, *KSS1* p.66.

aeon(s) (Gk. *aion*) *Lit.* an immeasurably long period of time; in gnosticism, a power, emanation or realm; a Greek term used by the gnostics, who invested it with a wide spread of meaning. It referred to the higher regions as well as the powers that rule them, both of which were considered to have emanated from God. Sometimes, God and eternity were also referred to as *aeons;* so too were the divine, creative Power and the Saviour.

In the *Acts of John,* John – in a long speech concerning Jesus – identifies the *aeons,* as well as other focuses of power in the creative hierarchy ("all authority and all power and … all angels"), as less than God:

It is not a man whom I preach to you to worship,
but God unchangeable, God invincible,
God higher than all authority and all power,
and elder and mightier than all angels
and creatures that are named, and all *aeons*.
If then you abide in him and are established in him,
you shall possess your imperishable soul.

Acts of John 104; cf. ANT p.256

Many of the gnostic texts describe the creation as consisting of a large number of these *aeons,* arranged in a complex hierarchy, the ones above creating those below. Thus, the author of the *Tripartite Tractate* speaks of the *"aeons* of the *aeons",* meaning the greater *aeons* from which the lesser *aeons* are emanated:

> All those who came forth from Him, who are the *aeons* of the *aeons,* being emanations and offspring of His procreative nature, they too, in the procreative nature, have given glory to the Father, as He was the cause of their establishment. This is what we said previously, namely that He creates the *aeons* as roots and springs and fathers, and that He is the one to whom they give glory.
>
> *Tripartite Tractate 67–68, NHS22 pp.218–21*

The same writer also says that all the powers in creation relate to God as the One they love and seek, but do not know:

> The entire system of the *aeons* has a love and a longing for the perfect, complete discovery of the Father, and this is their unimpeded agreement. Though the Father reveals Himself eternally, He did not wish that they should know Him, since He grants that He be conceived of in such a way as to be sought for, while keeping to Himself His unsearchable primordial Being.
>
> *Tripartite Tractate 71, NHS22 pp.224–25*

It was also understood that the *aeons* of the higher spiritual world were copied by the "great Demon", the negative power, in the formation of the realms within his jurisdiction:

The great Demon began to produce *aeons*
in the likeness of the real *aeons.*

Trimorphic Protennoia 40, NHS28 pp.412–13

The "real *aeons*" are the highest divine blueprint or pattern, so to speak, from which the lower *aeons* are formed.

In some instances, the *aeons* also refer to eternity, the eternal home of the soul, as in a Manichaean psalm addressed to Jesus:

> Your good fight I have set myself to....
> I will strip myself of the body of destruction,
> the habitation of the powers of death,
> and ascend on high to your *aeons*
> from which I was once separated;
> That I may receive your gifts,
> my merciful God, my Saviour, my Rescuer.
> *Manichaean Psalm Book CCLXVIII; cf. MPB pp.86–87*

Eternity is thus also known as the *"aeon"* or the "perfect *aeon*", as in the *Apocryphon of John,* where the writer has Jesus say:

> Behold, now I shall go up to the perfect *aeon.* I have completed everything for you in your hearing. And I have said everything to you that you might write them down and give them secretly to those of like spirit.
>
> *Apocryphon of John 31; cf. NHS33 p.175*

And:

> To Him belongs immeasurable purity....
> He is an *aeon*-giving *aeon*....
> He is life-giving Life....
> He gives the immeasurable, incomprehensible Light.
>
> How am I to speak with you about Him?
> His *aeon* is indestructible,
> at rest and existing in silence, reposing,
> being prior to everything.
> For He is the head of all the *aeons,*
> and it is He who gives them power in His goodness.
> *Apocryphon of John 4; cf. NHS33 pp.27, 29*

af'āl (A/P) *Lit.* acts; in Sufi terminology, the first plane above the physical is the world of Acts *('ālam al-Af'āl),* corresponding to the astral region. The world of God's Acts brings about the results seen in the physical plane, called the world of (God's) Signs or Works *('ālam al-Āthār).*

See also: **'olam ha-'assiah**.

āftāb (P) *Lit.* sun; equivalent to the Arabic *shams;* the solar aspect of physical manifestation; an aspect of *'ālam al-shahādah* (the visible world). In Islamic lore, *āftāb* is the abode of Jesus, though whether this is to be understood literally or mystically depends on the context. For Rūmī, the meaning would have been mystical:

When Jesus … found the ladder of God's light,
he hastened to the top of the fourth dome.
Rūmī, Maśnavī II:920; cf. MJR2 p.269

From now on let me sit with Jesus
on top of the fourth heaven!
Rūmī, Maśnavī I:649; cf. MJR2 p.37

See also: **'ālam al-shahādah**.

afterlife Life after death, the hereafter, the next world, the future life; a colloquial expression for existence after the death of the physical body.

The belief in an afterlife is common to all human societies. The forms of the belief, however, exhibit considerable variation, from a vague and shadowy existence (*e.g.* ancient Greek mythology), to resurrection of the decomposed corpse (*e.g.* Judaism, Christianity), to the independent existence of an immortal soul (*e.g.* Greek mysticism, Hinduism, Sikhism, gnosticism, Manichaeism). The belief in an immortal soul is also commonly associated with a belief in reincarnation and transmigration of the soul.

The afterlife may be a paradise or a hell, the one to which an individual goes usually being deemed to depend upon his deeds and bent of mind in life. Paradise consists of a blissful immaterial heavenly existence free from suffering, while hell is the reverse. The beliefs concerning the destination of paradise and hell are not always based upon universally accepted ethical values, however. In Aztec belief, only those who died in war, by sacrifice, by lightning, by drowning, in childbirth, or by certain diseases were admitted into paradise. The remainder made a made a four-year journey, beset with perils, through the nine hells of the underworld, *Mictlan* (under the northern deserts). Reaching the ninth, where dwelt the skull-faced god of death, *Mictlantecuhtli,* they either disappeared or found rest. Similarly, in Islam, it is believed that those who die a martyr's death in *jihād* (holy war), enter immediately into paradise *(al-jannah),* their sins being annulled and the formalities of judgment waived.

A few cultures have regarded the tomb as the actual dwelling place of the deceased. Thus, some graves in ancient Crete and the ancient Syrian city-state of Ugarit (now Ras Shamra) were equipped with pottery conduits to the surface to facilitate libations to the dead. Often, the grave has been perceived as the entrance to a vast subterranean realm, a dark and sombre pit or cavern, as in the Mesopotamian *kurnugia* (*lit.* land of no return), the Greek *Hadēs,* the Hebrew *Sheol,* and the Scandinavian *Hel.* Other dwelling places for the dead, reached by uncertain means, include the ancient Germanic *Niflheim* and the Aztec *Mictlan.* In such places, the dead may merely survive in a joyless eternity, or – if the afterlife is understood as a place of retribution – they may be tortured for their past misdeeds, in contrast to the heavenly abode to which the good have gone. Sometimes the underworld is under the dominion of an awesome ruler, such as the Mesopotamian *Nergal,* the Greek *Hadēs* or *Pluto,* the Hindu and Buddhist *Yāma,* or the Aztec *Mictlantecuhtli* and his wife *Mictecacíhuatl.*

In ancient Egypt, funeral rites presumed that the future welfare of the dead depended upon the adequate provision of material needs and comforts, although there is contemporaneous evidence of scepticism concerning the belief. Mortuary practices therefore included mummification and the provision of various articles such as pottery, jewellery, and amulets and charms of various kinds. Even the favourite dog of the deceased was sometimes sacrificed and interred with him for companionship and protection in the afterlife. Small statuettes, often holding implements such as hoes, were also included so that the deceased would be able to perform any menial tasks the gods might demand of him.

Christianity, which came to believe in both immediate retribution and a final Day of Judgment, developed the idea of a purgatory where the souls suffer for their venial sins in a disembodied state while awaiting physical resurrection. Likewise, the heavens and hells of Hinduism and Buddhism are places of reward or punishment before eventual reincarnation.

See also: **al-ākhirah**, **paraloka**.

air, **air of joy**, **airy-earth** Air is a term occasionally found in an esoteric or mystic context in ancient writings. Since terms for 'spirit' and 'wind' are the same in Greek, Hebrew and some other languages, the words for 'air' seem to have benefited by the closeness of meaning, and have become imbued with a spiritual undertone when used in esoteric literature.

The astral body, for example, was sometimes called the body of fire, while the more subtle causal body was known as the body of air.[1] These uses are metaphorical. The astral body glistens and sparkles as if sprinkled with stardust – hence the term 'astral' and the expression 'body of fire'. Likewise, the causal body, being more subtle than the astral, was said to be as if composed of air.

Interestingly, Paul speaks of Satan as the "Prince of the power of the air", certainly referring to him as a subtle power, possibly as a more specific reference to the devil as the force of negativity in the lower realms of creation that include this world. He is:

> The Prince of the power of the air,
> the spirit that now worketh
> in the children of disobedience.
>
> *Ephesians 2:2, KJV*

The term was also used as a general expression for the higher realms, like the term 'water'. In the gnostic text, the *Teachings of Silvanus,* for example, the realms and forces of negativity are described as "this kind of air which is full of powers":

> My son, prepare yourself to escape from the world-rulers of darkness and of this kind of air which is full of powers. But if you have Christ (the Saviour), you will conquer this entire world.
>
> *Teachings of Silvanus 117, NHS30 pp.366–67*

Similarly, in the revelational *Ascension of Isaiah,* the 'space' of each region is described as the "air" of that realm. It is an interesting term, for it implies something both subtle and spiritual, beyond all physical space, and beyond the capacity of earthly language to describe:

> And he (an angel) took me up into the air of the sixth heaven, and I beheld a glory I had not seen in the five heavens while I was being taken up, and angels resplendent in great glory.
>
> *Ascension of Isaiah 8:1–2, AOT p.800*

Likewise, speaking of those souls destined to be mystically baptized or initiated as the "generation of those men whom he had chosen for himself", another gnostic writer speaks of the advent of the Saviour, "out of a foreign air, from a great *aeon*". By "foreign" is implied the altogether otherworldliness of the spirit and of God in comparison to this world:

> Out of a foreign air, from a great *aeon,*
> the great Illuminator came forth.
> [And he made] the generation of those men
> whom he had chosen for himself, he made to shine.
>
> *Apocalypse of Adam 82–83; cf. NHS11 pp.188–89*

In *Zostrianos,* another writing in the revelational genre, the author speaks of being baptized and taken up into the higher realms, away from the "airy-earth", the aethereal or subtle realm, probably a reference to the astral regions or heavens just above the physical universe:

Then I knew that the Power in me
was greater than the darkness,
because it contained the whole Light.
I was baptized there,
and I received the image of the glories there.
I became like one of them.

I passed through the airy-[earth]
and passed by the copies of the *aeons,*
after washing there seven times in Living Water,
once for each of the *aeons.*
I did not cease until I had seen
all the waters (inner realms)....

I passed by the sixth *aeon.*
I ascended to the [seventh?]....
I stood there after having seen light
from the Truth which really exists,
from its self-begotten Root.

Zostrianos 5–6; cf. GS p.127, NHS31 pp.38–41

Zostrianos is not without its similarities to the *Ascension of Isaiah.* It speaks of the higher creation as divided into the seven heavens or *"aeons"* or "waters", for example. It also points out that the first heavens (the "airy-earth") passed through immediately upon leaving the physical universe are "copies of the *aeons*" – the higher *aeons,* that is.

Later in the same text, the writer repeats the expression and elucidates to some degree the meaning of "*aeon* copies" and the "airy-earth". They come, he says, from the Word; but unfortunately the document is full of *lacunae,* and the remainder is difficult to decipher:

> The great ruler on high, *Authrounios,* said to me: "Are you asking about those (regions) through which you have passed? And about this airy-earth, why it has a cosmic archetype? And about the *aeon* copies, how many there are, and why they do not suffer?" ...
>
> The great ruler on high, *Authrounios,* said to me, "The airy-earth came into being through a Word."
>
> *Zostrianos 8–9; cf. GS p.128, NHS31 pp.44–47*

As before, the "airy-earth" seems to refer to the lowest of the inner realms, and as such would equate to the astral realm of more modern terminology. This realm was regarded by the writer as a copy of higher realms. Literally translated, the term might be something like 'land of air', implying the subtlety of substance, an interweaving of mind and spirit of which both the astral and causal realms consist.

Reading these passages, it becomes clear that the biblical accounts of the prophet Elijah being taken up "by a whirlwind into heaven",[2] or of Jesus being "taken up ... into heaven" and "received by a cloud",[3] or of Paul's assertion that at the final resurrection (which he imminently expected), the faithful would be "caught up ... to meet the Lord in the air"[4] are not to be taken literally. They make much more sense when read as being 'taken up in the spirit' or 'meeting the Lord in the spirit'. The ascension was spiritual, not physical.

As a metaphor for the spirit, the term 'air' is also found in the Manichaean writings. In one psalm, for instance, the Perfect Man, the Master or Helmsman, is specifically hailed as both the "mooring harbour" and the "clear air":

> Hail, Perfect Man, holy path that draws to the Height,
> clear air, mooring harbour of all that believe in him:
> Open to me your secrets, and take me to you from affliction.
> As I come unto you today, O Kings of Light,
> O Helmsmen, open to me your doors
> and take me in unto you.
>
> *Manichaean Psalm Book CCLXVI; cf. MPB p.83*

In another psalm, the creative Power is referred to as "Wisdom", "Root" and "Air":

> I bless you, O glorious seat,
> the Sign of Wisdom;
> We worship the Sign of your greatness
> and your mysteries ineffable.
> You are the blessed Root....
> You are the gift of the Air.
> You are the manifestation of the victory of the Light.
>
> *Manichaean Psalm Book CCXXX; cf. MPB p.26*

In another, the soul encourages itself to rise up from the pleasures and enticements of the senses, mind and body "into the air of joy":

> Come to me, my Saviour, the haven of my trust.
> Bestir yourself, O my soul that watches in chains
> that have long endured,
> and remember the ascent into the air of joy;
> For a deadly lure is the sweetness of this flesh.
>
> *Manichaean Psalm Book CCXLV; cf. MPB p.52*

See also: **bird** (5.1), **Living Air** (3.1), **wind** (3.1).

1. *Untitled Text* 256–57:16, *BC* pp.274–77.
2. *2 Kings* 2:11, *KJV.*
3. *Acts* 1:9–11.
4. *1 Thessalonians* 4:17, *KJV.*

ākhirah, al- (A), **ākhirat** (P) *Lit.* the hereafter; often as *al-dār al-ākhirah* (the home of the hereafter); that place or state to which the soul goes after death; specifically, heaven, earned as a result of a good life:

> That home of the hereafter *(al-dār al-ākhirah),*
> we will give to those
> who intend not high-handedness or mischief on earth:
> And the end is (best) for the righteous.
>
> *Qur'ān 28:83, HQSA*

Mystics have never regarded life in this world as real life. It is the "hereafter" that holds true life:

> What is life of this world
> but amusement and play?
> But verily the home of the hereafter *(al-dār al-ākhirah)* –
> that is life indeed, if they but knew.
>
> *Qur'ān 29:64, HQSA*

In Islam, as in other religions, religious practices are often performed for the sake of earning merit *(thawāb)* in the hereafter, to ensure a place in heaven and to avoid hell. Describing heaven as 'the hereafter *(al-ākhirah)*' implies that it is to be experienced after death. The Sufi, by contrast, seeks the spiritual intoxication of union with God, higher even than the bliss of the heavenly realms, while still living in the body. Ḥāfiẓ, describing such a devotee as a "drunken one", writes:

> How fortunate is that drunken one
> who has thrown this world and the next *(ākhirat)* to the winds,
> without regret!
>
> *Ḥāfiẓ, Dīvān, DHA p.28, DHM (92:7) p.114, DIH p.75; cf. DHWC (70:7) p.171, in SSE3 p.191*

See also: **afterlife**, **'ālam**, **al-dunyā** (6.2), **paraloka**.

akhtar (P) (pl. *akhtarān, akhtar'hā*) *Lit.* star; in a mystical context, the inner heavens. Referring to the astrological association of the physical stars with a person's temperament, for example, Rūmī speaks metaphorically of the "stars" in the spiritual "heavens", "immanent in the radiance of the light of God":

Anyone who has an affinity with a star *(akhtar)*
has a concurrence with his star *(akhtar)*
If his ascendant star *(ṭāli')* be Venus,
his whole inclination and love and desire is for joy;
And if he be born under Mars,
one whose nature is to shed blood,
he seeks war and malignity and enmity.

Beyond the (material) stars *(akhtarān)* are stars *(akhtarān),*
in which is no conflagration *(iḥtirāq)* or sinister aspect.
(Stars) moving in other heavens,
not these seven heavens known to all;
(Stars) immanent in the radiance of the light of God,
neither joined to each other nor separate from each other.

Rūmī, Maśnavī I:751–56, MJR2 p.43

Here, an *iḥtirāq* (conflagration, burning) is an astronomical term for the disappearance of Venus, Mercury, Mars, Jupiter or Saturn due to closeness to the sun when viewed from earth, a configuration considered astrologically significant.

See also: **'ālam al-shahādah, tārā**.

akshar(a) (S/H) *Lit.* not *(a)* perishable *(kshar);* imperishable; hence, not of this perishable *(kshar)* world; indestructible, undecaying, unchanging, immutable; mystically, the imperishable One, the supreme Lord.

Kshar (perishable) is used as a term for *māyā* (illusion). Hence, *akshar* is also used as a name for the spiritual realm, also called *daswān dwār* (*lit.* tenth door) and *sunn* (*lit.* void), above *māyā* or *kshar*. Beyond *akshar* lies a region that some Saints have called *mahā sunn* (great void). Thus, Swāmī Shiv Dayāl Singh writes:

Only Saints have spoken of *mahā sunn,*
which is beyond *akshar.*
The *Vedas* have their origins in *akshar,*
but they do not know exactly what *akshar* is....

The reach of the *Vedas* and other holy books is below *akshar* or *sunn*.
None knew what lay beyond, Saints alone have revealed it.

Swāmī Shiv Dayāl Singh, Sār Bachan Poetry 11:1.61–62, 64–65, SBP p.100

Kabīr has called the ruler of this region *akshar Brahm* (lord of *akshar*), likening the divine Music of this realm to that of the Indian stringed instruments, the *kingrī, sārangī* and *sitār:*

The music of the *kingrī, sārangī* and *sitār* play continuously
in the *sunn* of *akshar Brahm*.

Kabīr, Shabdāvalī 1, Bhed Bānī 22:18, KSS1 p.66

See also: **akshara** (2.1), **kshara** (6.2), **nihakshar**.

'ālam (A/P) (pl. *'ālamīn;* A. *'ālamūn, 'awālim;* P. *'avālim*) *Lit.* universe, world, realm, region, domain; also, condition, state (of being). In the *Qur'ān*, the term is always used in the plural, *'ālamīn:* worlds, universes, creatures, nations. One of the more frequently used terms for God is *Rabb al-'ālamīn* (Lord of the worlds), which conveys the idea of God as the caring Sustainer of His creation. Indeed, the *Qur'ān* opens with the line:

Praise be to *Allāh*,
the Cherisher and Sustainer of the worlds *(Rabb al-'ālamīn).*

Qur'ān 1:2, HQSA

The implication is that the creation includes many worlds or many universes, not merely the material universe visible to the physical eyes; hence the expression, *'awālim al-kullīyah,* meaning 'all the worlds together', the entire creation.

In the *Qur'ān* itself and in most early Islamic writings, the emphasis is generally on only two *'ālamīn:* this transitory world *(dunyā)* and the next, the hereafter *(ākhirah)*. These are referred to in a number of ways and, in each case, pairing is used to emphasize that the spiritual world, though unseen, is more real and lasting than the transitory world. Thus, *'ālam al-shahādah* (visible, manifest world) is contrasted with *'ālam al-Ghayb* (world of the Unseen). *'Ālam al-khalq* (world of the creation) is brought into existence by the *'ālam al-Amr* (world of the Command). Sometimes, *'ālam-i khāk* (world of dust, clay or earth) or *'ālam-i suflī* (low world) are contrasted with *'ālam-i 'ulvī* (high or sublime world).

'Ālam al-mulk (world of the kingship) is another name for the physical world, which is ruled over by *'ālam al-malakūt* (world of the kingdom). Both of these terms are used in the *Qur'ān*. Al-Ghazālī says that there are two

doors in man's spiritual heart, one leading to *'ālam al-mulk,* the other to *'ālam al-malakūt.* The physical world is also called the *'ālam al-ḥiss* (sensory world).

Sufis have generally described the creation as divided into three, four, five or more *'ālamīn,* one above another. Each realm is governed by the one above it, and each realm provides energy to the one below it. The ultimate light of the Creator is thus refracted downward through all the levels of creation.

These realms are arranged not in space, but in being or consciousness. They are expressions or creations of the Supreme Being or Universal Consciousness. The distinguishing feature of each realm is the nature of the spiritual consciousness that pertains there. The journey of the individual soul back to its Source consists of progressive ascension through these realms. In each higher realm the consciousness is more and more refined, until at the ultimate height there is only consciousness of the Absolute. Different mystics may identify spiritual realms in varying ways, separating them into different numbers of levels. But the primary characteristic of ascending purity of spiritual consciousness is common to all.

A frequently encountered Sufi description of the *'ālamīn* consists of four or five realms: *'ālam al-mulk* is the lowest level or the physical plane; *'ālam al-malakūt* is the next higher, of which *'ālam al-mulk* is said to be a reflection. Above that lies *'ālam al-jabarūt* (world of power), the domain of angelic manifestation, surrounding and containing the realms below it. Above that, *'ālam al-lāhūt* (world of divinity), also called *'ālam al-'izzah* (world of glory), is sometimes used to include all the realms of pure spirit, including the Essence of God Himself. Sometimes, this highest spiritual realm is further divided into *'ālam al-lāhūt* and *'ālam al-hāhūt,* the former representing divinity as being, the latter as undifferentiated Essence.

Many Sufis have used the term *'ālam al-nāsūt* (world of humanity) in place of *'ālam al-mulk* to refer to the lowest plane of the creation. The use of *'ālam al-nāsūt* implies both the physical world itself, as well as the normal consciousness of the ordinary human being. It is typical of the *'ālamīn* terms to denote realms in the hierarchy of creation, as well as the characteristics of consciousness inherent in those realms. A normal, spiritually undeveloped human being perceives only through his physical senses; he does not perceive the subtle realms, and thus functions within the *'ālam al-nāsūt. Lāhūt* (divinity or the divine nature) and *nāsūt* (humanity or human nature) are antonyms. In common usage, the terms imply two poles of reality – limited human nature and the unlimited divine nature.

In another descriptive system, the physical world is called *ḥaḍrat al-shahādah al-muṭlaq* (manifestation of the totally visible); *malakūt* and *jabarūt* are referred to jointly as *ḥaḍrat al-Ghayb al-muḍāf* (manifestation of the relative Unseen); and the realm of pure divinity is called *ḥaḍrat al-Ghayb al-muṭlaq* (manifestation of the totally Unseen). Therefore, while *'ālam al-malakūt* (world of the kingdom) and *'ālam al-jabarūt* (world of power) are subtle realms relative to the physical world, they are within the 'qualified Unseen', and do not belong to the highest realms of refined spirit. *Kashf* (unveiling) consists of the soul's ascent from the physical realm through these increasingly pure and subtle worlds.

Another description divides the levels of creation into three *'ālamīn.* These are, in ascending order: *'ālam al-ajsām* (world of bodies), *'ālam al-mithāl* (world of likenesses or patterns) and *'ālam al-arwāḥ* (world of spirits). *'Ālam al-ajsām* represents the lower plane(s), where the soul is clothed with gross and subtle bodies. *'Ālam al-mithāl* is an intermediate world, refracting light from *'ālam al-arwāḥ.*

Mithāl – variously translated as likenesses, similitudes, patterns, ideas, image exemplars, archetypes, prototypes or blueprints – refers to the subtle unseen forms and forces that shape events in the world of bodies. The physical realm is a reflection of or a projection from subtle patterns that are hidden in *'ālam al-mithāl.*

Yet another Sufi cosmology describes seven levels of consciousness. The lowest three are considered *tashbīh* (to which some comparison can be made, hence perceptible, capable of description); these are the familiar *'ālamīn: ajsām, mithāl* and *arwāḥ.* Above the *tashbīh* planes are the *tanzīh* (stainless, beyond comparison, imperceptible, beyond all description); these are given names, all meaning 'oneness', but in various degrees *(wāḥidīyah, waḥdah* and *aḥadīyah).* Above this is the Essence of God *(al-Dhāt).*

Following the Islamic belief that there is no reality but God, some Sufis have described the creation as descriptions of aspects or levels of the Lord's own being. In descending order these are: the world of God's Essence *('ālam al-Dhāt),* the world of God's Names *('ālam al-Asmā'),* the world of God's Attributes *('ālam al-Ṣifāt),* the world of God's Acts *('ālam al-Af'āl),* and the world of God's Signs *('ālam al-Āthār).* Shabistarī associates God's Signs with *'ālam al-mulk* (the physical plane), God's Acts with *'ālam al-malakūt* (world of the kingdom), God's Attributes with *'ālam al-jabarūt* (world of power), and God's Essence with *'ālam al-lāhūt* (world of divinity), the stage of merging in the Lord.

In this descriptive system, all of creation, from the most subtle to the most coarse level of manifestation, is regarded as aspects of the one divine Being. The planes of consciousness that make up the creation range from the most inward, essential level of that Being to His most outward and superficial expressions.

At the physical level, only His Signs *(Āthār),* the results of His Acts, can be observed; but neither He nor His Acts can be seen. In the realm above, His Acts *(Af'āl),* of which the physical world is the result, can be observed. Above that, the Attributes *(Ṣifāt)* giving rise to the Acts, can be observed. Beyond that, the divine realities called divine Names *(Asmā'),* which bring the Attributes into being, can be observed. At the level of the ultimate Reality is found the innermost Essence *(al-Dhāt)* of the divine Being.

Seeming inconsistencies are found in Sufi literature, however, and different names have been used by different writers for the same regions. Likewise, the same names have been used for different regions. These differences may be attributable in part to shifts in nomenclature, as Sufism spans many centuries, many countries and a number of languages. Thus, in the writings of some of the earlier Sufis, including al-Ghazālī and Ibn 'Aṭā' Allāh, the term *malakūt* is used for the realm above *jabarūt. Malakūt* is portrayed as the realm of angels and 'light substances', while *jabarūt* is an intermediate world or isthmus *(barzakh)* refracting the light from *malakūt.* But Sufis of the *Waḥdah al-Wujūd* (Oneness of Being) school – Ibn 'Arabī and his followers – and most Sufis who came later, used these two terms in the opposite order, with *jabarūt* above *malakūt.*

In addition to terminology using *'ālam,* the Sufis also described the subtle realms traversed by the soul on its spiritual ascent as a series of *maqāmāt* (stations) or *manāzil* (abodes, stages) or *marātib* (stages) or *ta'ayyunāt* (entifications, individuations of the one Lord) or *ḥaḍarāt* (manifestations).

See also: **aṇḍa**, **'olam**, **regions**.

'ālam al-Amr (A), **'ālam-i Amr** (P) *Lit.* realm *('ālam)* of the Command *(Amr);* the world or universe of Command; that which takes its existence from the Real without secondary cause. The world of creation *('ālam al-khalq)* and the world of Command *('ālam al-Amr)* are contrasted in the *Qur'ān.*[1] *Khalq* is 'the created' and *Amr* is the creative Power. R.A. Nicholson defines *'ālam al-Amr* as the "spiritual world brought into existence immediately and directly, without space and time, by the divine fiat, '*Kun* (Be)!'"[2] Rūmī says:

> The pomp and grandeur belonging
>   to the world of creation *(khalq)* is a borrowed thing;
> The pomp and grandeur belonging
>   to the (world of) Command *(Amr)* is an essential thing.
>
> *Rūmī, Maśnavī II:1103, MJR2 p.278*

See also: **'ālam**, **al-Amr** (3.1), **jihah** (5.2), **al-khalq**.

1. *Qur'ān* 7:54.
2. R.A. Nicholson, *Commentary on Maśnavī* II:1103, *MJR7* p.280.

'ālam al-arwāḥ (A), **'ālam-i arvāḥ** (P) *Lit.* world *('ālam)* of spirits *(arwāḥ), arwāḥ* being the plural of *rūḥ* (spirit). Sufis sometimes spoke of three worlds, in ascending order: the world of bodies *('ālam al-ajsām),* the world of patterns *('ālam al-mithāl)* and the world of spirits *('ālam al-arwāḥ).* Each world is a reflection of the one above it. The world of spirits is sometimes also called *'ālam al-ma'ānī* (world of meanings).

See also: **'ālam**, **ñe'eng-güery**.

'ālam al-Ghayb (A), **'ālam-i Ghayb** (P) *Lit.* world *('ālam)* of the Unseen *(al-Ghayb);* the unseen world, the invisible world, the hidden world. Refers to all the *'ālamīn* (realms) beyond the physical world; all that is hidden from the physical senses. Sometimes separated into *al-Ghayb al-muṭlaq* (the totally Unseen) representing the highest of the subtle realms, and *al-Ghayb al-muḍāf* (the qualified Unseen) representing the lower of the subtle realms.

See also: **'ālam**, **al-Ghayb**.

'ālam al-iṭlāq (A), **'ālam-i iṭlāq** (P) *Lit.* world *('ālam)* of release *(iṭlāq);* world of liberation; world of Nonexistence, where the soul has no existence separate from that of God. Before a soul is embodied in a created form, it is in the *'ālam al-iṭlāq.* When the soul is placed in a human body, it is in the *'ālam al-taqayyud* (world of binding), imprisoned by the limitations of separated earthly existence:

> In the *'ālam-i iṭlāq* (world of Nonexistence), God was my Beloved. In childhood, after I came into the *'ālam-i taqayyud* (binding world), I had faint glimpses of Him. But the older I grew, the more my bodily senses were darkened, and I became further and further removed from God.
>
> *Anon., in SROH p.24*

See also: **'ālam al-taqayyud**.

'ālam al-'izzah (A), **'ālam al-'izzat**, **'ālam-i 'izzat** (P) *Lit.* world *('ālam)* of the glory *('izzah);* also called *'ālam al-lāhūt.* According to one system of Sufi nomenclature, the ascending realms above the physical plane are called, in order: the kingdom *(malakūt),* the power *(jabarūt)* and the glory *('izzah).*

See also: **'ālam**.

'ālam al-jabarūt (A), **'ālam-i jabarūt** (P) *Lit.* world *('ālam)* of power *(jabarūt);* derived from *jabr* (force, compulsion); a term for the second or sometimes the third subtle realm above the physical world.

See also: **'ālam**.

'ālam al-khalq (A), **'ālam-i khalq** (P) *Lit.* realm *('ālam)* of the creation *(khalq);* the physical world, brought into being from the *'ālam al-Amr* (world of the Command).

See also: **'ālam, al-khalq**.

'ālam al-malakūt (A), **'ālam-i malakūt** (P) *Lit.* world *('ālam)* of dominion *(malakūt);* the first or sometimes the second realm above the physical realm; the location of many of the paradises mentioned in various scriptures. *'Ālam al-malakūt* is entered after the awakening of the faculties of inner perception, when the spiritual soul breaks free from the confinement of the physical body. The transition from the physical plane to the *'ālam al-malakūt* is for this reason called *mawt ikhtiyārī* (voluntary death, mystical death).

See also: **'ālam, Malkut**.

'ālam al-mithāl (A), **'ālam-i miśāl** (P) *Lit.* world *('ālam)* of patterns *(mithāl);* the world of likenesses, similitudes, symbols, archetypes; sometimes translated as the world of imagination, of image exemplars, or even of blueprints or prototypes. Sufi cosmology points out that each realm is a reflection of the realm above it. Thus, the physical world is a reflection of *'ālam al-mithāl,* which contains the subtle essences or patterns, the subtle forms and forces from which this world is derived. *'Ālam al-mithāl* is in turn a reflection of the next higher, vaster and 'more real' region, *'ālam al-arwāḥ* (world of spirits) or *'ālam al-ma'ānī* (world of meanings). *'Ālam al-mithāl* has sometimes been used for *'ālam al-malakūt* (world of dominion), sometimes for *'ālam al-jabarūt* (world of power) and sometimes for both at the same time, since both are patterns or exemplars of the worlds below.

These are not patterns or similitudes in the sense of metaphors, but real essences or energies that are the seed form, so to speak, of what lies below. *'Ālam al-mithāl* probably corresponds to Plato's 'world of ideas'. Scholars have commonly taken such descriptions to be an intellectual system, having no reality in terms of something that actually exists. Mystics differ.

'Ālam-i miśāl is also called *'ālam-i khayāl, khayāl* meaning fantasy or imagination. The term embodies the reality taught by mystics that this world

is the expression of mental impressions – of dreams and fantasies. There is a saying *(ḥadīth),* traditionally attributed to Muḥammad: "Men are asleep, and when they die, they awake."[1]

See also: **'ālam**, **khayāl** (5.1).

1. *Ḥadīth, AMBF* 222, in *MDI* p.382.

'ālam al-mulk (A), **'ālam-i mulk** (P) *Lit.* world *('ālam)* of the kingship *(mulk);* the physical world.

See also: **'ālam**, **Malkut**.

'ālam al-nāsūt (A), **'ālam-i nāsūt** (P) *Lit.* world *('ālam)* of humanity *(nāsūt);* the material world that is perceived through the physical senses. *'Ālam al-nāsūt* also indicates the ordinary condition of human consciousness, limited to physical perception and intellect, before the mystic journey is begun. This identification of a plane of the creation with the consciousness pertaining to it is characteristic of Sufi teaching. *Nāsūt* is the natural human state in which a Muslim lives when following the rules of the *sharī'ah* (the religious law), including both the teaching of the *Qur'ān* and of the traditional sayings of Muḥammad.

See also: **insānīyah**.

'ālam al-shahādah (A), **'ālam-i shahādat** (P) *Lit.* world *('ālam)* of witnessing *(shahādah);* the visible world, the manifested world; the world that is visible to the physical senses; the physical universe. *'Ālam al-shahādah* is considered to lie below the spiritual world, also called the world of Command *('ālam al-Amr)* and the world of the Unseen *('ālam al-Ghayb).*

Sufis generally describe *'ālam al-shahādah* as comprised of seven aspects of manifestation:

1. *Sitārah*	stellar.
2. *Mahtāb*	lunar.
3. *Āftāb*	solar.
4. *Ma'danīyah*	mineral-ness, the mineral kingdom.
5. *Nabātīyah*	vegetable-ness, the vegetable kingdom.
6. *Ḥayavānīyah*	animal-ness, the mineral kingdom.
7. *Insānīyah*	human-ness, mankind.

The realm of minerals is an aspect of God's manifestation in the visible world. It is also a station or stage of spiritual development; the beings in the station of minerals *(ma'danīyah)* have a particular type of mind or life.

Similarly, the vegetable kingdom *(nabātīyah)* and the animal kingdom *(ḥayavānīyah)* are aspects of God's manifestation in the visible world, and are also stations or stages of spiritual development.

The human aspect or station *(insānīyah)* is the crown of all, because from this station the soul can reach the spiritual world, beyond the limits of the visible universe. But few souls in the visible world reach the station of true humanness, though many have the human form.

The first three aspects of manifestation of the visible world – *sitārah* (stellar), *mahtāb* (lunar) and *āftāb* (solar) – are related to the nine heavens of traditional Islamic cosmology, based upon the geocentric system of the Greeks and also used in descriptions of the visible world:

1. The firmament of the Moon or *mahtāb.*
2. The firmament of Mercury.
3. The firmament of Venus.
4. The firmament of the Sun or *āftāb.*
5. The firmament of Mars.
6. The firmament of Jupiter.
7. The firmament of Saturn.
8. The firmament of the fixed stars or *sitārah,* also called *al-kursī* (God's footstool).
9. The starless heaven, also called *al-'arsh* (God's throne).

These nine heavens, however, are variously described. In other descriptions, they include the seven paradises or heavens *(sab' samāwāt),* and in that context are clearly beyond the boundaries of the physical universe.

Some descriptions of the aspects of manifestation in the visible world *('ālam al-shahādah)* include only *al-'arsh, al-kursī, āftāb, mahtāb,* and the four types of forms made up of the gross elements and perceptible to the gross senses: animal, mineral, vegetable and human.

See also: **'ālam**.

'ālam al-taqayyud (A), **'ālam-i taqayyud** (P) *Lit.* world *('ālam)* of binding or confinement *(taqayyud);* the realm in which the soul is bound or imprisoned; hence, the material realm.

See also: **'ālam al-iṭlāq**, **prison** (6.3).

'ālam-i khāk (P) *Lit.* world *('ālam)* of dust *(khāk);* world of clay, world of earth; the physical world, contrasted with the *'ālam-i 'ulvī* (high world), as in a verse of uncertain authorship, and attributed to both Ḥāfiẓ and Rūmī:

> I know for certain that my essence (soul)
> is from the higher worlds *('ālam-i 'ulvī).*
> I intend to return wherefore....
>
> I am a bird of paradise,
> not from this world of dust *('ālam-i khāk).*
> For a few days I am imprisoned in this body.
>
> *Rūmī, Dīvān-i Shams-i Tabrīz, GDST pp.114–15, GGS p.5*

All (the) A gnostic term referring to the entire creation, as in the *Gospel of Thomas:*

> Jesus said,
> "It is I who am the Light that is above them all,
> it is I who am the All.
> From me did the All come forth,
> and unto me did the All extend.
> Raise the stone and there you will find me,
> cleave the wood and there I am."
>
> *Gospel of Thomas 46:77, Oxyrhynchus Papyri 5:2; cf. NHS20 pp.82–83, SOL pp.12*

Hence, the writer of the *Acts of Peter* has Peter say of Jesus, in a devotional prayer:

> You are the All and the All is in you:
> You *are,*
> and there is nothing else that *is* save you alone.
>
> *Acts of Peter XXXIX; cf. ANT p.335*

In an untitled gnostic text from the *Bruce Codex,* God is described as the "First Source" and "First Father of the All". It is also said that the "All" comes into being through the "First Sound":

> He is the First Father of the All,
> He is the First Eternity....
> He is the First Source.
> He it is whose Voice has penetrated everywhere.
> He is the First Sound
> whereby the All perceived and understood.
>
> *Untitled Text 226:1; cf. BC pp.214–15, FFF p.547*

Similarly, in the *Trimorphic Protennoia,* the creative Power 'speaks' as the underlying force that creates and sustains the "All":

> I am the invisible One within the All....
> I am immeasurable, ineffable, yet whenever I wish,
> I shall reveal myself of my own accord.
> I am the head of the All.
> I exist before the All, and I am the All,
> since I exist in everyone....
> I am the One who gradually put forth (manifested)
> the All by my Thought.
>
> *Trimorphic Protennoia 35:24,28–32, 36:6–8, NHS28 pp.402–5*

The description of the creative hierarchy that makes up the All is considered by the writer of the *Pistis Sophia* to be secret, when he has Jesus say:

> I will not tell you these things now, but when I begin to tell you of the expansion of the All, I will tell them all to you, one by one: namely its expansion and its description of how it is, and the harmony of all its members that belong to the organization of the only One, the true, inaccessible God.
>
> *Pistis Sophia 243:98; cf. PS pp.486–87, PSGG p.202*

The same writer also indicates that the All is not eternal, but will suffer dissolution at some later time:

> All this which I have told you will not happen at this time, but it will happen at the end of the *aeon,* that is, at the dissolution of the All.
>
> *Pistis Sophia 196:86; cf. PS pp.392–93, PSGG p.164*

As regards the seekers of God, they are advised in the same book to escape from the All, to leave the creation and return to God:

> Say to them (the God-loving): "Renounce the All, that you may receive the mysteries of the Light, and go to the Height, to the kingdom of the Light."
>
> *Pistis Sophia 261:102, PS pp.522–23; cf. PSGG p.218*

amṛit sar (H), **amrit sar** (Pu) *Lit.* lake *(sar)* of Nectar *(amṛit),* pool of Nectar; a shortened form of *amṛit kā sarovar,* from the Sanskrit *amṛit* and *sarovar* (lake). Generally, the term refers to the all-pervading spiritual bliss and nourishment of the creative Power by which the soul is encompassed and permeated in the higher realms. It is similar to such expressions as the well of Living Water and the Fountain or Spring of eternal life.

Specifically, *amṛit sar* refers to the state of bliss, tranquillity, equipoise – a condition or a degree of spiritual purity or divine consciousness obtained in the regions beyond the realms of mind and matter where all desire ends. There, the soul, washed clean of all sins, impurities and imperfections, and rid of the physical, astral and causal bodies, finds itself fully awakened and energized and, in its natural and pristine glory, begins the final process of identification with the Creator – its true Source. In this sense, *amṛit sar* is equivalent to the term *mānsarovar.* Guru Amardās writes:

> In the body is the true pool of nectar *(amrit sar),*
> and the soul indrinks it with love and devotion.
>
> *Guru Amardās, Ādi Granth 1046, MMS*

Guru Rāmdās writes that the *Satguru,* the Master, is the *amrit sar:*

> God incarnate, the true *Guru,* is the pool of nectar *(amrit sar):*
> the fortunate ones come and bathe therein.
> Their filth of many births is washed off,
> and the immaculate Name *(nirmal Nām)* is implanted within them.
>
> *Guru Rāmdās, Ādi Granth 40, MMS*

Amritsar, first known as Rāmdāspur, is also the name of a city in the Punjab, held sacred by the Sikhs, having grown out of the small community founded by Guru Rāmdās in 1564 CE.

See also: **mānsarovar**.

aṇḍ(a) (S/H) *Lit.* egg, egg-shaped; mystically, the astral region. Kabīr, Swāmī Shiv Dayāl Singh and the Masters following him have spoken of the creation as divided into three grand divisions, above which is the realm of the Godhead. By creation here is meant not only the physical universe, but also all the higher, finer, more subtle regions.

The three divisions are: *piṇḍa,* the physical universe, experienced through the physical body below the level of the eye centre; *aṇḍa,* the astral region from the eye centre to the bottom of *trikuṭī* (*lit.* three peaks); and *brahmāṇḍa,* from *trikuṭī* to the top of *bhanwar guphā* (*lit.* rotating cave). Beyond these three divisions lies *sat desh* (true or real country), the eternity of God. As understood in Hindu mythology, where the term originates, *brahmāṇḍa* is actually a general term for the created worlds. In the present context, the term is given a more specific meaning.

Piṇḍa, the physical universe, is composed of matter of varying density, but essentially coarse in quality. It includes the six bodily *chakras* or subtle energy centres, and their corresponding subtle planes. Here, spirit, in the form of the creative Power or Word, is greatly obscured. Spirit is the only thing that is self-existent – without it, matter would not exist. Matter may be considered as spirit in a much depleted form. It has a low intensity of vibration. Compared to the eternity, it is pitch dark here, and life is scarcely perceptible. It is full of imperfections, and is marked by a state of heavy inertia. As the soul leaves this lowest phase and ascends into higher realms of consciousness, light increases, and there is more vibration, more life, beauty and happiness.

Aṇḍa is the next grand division, above and beyond *piṇḍa.* It extends from the eye centre to the threshold of *trikuṭī.* The words 'above' and 'beyond' are not used in a physical, but in a spiritual sense. These higher worlds could just as well be described as planes of consciousness. But when a soul passes from one plane to another, it feels as if it is traversing immense space. *Aṇḍa* is far greater in extent than *piṇḍa,* it has a much finer composition and vibratory character, and the all-pervading Spirit is less concealed. Its central powerhouse or headquarters is *sahans dal kanwal* (the thousand-petalled lotus), also called *sahasrāra* (*lit.* thousand-spoked). This great group of one thousand lights, each one said to possess a different hue, is the powerhouse from which flows the energy that creates and sustains all the worlds below, including the physical universe. Extraordinarily beautiful, it is far superior to anything seen on the earthly plane.

Aṇḍa is the astral plane, the 'heaven' of most religions. It is probably the region referred to by Plato when he speaks of a more perfect world: a world of 'ideals', images or patterns of which the physical world is an imitation.[1] Just as the soul has contact with the physical world through a physical body and a physically oriented mind, so too is it in contact with *aṇḍa* through an astral body *(sūkshma sharīr)* and an astral mind *(aṇḍī man).*

The third grand division, lying beyond *aṇḍa,* is called *brahmāṇḍa.* It extends from the upper part of *trikuṭī* to the gateway of *sat desh.* It is of far greater extent than *aṇḍa,* more refined and more luminous. Spirit predominates here as does matter in *piṇḍa,* while *aṇḍa* is intermediate between the two. The lower aspect of *trikuṭī* faces *aṇḍa* and the higher aspect faces *daswān dwār. Trikuṭī* is also known as the causal region or universal mind. It is practically all mind, which is matter of the most refined order, with a high admixture of spirit. The soul remains in contact with the causal plane through a causal body *(kāraṇ sharīr)* and a causal mind *(kāraṇ man)* of corresponding subtlety.

The part of *brahmāṇḍa* beyond *trikuṭī* is known as *pārbrahm* (beyond *Brahm*). Here, the ascending soul bathes in the lake of immortality, *mānsarovar,* severing forever its ties to the lower regions. Here, too, it knows itself as soul for the first time. After travelling through *mahā sunn* (great void), an area of intense darkness that the soul can only cross with the help of a perfect Master, it reaches *bhanwar guphā.*

The realm above *piṇḍa, aṇḍa* and *brahmāṇḍa* is *sat desh.* It is the region of divine Truth or ultimate Reality, of eternity, of pure spirit, limitless in extent and full of light and beauty. It is known only to the mystics of the highest order, who have observed that it cannot be described in words or comprehended by the intellect since it is utterly beyond the frontiers of mind. The lowest aspect of this region is called *sat lok* (true realm) or *sach khaṇḍ* (true region), both of which mean true or real region. It is inhabited by countless pure souls who know no stain or imperfection, no sorrow, and no death. They are perennially in a state of perfect bliss. It is the beginning and end of all else. From this centre of all light, life and power, the great creative Current flows outward and downwards to create, govern and sustain all regions.

Sat desh is the region of immortality, untouched by dissolution *(pralaya)* or grand dissolution *(mahā pralaya).* It has four aspects, although the differences between them are very slight. In ascending order, they are: *sach khaṇḍ* or *sat lok, alakh lok* (invisible place), *agam lok* (inaccessible region) and *anāmī dhām* (nameless home).

Brahmāṇḍa, aṇḍa and *piṇḍa* are subject to occasional dissolution *(pralaya),* on a cyclic basis. There are two kinds of *pralaya:* one includes the regions up to *trikuṭī,* and occurs after vast aeons of time. The other *(mahā pralaya)* occurs after even longer spans of time, and encompasses all regions up to the threshold of *sat desh.* After a period of darkness or quiescence, a new creation takes place.

The three grand divisions comprising the creation have a great many regions within them, the numbers stated depending on the way they are described by a particular mystic. All these divisions and subdivisions blend into one another, and this partly accounts for the many different descriptions of the regions found in mystic literature, and the great variety of names assigned to them. When asked whether there were four regions or grand divisions (counting *sat desh* as a grand division), Mahārāj Charan Singh pointed out the limitations of language to describe the spiritual world:

> Many Saints have tried to explain those regions. Mostly the Saints have tried to explain them in the same number of divisions, but many mystics, even Indian mystics, have just referred to two regions – one consisting of what lies below *trikuṭī* and the other as all that which is above *trikuṭī;* one region under the reign of mind and *māyā,* and the other region above the reign of mind and *māyā.* But others have referred to five regions, and still others have subdivided the fifth region.
>
> We should not get confused with how many regions or stages have been described. Actually, it is the same journey, and they are not

> watertight compartments. The thing has to be described in one way or another; so these languages just describe them. Some have described just two regions; some have classified the two regions into four, and some into five and some into eight regions. Actually, it is the same journey, and covers the same territory, whether classified as consisting of two, four, five or eight regions.
>
> *Mahārāj Charan Singh, The Master Answers 352, MA pp.385–86*

The Microcosm and the Macrocosm

What lies below is a reflection of what lies above. Speaking here of *brahmāṇḍa* as extending from "the bottom of *trikuṭī* up to the border of *daswān dwār*",[2] Mahārāj Sāwan Singh explains:

> *Brahmāṇḍa, aṇḍa* and *piṇḍa* are related to one another as the image is related to the object. *Aṇḍa* is the reflection of *brahmāṇḍa,* and *piṇḍa* is the refection of *aṇḍa.* Just as the sun and its reflection in water and the reflection on a wall from the surface of water are related to one another.... The reflection on the wall is only a hazy patch of light, distorted and devoid of glory. *Piṇḍa* is a copy of *aṇḍa,* and *aṇḍa* is a copy of *brahmāṇḍa.* The so-called man is thus a copy of the copy, leaving aside the pure spirit.
>
> *Mahārāj Sāwan Singh, Spiritual Gems 145, SG p.220*

In each region below the eternity of *sat desh,* there are energy centres, known as *chakras* or lotuses *(kamalas).* Each of these centres has particular energy aspects, each associated with its particular functions, commonly described in Indian mystical literature as the petals of a lotus flower. Although there are a great many higher realms, mystics such as Kabīr and Swāmī Shiv Dayāl Singh have spoken of eighteen major centres lying within the microcosm of the human form: six in *piṇḍa,* six in *aṇḍa* and six in *brahmāṇḍa* (here including *trikuṭī* and the realms up to but not including *sat desh*). The six centres in *piṇḍa* are a reflection of the centres in *aṇḍa,* which in turn are a reflection of the centres in *brahmāṇḍa.*

These sets of centres are depicted schematically in the adjoining table, giving an admittedly inadequate idea of how the vast regions of *bhanwar guphā, pārbrahm, trikuṭī* and *sahans dal kanwal,* when traced downwards through the creative hierarchy, are finally contained as reflections in the microcosm of the human form. The aspects of eternity within the Godhead are also shown.

Before studying this table, perhaps it also needs to be reiterated that both words and charts can be entirely misleading when attempting to convey something of the way in which the hierarchy of creation is put together.

	No. of Petals	Names of the levels, stages, regions or planes of consciousness			
		Anāmī *Agam* *Alakh* *Sat lok*	Nameless Inaccessible Imperceptible True region	GOD	
Brahmāṇḍa	2	*Bhanwar guphā* *Sohang*	Whirling cave I am He	Spiritual Planes	*Mahā Pralaya*
	16	*Mahā sunn*	Great darkness		
	12	*Achint dīp*			
	8	*Pārbrahm* (upper)	Beyond *Brahm*		
	6	*Pārbrahm* (lower) *Daswān dwār*	Tenth door		
	4	*Trikuṭī* (upper)	Three peaks Universal mind	Causal Planes	
Aṇḍa	2	*Trikuṭī* (lower)	Three peaks Universal mind		*Pralaya*
	16	*Set sunn*	White void	Astral Planes	
	12	*Sahans dal kanwal,* *Sahasrāra*	Thousand-petalled lotus		
	8	*Asht dal kanwal* *Tīsrā til*	Eight-petalled lotus Third eye		
	6	*Khaṭ dal kanwal*	Six-petalled lotus		
	4	*Antaḥkaraṇa*	Inner organ Instrument of thought		
Piṇḍa	2	*Ājñā* *Do dal kanwal*	Eye centre Two-petalled lotus	Physical Plane	Physical death
	16	*Vishuddha*	Throat centre		
	12	*Hṛidaya*	Heart centre		
	8	*Maṇipūraka,* *Nābhi*	Navel centre		
	6	*Svādhishṭhāna*	Genital centre		
	4	*Mūlādhāra,* *Gudā*	Rectal centre		

The Grand Hierarchy of Creation[3]

Words and graphical representations convey things in entirely physical terms, and give entirely the wrong impression. The inner creation is an ocean of scintillating energies and consciousness in an ultradynamic interactive drama which follows 'principles' that are utterly beyond the understanding of even the finest human intellect. If words or graphs are taken as more than mere indicators of a very sketchy nature, they can even form preconceptions that can be counterproductive to the inner quest.

It can be seen, for example, how the four-petalled lotus in *trikuṭī* (*lit.* three peaks, the universal mind) is reflected as the *antaḥkaraṇa* (human mind centre), and again as the *mūlādhāra* or rectal *chakra.* The colours of *trikuṭī* are said to be red and golden, like those of the setting sun. Similarly, the *antaḥkaraṇa* and the *mūlādhāra chakra* are described as possessing a dull reddish colour.

Again, the *ākāsha tattva* is administered or located in the *vishuddha chakra* of the physical form. This, however, is reflected from the *set sunn* (white void), the 'sky' of the astral zone, the 'zero point' or 'vacuum' separating the astral from the causal regions (lower *trikuṭī*) lying above. And this is again reflected from the *mahā sunn,* the great and final gulf separating the lower spiritual regions from the higher. It is often described as an area of intense darkness, just as human beings are separated from the astral zone by the 'darkness' of the human mind.

It may also be observed how there is a link between the top of one set of centres and the bottom of the set immediately above. The *antaḥkaraṇa,* for example, provides the energy centres that are experienced as the physical *(piṇḍī)* or human mind. In fact, the area from the *ājñā chakra* up to and including the *ashṭ dal kanwal* is sometimes called the 'sky' of the body.

Similarly, the great divide of the three worlds of the mind from the higher spiritual regions is not so clearly delineated as it is sometimes described. Just as the highest and purest of human thoughts already link up to the lower astral levels, so too is the universal mind interlinked with the spiritual realms above. The lower is always a reflection of the higher.

It is also possible, within this scheme, to understand how individual death takes place. Individual death is simply the dissolution of the individual set of six physical *chakras* that underlie the physical form. But the seeds of all mental processes, and therefore of all deeds and desires, are still contained within the human mind, within the *antaḥkaraṇa.* This centre, being of the lower astral, is not destroyed at physical death. In fact, it is from the energies or patterns stored in this centre that the next physical life is determined or precipitated. Upon rebirth, the memory of past lives is usually no longer accessible, but the general impressions or *sanskāras* remain.

Since the *antaḥkaraṇa* performs the functions that are experienced as the human mind, it can be seen how the *sanskāras* of previous lives become the underlying trend or personality of future lives. This is how Mozart was able to compose concertos when only aged six. And this is how all human beings are born with a personality, talents and nature that may develop or change to some degree during the course of life, but yet – in essence – remain constant and recognizable.

Pralaya, the dissolution, or death of the entire mind area, takes place up to the lower part of *trikuṭī,* leaving the seed forms of the mind creation still encoded into the lower spiritual regions, just as the seeds of physical life are impressed into the *antaḥkaraṇa* of the lower astral. The seeds for the next 'life' or creation of the mind are thus stored in readiness for the next out-breathing in the cycle of creation and dissolution.

Similarly, in the grand dissolution or *mahā pralaya,* the spiritual centres up to the gateway of *sat lok* are also dissolved. In no case is only *part* of *aṇḍa* or *part* of *brahmāṇḍa* dissolved. All are dissolved together, at the same time. They are also created in that way, too.

Similarly, death does not take place only up to the navel, for instance, or the heart. Even during withdrawal of consciousness from the body during meditation, the normal biological life functions continue. The physical body is a whole and integral affair. Life animates all of it or none at all. A person may lose a limb – an extension lever, so to speak – but a large area of the torso cannot be lost and life maintained. An individual cannot remain alive with any of the physical *chakras* missing.

Again, from a study of the table, it can be seen how confusion sometimes arises as to the nature and location of the third eye. The eye centre, the *ājñā chakra* or two-petalled lotus is often called the third eye – the point where a practitioner initially focuses attention in all systems of *yoga* or meditation designed to withdraw the mind and soul currents from the physical body.

Strictly speaking, however, this is not the true third eye *(tīsrā til)* or actual entrance to the astral zones. That gateway – the eight-petalled lotus *(ashṭ dal kanwal)* – is a little higher up or further within. This, too, is where initiates meet the radiant, astral form of their *Guru* on the inner ascent.

Likewise, the human body is often described mystically as the house with ten doors. Nine of these doors open outward: the two eyes, two ears, two nostrils, the mouth and the two lower apertures. Through these, the attention of the mind goes out into the physical world. Due to this activity of the mind, most people remain deeply involved in the world, and the tenth door, leading inwards, remains undiscovered. This 'passage' or 'tunnel' between the physical and lower astral zones 'starts' at the eye centre and opens into the true astral world at the third eye. On passing out of this tunnel, a soul is met by other souls whose nature reflects the contents of that individual's own mind. Goodness and light are drawn to goodness and light, while the converse is true for a darker mind.

It is not an easy matter to pass through this valve, gateway or tunnel into the astral realms. The 'flow' of *karma,* the mental impetus and destiny for life in this physical world, is like a waterfall arising from the impressions within and flowing out into this world. Moreover, a strong sense of attachment and identification or ego is associated with this continuous flow of events. As a consequence, the individual not only fails to pierce this inner veil or traverse this inner tunnel until the downward flow of destiny ceases at death, but – because this flow of destiny is so powerful – he also fails to realize that he is exiled from the inner realms of mind and spirit. He is unaware of his true spiritual heritage. He does not know who or what he is, nor how he is put together as an entity of body, mind and soul.

Again, one of the names of the realm immediately above *trikuṭī* is *daswān dwār,* meaning 'tenth door', because there are ten 'doors' in *trikuṭī,* nine leading downwards and one opening upwards. In this, the reflective process can once again be seen at work.

When the soul passes through this tenth door, finally ridding itself of all coverings of the mind, it emerges at last as a free soul. This is the highest form of self-realization, for the real self is the soul, and the soul cannot know itself while still trapped within the three regions of the mind.

This process is again reflected in the human form where, as an individual begins to rise above the subconscious emotions of physical being – as he withdraws his mind and consciousness towards the eye centre – a far greater self-awareness or realization of his psychological make-up is experienced. This is not the highest mystic self-realization, which only happens when the soul gets release from the mind. But it shows, yet again, how the lower is reflected from the higher, and can even be mistaken for the higher, thereby putting a ceiling to the ascent before the journey has even begun. The human and psychological self-realization is essential for a person to come to terms with himself and to know what he really wants out of life. But it is only the base upon which to build the higher edifice of spiritual enlightenment.

Again, Indian mystics have described the spiritual journey as starting at the soles of the feet and ending at the top of the head.[4] From an understanding of how the hierarchy of creation is organized, the meaning of this can be glimpsed. The human form is a microcosmic reflection of the entire creation. The whole of the original is contained within the part. What lies above, comes together and creates what lies below. This is the process by which the creation is projected. It is a multireflecting projection system, emanating from within out. To reach God, a human being has to withdraw all consciousness from the body, starting from the feet and moving up through the bodily *chakras,* and thence through the higher regions, back to God. All this takes place within the human body. The crown of the head reflects the highest point of consciousness, the Lord Himself.

In reality, the inner creative process cannot be described. It is immensely complex, beyond the capacity of words and intellect to depict. From the descriptions of others, therefore, it is almost impossible to tell just what is being described. The *Vedas* and *Upanishads,* for example, talk of *Brahman* as the highest Reality. Some Saints, however, have said that the supreme Reality lies beyond *Brahman.*

All regions have their own distinctive light and sound; that is, their own particular vibrational quality, experienced as light and sound. Once again, these are reflected downwards. Thus, a practitioner who enters the heart *chakra* will hear sounds and see sights bearing reflected resemblances to those that he would hear in the astral or still higher regions. Yet the difference between the two is clear. In one case, the practitioner has not escaped from the physical body. In the other, he is out of the body, perhaps beyond the regions of the universal mind, beyond the reach of birth and death on the physical plane.

Kabīr, Swāmī Shiv Dayāl Singh and other mystics have described this deceptive show of creation in a variety of ways. Some have also pointed out that the entire creation and the supreme region itself is all reflected within the astral zone alone. Thus, Kabīr says:

> Primal *māyā* has played a clever trick:
> she has created a false show in *piṇḍ.*
> In *aṇḍ,* she created a creation of a lower order,
> a reflection of which she has cast below (as *piṇḍ*).
> *Kabīr, Shabdāvalī 1, Bhed Bānī 22:31, KSS1 p.67*

In another, more extensive poem, attributed perhaps incorrectly to Kabīr, the sequence of *sunnas* (*lit.* voids) or focal points of creative energy in creation is described. It is indicated how the lower focal points in *aṇḍa* contain a reflection of the highest realms of the Godhead. He is describing the same reflective process of creation, but in a different way:

> *Kāl* has made an imitation in *aṇḍ*
> of the eternal stronghold.
> It is the seat of pure *(shuddh) Brahm,*
> but it is named *Anāmī.*
>
> The seventh *sunn* in *aṇḍ,*
> he has made as an imitation of the resplendent region.
> *Mahā Kāl* dwells there,
> but it is called *Agam Purush.*
>
> The sixth *sunn* in *aṇḍ,* he has made
> as an imitation of the realm of light.
> *Nirguṇ Kāl* dwells there,
> but it is called the transcendent *Alakh Purush.*

The fifth *sunn* in *aṇḍ,* he has made
as an imitation of *sat lok.*
Nirañjan dwells there with *māyā,*
but it is termed *Sat Purush.*

The fourth *sunn* in *aṇḍ,* he has made
as an imitation of *nirvāṇa pad* (the place of *nirvāṇa*).
A power of a lower order appears there as *Satguru,*
but it appears to be *sohang.*

Kabīr, Shabdāvalī 1, Bhed Bānī 23:3–7, KSS1 p.68

Mystics point out that the creation – though much of it is beguiling, intriguing and blissful – is a vast labyrinth designed to keep souls imprisoned. Were this not so, all souls would follow their most natural and fundamental inclination, and return to God. The absorbing, enticing and almost inextricable character of the creation is therefore essential for the drama to continue. It is for this reason that Saints say that it is only when the Lord wishes a soul to return to Himself that the exit is made clear. Only then does the true guide or perfect Master appear upon the scene and initiate the soul into the only power in creation that can bring about salvation – the Creative Word of God.

See also: **brahmāṇḍa**, **piṇḍa**.

1. Plato, *Republic* 6:508b, 509d, 7:517b, 532a–b. Also, throughout Plotinus, *Enneads.*
2. Mahārāj Sāwan Singh, *Spiritual Gems* 145, *SG* p.220.
3. *cf.* Lekh Rāj Puri, *Mysticism: The Spiritual Path* II, *MSP2* p.372.
4. *e.g.* Mahārāj Charan Singh, *Light on Sant Mat* 19, *LOSM* p.60.

aṇḍī (H) *Lit.* relating to *aṇḍa;* pertaining to the astral world.

'āqibah (A), **'āqibat** (P) *Lit.* end, outcome, consequence; often used in the *Qur'ān* to refer to the afterlife. Referring to the afterlife as the 'consequence' points to the principle by which the soul receives the fruit of its own actions.

See also: **al-ākhirah**.

ashṭ dal kanwal (H) *Lit.* eight *(ashṭ)* -petalled *(dal)* lotus *(kanwal);* a centre in *aṇḍa* situated below *sahans dal kanwal* (thousand-petalled lotus), where an initiate of a perfect Master first consciously meets the astral or radiant form of his Master. For a soul ascending from the human body, it is the threshold of the astral realms; also called *tīsrā til* (third eye), since it is the door or window through which the soul enters the astral realms.

The navel *chakra* of the physical body is also known as the *ashṭ dal kanwal,* this being a reflection in *piṇḍa* of the higher centre in *aṇḍa.* Of the navel or *nābhi chakra,* Kabīr says:

> At the *nābhi chakra,*
>   there is an eight-petalled lotus *(ashṭ dal kanwal).*
> There, *Vishṇu* sits on a white throne,
>   repeating the refrain *'hiring'.*
>
> *Kabīr, Shabdāvalī 1, Bhed Bānī 22:5, KSS1 p.65*

The centre in *aṇḍa* is itself a reflection of a higher eight-petalled centre in *pārbrahm,* above the universal mind *(trikuṭī),* where the soul first sees itself as pure soul. The 'sky' of *trikuṭī* is known as *gagan.* Of this higher centre, the sixteenth-century Indian mystic, Dādū, writes:

> The unstruck Word *(anhad Nād)* resounded
>   in the citadel *(gaṛh)* of *gagan.*
> I drank deep of the nectar within....
> In the *ashṭ dal kanwal,* seen within,
>   I saw my very own self.
>
> *Dādū, in Ghaṭ Rāmāyaṇ 1:2, 4, GR2 p.8*

See also: **aṇḍa**.

'assiah (He) *Lit.* making.

See **'olam ha-'assiah**.

astral plane, **astral realm**, **astral region**, **astral world** See **regions**.

asur(a) lok(a) (S/H) *Lit.* place *(lok)* of the demons *(asuras);* according to Hindu mythology, the region where the *asuras* (demons) dwell.

See **asura** (4.2).

athīr (A), **aśīr** (P) *Lit.* ether; from the Greek, *aether;* the outermost of the nine celestial spheres surrounding the earth, according to traditional Islamic cosmology, based upon the geocentric system of the Greeks; thus, the empyrean, as the highest of the spherical heavens, the sphere beyond the fixed stars; sometimes identified with *al-falak al-aṭlas* (crystalline sphere).

See also: **al-'arsh**, **ether** (5.1), **sab' samāwāt**.

avyākṛit(a) (S/H) *Lit.* not *(a)* separated or differentiated *(vyākṛita);* undeveloped, unexpounded, unanswered, unmanifested; hence, secret; not open to view; mystically, the unmanifested source; one of the three aspects of *Brahman,* the other two being *hiraṇyagarbha* (*lit.* the golden womb, manifested source) and *vishvarūpa* (all-inclusive form), also called *virāṭrūpa* (*lit.* huge or expanded form, the grossly manifested, physical universe) and *vaishvānara* (*lit.* consisting of all men, common to all men, universal, omnipresent).[1]

Avyākṛita is the seed or most subtle form of *māyā,* being *māyā* in undifferentiated or unmanifested form, as found in the highest reaches of the causal plane. The term is used in the *Bṛihadāraṇyaka Upanishad* and hence in the *Vedānta* and *Sānkhya* schools of Indian philosophy:

> At that time, this (universe) was undifferentiated *(avyākṛita).*
> Later, it became differentiated by name and form.
>
> *Bṛihadāraṇyaka Upanishad 1:4.7*

In Buddhism, *avyākṛita* specifically means unanswered or unexpounded, and is applied to certain metaphysical questions that the Buddha regarded as irrelevant to spiritual practice. These questions, numbering ten in Pali Buddhism and fourteen in Sanskrit, include: "Does the universe have an origin in time?" And: "Is the universe limitless or does it have a boundary?" According to the Buddha, these questions were improperly formed, meaning that they were based on a logical muddle. *Avyākṛita* can also be interpreted to mean that the answers to these questions were 'inexpressible'; and that because the Buddha would not address them, he left them unanswered.

See also: **hiraṇyagarbha**, **virāṭrūpa**, **vishvarūpa**.

1. For *avyākṛita,* see *Bṛihadāraṇyaka Upanishad* 1:4.7; for *hiraṇyagarbha,* see *Shvetāshvatara Upanishad* 3:3, 4:12, *Nṛisiṃha Uttara Tāpinīya Upanishad* 1; for *vaishvānara,* see *Māṇḍūkya Upanishad* 3, *Prashna Upanishad 1:7, Bhagavad Gītā* 15:14, *Vedāntasāra* 91; for *virāṭrūpa,* see *Vedāntasāra* 91; for *vishvarūpa,* see *Prashna Upanishad* 1:7, *Bhagavad Gītā* 11:16, *Rām Charit Mānas* 4:21.2, 6:14.

aẓilut (He) See **'olam ha-aẓilut**.

baḥr (A/P) *Lit.* sea, ocean; metaphorically, the divisions or realms of creation, as in:

baḥr-i ẓuhūr:	sea of manifestation.
baḥr-i a'yān:	sea of (self-)evident, apparent sea, visible sea.
baḥr-i hastī:	sea of existence.

The metaphor is related to the term *barzakh* (isthmus), which denotes the boundaries between the various realms. 'Irāqī states that both the lowest 'sea' (the outward, physically manifest) and the highest, meet and combine within himself:

> The sea of manifestation *baḥr-i ẓuhūr*
> and the pre-existent inner sea *(baḥr-i baṭūn):*
> Behold, both are within me:
> a combination of the two great seas *(baḥrayn-i akbar)* am I.
>
> *'Irāqī, in FLI p.187*

See also: **baḥr** (2.1).

baikuṇṭh (H/Pu) See **vaikuṇṭha**.

bank nāl, bank kamal (H) *Lit.* crooked or curved *(bank)* tunnel *(nāl)* or lotus *(kamal);* the crooked tube; the name of a 'passage', 'valve' or 'gateway' lying between *sahans dal kanwal* and *trikuṭī;* a passage 'finer than the eye of a needle' through which the soul passes when ascending from the first to the second spiritual regions.

The creation is arranged in such a way that from any region it is far easier to go down and out, rather than in and up. The means of ascent is concealed by the downflow of creative energy, since the point of ascent from one level to another is the same point at which the creative energy is streaming down from above, enlivening the realms below. It thus becomes far easier for souls to take the line of least resistance, following the creative impulse out into the surrounding region, rather than gathering together all their powers of concentration, devotion and love, and finding the way through into the next higher realm.

This is why, for example, although all souls in this world will be forced at death to take the narrow passageway that leads out of the body into the subastral realms, very few are even aware of the existence of this passage within their own head, nor do they seek to find it. The incessant outflow of energy that creates the karmic pattern of life dominates and forms human existence to such an extent that few are able to even perceive that there is a way of escape until death overtakes them, and they are forced, willingly or unwillingly, to pass through the narrow gateway.

Such points of focus are known as 'gateways', 'valves', 'skies', 'passageways', 'doors', 'trap doors', 'tunnels', 'eye of a needle' or – in the case of the *bank nāl* – the 'crooked tunnel'.

Writing of the ascent from *sahans dal kanwal* to *trikuṭī,* Sardār Bahādur Jagat Singh says:

> After the thousand-petalled lotus, comes the land of *Brahm,* lord of the second spiritual region. He is the creator, the sustainer and the destroyer of the universe. Connecting the two regions is an oblique passage, called the *bank nāl.* Only after crossing this tunnel, does the soul reach the realm of *Brahm.* Here, the attributes of the mind drop off, and thereafter the soul ascends alone. *Trikuṭī* is the source of the mind. Once it reaches its home, it merges in it, thereby setting the soul free.
>
> *Sardār Bahādur Jagat Singh, Science of the Soul I:2, SOS p.21*

Similarly, Kabīr writes:

> Hear the sound of the gong and conch:
> The divine Music flows out ceaselessly
> from the refulgent thousand-petalled lotus *(sahas kanwal).*
> There behold the creator (of all below).
> Now enter and pass through the *bank nāl....*
>
> *Trikuṭī* is the source of knowledge,
> where thunder resounds like a big drum,
> and the light of the red sun glows brightly.
> There you will find the four-petalled lotus
> from which the ceaseless sound of *Onkār* arises.
>
> *Kabīr, Shabdāvalī 1, Bhed Bānī 22:12, 15, KSS1 p.66*

Dariyā Sāhib, an eighteenth-century Indian Saint of Bihar, uses the variant expression *bank kamal.* He writes of the journey through the *bank kamal* into *trikuṭī,* and onward to an area above *trikuṭī* known as *triveṇī:*

> Enter the illumined curved lotus *(bank kamal),*
> and see and experience its scent and fragrance.

> Drink the nectar of love to your fill,
> and fill your vessel on the banks of *triveṇī.*
>
> *Dariyā Sāhib, Gyān Dīpak, Chaupaī 891–92, DYD p.134, GD p.201; cf. DSSB p.66*

See also: **haṃsnī nāl**.

barzakh (A/P) *Lit.* isthmus; a narrow strip of land, with the ocean on either side, connecting two larger land areas; hence, a passage lying between two less or completely unrestricted areas. Originating in the *Qur'ān,* Sufis have used the metaphor in several contexts. In descriptions and explanations of the structure of the creation, they have used the image to convey that which lies between its higher and lower levels. For example, the *'ālam al-mithāl* (world of patterns) is considered a *barzakh* between the *'ālam al-ajsām* (world of bodies) and the *'ālam al-arwāḥ* (world of spirits). The variant uses of *barzakh* have been developed largely by Ibn 'Arabī.

Sometimes, *barzakh* conveys the idea of a barrier, an obstacle, an interval, a bar or partition:

> The distance between two things is referred to as a *barzakh.* In *Ṣūfī* language, it denotes the world of patterns *('ālam-i miśāl)* which is a barrier between the gross world and the world of incorporeal spirits *('ālam-i arvāḥ).*
>
> *Al-Qāshānī, Iṣṭilāḥāt al-Ṣūfīyah, ISJ p.36, in FNI3 pp.153–54*

Barzakh can also convey the idea of a link or a bridge rather than a barrier. The narrow strip of land that borders two different oceans is in touch with the characteristics of both. The oceans cannot see, touch or know each other, but the isthmus between them can convey knowledge of the one ocean to the other. Thus, the *'ālam al-mithāl* is seen as refracting the light from the realms above it, projecting and reflecting spiritual light and power into the worlds below:

> A state or a thing between two things is a *barzakh.* The present is a state of *barzakh* between past and future. This state has a share or influence from both sides. The present is the result of the past and the beginning of the future. So the world of patterns *('ālam-i mithāl)* which separates the gross world *('ālam-i kaśīfah)* from the world of incorporeal spirits *('ālam-i arvāḥ-i mujarradah)* is called *barzakh.*
>
> *Shāh Ni'mat Allāh Valī, Rasā'il, RNV4 p.16, in FNT3 p.150*

In the terminology of Ibn 'Arabī, followed by others, the unmanifested Essence of God *(Dhāt)* permeates the creation through a process of descent *(tanazzul)* and 'entification *(ta'ayyun)*' or individuation. That is, the one Lord 'entifies' in a descending series of planes of consciousness. Thus, the first entification below the level of *Dhāt* is called *al-Barzakhīyah al-Ūlá,* the First Isthmus Nature or the Supreme Isthmus Nature.[1] In this sense, it is also identified by Ibn 'Arabī with the Breath of the All-Merciful *(al-Nafas al-Raḥmān),* the Cloud *(al-'Amā')* and a number of other terms for the first expression of God in His process of manifesting the creation.[2]

The Perfect Man, who is manifestly a part of this world while at the same time embracing all the inner realms of light, has also been called a *barzakh.* He is the point at which the two worlds meet. Like a connecting link between this realm and that, he can guide human beings across. Even the ordinary man has been called a *barzakh,* since he has the potential to live on both sides of death, to become divine while still incarnate.

In the *Qur'ān, barzakh* is described as a barrier between the two seas, the bitter and the sweet:

> And it is He who let forth the two seas:
> this one sweet, grateful to taste,
> and this salt, bitter to the tongue;
> And He set between them a barrier *(barzakh),*
> and a ban forbidden.
>
> *Qur'ān 25:53, KI*

> And he set forth the two seas that meet together:
> between them a barrier *(barzakh)* they do not overpass.
>
> *Qur'ān 55:19–20, KI*

Mystics such as Rūmī see the "bitter sea" as this world, and the "sweet sea" as the beyond. He advises going beyond both to the divine Source of all:

> In this world, the bitter sea
> and the sweet sea are divided;
> Between them is "a barrier *(barzakh)*
> which they do not seek to cross".
> Know that both these flow from one origin.
> Pass on from them both: go to their origin!
>
> *Rūmī, Maśnavī I:297–98, MJR2 p.19*

In traditional Islam, this *barzakh* is generally understood to mean purgatory, the 'intermediate stage' or the 'intermediate world' where the souls of those who have died await judgment. It implies a dark and uncertain time of waiting between death and the future placement of the soul. Stressing the impassability of this *barzakh,* the *Qur'ān* also says:

Till when death comes to one of them, he says,
"My Lord, return me (to the world);
Haply I shall do righteousness in that I forsook."
Nay, it is but a word he speaks,
  and there, behind them, is a barrier *(barzakh);*
Until the day that they shall be raised up.

Qur'ān 23:99–100, KI

But Rūmī is again specific when he identifies the physical world as the dark and uncertain *barzakh:*

O world, you are like the intermediate state *(barzakh).*
The everlasting light is beside this low world,
  the pure milk is beside rivers of blood.
When you take one step without precaution,
  your milk will be turned to blood through commixture.

Rūmī, Maśnavī II:12–14; cf. MJR2 p.222

1. W.C. Chittick and P.L. Wilson, *Divine Flashes, DF* p.11.
2. W.C. Chittick, *Sufi Path of Knowledge, SPK* pp.15, 125, 127, 133, 135, 139.

bhanwar guphā, **bhanwar kamal** (H) *Lit.* rotating, revolving or whirling *(bhanwar)* cave *(guphā)* or lotus *(kamal);* a name given by some Indian Saints to the fourth spiritual region on the soul's journey within, immediately prior to the eternal region. In normal parlance, a *bhanwar* is a whirlpool or eddy, and the name indicates the state of the soul as it collects its strength, like a whirlwind rising upwards, to reach eternity and attain union with the Divine. It suggests the powerful surging or swinging of blissful currents of the creative Life Stream from which the soul derives the power and strength to make the final ascent.

Descending, *bhanwar guphā* is the first created realm in the Lord's creation. Here, vortices appear, forming as energy whirls like hollow caves, forming the first extremely subtle manifestation of the multiplicity that characterizes the lower creation. Bright, all-round light or radiance and swinging, rhythmic motions constitute the essence of this stage, and the sound heard there is said to be like that of a flute, vibrating with the intense longing of the soul for union with the Lord. The sound is said to be that of *sohang* (I am He) or *anā Hū* (I am He),[1] for here the ascending soul begins to truly comprehend its union with God who is realized to be so close at hand.

Writing of this region and of the approach to *sach khaṇḍ* (true region) lying above it, the nineteenth-century Indian mystic, Swāmī Shiv Dayāl Singh, says:

The soul beheld the mountain of *bhanwar guphā,*
approaching which it heard the sound of *sohang.*
There, the piercing melody of the flute arises,
and the soul sees the intense radiance of the white sun.
The region is exceedingly beautiful and sweet,
full of light and glory.
There, an infinite Melody plays on forever.

There, the souls live on the *Shabd* as their food.
Playing about on the great plane are groups of *haṃsas,*
and with them are many devotees.
There are vast and innumerable planes and worlds,
abounding with a variety of creations,
inhabited by countless devotees.
Nām is the staff of their existence,
and they drink eternally of its nectar.

Swāmī Shiv Dayāl Singh, Sār Bachan Poetry 26:4.7–11, SBP p.228

Bhanwar guphā has also been called the *bhanwar kamal,* the revolving or whirling lotus:

How can anyone describe its bliss and taste,
once the nectar of *bhanwar kamal* has permeated the soul?
How can anyone ask a moth to describe the lamp,
when it has already become one with its flame?

Keshavdās, Amīghūnt 8:2, KDA p.4

See also: **baṃsarī** (3.2), **muralī** (3.2).

1. Swāmī Shiv Dayāl Singh, *Sār Bachan Poetry* 38:6.31, *SBP* p.342.

bihisht-u dūzakh (P) *Lit.* heaven *(bihisht)* and *(u)* hell *(dūzakh);* the afterlife, where the fruits of human life are harvested. In orthodox Islam, heaven is the prized reward of the devout Muslim, hell is for sinners and unbelievers, a viewpoint arising from a literal interpretation of the *Qur'ān* where heaven and hell are graphically portrayed. Sufis and others, however, have commonly understood the descriptions in the *Qur'ān* to be metaphorical. This point of view stems from the *Qur'ān* itself, which says that some verses in it are definite in meaning, the rest figurative, no one knowing the hidden meaning of the latter "except God" and "those gifted with insight":

He it is who has sent down to thee the Book.
Some verses of it are definite in meaning.
These form the mother of the Book (the basic therein),
and the rest are figurative.
But they in whose minds there is a tendency to deviate from truth,
take the figurative (in their literal sense), craving discord,
and craving to give them their own interpretation,
although none knoweth the reality about them except God.
And those too who make a right approach to knowledge
could only say, "We believe therein: all is from our Lord."
None can catch their significance except those gifted with insight.

Qur'ān 3:7, QAL

In addition to this general principle, there are also specific sayings in the *Qur'ān* to suggest that descriptions of heaven and hell are intended figuratively. An extensive portrayal of paradise, for instance, is described as a "similitude".[1]

Although Sufis have acknowledged the actual existence of heaven and hell, they have characteristically stressed the quality of consciousness in the here and now, and have consequently interpreted heaven and hell metaphorically. Thus, to those who know the great bliss of contact with the Divine, human imperfections are hell. Laying emphasis on the value of the present moment, 'Aṭṭār equates heaven and hell with the quality of a person's thoughts:

If that which is bad thought is hell *(dūzakh),*
then that which is good thought is heaven *(bihisht).*

'Aṭṭār, Asrār-Nāmah 1493, AN p.92

The *Qur'ān* itself, though repeatedly portraying hell as a place where sinners and especially nonbelievers will be consigned, also indicates that it is to be understood as a state of mind, a state of spiritual distress and deprivation. Speaking of the "wealthy slanderer", it says:

Mark! He will certainly
be flung into the fierce fire *(ḥuṭamah);*
And who shall make thee understand
what the fierce fire *(ḥuṭamah)* is?
It is God's kindled fire,
which riseth up to the hearts (of men,
or the feeling of terror which seizeth their hearts
when they have committed a heinous crime
and are anxious to flee from its results).

Qur'ān 104:4–7, QAL

In Sufi thinking, hell is inextricably linked with the *nafs* (lower mind). Rūmī says, "This carnal self *(nafs)* is hell *(dūzakh),*"[2] and, "This self of ours is a part of hell *(dūzakh),* and all parts have the nature of the whole, to God alone belongs the power to kill it."[3] Depicting the highest heaven as a garden, he says that human beings have become obsessed with "two or three bunches of flowers" of the earth that rapidly fade, and have "shut the garden door" of the *Logos,* where eternally fresh flowers are found in abundance.[4] Having lost the "keys" to that divine garden, he continues, "greed", "lust" and other imperfections have become the "seven-headed dragon" of "hell", alluding perhaps to the seven deadly sins, and comparing them to the seven stages of hell. "Greed", he concludes, baits the "snare" of "hell", which he equates with the rented accommodation of the body:

Alas, dear soul, that on account of (greed for) bread,
  such keys drop continuously from your fingers!
And if for a moment you are relieved
  from your preoccupation with bread,
  then you give yourself up to your passion for women;
And then, when the sea of your lust breaks into billows,
  you must needs have, at your command,
  a whole city full of bread and women.

At first you were only a snake:
  now indeed you have become a dragon.
You had only one head: now you have seven heads.
Hell *(dūzakh)* is a seven-headed dragon:
  your greed is the bait, and hell *(dūzakh)* the snare.
Pull the snare to pieces, burn the bait,
  and open new doors in this tenement!

Rūmī, Maśnavī VI:4653–58; cf. MJR6 p.515

'Aṭṭār, too, refers to this world as "hell" when he relates a dialogue between the "tortured souls in hell" and "those in paradise". "When we glimpse that radiant Face," say the souls in hell, "such longing seizes us," that the troubles of hell are all forgotten. Then, indicating that he is also speaking of this world, 'Aṭṭār goes on to speak about "the man who feels such longing":

Shaykh Bū 'Alī Ṭūsī's long pilgrimage,
  (he was the wisest savant of his age),
  conducted him so far that I know none
  who could draw near to what this man has done.
He said: "The wretches damned in hell *(dūzakh)* will cry
  to those in paradise *(jannat):* 'O testify

to us the nature of your happiness;
Describe the sacred joys which you possess!'

"And they will say: 'Ineffable delight
shines in the radiance of His face; its light
draws near us, and this vast celestial frame –
the eightfold heaven *(khuld)* – darkens, bowed by shame.'

"And then the tortured souls in hell *(dūzakh)* will say:
'From joys of paradise *(firdaws)* you turn away;
Such lowly happiness is not for you –
all that you say is true, we know how true!
In hell's *(dūzakh)* accursèd provinces we reign,
clothed head to foot in fire's devouring pain;
But when we glimpse that radiant Face, and know
that we must live forever here below,
cut off through all eternity from grace –
Such longing seizes us for that far Face,
such unappeasable and wild regret,
that, in our anguished torment, we forget
the pit of hell *(dūzakh)* and all its raging fire;
For what are flames to comfortless desire?'"

The man who feels such longing takes no part
in public prayers; he prays within his heart.
Regret and sighs should be your portion here;
In sighs rejoice, in longing persevere –
and if beneath the sky's oppressive dome
wounds scar you, you draw nearer to your home;
Don't flinch from pain or search here for its cure,
uncauterized your wounds must bleed; endure!

'Aṭṭār, Conference of the Birds 3197–215, CBD pp.164–65

Emphasizing that hell is the forgetfulness of God, Rūmī goes so far as to say that souls in hell are less miserable than the souls in this world:

The inhabitants of hell *(dūzakh)* are happier in hell *(dūzakh)* than they were in this world, since in hell they are aware of God, but in the world they were not. And nothing is sweeter than the awareness of God. So the reason they wish to return to the world is to do something in order to become aware of the manifestation of divine grace, not because the world is a happier place than hell *(dūzakh)*.

Rūmī, Fīhi mā Fīhi 65:1–4, KFF p.229; cf. DRA p.236, in SPL p.107

Like many other mystics, Sufis have also taught that God should be loved without the hope of heaven or the fear of hell. They have no concern with either. Their only concern is to annihilate themselves in the Beloved. ʻAṭṭār quotes Kharaqānī, who says that he is only concerned with the uncreated God, not with His creation, whether it be heaven or hell:

> I do not say that heaven and hell *(bihisht-u dūzakh)* do not exist.
> I say that heaven and hell *(bihisht-u dūzakh)*
> have no place around me, for both are created things;
> And where I am there is no place for that which is created.
>
> *Kharaqānī, in Tadhkirat al-Awliyā' 2, TAN2 p.216, in SSE3 p.209*

Other Sufis have spoken similarly. To be with God is heaven; to be separated is hell:

> Union and separation are also interpreted as heaven *(bihisht)* and hell *(dūzakh).*
>
> *Javad Nūrbakhsh, Sufi Symbolism, FNI3 p.168; cf. SSE3 p.209*

> My Lord, why should I be proud of heaven *(bihisht)* and houris?
> Bestow upon me that eye
> with which I can make a paradise *(bihisht)* of every sight.
>
> *Anṣārī, Rasā'il, RAA p.105, in FNI3 p.168*

Like other mystics, Ḥāfiẓ speaks of finding God now, rather than hoping for heaven after death:

> Why should I, who can have heaven *(bihisht)* in hand today,
> put my faith in the cleric's promise of (heaven) tomorrow?
>
> *Ḥāfiẓ, Dīvān, DHA p.205, DHM (437:11) p.397, DIH p.333, in SSE3 p.209*

Given the vivid warnings of hell's torture and descriptions of the delights of paradise, they are traditionally understood in a literal manner. People, therefore, worship God from the fear of hell and the hope of heaven. Mystics, however, have another point of view. Rābiʻah of Baṣrah is famed for saying:

> O my Lord, if I worship You
> from the fear of hell *(dūzakh),*
> burn me in hell *(dūzakh).*
> And if I worship You from hope of paradise *(bihisht),*
> exclude me thence;
> But if I worship You for Your own sake,
> then withhold not from me Your eternal beauty.
>
> *Rābiʻah, in Tadhkirat al-Awliyā' 1, TAN1 p.73; cf. RM p.30*

See also: **Hadēs**, **heavens**, **hell**, **jahannam**, **al-jannah**, **naraka**, **svarga**, **vaikuṇṭha**.

1. *Qur'ān* 47:15.
2. Rūmī, *Maśnavī* I:1375, *MJR2* p.76.
3. Rūmī, *Maśnavī* I:1382–83, *MJR2* p.76.
4. Rūmī, *Maśnavī* VI:4648–52; *cf. MJR6* p.515.

Binah (He) *Lit.* understanding, intelligence; mystically, spiritual understanding. According to the system of the medieval Kabbalah, *Binah* is the third of the ten *sefirot* (divine qualities), through whose emanation the creation took place. *Ḥokhmah* (Wisdom) is the creative Power, likened to the masculine or positive energy of creation. *Ḥokhmah*'s activity takes place within *Binah. Binah* is the feminine or receptive aspect of Wisdom in the sense that she is the 'womb' or 'field' in which Wisdom projects itself. In the *Zohar,* she is also called the Palace or Building, suggesting a location in which the lower *sefirot* reside, or exist in potential. The union of *Ḥokhmah* and *Binah* produces a subtle or 'shadow' *sefirah* of *Da'at* (spiritual knowledge), from which the seven lower *sefirot* are born. Thus, *Binah* is often called the mother of the seven lower *sefirot.* She is the womb from which all life originates.

See also: **sefirot**.

Brahmaloka, **Brahmapura**, **Brahmapurī** (S), **Brahm lok**, **Brahm purī** (H/Pu) *Lit.* place *(lok)* or city *(purī)* of *Brahman (Brahm);* the station of the Ultimate, the highest Reality, as described in the *Upanishads;* also, depending on the context, the heaven of the Hindu deity, *Brahmā,* the highest of the seven heavens of Indian mythology, also called *satyaloka;* also, the human body, understood as the dwelling place of *Brahman,* the 'city' in which *Brahman* is to be found. The *Chhāndogya Upanishad* uses *Brahmapura* to mean both the human form and the dwelling place of *Brahman:*

> There is, in this city of *Brahman (Brahmapura),* a dwelling in the form of a small lotus; within it, there is an inner space *(ākāsha).* That which is within that inner space is to be sought after; it is that which one should desire to know.
>
> Should someone ask, "With regard to this dwelling, the lotus within the city of *Brahman (Brahmapura),* and the space that is within it – what is within it that it should be sought after, and what is there that one should desire to know?"

> Then he should reply: "Truly, as (great as) is the vast space without, so extends the space within the heart. Truly, both heaven and earth are contained within it, as are fire and air, sun and moon, lightning and the stars – whatever is possessed and whatever is not possessed – all that is contained within it."
>
> Should someone ask, "If all that exists – all beings and all desires – is contained within this city of *Brahman (Brahmapura),* then what is left of it when old age comes upon it or when it perishes?"
>
> Then he should reply: "It (the self within) does not age when the body ages, nor die when the body dies. That is the true city of *Brahman (Brahmapura).* In It are contained all desires. It is the soul *(ātman)* – free from sin, free from old age and death, free from suffering, free from hunger and thirst."
>
> *Chhāndogya Upanishad 8:1.1–5*

The same *Upanishad* adds:

> Just as those who do not know the place in a field where a treasure is buried will walk over it again and again without finding it, so do all beings go on, day after day, never finding the world of *Brahman (Brahmaloka)* within, for they are carried away by unreality.
>
> *Chhāndogya Upanishad 8:3.2*

See also: **Brahmā**, **Brahman** (2.1), **Indraloka**, **loka**, **Shivaloka**, **Vishṇuloka**.

brahmāṇḍ(a) (S/H), **brahmaṇḍ** (Pu) *Lit.* egg *(aṇḍa)* of *(Brahmā).* According to the *Manu Smṛiti,* the self-existent One first creates the primordial 'waters', depositing a seed therein. This seed becomes a golden egg *(hiraṇyāṇḍa),* resplendent as the sun. From this primordial egg is born *Brahmā* – the creator of all the worlds. *Brahmā* brings about creation by dividing the egg into two parts, with which he constructs the heavens and the earth, going on to create the ten *Prajāpatis,* the 'mind-born sons', who complete the work of creation. The creation so formed is known as *brahmāṇḍa:*

> This (universe) existed in the shape of darkness,
> unperceived, destitute of distinctive marks,
> unattainable by reasoning, unknowable,
> wholly immersed as though in deep sleep.
>
> Then the divine Self-Existent,
> invisible, but making visible the elements and all the rest,
> appeared with irresistible (creative) power,
> dispelling the darkness.

He who can be perceived by the internal organ alone,
who is subtle, invisible and eternal,
who contains all created beings and is inconceivable,
shone forth of His own will.

He, desiring to produce beings
of various kinds from His own body,
first created the waters with a thought,
and placed His seed in them.

That seed became a golden egg *(hiraṇyāṇḍa),*
in brilliancy equal to the sun;
In that egg, He Himself was born as *Brahmā,*
the progenitor of the whole world.

The waters are called *nārāh,*
for the waters are, indeed, the offspring of *Nāra;*
And because they were his first residence *(ayana),*
he *(Brahmā)* is therefore named *Nārāyaṇa....*

That divine one resided in that egg all year long,
then he himself, by his thought (alone),
divided it into two halves;

And out of those two halves,
he formed heaven and earth,
between them the middle sphere,
the eight points of the horizon,
and the eternal abode of the waters.

Manu Smṛiti 1:5–10, 12–13; cf. LM pp.2–6

Although the details of this account differ in the various texts, *brahmāṇḍa* is generally understood in Indian mythology to comprise the whole created cosmos, arranged in three principal strata known as *triloka* (three worlds). These three worlds are: *loka,* the heavens, high above the earth; *tala,* the subterranean regions; and *naraka* or hells far below the earth. Each division of the *triloka* is said to be further subdivided, making twenty-one regions *(lokas)* in the entire creation. Details vary from one description to another, but these regions are generally listed as:

1. *Loka* Seven regions or worlds, including the heavens of the gods, as well as atmospheric and terrestrial spheres: *bhūloka, bhuvaloka, svarloka* or *Indraloka, maharloka, janaloka, tapoloka* and *satyaloka* or *Brahmaloka.*

2. *Tala* The seven subterranean regions: *atala, vitala, sutala, rasātala, talātala, mahātala* and *pātāla.*[1]

3. *Naraka* The seven hells: *put, avīchi, saṃhāta, tāmisra, ṛijīsha, kudmala* and *kākola.*

Indian mystics from medieval times onwards have used *brahmāṇḍa* in a number of ways. In a general sense, it is used to mean the universe, the entire creation up to the threshold of eternity. Thus, Rāja Pīpā writes:

> He who is in the universe *(brahmaṇḍ),*
> that also abides in the body:
> And whoever seeks, he finds Him there.
>
> *Pīpā, Ādi Granth 695, MMS*

There is also a verse from Kabīr, using almost identical words.[2]

The nineteenth-century Swāmī Shiv Dayāl Singh and the mystics following him, in keeping with their identification of *Brahm* or *Brahman* as the region of *trikuṭī,* also known as the universal mind *(brahmāṇḍī man),* have used *brahmāṇḍa* more specifically. Firstly, it is the creation above the physical universe, up to the level of *Brahm:*

> The region of *sahans dal kanwal* (astral) begins above the eyes, and this is the beginning of *brahmāṇḍ.* This ends below the plane of *daswān dwār....* The region above that is called *pār brahmāṇḍ.*
>
> *Swāmī Shiv Dayāl Singh, Sār Bachan Prose 1:26, SB p.15*

In this context, *brahmāṇḍa* refers only to the astral and causal worlds, the regions of the mind. *Daswān dwār* (tenth door) is the realm lying immediately above the mind.

Brahmāṇḍa, however, is also used to mean the third grand division in creation, the first two being *piṇḍa* (physical) and *aṇḍa* (astral). Here, *brahmāṇḍa* refers to those realms of creation extending from, and including, the upper part of *trikuṭī* up to the portals of eternity *(sat desh):*

> The lower portion of *brahmāṇḍa* (is) named *trikuṭī.* The upper portion of *brahmāṇḍa* is called *pārbrahm.*
>
> *Julian Johnson, The Path of the Masters 4:4, POM p.228*

In this context, *pārbrahm* (beyond *Brahm*) refers to the regions between *trikuṭī* and *sach khaṇḍ.*

See also: **aṇḍa**, **hiraṇyagarbha**, **Nārāyaṇa** (4.2).

1. See Sadānanda, *Vedāntasāra* 2:104.
2. Kabīr, *Ādi Granth* 1162.

branch A metaphor associated with that of the Tree of Life as the creative Power, the branches being the souls, the realms of creation and so on – depending upon the context; a term also translated as 'shoot'. Sometimes, the branch or shoot also refers to the Messiah or Saviour.

In the gnostic *Tripartite Tractate,* the writer – while trying to describe how the One can be found in the manyness of this creation – portrays the Father as a single root from which arise the branches and fruit of creation:

> He existed before anything other than Himself came into being. The Father is a single one … Yet He is not like a solitary individual. Otherwise, how could He be a father? For whenever there is a 'father', the name 'son' follows. But the single One, who alone is the Father, is like a root with tree, branches and fruit.
>
> *Tripartite Tractate 51, NHS22 pp.192–93*

He also portrays the "*aeon* of Truth" – an epithet of the Father – as being

> like a spring – which is what it is – yet flows into streams and lakes and canals and branches; or like a root spread out beneath trees and branches with its fruit; or like a human body, which is partitioned in an indivisible way into members of members, primary members and secondary, great and small.
>
> *Tripartite Tractate 73, NHS22 pp.228–29*

See also: **Righteous Shoot** (▸2), **Root** (3.1), **Tree of Life** (3.1).

briah (He) *Lit.* creation.

See **'olam ha-briah**.

bustān (A/P) *Lit.* place of fragrance; the place where fragrances can be enjoyed; an abode of perfumes; hence, a garden; metaphorically, the inner being of the contemplative, the inner condition of the mystic; also, a pleasurable state of the mind. Like *jannah* (garden), *bustān* sometimes refers to paradise or the inner realms. It also appears in other metaphorical contexts. Rūmī, for instance, speaks of eternity as the "garden *(bustān)* of God",[1] while Ḥāfiẓ begs for the "dawn wind" and "fragrance" of the divine grace that comes from the eternal "rose garden *(bustān)*":

Along with the dawn wind *(ṣabā),*
send from Your cheek, a handful of roses:
Then, maybe, I will discern some fragrance
from the dust of Your rose garden *(bustān).*
Ḥāfiẓ, Dīvān, DHA p.2, DHM (2:6) p.34, DIH p.30; cf. DHWC (2:8) p.16

See also: **gardens**, **al-jannah**.

1. Rūmī, *Maśnavī* I:72, *MJR2* p.8.

causal plane, **causal realm**, **causal region**, **causal world** See **regions**.

chamber(s) See **rooms**.

chandra (S/H/Pu), **chand** (H/Pu) (pl. *chandā*) *Lit.* the moon; used mystically in reference to the 'moon region', one of the subtle, subastral realms lying within the 'sky' of the body. This region is traversed as the soul leaves the body, and is situated between the eye centre (*ājñā chakra,* the two-petalled lotus, the topmost *chakra* in the human body) and the *ashṭ dal kanwal* (eight-petalled lotus), on the threshold of the astral realms). The moon region is so-called because the light there is experienced as circular, like the end of a tunnel, and as calming and steady, like the light of the full moon. In fact, to begin with, the soul experiences quavering and intermittent light like the stars at night. Then, the light appears to focus and become bright like that of the sun. Then, it steadies into the clear light of the moon. After that, the soul steps out into the lower reaches of the astral world. This process is described in the *Bṛihadāraṇyaka Upanishad:*

When a man departs from this world,
he reaches the air (inner sky).
The air opens there for him,
as wide as the hole of a chariot wheel.
Through this (opening),
he ascends and reaches the sun.
The sun opens there for him,
as wide as the hole of a *lambara* (a small drum).
By this (opening) he ascends
and reaches the moon *(chandra).*
The moon opens there for him,
as wide as the hole of a *dundubhi* (a large drum)

By this (opening) he ascends,
  and reaches a world free from grief and cold.
There he dwells for endless years.

Bṛihadāraṇyaka Upanishad 5:10.1, U3 p.333

Being "free from grief and cold" symbolizes freedom from mental and physical suffering. Many mystics have spoken of these realms. Dariyā Sāhib of Bihar writes:

The sun *(sūr)* and moon *(chand)* come into sight,
  then both set as the soul rises.

Dariyā Sāhib, Gyān Dīpak, GD pp.527–28; cf. DSSB p.65

In other instances, it is unclear whether the mystic is referring to these initial stages in the soul's ascent or whether the allusion is a general reference to the light within, symbolized as the sun and moon:

Where there are no suns, I saw a sun;
Where there are no moons *(chandā),* I saw a moon *(chand);*
Where exist no stars, there I saw them twinkle:
Boundless was Dādū's joy.

Dādū, Bānī 1, Parchā 90, DDB1 p.49

Mystics have also spoken of the light of the *sahaj* (easy, natural, peaceful) region, also called *daswān dwār* (*lit.* tenth door), the first of the regions beyond those of the mind, as being like the white light of the full moon:

On the day of the full moon,
  the moon *(chand)* is full in the heavens.
With the might of its beams,
  the gentle (*sahaj,* peaceful) light is diffused.

Kabīr, Ādi Granth 344, MMS

See also: **tārā**.

curtain See **veil**.

da'at (He) *Lit.* knowledge; inner knowledge; mystic knowledge of God; inner spiritual awakening; derived from a Hebrew word meaning 'attaching' or 'joining', implying the condition of union or merging that is characteristic of mystic knowledge.

In the system of the ten *sefirot* (emanations), *Da'at* is the 'shadow' *sefirah* – the assumed axis upon which the *sefirot* of *Ḥokhmah* and *Binah* blend to form one harmony and unity, exchanging and combining their individual essences to give birth to the seven lower *sefirot.*

See also: **sefirot**.

dā'irat al-imkān (A), **dā'irah-'i imkān** (P) *Lit.* sphere *(dā'irat)* of possibility *(imkān). Dā'irat* means sphere, circle, jurisdiction, hence, the world. *Imkān* means possibility, contingency, potentiality, existence.

The expression refers to all creation below that which is real, eternal and unchanging, since everything created is 'contingent' on God's will. God is the only 'Necessary Being *(Wājib al-Wujūd)*'. That is, only God is and necessarily must be. All other beings are called contingencies *(imkān).* However, even the *imkān* is an aspect of God or is God. Sufis have expressed this by describing the 'necessary' and the 'contingent' as the 'two hands *(yadān)* of God'.

See also: **mumkin**, **Wājib al-Wujūd** (2.2).

daswān dwār (H), **dasam duār**, **daswain duār** (Pu) *Lit.* tenth *(daswān)* door *(dwār);* the tenth gate; the spiritual realm that lies immediately above that of the universal mind or *trikuṭī* (*lit.* three peaks) in which the soul, for the first time since it left its eternal home with God, knows itself as pure soul, free of all coverings of the mind. *Daswān dwār* is therefore said to be the realm of true or mystic self-realization, though the soul has yet to realize its identity with God (God-realization). The soul at this stage has also achieved liberation from the wheel of birth and death.

Trikuṭī is described as being like a fortress or citadel *(gaṛh)* possessing nine gates opening downward and one gate – the tenth gate – leading inward. Because of the difficulty both of locating and ascending through this tenth gate, it is normally said to be closed. It is from this characteristic that *daswān dwār* gets its name, since it lies beyond the tenth door.

From the vantage point of *daswān dwār,* the soul's entire past history of transmigration is crystal clear, like looking into a mirror. But by the time it reaches this level on its journey homewards, the soul is not interested in knowing its past. It always looks ahead or upwards, towards the divine Source of all. The soul here has the urge to continue higher, since it has not yet reached eternity – *daswān dwār* and the spiritual realms below eternity being subject to grand dissolution *(mahā pralaya).*

The created realms below *daswān dwār* are known generally as *triloka* (three worlds). Hence, Guru Amardās writes:

He alone is emancipated who conquers his mind,
and mammon (*dhāt,* dirt) clings not to him again.
He abides in the tenth gate *(daswain duār),*
and obtains the knowledge of the three worlds *(tribhavaṇ).*

Guru Amardās, Ādi Granth 490, MMS

Kabīr, speaking of India's innumerable wandering holy men *(sādhus),* writes of rising above *trikuṭī* by passing through the tenth door:

A (true) *sādh* (holy man) is he who conquers this fort (of *trikuṭī*).
Going beyond the nine manifested doors to the tenth,
he opens that which is locked.

Kabīr, Shabdāvalī 1, Bhed Bānī 22:16, KSS1 p.66

Charaṇdās also speaks of passing through *daswān dwār* in the 'sky' of *trikuṭī:*

They who worship the Lord
and focus their attention in *gagan maṇḍal* (the sky of *trikuṭī*)
in which is found the tenth door *(daswān dwār)* –
It is they, says Charaṇdās, who reach the Lord's court.

Charaṇdās, Bānī 1, Sumiran Vidhi 22, CDB1 p.32

The human form is also described by mystics as a city with nine gates. The nine sensory openings lead out while one, the tenth gate or eye centre, also known as *daswān dar* (tenth door) or *daswīn galī* (tenth lane), leads within. It is the gateway leading from *piṇḍa* to *aṇḍa,* from the physical to the astral realms. A *dar* is a less prestigious kind of a door than a *dwār.* The former is an ordinary house door. A *dwār* is the door to a temple or palace, or to the residence of a superior, approached meekly when seeking an audience or a favour. *Daswān dar* is a reflection of the tenth gateway at the top of *trikuṭī* that leads into the region known as *daswān dwār.*

See also: **daswān dwār** (▸2), **kingrī** (3.2), **sārangī** (3.2).

devaloka (S), **devlok** (H/Pu) *Lit.* realm or world *(loka)* of the gods *(deva);* the world or sphere of any deity; heaven or *svarga;* more specifically, the highest of the three worlds *(triloka)* of Vedic and Puranic tradition. The *Bṛihadāraṇyaka Upanishad* says that *devaloka* can be reached "through *vidyā*", *vidyā* (*lit.* knowledge) in this context meaning *gnosis* – divine knowledge or experience:

Verily, there are three worlds *(lokatraya):*
  the world of men,
  the world of the ancestors,
  and the world of the gods *(devaloka)....*

The world of the gods *(devaloka)*
  (can be reached) through *gnosis (vidyā).*
The world of the gods *(devaloka)*
  is the best of the worlds.
Therefore, they praise *gnosis (vidyā).*

Bṛihadāraṇyaka Upanishad 1:5.16

According to Hindu religious tradition, there are a great many lesser gods, deities or rulers, many of which have their own heavenly realms, such as *Vishṇuloka, Brahmaloka, Shivaloka, Indraloka* and so on. According to mystics, such heavens would lie within the astral and causal realms, that is, within the domain of the universal mind. As such, they are subject to the cycle of creation and dissolution.

Thus, the *Bṛihadāraṇyaka Upanishad* indicates that *devaloka* is not the highest world. The worlds of *Indra* and *Virāj (Prajāpati)* are higher. And beyond these lies *hiraṇyagarbha* (the golden womb), the first manifestation of *Brahman* in the process of creation. According to the story related in this *Upanishad,* the woman philosopher, Gārgī, has asked the sage Yājñavalkya about the origin of things. According to Hindu mythology, the world originated from and is supported or pervaded by water. "But what," she asks, "pervades the water?"

He replies, "the wind." "And what," she continues, "pervades the wind?" And so begins a series of questions and answers, as Yājñavalkya enumerates a number of the worlds of Indian mythology, each one, he says, supporting the one below. The water is supported by the wind, the wind by *bhuvaloka* (world of the atmosphere), and that in turn by the worlds of the *ghandarvas* (heavenly musicians), the *āditya* (sun), the *chandra* (moon) and the *nakshatras* (stars). The imagery used for pervading or supporting is that of weaving, in which each successively lower world is woven as "warp and weft" upon the world above. Gārgī presses Yājñavalkya relentlessly:

"On what is the world of the stars woven, warp and weft?"
"On the world of gods *(devaloka),* O Gārgī."
"On what is the world of the gods woven, warp and weft?"
"On the world of *Indra,* O Gārgī."
"On what is the world of *Indra* woven, warp and weft?"
"On the world of *Virāj,* O Gārgī."
"On what is the word of *Virāj* woven, warp and weft?"

"On the world of *hiraṇyagarbha* (golden womb), O Gārgī."
"On what, pray, is the world of *hiraṇyagarbha* woven, warp and weft?"
"Gārgī," said Yājñavalkya, "do not question so much, lest your head fall off! Truly, you question too much about a deity about whom further questions cannot be asked. Gārgī, do not question so much."

Thereupon, Gārgī, the daughter of Vāchaknavī, held her peace.

Bṛihadāraṇyaka Upanishad 3:6.1

See also: **loka**, **triloka**.

dharam khaṇḍ (Pu) *Lit.* region *(khaṇḍ)* of *dharam;* used by Guru Nānak for the physical world *(piṇḍa). Dharam* includes in its meaning, justice, duty, right living, righteousness and religion, all of which are characteristics of human existence.

See also: **khaṇḍ**, **piṇḍa**.

Din (He) *Lit.* judgment, law; the fifth of the ten *sefirot* or emanations; also called *Gevurah* (Might, Power). According to Kabbalistic thought, *Din*'s role is to channel God's abundant love and mercy (embodied as the fourth *sefirah* of *Ḥesed,* Love) into the creation. The creation is unable to receive the full potency of God's love, and *Din* represents the first limitation or channelling of His love. In the language of Kabbalist Isaac Luria, *Din*'s limiting activity mirrors the initial *ẓimẓum* – the contraction of the Godhead into itself – which preceded the first expression of the divine will. Through its limiting activity, *Din* contains the 'seed' or potential of evil, which manifests in the lower realms.

Through this imagery, Kabbalists explain how evil originates from within God, who is purely spiritual, without even a trace of matter or negativity. It depicts how the potential of both positive and negative principles are embodied within God who transcends all.

See also: **sefirot**.

dominion(s) A land or province under the rule of some prince, lord or other authority; mystically, a term sometimes used for the inner realms, meaning much the same as principality and sovereignty. As one of the gnostic writers says:

In this (the structure of the creation) many dominions and divinities (gods, rulers) came into existence.

Treatise on the Resurrection 44, NHS22 pp.148–49

The term was also used for the eternal realm or "dominion":

> Blessed be the eternal dominion,
> the fortunate divine Lord of the strong.
> *Manichaean Hymns, MM3 p.885, RMP bn, ML p.139*

See also: **principality**, **sovereignty**.

dunyā wa-ākhirah (A), **dunyā-u ākhirat** (P) *Lit.* this world *(dunyā)* and the afterlife *(ākhirah);* this world and the next, this world and the world to come; an expression embodying the teaching of the *Qur'ān* that while living in this world *(dunyā),* the hereafter *(ākhirah)* should not be forgotten:

> O my people! Lo! this life of the world *(al-dunyā)*
> is but a passing comfort.
> And lo! the hereafter *(al-ākhirah),*
> that is the enduring home.
> *Qur'ān 40:39, MGK*

In fact, the *Qur'ān* counsels living life with a view to entering the hereafter after death. Hence, the advice to spend wealth in charity and good deeds, since everything comes from *Allāh* and should be spent in His service:

> But seek with the (wealth) which *Allāh* has bestowed on thee,
> the home of the hereafter *(al-dār al-ākhirah);*
> Nor forget thy portion in this world *(dunyā):*
> But do thou good, as *Allāh* has been good to thee,
> and seek not (occasions for) mischief in the land:
> For *Allāh* loves not those who do mischief.
> *Qur'ān 28:77, HQSA*

There is a *ḥadīth* (traditional saying of Muḥammad) which similarly says that what you sow here, you will reap hereafter: "This world *(dunyā)* is the seedbed for the other world *(ākhirah).*"[1]

For Sufis, the real meaning of *dunyā* is not only the more obvious temptations of the world, but anything that diverts the attention from God. They also stress valuing neither *dunyā* nor *ākhirah,* this world or the hereafter. They repeatedly say that they care neither for this world nor for the next, but only for pleasing the Beloved. Dhū al-Nūn said:

> O God, if I have a share in this world *(dunyā),* I donate it to the heathen (those not knowing God); and if I have savings in my account

> in *ākhirah,* I give it to the religious minded. The remembrance of You while in this world *(dunyā)* and seeing You in the next *(ʻuqbá)* are enough for me. This world *(dunyā)* and the next *(ʻuqbá)* are both goods or merchandise with a price to be paid; but seeing You is cash freely bestowed.
>
> *Dhū al-Nūn Miṣrī, in Kashf al-Asrār, KA2 p.319, in FNI3 p.153*

Sufi reasoning for only desiring the Beloved is that the fundamental nature of the world is impermanence. This is expressed by al-Ghazālī:

> The first magical thing about *dunyā* is that it presents itself to you as motionless or stationary, whereas it is really moving ever so gradually, bit by tiny bit. It is like a shadow; when you look at it, it stands still; but in reality, it is constantly moving. Therefore, it should be clear that your life too is passing by constantly, gradually decreasing every moment. It is *dunyā* which is escaping from you, that bids you farewell; yet you are unaware of it....
>
> Know that the plans of this *dunyā* look simple and small, but a whole lifetime will be the required investment for the fulfilment of even one of these schemes. Jesus said, "A seeker of the world is like one who drinks the water of the sea. The more he drinks, the thirstier he becomes. He keeps drinking it until he dies, and that thirst will never leave him." And Muḥammad said, "In the same way that it is not possible to go to the water and not get wet, it is not possible to be in the world and not be tainted by it."
>
> *Al-Ghazālī, Kīmiyā-yi Saʻādat 4, KS pp.66, 68*

Rūzbihān continues in the same vein by pointing out that letting go of desires for the world opens the way to the higher Reality:

> Whenever a devotee can pass through the veils of the world and cleanse his mind of desires, he will reach the door of the heart. And when, with the key of servitude, he opens the heart's door and attains the vantage point of the soul, he perceives the world of wisdom, unseen lights and brides of faith and certitude. He also sees the reality of the angelic forms in the mirror of his heart, and has reached the level of *ākhirah* where exist heaven, hell, doomsday, resurrection, Judgment Day, firmament, empyrean, levels and ranks of spiritual progress, conditions, feelings, forms, palaces, union, separation, discovery and beholding of visions.
>
> This heart is unseen, and within it lies yet another unseen wherein are veils of divinity, might, glory, eternity and infinity. Whoever knows these divine halting stations will know *ākhirah* and all it contains.

> In the mirror of the heart of the Saints, *ākhirah* is revealed. But this state cannot be attained except through experiencing the stages of meditation.
>
> *Rūzbihān, Mashrab al-Arwāḥ, MAR p.61, in FNI3 p.152*

See also: **al-ākhirah**, **al-dunyā** (6.2), **paraloka**.

1. *Ḥadīth, AMBF* 338, in *MDI* p.107.

dūzakh (P), **dozakh**, **dojak** (Pu) *Lit.* hell; the place of torture; the place where punishment for bad deeds is meted out. *Dūzakh* is contrasted with *bihisht* (heaven). *Dūzakh* also refers to sensual desires that ensnare people into unrighteous living and entrap them in the limitations of the physical world. The term also means 'stomach', comparing physical appetite to the fires of *dūzakh*.

Sufi mystics acknowledge the existence of hells in the subtle regions, but their emphasis is on the quality of consciousness in the here and now: a person whose thoughts are filled with evil and hurtfulness is already in hell.

See also: **bihisht-u dūzakh**, **Gehenna**, **Hadēs**, **hell**, **jahannam**, **naraka**, **Pit**, **Sheol**.

dvīp(a) (S/H), **dīp** (H/Pu) *Lit.* island; geographically, a continent; mythologically, one of the seven insular land masses that, according to the *Purāṇas,* comprise the known world. The *Vishṇu Purāṇa*[1] names these *dvīpa* after trees or plants that grow on them or after other identifying features. They are *jambu* (rose apple tree), *plaksha* (fig tree), *shālmali* (silk-cotton tree), *kusha* (a sacred grass used in various religious ceremonies), *krauncha* (a heron, the name of a mountain), *shāka* (teak tree) and *pushkara* (a blue lotus). The seven *dvīpa* are surrounded respectively by seven great seas, *viz.* the sea of salt water *(lavaṇa),* of sugar cane juice *(ikshu),* of wine *(surā),* of clarified butter *(sarpish),* of curds *(dadhi),* of milk *(dugdha)* and of fresh water *(jal).* These seas all symbolize fertility. This mythological geography did not actually influence Indian astronomers of the past, who knew that the world was spherical, nor Indian sailors who were naturally aware that there was salt water in the oceans.

Esoterically, *dvīpa* is used either for certain areas within the spiritual regions or for the spiritual realms themselves. The term has sometimes been translated as island universes. Galaxies, being widely spaced clusters of stars and solar systems within the physical universe, could be regarded as island universes of *piṇḍa,* for instance.

The eighteenth-century Indian mystic, Dariyā Sāhib, has described seven regions from the highest down to the physical universe, calling them somewhat enigmatically: *dayā dvīp* (island of grace), *puhup dvīp* (flower island), *ambu dvīp* (island of water), *sahaj dvīp* (island of peace), *pāyar dvīp* (island of paddy straw), *shālmali dvīp* (island of the silk-cotton tree, *mānsarovar)* and *jambu dvīp* (island of the rose apple, the physical universe).[2] In one of his verses, using the human body symbolically, he describes the all-pervading extent of *Sat Purush:*

> The Name of *Sat Purush* is incomparable:
> His Form none can describe.
> His divine eyes are lustrous:
> boundless and beyond reach is their brilliance.
> In comparison to the splendour of His forehead,
> even the sun seems pale....
> Extremely mighty are His arms, which extend
> to the seven regions *(dvīpas)* and nine realms *(khaṇḍas).*
> The fragrance of Truth emanates from His body and chest,
> a sweet aroma arises from every pore of His body.
> *Dariyā Sāhib, Gyān Dīpak, GD pp.24–25; cf. DSSB pp.91–92*

See also: **khaṇḍ**, **puhup dvīp**.

1. *Vishṇu Purāṇa* 2:2.
2. See *DSSB* p.92 (n.4); used throughout the works of Dariyā Sāhib.

dwelling(s) A place of residence; mystically, a name given to the inner regions of the creation in Judaic, Christian, Mandaean, Manichaean and other allied ancient Middle Eastern mystical writings; sometimes rendered in translation as 'habitations'. In Mandaean literature, 'dwelling' is commonly translated from *shkinta* (pl. *shkinata*). The Supreme, for instance, is described as

> the great Father of Glory by whose Word
> worlds were created, and by whose utterance
> dwellings *(shkinata)* came into being.
> *Mandaean Prayer Book 376, CPM p.276*

In later times, demonstrating the processes of externalization of mystic teachings, the sacred cult or priestly huts in Mandaeanism used for initiation were also known as *shkinata.*

See also: **habitations**, **mshunia kūshṭā**, **regions**, **shkinta**.

emanation(s) Something that issues or proceeds from a source; an effusion or flowing forth; mystically, the creation, as the emanation or projection of God as the source or root of everything. The term is frequently found in gnostic and mystic literature, as in the *Gospel of Truth.* Here, *pleromas* ('fullnesses') are blueprints or archetypes, the seed forms or patterns of all that is further created from them. The writer says:

> All the emanations of the Father are *pleromas;*
> And the Root of all His emanations
> is in the One who made them all grow up in Himself:
> He assigned them their destinies.
> Each one then is manifest.
>
> *Gospel of Truth 41, NHS22 pp.114–15*

In the *Pistis Sophia,* using the term in a similar manner, Jesus describes the inner journey to his disciples:

> For this cause, therefore, you will go to the Height; you will enter into all the regions of all the great emanations of the Light, and become rulers (kings) in the eternal kingdom of the Light.
>
> *Pistis Sophia 252:100; cf. PS pp.504–5, PSGG p.209*

In the *Wisdom of Solomon,* Wisdom, as the creative Power, is described as a "pure emanation":

> She is a Breath of the Power of God,
> pure emanation of the glory of the Almighty;
> Hence nothing impure can find a way into her.
>
> *Wisdom of Solomon 7:25, JB*

This passage is echoed in the gnostic *Teachings of Silvanus,* describing Christ:

> For he is light from the Power of God,
> and he is an emanation of the pure glory of the Almighty.
>
> *Teachings of Silvanus 112–13, NHS30 pp.354–55*

The Kabbalah, the system of medieval Jewish mysticism, also describes the creation as a hierarchy of emanations *(sefirot)* from the divine Source *(Ayn-Sof).*

See also: **sefirot**.

field(s) See **gardens**.

firdaws (A/P) *Lit.* paradise; *firdaws* is derived from the old Persian *paridaiza,* from the Avestan *pairdaeza,* with the original meaning of an enclosure; hence, an enclosed garden; sometimes as *firdaws-i barīn* (supreme paradise, highest heaven). The English word 'paradise' comes from the Greek, *paradeisos* (garden), also from the old Persian.

See also: **bihisht-u dūzakh**, **heavens**, **al-jannah**, **paradise**.

firmament The expanse of the sky or the heavens. In religious and mystic literature, the term is used loosely, particularly in translations. Sometimes, however, it seems to have a more definitive meaning, referring to the inner 'sky' between the eye centre and the subastral realms.

In the *Ascension of Isaiah,* for instance, the writer describes how Isaiah – who has been taken up into the highest heaven – witnesses Jesus receiving instructions to descend to this world:

> And I heard the Voice of the Most High, the Father of my lord, saying to my lord the Christ, who will be called Jesus, "Go forth, and descend through all the heavens: descend to the firmament and through that world as far as the angel who is in *Sheol;* but to *Hagu'el* (perdition, hell) you shall not go. And you must transform yourself so as to be like all those who are in the five heavens. And you must take care to transform yourself so as to be like the angels of the firmament as well, and also like that of the angels who are in *Sheol.* And none of the angels of that world will know that you are lord with me of the seven heavens and of their angels."
>
> *Ascension of Isaiah 10:7–11; cf. AOT pp.806–7, OTP2 p.173*

The Master, in this case Jesus, is appointed or commissioned by the "Voice of the Most High" to descend to earth. But he has to travel incognito. In each realm, he takes on the form or garment of that world, and appears to be like the inhabitants of that region, just as in this world he comes in the garb of a human being, only revealing himself to his chosen ones.

Here, *Sheol* (*lit.* the Pit) probably refers to this world, as it does in many other places in this kind of mystic literature; but, in the text as it stands, the precise identification of the various realms is uncertain. The "firmament", however, also translated as the 'vault of heaven' or the 'sky of heaven', together with the "angels who are in *Sheol*", probably refers to the subtle side of the physical universe – the subtle administration system, so to speak, by which the physical universe is governed. In other mystic traditions, this realm is known as the 'sky of the body' or – in Indian terminology – *chidākāsha* (*lit.* sky of consciousness), being the subastral realm lying between the single eye and the true astral plane.

This suggestion is borne out by what are probably explanatory interpolations found both in the Slavonic and in one of the Latin texts of the *Vision of Isaiah* – a document that contains this part of the *Ascension of Isaiah.* At the beginning of Isaiah's ascent through the heavens, he is first taken to the "firmament" that lies below the first heaven. Here he sees the pattern or blueprint of what goes on below, on earth. And the writer, through Isaiah, quotes the ancient Hermetic axiom:

> As above, so also on earth, for the likeness of what is in the firmament is here on earth. What happens in the firmament happens similarly here on earth.
>
> *Ascension of Isaiah 7:10; cf. AOT p.797, OTP2 p.166*

The vision then continues:

> After this, he took me up into the regions above the firmament; this is the first heaven.
>
> *Ascension of Isaiah 7:13; cf. AOT p.797, OTP2 p.166*

"Into the regions" and "this is the first heaven", however, are explanatory interpolations, found only in the Slavonic and in one of the Latin texts, and introduced either by the translator or some subsequent hand. It is known that these texts were used by the medieval Bogomils of Eastern Europe and other gnostically minded groups who had some knowledge of the inner realms, and it is they who may have been responsible for this later attempt at elucidation.

See also: **heavens**.

Five Divine Presences See **al-Ḥaḍarāt al-Ilāhīyah al-Khams**.

Five Greatnesses One of the ways used by the third-century Persian mystic, Mānī, to describe the hierarchy of heavens in creation. Mystics have used many 'systems' in their attempt to describe the indescribable. Although mentioned in a number of Manichaean writings, only fragments of Mānī's teaching concerning these five heavens remain and, among these, the most detailed is not only rather brief, but the description of the first two heavens is lost. In this system, the fifth heaven is "self-existent" and eternal. The description begins in the third heaven:

... the third, the blessed *aeons* without count and number,
wherein dwell the light gods, angels, elements,
the powers in great bliss and joy.

The fourth: the unborn Air
in the paradise of light,
wondrous, beautiful to behold,
immeasurable its goodness for them.
By supernatural power it shall, by itself,
bring into being the gods' marvellous dress and garment,
throne, diadem, and fragrant wreath,
ornaments and finery of all kinds.

The fifth: the light earth (land of light),
self-existent, eternal, miraculous;
In height, it is beyond reach,
its depth cannot be perceived.
No enemy and no attacker walk this land.
Its divine pavement is of the substance
of diamond that never shakes.
All good things are born from it:
beautiful, graceful hills wholly covered with flowers,
grown to perfection;
Green fruit-bearing trees
whose fruits never drop, nor rot,
and never have worms;
Springs flowing with ambrosia
that fill all of paradise, its groves and plains;
Countless mansions and palaces,
thrones and seats that exist in perpetuity,
for ever and ever.

Thus is paradise arranged in these Five Greatnesses.
They (who dwell there) are serenely peaceful,
knowing no fear.
They live in the light, where they have no darkness;
In eternal life, free from death;
In health without sickness;
In a joy free from sorrow;
In love without hatred;
In the company of friends, without separation;
In a form that is not destroyed;

In a divine body where there is no decay;
On ambrosial food without limit,
enduring no toil or hardship.

Their appearance is beautiful, their strength powerful,
their wealth bountiful:
They do not even know the name of poverty.
Rather, they are equipped, beautiful and adorned:
no harm befalls their bodies.
Their garment of joy is a finery that is never soiled,
of seventy myriad kinds, set with jewels.
Their homes are never destroyed.

Manichaean Text, M178 (Sogdian); cf. SFMC p.308

Mystics have no words to describe the inner mansions of the soul. Words describe only the things of this world and, even that, quite inadequately. No experience, even of physical things, can be transmitted or conveyed by words. Experience and words are fundamentally different. Mystics have therefore consistently described the inner realms in terms of the most beautiful, fabulous and enduring things of this world. But to know what those regions are really like, the individual must go there and find out for himself.

There are other Manichaean references to these Five Greatnesses. None, however, is complete and definitive. In one of the Manichaean psalms, for example, the distinction is drawn between the "two natures" – that of "light" and that of "darkness". The Saviour comes as the Holy Spirit and teaches the difference between the two:

Let us worship the Spirit of the Paraclete.
Let us bless our Lord Jesus
who has sent to us the Spirit of Truth.
He came and separated us from the Error of the world;
He brought us a mirror, we looked:
we saw the universe in it.

When the Holy Spirit came,
he revealed to us the way of Truth,
and taught us that there are two natures:
That of light and that of darkness,
separate, one from the other, from the beginning.

The kingdom of light, on the one hand,
consisted in Five Greatnesses:

And they are the Father and His twelve *aeons*
and the *aeons* of the *aeons,* the Living Air,
the land of light;
The great Spirit breathing in them,
nourishing them with His Light.

Manichaean Psalm Book CCXXIII, MPB p.9

The inner realms of light are five in number; they consist of "Five Greatnesses" projected from the Father and his twelve subpowers, aspects of the Word, the "*aeons* of the *aeons,* the Living Air, the land of light", the Source. Within these "Five Greatnesses" the "great Spirit" breathes, giving them existence or nourishment through "His Light".

But the kingdom of darkness
consists of five storehouses,
which are smoke and fire and wind
and water and darkness;
Their counsel creeping in them,
moving them and inciting them
to make war with one another.

Manichaean Psalm Book CCXXIII, MPB p.9

The "kingdom of darkness", on the other hand, is comprised of five basic 'elements' or conditions of matter, which remain incompatible with each other. The precise esoteric meaning of these five elements is unclear from the Manichaean texts, but fire, for example, creates turbulence in water and wind. Likewise, the other elements have their own characteristics and "make war with one another".

In another fragmentary psalm, there is a reference to the five rulers of the five realms. And here, the fifth realm is the "Living Air" itself, the source of the divine creative impulse, the "first-born of his Father":

The five spirits (rulers) of the Five Greatnesses,
servants of the land of light,
that receive fragrant Life….

The fifth essence, which is the Living Air,
the first-born of his Father.
The armour which was not stained,
the clothing which was not defiled.

Manichaean Psalm Book; cf. MPB pp.136–37

See also: **'ālam**, **al-Ḥaḍarāt al-Ilāhīyah al-Khams**, **heavens**.

gagan(a) (S/H/Pu), **gagan maṇḍal** (H) *Lit.* sky, heaven, firmament *(gagan);* sphere *(maṇḍal)* of heaven *(gagan),* realm of heaven, a *maṇḍal* being anything circular or circumscribed, such as an orbit, a sphere, a halo, a zone, a division and so on. The terms are used in a number of ways; mystically, the inner heavens or regions:

Invert your attention at the eye centre *(do dal kanwal)*
and ascend to the (inner) sky *(gagan).*
Then you will become enraptured,
and hear the ringing of the Sound *(Nād).*
Swāmī Shiv Dayāl Singh, Sār Bachan Poetry 13:1.43–44, SBP p.108

In the sky *(gagan)* within is an inverted well,
wherein burns a lamp.
Wherein burns a lamp without a wick,
without any oil.
Paltū, Bānī 1, Kuṇḍalī 169:1–2, PSB1 p.71

I am so mad with love
that nobody can understand my suffering.
My bed is on a gallows,
how can I possibly sleep!
The Lord's bed is in *gagan maṇḍal,*
How can I ever meet Him?
Mīrābāī, Shabdāvalī, Virah aur Prem 3:1, MBS p.4

Gagan is also used in a particular sense for the region of *trikuṭī* (*lit.* three peaks, the highest of the mind regions, the universal mind):

Below the region of *sunn* (void) or *daswān dwār* (tenth door) is the region of *trikuṭī,* also called *gagan.*
Swāmī Shiv Dayāl Singh, Sār Bachan Prose 1:14, SB p.11

More specifically, it also means the 'sky' or highest part of *trikuṭī.* Thus, Swāmī Shiv Dayāl Singh describes the ascent of the soul from the realms of the mind, characterized by the *tattvas* (elements), *prakṛitis* (natures) and *guṇas* (attributes), up to *gagan maṇḍal* in the realm of *Kāl* (used here as a name for the negative power), on through the *sunn* (void) region and finally to the inaccessible *(agam)* realm of the Supreme:

Having been released from the five *tattvas,*
the twenty-five *prakṛitis* and the three *guṇas,*
the soul ascended to the *gagan maṇḍal,*
and laid siege to the *Kāl maṇḍal.*

It conquered the fort of *sunn maṇḍal,*
and went on to reach the *agam maṇḍal.*
Swāmī Shiv Dayāl Singh, Sār Bachan Poetry 6:8.12–14, SBP p.57

Esoterically, a 'sky' or firmament refers to the 'space' or 'energy field' out of which a region is created. Thus, physical space *(ākāsha)* is the energy field from which all physical creation comes into being. A 'sky' also effectively demarcates one region from another giving the illusion, when looking from the lower region, that that region is the last (or only one). This is true of the physical world, bounded by all-pervading physical space, where the majority of souls feel that it is the only universe in existence. Similarly, the *gagan* or 'sky' of *trikuṭī* gives the illusion to those who have no one who can take them beyond it, that the universal mind is the ultimate and final cause of all creation.

Kabīr uses the term for the region of *sunn,* the realm beyond *trikuṭī,* for he says that by reaching *gagan,* the soul is freed from birth and death:

By listening to the divine Melody,
the mind will be absorbed in *gagan,*
and will then cease its coming and going (in birth and death).
Listening to the *Shabd* in (the realm of) *sunn,*
it will become unwavering.
Kabīr, Sākhī Sangrah, Shabd 47, KSS pp.96

Bullā Sāhib implies the same:

He who makes his dwelling in the *gagan maṇḍal*
for him, there is no more coming and going *(āvāgavan).*
Bullā Sāhib, Shabd Sār, Chetāvnī 3:3, BSSS p.7

And Guru Nānak has used *Gagan* as a term for God:

When the infinite Lord *(Gagan)* abides
in the man's mind-firmament (*gaganantar,* firmament within),
he sings the Lord's praise and dwells in celestial peace *(sukh sahaj)....*
My Master *(Gagan)* is unapproachable, self-dependent and unborn.
Guru Nānak, Ādi Granth 932, MMS

See also: **sky**.

gan (He) *Lit.* garden; mystically, the heavens or spiritual regions, as in *gan be-'Eyden* (the garden in Eden).

See also: **gardens**.

garden(s), garden of Adam, garden of Eden, garden of ether spirit, garden of Life, gardens of light, garden of the Lord, gardens of fragrance A garden is an area of land planted with trees, shrubs, flowering plants and so on, generally conceived as a place of vitality, peace and beauty; one of the commonest terms used for the inner heavens in the mystic and religious literature of the Middle East. The term *(al-jannah),* for instance, found in the *Qur'ān,* is used consistently by the later Sufi writers for the higher heavens.

As a simile for the inner realms, the image is appropriate. Gardens are associated with peace, happiness, beauty, colour, fragrance, warmth, refreshing breezes, abundance of life, fecundity, and all those things that lend a sense of equanimity and contentment to life. These are also the characteristics of the heavenly regions.

The origin of these terms goes back to earliest Jewish times, and probably before that into Mesopotamian literature. The garden planted in Eden is one of the first images encountered in the Bible – Eden symbolizing eternity and the garden representing the higher realms of creation. Similarly, the garden of Life was an ancient Mesopotamian myth that is likely to have had its origins in mystic teachings.

The *Genesis* story was probably written between the ninth and the sixth centuries BCE. The derivation of Eden (pronounced Eyden in Hebrew) is uncertain. It either comes from a Hebrew root meaning 'pleasure' or 'delight', or from an Ugaritic root, *'dn,* meaning a place that is 'well watered throughout', or from the Akkadian, *edinu,* borrowed from the Sumerian *eden,* meaning a 'plain' or a large expanse of open country. The latter is the closest word to the actual Hebrew.

In Jewish teachings, Eden is referred to as the garden in Eden *(gan be-'Eyden),* the garden of Eden, the garden of *Yahweh,* the garden of God and Eden of blessing.

In the *Septuagint,* the early Greek translation of the Bible made around 300 BCE, the garden of Eden is translated as the 'paradise of delight'. The term paradise comes from the Greek, *paradeisos,* in turn derived from the old Persian, *paridaiza,* meaning 'an enclosure', hence, 'an enclosed garden'. In post-biblical Hebrew literature, the related term *pardes* was often used for the garden of Eden or, mystically, for the heavenly regions.

The first occurrence of garden metaphors in extant Jewish literature is in the *Genesis* allegory, where it is said:

> And the Lord God planted a garden eastward in Eden,
> and there He put the man whom He had formed.

And out of the ground made the Lord God to grow
every tree that is pleasant to the sight,
and good for food;
The Tree of Life also in the midst of the garden,
and the Tree of Knowledge of Good and Evil.
And a river went out of Eden to water the garden.

Genesis 2:8–10, KJV

Eden represents eternity, within which everything else exists. The "garden planted eastward in Eden" represents the heavenly realms. "Eastward" is the place from which the sun arises, symbolizing the source of divine Light from which the creation comes into being. The hierarchy of creation with all the heavenly realms are thus "planted … in Eden". The power that sustains these realms is the "Tree of Life", which is therefore said to be planted "in the midst of the garden".

Also in this garden of creation are the regions of the negative power. Hence, the Tree of Knowledge of Good and Evil is a part of the garden. And this mystic garden is watered by a "river" of Living Water flowing out of Eden – having its source in eternity.

Underlining the mystical and allegorical interpretation of this passage in *Genesis* is a Mandaean poem alluding to the *Genesis* allegory, where God's creation is described symbolically as the "garden of Adam":

On yonder side among the fruits of splendour,
in the farmyards of light,
in the house of perfection,
within you, garden of ether spirit, …
within you, garden of Adam,
the Voice of Life (is crying out)
what the Great One is saying.

Mandaean John-Book, JMM p.241; cf. JM p.221, MEM p.19

Here it can not only be seen how "on yonder side" – on the other side of death – is equated with "within you", but also that "the Voice of Life" is only audible in those realms, not in this world.

In another Mandaean poem, the mythical Saviour, Hībil-Zīwa, is praised by the celestial *'uthras* or divine beings:

Sweet is your Voice, youth Hībil,
when you speak in the garden of Adam
and chant sublime hymns.
Sweet is your Voice!
And its Sound went thither.

Mandaean Prayer Book 204; cf. CPM pp.173–74

The "sublime hymns" and the sweet "Voice" are the "Sound" of the divine Music, heard in the "garden of Adam". Likewise, in the Judaic *Book of Enoch,* the initiates are described as:

> All the elect who dwell in the garden of Life.
>
> *1 Enoch 61:12, BE p.80*

Where 'garden' metaphors appear in the Bible, the full context is worth exploring for a possible mystic sense. There is a passage in *Amos,* for instance, where the "captivity of my people of Israel" is probably to be taken metaphorically to mean the captivity of souls in the physical universe. The "waste cities" that are to be rebuilt with "vineyards" and "gardens" are the souls in human form, in need of spiritual renewal, having lost all the higher glory of their former state:

> "And I will bring back the captivity of my people of Israel,
> and they shall build the waste cities,
> and inhabit them;
> And they shall plant vineyards,
> and drink their wine;
> They shall also make gardens,
> and eat the fruit of them.
> And I will plant (initiate) them upon their land,
> and they shall no more be plucked up
> out of their land which I have given them,"
> says the Lord thy God.
>
> *Amos 9:14–15, KB*

In other places, the meaning is more explicit. One of the most poignant and certainly most revealing of all the biblical passages comes in the epilogue to the biblical *Song of Songs.* There, an unknown devotee, clearly moved by the content of the *Song,* points to the mystical interpretation by which he or she understood it:

> You who dwell in the gardens,
> the companions listen for your voice;
> Deign to let me hear it.
>
> *Song of Songs 8:13, JB*

The "you" is the divine Beloved, the Master; the "gardens" are the inner realms where the Master dwells; and the "Voice" is the divine Music, the Voice of God, which every disciple of a Master longs to hear. But he knows that such inner hearing is only opened when the Master "deigns" – when he sees fit.

Extensive use is made of garden metaphors in the *Song of Songs,* where there are a number of references to gardens as the inner realms of creation. The gardens, for instance, are identified with the "pastures" of the Shepherd, the divine Beloved who guides his flock of souls through the heavenly regions, back to God. The lover says:

My Beloved went down to his garden,
  to the beds of spices,
  to pasture his flocks in the gardens,
  and gather lilies.
I am my Beloved's, and my Beloved is mine.
He pastures his flock among the lilies.

Song of Songs 6:2–3, JB

Among the Christian writers of the Eastern Church, in a passage attributed to the fourth-century Ephraim Syrus, the pure "bridal chamber" is equated with the "glorified garden", both referring to the realm of eternity, and given to the "King, fashioned from the dust" – the Saviour who incarnates in this world, taking a physical body of matter or "dust":

The glorified garden, the bridal chamber of chastity,
  he gave unto that King, fashioned from the dust.

Ephraim Syrus, ESR p.342, MEM p.122

In the Manichaean writings in Parthian, a story is related about a certain Mihrshāh, brother to Shāpūr, the king. While Shāpūr gave Mānī protection throughout his lands, Mihrshāh was deeply hostile to Mānī and his teachings. Hatred, however, is only the other side of love, and a person who is either positively or negatively obsessed with a mystic may ultimately derive some benefit from that association. Only someone who has no interest in a subject can remain untouched by it, while a hostile person declares his interest by his hostility. The story concerns the difference between inner and outer gardens:

Shāpūr, the king of kings, had a brother, lord of Mesene (a district of Baṣrah in Mesopotamia), and his name was Mihrshāh, who was extraordinarily hostile to the path of the Apostle (Mānī). And he had arranged a garden which was fine, lovely and wonderfully spacious, the like of which no other man had ever possessed.

Then the Apostle knew that the time of (Mihrshāh's) salvation had come near. And he arose and came before Mihrshāh who was seated in his garden, greatly enjoying a feast.… Then he (Mihrshāh) said to the Apostle: "In the paradise of which you speak, was there ever a

> garden such as mine?" At this, the Apostle perceived his sceptical thoughts. And by his miraculous power he showed him the paradise (garden) of light with all the gods, divine beings and the immortal Breath of Life, and every kind of garden, and also other splendid things there.
>
> Thereafter, he (Mihrshāh) fell to the ground unconscious for three hours, and what he saw he kept as a memory in his heart. Then the Apostle put his hand upon his head. He regained consciousness. When he had risen, he fell down at the Apostle's feet and clasped his right hand.
>
> *Manichaean Text, HR2 pp.82–84, MBB p.103, RMP f; cf. ML p.20*

By his own spiritual power, Mānī takes Mihrshāh into the inner realms. As a consequence, Mihrshāh loses all consciousness of this world and is caught up in a state of superconsciousness, inside. He lay "unconscious (of this world) for three hours, and what he saw he kept as a memory in his heart" – he kept his inner visions secret. Having taken him up, Mānī had to bring him back to this world by placing his hand upon Mihrshāh's head, again using his spiritual power to bring him down. And when Mihrshāh returned, his first act was to pay obeisance to Mānī, for now he had glimpsed just who Mānī really was.

Elsewhere in the Manichaean texts in Parthian, the inner regions of the soul, "these blessed gardens of fragrant flowers", are also called "monasteries", "places" and "cabins":

> The monasteries and abodes of the gods, the places and cabins,
> where the radiant *Vahman* (*Vohu Manō,* the Primal Mind)
> fulfils the (soul's) desire of becoming divine:
> The powerful gods, the strong Apostles, … the glories,
> the spirits, the sons of the Right Hand who have entered there –
> may they come in peace.
> Peace and blessing
> upon these blessed gardens of fragrant flowers.
>
> *Manichaean Hymns, MM2 p.323ff., RMP cm; cf. ML p.30*

"The strong Apostles" are the Masters, the spiritual leaders of their community of chosen disciples, while the "powerful gods", the "glories" and the "spirits" are beings who dwell in the inner realms. The "sons of the Right Hand" are the disciples of the Master, his mystic "sons". All of them dwell – now or later – within the inner domains of light, in the "blessed gardens of fragrant flowers".

The metaphor was used extensively in the Manichaean literature. In a Coptic psalm, for instance, in praise of Mānī as "the sage, the Paraclete", it is said that all the powers, realms and souls in creation "render glory" to him. Included among those that render obeisance are the "gardens of fragrance" and the "blossoming trees", refreshed and vitalized by the "Breath of the Wind" or Spirit:

> The blossoming trees, the gardens of fragrance,
>   and the Breath of the Wind (Spirit) –
> They render glory to this imperishable one,
>   the sage, the Paraclete.
>
> *Manichaean Psalm Book CCXXXVII; cf. MPB p.37*

The same psalms also relate the story of a soul who, having "reached the door of the garden" – having concentrated sufficiently at the single eye – scents the "fragrant smell of the trees", and is impelled by longing to enter the inner gardens. By means of a parable, the psalmist then points out that all the money and riches in the world cannot buy access to these "gardens". Rather, such wealth only serves to attach the soul to this world, keeping her away from the inner treasures.

The soul offers to buy her way into the inner realms. But emphasizing the point that Masters are always the givers, never charging for their supreme gift, the Master – the "Great One" sent from the "Height of Truth" – responds, "[are we some hired] porter [standing at the door]?" However, a payment is to be made for entrance to the "garden", not in cash, but in fasting from the attachments of the world, and in withdrawing the mind from all human imperfections:

> I reached the door of the garden,
>   the fragrant smell of the trees spread to me;
> I lifted up my face, saying:
> "Who will take from me ten talents,
>   and take me in to the garden?
> Twenty silver staters in all,
>   who will take them from me,
>   and make me sit beneath the shade of the garden?
> Thirty silver staters in all,
>   who will take them from me,
>   and make me stand in its midst?
> Fifty-seven in all,
>   who will take them from me,
>   and take me in to their midst?
> A full hundred entire,
>   who will take them from me,
>   that I may be counted worthy to be one of them?"

They came from the Height of Truth,
they said to me, even the Great Ones,
"What have you to do with ten silver staters?
[are we some hired] porter [standing at the door]?
What have you to do with twenty,
what have you to do with thirty,
standing at the door of the garden?
What have you to do with this whole hundred?
(Because of this) you will be tortured by your enemies;

"But if you fasted with fasting,
then shall you be taken into the garden;
If your eyes glance not evilly,
they will make you sit
beneath the shadow of the garden;
If your mouth speaks truly,
they will show you their Image (light form);
If your hands are pure from [all dishonesty and greed],
they will hear the accents of your pleading.
If your heart is steadfast,
they will [raise you up from your body],
and make you stand in their midst.
If your feet walk in the path of Truth,
they will make you one of them.
If you do these things indeed,
and sleep not, you shall go up,
and see the land of light.

Psalms of Thomas XVIII, Manichaean Psalm Book; cf. MPB pp.224–25

Here, the ending of the story makes it evident that the "garden" is to be equated with the "land of light".

Following in this Middle Eastern tradition, the *Qur'ān* is one of the most frequent users of garden imagery for the heavenly realms:

The righteous (will be) amid gardens *(jannāt)*
and fountains *('uyūn)* (of clear flowing water);
(Their greeting will be):
"Enter here in peace and security."

Qur'ān 15:45–46; cf. AYA

As a metaphor, gardens sometimes appear in mystical literature with meanings other than that of the heavenly realms. In the *Song of Songs,* for instance, the Beloved describes his lover, the soul, as a "garden enclosed":

She is a garden enclosed,
  my sister, my promised bride;
A garden enclosed,
  a sealed fountain.

Song of Songs 4:12, JB

The soul is a "garden enclosed" or a "sealed fountain" because she is still enmeshed in the snares of a human body and human life. Peace and beauty are within her – but have yet to be revealed. This is why the Beloved adds:

The rarest essences are yours: …
  with the subtlest odours.
Fountain that makes the gardens fertile,
  well of Living Water,
  streams flowing down from Lebanon.

Song of Songs 4:13–15, JB

Fragrance, fountains, a "well of Living Water", streams flowing out of Lebanon (here symbolizing eternity) – all these lie within the soul, bringing life and fertility to her garden.

The soul responds by asking the "wind" to blow: to breathe over her garden, to bring the fragrance of the divine Music and the Beloved himself into the garden of her soul – wind, breath and fragrance being common metaphors for the Spirit:

Awake, north wind,
  come, wind of the south!
Breathe over my garden,
  to spread its sweet smell around.
Let my Beloved come into his garden,
  let him taste its rarest fruits.

Song of Songs 4:16, JB

The Beloved then responds:

I come into my garden,
  my sister, my promised bride.

Song of Songs 5:1, JB

Such usage, however, is less common than its use as a term for the higher regions.

See also: **bihisht-u dūzakh**, **bustān**, **al-jannah**, **Tree of Life** (3.1).

Gehenna (He. *Gehinnom*) In biblical times, the valley below Jerusalem, the "valley of the son of Hinnom", where idolatry was practised and children were sacrificed.[1] By the time of Jesus and the early Christian era, the term had come – not unnaturally – to mean 'hell'.

The Bible has very little to say on the nature of hell, but later Jewish sources, especially rabbinic and Kabbalistic writers, have expanded on the theme. The thirteenth-century *Zohar,* for instance, contains a number of discussions concerning the nature of Gehenna, which are probably derived from earlier legends and beliefs that developed in the *Midrash, Talmud* and other post-biblical rabbinic sources, as well as in the early Kabbalah. The *Zohar* describes the departure of souls from this world:

> God shows kindness to His creatures in not divesting them of their earthly garment until other garments, more precious and finer than these, are prepared for them. But the wicked, they who have never turned to their Lord with a perfect repentance – naked they came into this world, and naked they must return from it, and their souls go in shame to join the other souls in like plight, and they are judged in the earthly Gehenna by the fire from above. Some of them flutter upward after a time; these are the souls of the sinners who had intended to repent, but died before they had carried out their intentions. These are judged first in Gehenna, and then flutter upward.
>
> See how great is the mercy of the Holy One towards His creatures! (It is true that) the most wicked sinner, if he has intended repentance, but dies without carrying out his resolve, is … punished for having gone out of this world without having repented, but his good intention is not lost; … it (the soul) ascends to the supernal King, and there remains until the Holy One, seeing it, prepares for that soul a place of refuge in *Sheol,* where it twitters repentance.
>
> For the good intention issues from before the Holy One and, breaking all the strong gates of the habitations of Gehenna, reaches at last the place where that sinner lies. It smites him and awakens in him again that intention which he had had on earth, causing the soul to struggle and ascend from the abode of *Sheol.*
>
> *Zohar 2:150a–b, ZSS4 pp.26–27, JCL*

In another passage, the author explains that there are several regions or "storeys" in Gehenna:

> There are storeys in *Gehinnom,* one above another; there is *Sheol* and below it *Abaddon.* From *Sheol,* it is possible to come up again, but not from *Abaddon.* Now those who have good works in this world, or reckoning or knowledge or wisdom, when they pass by to observe

> the sinners in *Gehinnom,* and hear them crying out from the grade of *Sheol,* are not left there, but ascend aloft to the place of illumination and delight, where God comes to have converse with the righteous in the garden of Eden.
>
> *Zohar 3:178a, ZSS5 p.241, JCL*

Another passage contains various legends and beliefs concerning Gehenna. Its notorious and fearsome heat and fire are said to correspond to the heat of human passions that are the cause of sinfulness, and ultimately result in the suffering of Gehenna. The passage continues with a detailed description of the levels of Gehenna, the kinds of sinner assigned there, and the punishments they must endure:

> Said Rabbi Judah: "Why are the sinners punished by the fire of Gehenna? Because the fire of Gehenna, which burns day and night, corresponds to the hot passion of sinfulness in man. There was once a period when, for some time, sin ceased to rule because it had been thrown into the iron ring in the abyss of the Ocean. During that period, the fire of Gehenna went out and did not burn at all. When sinfulness returned, and again began to burn in the hearts of sinners, the fire of Gehenna was started again, for it is the heat of sinful passion in the hearts of sinners that kindles and keeps alight the fires of Gehenna, causing them to burn day and night without ceasing.
>
> "Gehenna has seven doors which open into seven habitations; and there are also seven types of sinners: evildoers, worthless ones, sinners, the wicked, corrupters, mockers and arrogant ones; and corresponding with them are the habitations in Gehenna, for each kind a particular place, all according to grade. And over each habitation a special angel is appointed, all being under the direction of *Dumah,* who has thousands and myriads of angels under him, to punish sinners according to their deserts.
>
> "The fire of the Gehenna which is below comes from the Gehenna which is above, and is kindled by the heat of the sinners in whom the evil inclination burns, and there all the piles burn. In Gehenna, there are certain places and grades called 'boiling filth', where the filth of the souls that have been polluted by the filth of this world accumulates. There, these souls are purified by fire and made white, and then they ascend towards the heavenly regions. Their filth remains behind and the evil grades, called 'boiling filth', are appointed over that filth, and the fire of Gehenna rules over it.
>
> "There are certain sinners who pollute themselves over and over again by their own sins, and are never purified. They die without repentance, having sinned themselves and caused others to sin, being

stiff-necked and never showing contrition before the Lord while in this world. These are they who are condemned to remain forever in this place of 'boiling filth' and never leave it. Those whose ways upon earth have been corrupt and who have not considered the honour of their Lord in this world are condemned to remain there for all generations.

"On Sabbaths, new moons, special seasons and festivals, the fire is extinguished there, and they have a respite from punishment, but, unlike sinners of a lesser degree who are accorded relief, they are not allowed to leave that place even on such days."

Zohar 2:150b; cf. ZSS4 pp.26–27, JCL

See also: **Abaddon**, **abyss**, **dūzakh**, **Hadēs**, **hell**, **jahannam**, **outer darkness**, **Sheol**.

1. *2 Kings* 23:10, *Jeremiah* 19:6.

Gevurah (He) *Lit.* might, power; the fifth of the ten *sefirot* or divine emanations; also called *Din* (Judgment) or *Paḥad* (Fear); the quality that mitigates and controls the unrestrained outpouring of God's love, which is embodied as the fourth *sefirah* of *Ḥesed* (Lovingkindness, overflowing love and mercy). *Gevurah* is also a name used for the 'iron age' in the Kabbalistic system of cosmic cycles *(shemittot).*

See also: **Din**, **sefirot**.

Ghayb, al- (A/P) *Lit.* the Unseen, the Invisible, the Mystery, the Unmanifest; that which is hidden; that which is transcendental; the supernatural; the divine secret; a general name for realms of the creation that lie beyond perceptual and intellectual apprehension. *Ghayb* is an adjective meaning hidden, invisible, unseen and so on, as in *'ālam al-Ghayb,* the Unseen world. Sufism has also been called the science of the Unseen *('ilm al-Ghayb).*[1]

The *Qur'ān* puts a belief in the Unseen *(al-Ghayb)* among the first duties of man:

This is the Book (Scripture):
In it is guidance sure, without doubt to those who fear *Allāh,*
who believe in the Unseen *(al-Ghayb),* are steadfast in prayer,
and spend out of what We have provided for them.

Qur'ān 2:2–3, AYA

The *Qur'ān* also says that God has full knowledge of everything, seen or unseen, and everything obeys His command:

With Him are the keys of the Unseen *(al-Ghayb),*
the treasures that none knows but He.
He knows whatever there is on the earth and in the sea.
Not a leaf falls but with His knowledge:
There is not a grain in the darkness (or depths) of the earth,
nor anything fresh or dry (green or withered),
but is (inscribed) in a record clear (to those who can read).

Qur'ān 6:59; cf. AYA

The "record clear *(kitābin-mubīn)*" refers to the Well-Guarded Tablet *(Lawḥ al-Maḥfūẓ)* upon which all destinies are written. So, says the *Qur'ān,* since everything is in His hands, "put your trust in Him":

To *Allāh* do belong the unseen *(al-ghayb)* (secrets)
of the heavens and the earth;
And to Him goes back every affair (for decision):
Then worship Him, and put your trust in Him:
And your Lord is not unmindful of anything you do.

Qur'ān 11:123; cf. AYA

Among the realms of creation, *'ālam al-mulk* (the physical world) is called the 'manifestation of the totally visible'; *'ālam al-malakūt* and *'ālam al-jabarūt* are called the 'manifestation of the relative Unseen *(ḥaḍrat al-Ghayb al-muḍāf)*'; and *'ālam al-lāhūt* (world of divinity) and what lies beyond are called the 'manifestation of the totally Unseen *(ḥaḍrat al-Ghayb al-muṭlaq)*'. Shabistarī also associates *'ālam al-lāhūt* with *Huwīyat al-Ghayb* (the Unseen He-ness). *Al-Ghayb al-muṭlaq* and *Huwīyat al-Ghayb* are used by Sufis to express the nature of *Allāh.*

See also: **'ālam al-Ghayb**, **al-ḥijāb** (6.2).

1. *Qur'ān* 53:35.

Guru pad (H/Pu) *Lit.* place *(pad)* of the *Guru;* a name used by a number of Indian mystics for the highest of the three parts of *trikuṭī* (*lit.* three peaks), the highest region of the mind, the universal mind. The creation here is said to be so beautiful that the soul does not want to come back to this world, and continually desires to go there. Sardār Bahādur Jagat Singh explains:

> *Trikuṭī* has three prominences, the highest being called the *Guru pad.* It is a sublime stage beyond description. As the python draws its prey towards itself, so does the Melody (of this region) draw the soul towards it.
>
> *Sardār Bahādur Jagat Singh, Science of the Soul I:2, SOS p.21*

See also: **trikuṭī**.

gyān khaṇḍ (Pu) *Lit.* region or division *(khaṇḍ)* of knowledge *(gyān);* used by the Indian mystic, Guru Nānak, to denote the astral region, above the eye centre.

See also: **khaṇḍ**.

habitations A term found particularly in Manichaean writings, referring to the true home or habitation of the soul, as in a psalm where the soul is exhorted to embark on a ship of light and "sail to your habitations":

> O soul, … take your merchandise aboard,
> and sail to your habitations.
>
> *Manichaean Psalm Book; cf. MPB p.147*

See also: **dwellings**.

Ḥaḍarāt al-Ilāhīyah al-Khams, al- (A), **Ḥażarāt-i Ilāhī-i Khams** (P) *Lit.* the Five *(Khams)* Divine *(Ilāhīyah)* Presences *(Ḥaḍarāt);* the Five Divine Manifestations; the planes of consciousness, or the levels or realms of the creation; a way of describing the totality of creation; a terminology developed by Ibn ʻArabī, and used by later Sufis such as Qūnawī, ʻIrāqī and others.

Three of the five manifestations are the *ʻālam al-ajsām* (world of bodies), the *ʻālam al-mithāl* (world of patterns) and the *ʻālam al-arwāḥ* (world of spirits). These three constitute the full range of the created worlds; they are said to make up the *arbāb,* the creation over which *al-Rabb* (the Lord) rules with His cherishing and sustaining love.

The fourth *ḥaḍrat* or manifestation is the realm of the First Entification *(al-Taʻayyun al-Awwal),* also called *al-Fayḍ al-Aqdas* (Most Holy Emanation), and the First Isthmus Nature *(al-Barzakhīyah al-Ūlá).* This is, in the simplest terms, the level at which the unmanifested Essence of God *(Dhāt)* first begins the process of manifestation by becoming the Creator, the Merciful, the Bountiful. It is from this First Entification of God that the creation proceeds through the divine Creative Word. This First Entification is the speaker of the creative Command, "Be!"

The fifth manifestation is *al-Ḥaḍrat al-Jāmi'ah,* meaning the 'All-Comprehensive Manifestation' or the 'Synthesis of Manifestations'. It represents the consciousness of the Perfect Man *(al-Insān al-Kāmil)* that spans all the *ḥaḍarāt* from the physical plane to God Himself.

These five manifestations are sometimes expressed in the following terms:

1. The *ḥaḍrat al-shahādah al-muṭlaq* (manifestation of the totally visible), which represents the physical, phenomenal world.

2. The *ḥaḍrat al-Ghayb al-muḍāf* (manifestation of the relative Unseen), which represents the lower subtle realms of the spiritual-material creation.

3. The *ḥaḍrat al-Ghayb al-muṭlaq* (manifestation of the totally Unseen), which represents the higher, subtle realms of the spiritual creation.

4. The *ḥaḍrat al-Ta'ayyun al-Awwal* (manifestation of the First Entification), which represents the Lord, God, the Creator.

5. The *Ḥaḍrat al-Jāmi'ah* (All-Comprehensive Manifestation), representing the Perfect Man, who spans all the Presences.

In this latter set of five *ḥaḍarāt,* the totally visible, the relative Unseen and the totally Unseen can be compared to the worlds of bodies, the world of patterns and the world of spirits.

Some other Sufi systems also describe five levels. There are the five *'ālamīn* (worlds): *nāsūt, malakūt, jabarūt, lāhūt, hāhūt.* The hierarchy of worlds described by al-Jīlī, al-Shīrāzī and others also numbers five: the world of the divine Being, the world of His Names, the world of His Attributes or Qualities, the world of His Acts and the world of His Effects.

However, there is considerable scope for confusion when comparing one system of terminology with another, because, as well as the same regions being given different names, the same names are also used for different regions in different systems.

See also: **'ālam**, **Five Greatnesses**, **Five Trees** (3.1).

Hadēs (Gk) In ancient Greek mythology and belief, the lord of the underworld, also known as *Pluto;* brother of *Zeus* (ruler of the gods), *Poseidon* (god of the sea and earthquakes) and *Hera* (queen of the Olympian gods); also, the underworld itself, the place where the souls of all the dead go after physical existence, living out a sad and ghostly existence, regardless of the kind of human life they have led. Only the immortal gods, who – according to Greek legends – often behaved far worse than human beings, are saved from this fate. They live on forever in this world. This rather bleak picture of the afterlife was not the only religious belief entertained by the ancient Greeks. The teachings of the Greek mystics and philosophers, as well as the various mystery religions of the time, including mystical groups such as the Pythagoreans, offered alternative points of view.

In later Judaism, Christianity and popular usage, the term came to mean the hell that is commonly described by the various religions. The ancient Middle Eastern mystics, however, often referred to the physical world as *Hadēs,* as in the gnostic revelation, the *Apocryphon of John* where Jesus describes his descent into this world, picturing it as the "darkness and the inside of *Hadēs*" and the "prison of the body":

I entered into the midst of darkness
and the inside of *Hadēs*....
And I entered into the midst of their prison,
which is the prison of the body.
And I said, "He who hears,
let him get up from the deep sleep."

Apocryphon of John 30–31, NHS33 p.171

See also: **abyss**, **dūzakh**, **Gehenna**, **hell**, **jahannam**, **naraka**, **outer darkness**, **Pit**, **Sheol**.

haṃsnī nāl, haṃsnī surang (H) *Lit.* tunnel *(nāl, surang)* of the swan *(haṃsnī), haṃsa* being a common metaphor for the pure soul; the valve, gateway or passage said to lie between *daswān dwār* (tenth door) and *bhanwar guphā* (rotating cave), the third and fourth spiritual regions according to the descriptive system of some Indian Saints; one of the many barriers encountered by the soul in its upward ascent. The nineteenth-century Indian mystic, Swāmī Shiv Dayāl Singh, writes:

The soul then made ready for the fourth stage.
Catching the Sound,
it crossed the pass above the *haṃsnī nāl,*
and entered the *rukmiṇī nāl* (radiant tunnel).
It beheld an impressive passageway,
seeing which the *surat* (power to hear)
and the *nirat* (power to see) both became strong.

Swāmī Shiv Dayāl Singh, Sār Bachan Poetry 26:4.1–3, SBP p.228

See also: **bank nāl**.

havare pishyasū (Av) *Lit.* radiant *(havare)* with the sun *(pishyasū);* heavens radiant with the sun; the inner realms of light. In the extant *Gāthās* of Zarathushtra, very little is mentioned concerning the inner hierarchy of creation. He does speak of the eternal realm, the true home of the soul *(garō demāna),* but only describes the other heavenly regions in general terms. He calls them *havare pishyasū* – heavens radiant with the sun:

> How, O *Mazdā,* shall one who desires in life
> only things of selfish gain,
> ever seek the bliss of the higher creation?
> The followers of *Ashā* (Truth) shall dwell
> in heavens radiant with Your sun *(havare pishyasū);*
> Their place shall surely be in the abode of the wise.
>
> *Zarathushtra, Yasna 50:2; cf. DSZ p.736*

Havare pishyasū is identifiable with *khurshed paya* (the heaven of the sun) of the later Pahlavi writings on Zoroastrianism, where it is likely that some remnants of Zarathushtra's original teachings, not found in the *Gāthās,* have been preserved by tradition.

See also: **garō demāna** (2.1), **khurshed paya**.

ḥawḍ al-Kawthar (A), **ḥawż-i Kawśar** (P) *Lit.* pool *(ḥawḍ)* of *Kawthar. Kawthar* (*lit.* good in abundance) is a mythical spring or river, referred to in the *Qur'ān,* and generally understood as the abundant spiritual bounty that *Allāh* bestowed on Muḥammad:

> To you have We granted *al-Kawthar.*
>
> *Qur'ān 108:1; cf. AYA*

According to various *ḥadīth* (traditional sayings), there is a pool or lake *(ḥawḍ)* fed by the Spring of *Kawthar,* encountered at the entrance to paradise:

> Anas relates that the Prophet said that he saw the pond *al-Kawthar* on the night of his *Mi'rāj* or heavenly journey, and that it "was a river of water on each side of which there were domes, each formed of a hollow pearl".
>
> *Ḥadīth Ṣaḥīḥ al-Bukhārī 6:60.488, in "al-Kauṣar", DOI p.262*

Another *ḥadīth* describes this river:

> *Al-Kawthar* is a river in paradise, its two sides are made of gold, it runs on a bed of pearls and rubies, the fragrance of its sand is more perfumed than musk, its water is sweeter than honey and whiter than milk.
>
> *Ḥadīth 896, in RHP p.123*

Al-Ghazālī records:

> The Prophet said: "My pool *(ḥawḍī)* …; its water is whiter than yogurt and sweeter than honey, and its cups are the number of stars in the sky. He who drinks from it will never thirst."
>
> *Al-Ghazālī, Iḥyā 'Ulūm al-Dīn 4, IDB p.529*

According to 'Ināyat Khān:

> *Ḥawḍ al-Kawthar,* the sacred fountain of heaven, about which there is so much spoken in Islam, is a fountain of wine.
>
> *'Ināyat Khān, Sufi Message, SMIK9 p.218*

This 'pool' is so intoxicating and blissful, it is called 'wine'. Mystics of many languages and cultures have spoken of the blissful intoxication of experiencing the Creative Word, comparing it to wine; many have called it the Living Water or the Water of Life; some have spoken of a pool or lake of Living Water in which the soul bathes upon entry into the higher paradise beyond the domain of judgment and death.

See also: **amṛit sar**, **al-Kawthar** (3.1), **mānsarovar**.

heaven(s), heavenly regions, seven heavens In Christianity, heaven is the dwelling place of God and the angels. It is a place of communion with God after death, a place of eternal bliss and beatitude.

Probably all religions speak of heaven or heavens, using a variety of names. Generally, they are depicted as places where good people and believers go after death or on the Day of Judgment. Although their location is usually unspecified, there would seem to be only two possibilities – outside oneself or inside oneself. Some schools of thought, probably stemming from early Greek cosmology, believed in a hierarchy of heavens extending through the moon, the sun, the planets, the stars and the wide expanse of sky beyond the stars (the empyrean). Mystics, however, are in accord when they have said that the heavens lie within the sphere of consciousness. They also say that these heavens can be reached not only after death, but during a person's lifetime. In fact, it is the ability to leave the body and enter the inner heavens that characterizes a mystic.

The highest mystics are those who can leave their bodies, traverse the inner heavens and return to God, the "kingdom of heaven" as Jesus called it,[1] whenever they so desire. They can also return to their bodies whenever they wish. In fact, they can be in the body and with God at the same time, giving them all-knowledge and all-power, seeing God everywhere and in everything, even as human beings. According to the gospels of Luke and Matthew, when Jesus was baptized (initiated) by John the Baptist, he was immediately able to ascend into the inner heavens by means of the "Spirit of God":

> And Jesus, when he was baptized, went up straightway out of the water. And, lo, the heavens were opened unto him, and he saw the Spirit of God descending like a dove and lighting upon him.
>
> *Matthew 3:16, KJV; cf. Luke 3:21*

In Jewish and Islamic tradition, as well as early Christianity, the number of such heavens was commonly counted as seven, the seventh being the highest. This is the origin of the idiom, 'in the seventh heaven', expressing a state of the greatest happiness. But the belief in seven heavens was prevalent in other Middle Eastern religions. In *The Mysteries of Mithra,* Franz Cumont writes of the seven heavens as they were understood in the ancient Persian religion of Mithraism, which took the Persian deity *Mithra* as its focus. Mithraism spread widely throughout the Roman Empire during the first three centuries BCE, competing with Christianity as the religion of the empire:

> The heavens were divided into seven spheres, each of which was conjoined with a planet. A sort of ladder, composed of eight superposed gates, the first seven of which were constructed of different metals, was the symbolic suggestion in the temples of the road to be followed to reach the supreme region of the fixed stars. To pass from one storey to the next, each time the wayfarer had to enter a gate guarded by an angel of *Ormazd* (God). The initiates alone, to whom the appropriate formulas had been taught, knew how to appease these inexorable guardians.
>
> As the soul traversed these different zones, it rid itself, as one would of garments, of the passions and faculties that it had received in its descent to the earth. It abandoned to the Moon its vital and nutritive energy, to Mercury its desires, to Venus its wicked appetites, to the Sun its intellectual capacity, to Mars its love of war, to Jupiter its ambitious dreams, to Saturn its inclinations. It was naked, stripped

> of every vice and every sensibility, when it penetrated the eighth heaven to enjoy there, as an essence supreme, and in the eternal Light that bathed the gods, beatitude without end.
>
> It was *Mithra,* the protector of truth, that presided over the judgment of the soul after its decease. It was he, the mediator, that served as a guide to his faithful ones in their courageous ascent to the empyrean; he was the celestial Father that received them in his resplendent mansion, like children who had returned from a distant voyage.
>
> *Franz Cumont, Mysteries of Mithra, MMC pp.144–45*

Accounts of the seven heavens appear in early Jewish and Christian apocryphal literature, and later in the *Talmud,* their names and descriptions being commonly provided. Some Jewish *Merkavah* mystics also described seven heavens and their *archons* (angelic rulers). Others said that in the seventh heaven is found a hierarchy of seven further *hekhalot* (palaces), the seventh and highest being the divine Throne of God.

In Christianity, the idea of a hierarchy of seven heavens, each higher than the other in its innate spirituality, was inherited to a large extent from Judaism. Jesus himself speaks of "many mansions in my Father's house".[2] Paul also speaks of "a man in Christ" – generally understood to have been Paul himself – who was "caught up to the third heaven", which he equates with paradise:

> I will come to visions and revelations of the Lord. I knew a man in Christ above fourteen years ago – whether in the body, I cannot tell; or whether out of the body, I cannot tell: God knoweth – such an one caught up to the third heaven.
>
> And I knew such a man – whether in the body, or out of the body, I cannot tell: God knoweth – how that he was caught up into paradise, and heard unspeakable words (the unspeakable Word?), which it is not lawful (possible) for a man to utter.
>
> *2 Corinthians 12:1–5, KJV*

There are innumerable other references to this hierarchy of heavens in early Christian literature. In the *Acts of Thomas,* Judas Thomas speaks of the Holy Spirit as the "compassionate Mother … of the seven houses":

> Come, compassionate Mother….
> Come, she that reveals the hidden mysteries.
> Come, Mother of the seven houses (mansions),
> that your rest may be in the eighth house.
>
> *Acts of Thomas 27; cf. ANT p.376*

In this instance, eternal "rest" is "in the eighth house". There are also places where the inner regions are divided broadly into heaven, paradise and the city of God, the latter being the realm of eternity. At other times, it is paradise that refers to the eternal realm.

Some mystics have also said that the entire creation, including the created heavens, is liable to occasional dissolution. Only that which is truly eternal will remain forever, beyond all constraints of time. This must be the meaning of Jesus' saying as recorded in the *Gospel of Thomas:*

> Jesus said,
> "This heaven will pass away,
> and the one above it will pass away."
>
> *Gospel of Thomas 34:11, NHS20 pp.56–57*

One of the most complete descriptions of the seven heavens is to be found in the early Christian 'revelation', the *Ascension of Isaiah,* a 'revelation' being a common literary form of the times, employed when a writer wanted to speak of the inner realities, make predictions and prophecies (sometimes of a political or radical nature), and so on. Probably few, if any, of these 'revelations' related to actual experiences – nor, in the majority of cases, were their readers expected to believe so – and there is no reason to presume that the *Ascension of Isaiah* is any different. Even so, the revelational form is used quite deliberately by the unknown writer to describe something of the higher heavens, according to his understanding.

The account is a long one and, in this condensed version, the story is joined where *Isaiah,* who is giving a spiritual discourse – known as prophesying – is suddenly caught up by the Holy Spirit and, on hearing the Voice of the Holy Spirit, is taken on a trip through the seven heavens:

> And Isaiah began to talk to King Ḥezekiah about what was certain and sure, and all the princes of Israel and the eunuchs and the king's counsellors were seated round him; and there were forty prophets and sons of the prophets who had come from the villages and the mountains and the plains, when they heard that Isaiah had come from Gilgal to Ḥezekiah....
>
> And while Isaiah was talking about what was sure and certain to Ḥezekiah, they all heard a door open and the Voice of the Holy Spirit.... And when they all heard the Voice of the Holy Spirit, all of them worshipped and fell on their knees and glorified the God of Truth, the Most High – He who dwells in the upper world, the Holy One who sits on high, and who takes his rest among the saints. And they gave praise to Him who had thus graciously given a door in an alien world and had given it to a man.
>
> *Ascension of Isaiah 6:3–6, 8–13; cf. AOT pp.794–95, OTP2 pp.164–65*

The "Voice of the Holy Spirit" opens the single eye, the "door in an alien world", which has been "given … to a man" by God in His design of the human form. The text is confused at this point and the meaning could also have been that Christ, the Master, is the door who comes to this alien world in the form of a man. Many mystics have said that the soul, caught in the physical world is like a stranger in an alien land, while the single eye and the Master are both doors by which the soul may escape from this bondage.

> And while he was speaking in the Holy Spirit in the hearing of all, he suddenly became silent, and his spirit was caught up into heaven, and he no longer saw the men who were standing in front of him. But his eyes were open, although his lips were silent, and the spirit of his body was taken up from him. And only his breath remained in him, for he was in a vision. And the angel that was sent to explain things to him in the vision was not of this world, nor was he one of the angels of glory of this world, but had come from the seventh heaven.
>
> *Ascension of Isaiah 6:10–13; cf. AOT pp.795–96, OTP2 p.165*

Isaiah leaves his body and goes inside. Even though his eyes have remained open, his soul or spirit is so withdrawn from this world that he sees nothing. Only his "breath" – his vital life energy – remains to keep the body alive. Moreover, his soul is given a guide – an angel – to take him through the inner heavens. The guide, however, is no ordinary or even middle-ranking angel, but one from the "seventh heaven" itself. In this description, the "seventh heaven" is the highest realm, the place where the Lord dwells. The 'revelation' continues:

> And, apart from the circle of the prophets, the people who were there did not believe that the holy Isaiah had been caught up into heaven. For the vision that the holy Isaiah saw was not a vision of this world, but of the world that is hidden from man. After Isaiah had seen this vision he gave an account of it to Ḥezekiah and to his son Josab and to the other prophets who had come.
>
> But the officials and the eunuchs and the people did not hear it, but only Samnas the scribe and Joachim and Asaph the recorder, for they were doers of righteousness and the fragrance of the Spirit was in them. But the people did not hear it, for Micah and his son Josab had sent them away when the wisdom (perception, consciousness) of this world had been taken from him (Isaiah), and he had been left looking like a corpse.
>
> *Ascension of Isaiah 6:14–17; cf. AOT p.796, OTP2 p.165*

Isaiah had been discoursing to a group of people who included "prophets" – the spiritually minded. Since only they would understand what had happened to Isaiah, only they were permitted to stay, all others being ushered out. Isaiah himself then takes up the story, describing his ascent through the heavens, each one being of greater light, radiance, beauty and purity than the one below. Each heaven is also described as having its own "air", meaning its own 'place', spiritually speaking. The narrative is rejoined as Isaiah enters the "sixth heaven":

> And he (the angel) took me up into the air of the sixth heaven and I beheld a glory I had not seen in the five heavens while I was being taken up, and angels resplendent in great glory. And the praises there were sublime and wonderful....
>
> And ... I asked him and said to him, "Why are there no companions for the angels on the right?" And he said, "From the sixth heaven and above it there are no more angels on the left, nor is there a throne set in the middle, but they have their direction from the power of the seventh heaven, where He dwells that cannot be named, from the Chosen One, whose Name has not been revealed, and whose Name none of the heavens can learn."
>
> *Ascension of Isaiah 8:1–4, 6–7; cf. AOT p.800, OTP2 p.168*

References to the right- and left-hand paths, which generally signify the duality of creation, are found in the mystic literature of many traditions. Hence, in the lower heavens, each angel or power has its counterpart. According to the description of this writer, however, the sixth heaven and above transcend this duality, for the angels are described as having no "companions". The seventh heaven is the 'dwelling' of the "Chosen One, whose Name has not been revealed, and whose Name none of the heavens can learn". Describing Him, the angel continues:

> "For it is to His Voice alone that all the heavens and the thrones respond; and I have been empowered and sent to bring you up here so that you may behold this glory."
>
> *Ascension of Isaiah 8:8, AOT pp.800–1*

The "Voice" is the Sound or Creative Word of God that gives power to all the heavens and "thrones" – the centres of power and administration – in the hierarchy of creation. The 'revelation' continues:

> And I glorified and praised my lord (*i.e.* Christ), because through sharing in his lot I was to go up there. And he said to me, "Hear then

> this again from your companion. When by the angel of the Spirit you have been taken up there from that alien body of yours, then will you receive the garment that you will see, and you will also see other garments numbered and stored up there. And then you will be equal to the angels of the seventh heaven."
>
> *Ascension of Isaiah 8:13–15; cf. AOT p.801, OTP2 p.168*

The "garment" is the true nature of the soul – its inherent light and glory. Once it reaches the realm of God, the soul has the same nature and light as the pure souls or angels who already reside there. The writer then goes on to describe the "sixth heaven":

> And he took me up into the sixth heaven, and there were no angels on the left, nor was there a throne in the middle, but all the angels looked the same and their praises were equal. And strength was given to me, and I also sang praises with them, and the angel who was accompanying me also, and our praises were like theirs. And they glorified the Father of all and his Beloved, the Christ, and the Holy Spirit, all with one voice. But it was not like the voice of the angels who were in the five heavens, nor was it like their speech; but the voices were different there, and there was much light there.
>
> *Ascension of Isaiah 8:16–20; cf. AOT p.801, OTP2 p.169*

The Voice or Sound that emanates from and pervades all souls who dwell here is different from the Sound heard in the "five heavens" below; and this realm is filled with a light even brighter than that of the lower realms. All the souls here are full of the natural worship, glory and intense love of the supreme Father, of His beloved Son, the "Christ" and the Holy Spirit, the Word.

> And then, when I was in the sixth heaven, I thought that the light that I had seen in the five heavens was darkness. And I rejoiced and gave praise to him who had bestowed such light on those who await his promise. And I entreated the angel who was accompanying me that I might not have to return from there to the world of the flesh. For truth to tell, Ḥezekiah and Josab, my son, and Micah, there is great darkness here (in the physical world).
>
> *Ascension of Isaiah 8:21–24; cf. AOT pp.801–2, OTP2 p.169*

From the "sixth heaven", on the threshold of the highest heaven, even the great light of the lower heavens seems like such darkness that 'Isaiah' is full of a blissful gratitude and wonderment that such an incredible treasure of light and beatitude should be "bestowed … on those who await his promise"

– upon His chosen souls. Indeed, so great is his bliss and utter contentment that he begs that he may "not have to return" to his physical body, for by comparison this world is full of "darkness" and misery. But the angel tells him that his time to die has not yet come, though he gives him ample cause for happiness:

> And the angel who was accompanying me realized what I was thinking and said, "If you rejoice in this light, how much more will you rejoice in the seventh heaven when you see the light where the Lord is and his Beloved, and also the garments and the thrones and the crowns stored up for the righteous, for those, that is, who believe in that Lord who will descend in your human form. For great and marvellous is the light that is there. But as for your not returning to your body – the time has not come for your coming here."
>
> And when I heard this I was sad; but he said to me, "Be not sad."
>
> *Ascension of Isaiah 8:25–28; cf. AOT p.802, OTP2 p.169*

He describes the sixth heaven as supremely bright, making even the lower heavens seem dark by comparison. He also emphasizes that the "righteous", the chosen ones, are those who believe in the "Lord who will descend in your human form", that is – as the Saviour. In fact, earlier in this writing, the angel has said that one of the reasons why Isaiah was being taken up was:

> "So that you may see the Lord of all these heavens and of these thrones, transforming Himself until He becomes like you in form and in appearance."
>
> *Ascension of Isaiah 8:10, AOT p.801*

Isaiah is then taken up into the seventh heaven where he sees the Holy Spirit in the form of an angel:

> And I asked the angel who led me, and I said to him, "Who is this one?" And he said to me, "Worship him, for this is the angel of the Holy Spirit who speaks in you and also in the other righteous ones." And the eyes of my spirit were open, and I beheld the Great Glory.
>
> *Ascension of Isaiah 9:36–37; cf. AOT p.805, OTP2 p.172*

The Voice of the Word, the Holy Spirit, "speaks" in the soul of everyone, though only the initiated – "you and … the other righteous ones" – come to hear it in all its full glory and power; and then, only when the "eyes of the spirit" – the inner, spiritual eye – is opened. It is this power that transforms an individual, making him pure, subtle, bright, holy and truly "righteous".

> And I heard then the voices and the hymns of praise that I had heard in each of the six heavens – that I had heard as I ascended. And all the voices and the hymns were addressed to that Glorious One, whose glory I could not see.
>
> *Ascension of Isaiah 10:1–2; cf. AOT p.806, OTP2 p.172*

The highest realm of God is the source of all that lies below. Everything emanates from there. All the sounds or "voices" of the lower heavens are contained within the Sound or Voice of that realm. And with the Voice comes natural praise and worship. The soul automatically knows and understands the nature of true worship. The soul is entranced in the love, bliss and wonder of the divine Voice, and all such worship is automatically directed towards the Lord.

> And I heard and saw the praise that was being directed to Him. And the Lord and the angel of the Spirit heard everything and saw everything. For all the praise that comes up from the six heavens is not only heard, but seen.
>
> *Ascension of Isaiah 10:3–5; cf. AOT p.806, OTP2 pp.172–73*

Significantly, this worship is both visible and audible, "is not only heard, but seen" – these being the two faculties of the soul and the two characteristics of the Word or Voice.

> And I heard the angel, who was accompanying me, speaking to me; and he said, "This is the Most High of the high ones, who dwells in the high holy world, resting among His holy ones."
>
> *Ascension of Isaiah 10:6; cf. AOT p.806, OTP2 p.173*

The "holy ones" are the pure and holy souls who dwell with God. In the story, the "Lord the Christ" is then given his instructions, and the remainder of the revelation describes his appointment by the "Voice", and his descent through the lower heavens until he incarnates in a human form as Jesus.

Inevitably, all such accounts of the heavens are richly coloured by the personal belief systems, as well as the cultural and religious backgrounds, of their original writers, and often of their subsequent editors, too. Even so, the increasing intensity of spirit, bliss, light and love as the soul ascends, the heavenly Voice or Music that draws the soul upwards, and the darkness of human existence by comparison are features of practically all descriptions of the heavenly realms, whatever the religious tradition.

See also: **bihisht-u dūzakh**, **Hekhalot mystics** (▸2), **merkavah** (▸2), **sab‘ samāwāt**, **svarga**, **T’iēn**, **vaikuṇṭha**.

1. *Matthew* 4:17, 5:10,19–20, 7:21, 10:7, 11:11, 13:11,33,44,45,47,52, 16:19, 18:1,4,23, 19:12,14,23, 20:1, 22:2, 23:13, 25:1, *KJV*.
2. *John* 14:2.

heavens (Nahua) The Nahua people of Mexico were well known for their spiritual tradition and their poetry. Flowers and flower gardens are a favourite symbol, repeated frequently in contexts both spiritual and mundane. Here, the "divine gardens of sunrise" undoubtedly refer to the heavenly realms:

> The divine gardens of sunrise are blossoming: …
> flowers of the Lord of the near and close.
> Fragrant curds of dew glitter like the sun,
> most pleasing to the soul.
>
> *Nahua Poetry, in FIN p.42*

In other poems, the writer is explicit:

> It is there that I the singer hear the very essence of song;
> Certainly not on earth has true poesy its birth;
> Certainly it is within the heavens
> that one hears the lovely coyol bird lift its voice,
> that the various quechol and zacuan birds speak together.
> There they certainly praise the Cause of All.
> Ohuaya! Ohuaya!
>
> I, the singer, labour in spirit with what I heard,
> that it may lift up my memory;
> That it may go forth to those shining heavens,
> that my sighs may have borne on the wind,
> and be permitted to enter
> where the yellow humming bird
> chants its praises in the heavens.
> Ohuaya! Ohuaya!
>
> *Nahua Poetry, in ANP p.59*

One culture can very rapidly assimilate beliefs and traditions from another. In this poem, written sometime after the arrival of the Spanish in Mexico, Christian influences are clearly at work. "Ohuaya" is almost certainly a corruption of 'Hallelujah', while at other places in their poetry, alongside *Nahuaque,* the "Cause of All", is found the Spanish *Dios* (God). Cultures and languages change: only the inner Reality is ever constant.

See also: **gardens**.

hell, hellfire In Christianity, hell is the place or state of eternal punishment, ruled by Satan, experienced by the wicked after death. Hellfire is the punishment and torment of hell, depicted by Christian preachers as an eternal, fiery punishment for wickedness.

From a more mystical perspective, hell is a part of the subastral realms where souls suffer the consequences of their misdeeds and their desires for things of the material world. According to a number of mystics, the stay is only temporary, until the souls reincarnate once again in this world, though not necessarily in a human form.

Like all regions within the domain of the negative power, hell is essentially a realm of the mind, as is the physical universe. Moreover, the majority of souls in this world, whether in human or lower forms, are tortured by desires, passions and all the vicissitudes of physical existence. Consequently, they are already undergoing the torment of hell, though still physically incarnate. Speaking metaphorically, mystics have therefore frequently described this world as hell. This double meaning was also used in some instances as a veiled way of talking about reincarnation. Because of this, when hell is mentioned in sacred and especially mystic writings, it is necessary to study the context closely to determine precisely what is meant. Sometimes, both meanings are intended.

In John's gospel, for example, speaking of himself as the True Vine (the Word), Jesus says:

> If a man abide not in me,
> he is cast forth as a branch, and is withered;
> And men gather them, and cast them into the fire,
> and they are burned.
>
> *John 15:6, KJV*

The branch or soul that is not connected to the trunk of the True Vine – that does not abide in the Word – withers and dies, and is burnt in the fire. Traditionally, this is interpreted literally to mean that souls who are not good Christians will be sent to hell. This seems somewhat harsh, and their 'death' and 'burning' could also be meant metaphorically as their return to this world of birth and death.

In literature where reincarnation and transmigration are explicitly mentioned, the use of hell to describe this world is not infrequent. In the Manichaean texts from Chinese Turkestan, for example, the whirlpool of transmigration is specifically described as the "transmigration of hell", as well as the "eternal confinement", release from which can only be gained through contact with the "five Light-bodies", the five 'divisions' of the Word as it passes through the creation. The "*kalpa* (age) of destruction", or what is called the *kaliyuga* in Indian mythology, is the age of darkness through which the world is presently passing:

> If there are people who suffer in the transmigration of hell,
> in the fire of the *kalpa* of destruction
> and the eternal confinement,
> it is really because they do not recognize the five Light-bodies,
> and are therefore severed
> from the country of peace and happiness.
>
> *Manichaean Hymns, LSMH p.197:247*

Similarly, in a long Manichaean hymn cycle in Parthian in which the poet begs for release from the realm of birth and death, this world and its various bodily prisons are again described as hell:

> Who will lead me beyond rebirths,
> and free me from them all –
> and from all the waves, in which there is no rest?
> I weep for my soul, saying:
> "May I be saved from this,
> and from the terror of the beasts who devour one another!"
> The bodies of men, and of birds of the air,
> of fish of the sea,
> and four-footed creatures and of all insects –
> Who will take me beyond these and save me from them all,
> so that I shall not turn
> and fall into the perdition of those hells?
> So that I shall not pass through defilement in them,
> nor return in rebirth….
> Who will save me from the swallowing heights and the devouring deeps,
> which are all hell and distress?
>
> *Manichaean Hymns, Huwīdagmān IVa:5–10; cf. MHCP pp.82–83*

And likewise:

> [Those who dwell there]
> are struck by merciless blows in the deep;
> There is no health for all their sicknesses.
> Not all the lusts and the comfort of wealth
> will help them in that hellish place….
> Not all their idols, altars and images
> can save them from that hell.
> They are oppressed by anguish and by merciless [torment]….

Who will take me far from it,
  that I may not plunge into them,
  and that I may not tumble
  and fall into every bitter hell?
All who enter there find no way out.

Manichaean Hymns, Huwīdagmān V:9–10, 12–13, 19–20, MHCP pp.86–91

See also: **abyss**, **fire** (▸2), **Gehenna**, **Hadēs**, **outer darkness**, **Pit**, **Sheol**.

hereafter, the Life after death, the next world, the afterlife, the future life; a colloquial expression for existence after the death of the physical body.

See also: **afterlife**.

Ḥesed (He) *Lit.* lovingkindness, love, mercy, grace; the fourth of the ten *sefirot* (emanations); also called *Gedulah* (Greatness). As a quality of God, *Ḥesed* is His grace and love. It is the overflowing abundance *(shefa)* of His benign light and grace, the fount of the positive energy flowing into the creation. God's abundant *Ḥesed* is moderated by the fifth *sefirah* of *Din* (Judgment) so that it can be received by the creation in an ordered and controlled fashion.

The daily Jewish liturgy contains an invocation of *Ḥesed,* as well as other *sefirot.* Many of the daily prayers were composed by the Kabbalists as *kavvanot* (intentions), a way of calling upon the particular power or energy of these divine qualities. In one passage, the aspirant begs God to bestow upon him all the divine qualities embodied in the *sefirot,* through the same emanatory process by which He brought about the creation:

And from Your Wisdom *(Ḥokhmah),* O supreme God,
  emanate upon me (inspire me);
And from Your Understanding *(Binah),*
  give me Understanding;
With Your Lovingkindness *(Ḥesed),*
  enlarge me also.

Jewish Prayer Book; cf. PB p.3, DPB p.8

As a human quality, *ḥesed* is love and devotion for God, often called piety. It is from the same root as *ḥasid* – the pious one or devotee – a term used for both spiritual teachers and their disciples by various Jewish spiritual and mystical movements and orders at various times.

Ḥesed is also a name used for the age of righteousness, the 'golden age' in the Kabbalistic understanding of cosmic cycles *(shemittot).*

See also: **ḥesed** (2.1, ▸2), **sefirot**.

higher regions, higher worlds See **heavens, mansions, regions**.

hills, hill of frankincense See **mountains**.

hiraṇyagarbha (S/H) *Lit.* embryo *(garbha)* of gold *(hiraṇya);* the golden embryo. The earliest appearance of the term in Indian sacred literature is the *Ṛig Veda,* where *Hiraṇyagarbha* is the deity from whom all things came into being, although he himself arose from a prior source:

> Who is the god we should worship with our oblation?
> *Hiraṇyagarbha,* who arose in the beginning,
> who was manifest as the one Lord of creation.
> who held in place this earth and this sky.
>
> Who is the god we should worship with our oblation?
> He who gives life, who gives strength,
> whose command all the gods, his own, obey;
> His shadow is immortality – and death.
>
> Who is the god we should worship with our oblation?
> He who by his greatness became the one king of the world
> that breathes and blinks,
> who rules over his two-footed and four-footed creatures....
>
> Who is the god we should worship with our oblation?
> He by whom the awesome sky and the earth were made firm,
> by whom the dome of the sky was propped up, and the sun,
> who measured out the middle realm of space....
>
> Who is the god we should worship with our oblation?
> When the high waters came,
> pregnant with the embryo that is everything,
> bringing forth fire,
> he arose from that as the one life's breath of the gods.
>
> *Ṛig Veda 10:121.1–3, 5, 7; adapted from RV pp.27–28*

And:

> The Fashioner of all is vast in mind, vast in strength.
> He is the one who forms, who sets in order....
> He was the one whom the waters received
> as the first embryo *(garbha),* when all the gods assembled.
>
> *Ṛig Veda 10:82.2, 6; cf. RV p.36*

In later texts, *hiraṇyagarbha* undergoes a development, and the golden embryo becomes a golden egg *(hiraṇyāṇḍa),* from which the creation comes into being. The *Chhāndogya Upanishad* describes the process of creation in mythological terms:

> In the beginning, this (universe) was nonexistent.
> Then it became existent.
> It grew; it became an egg *(aṇḍa);*
> It lay for the space of a year; it broke open.
> Of the two halves of that eggshell,
> one was of silver and the other of gold.
> That which was of silver is this earth,
> that which was of gold is the sky.
> The outer membrane is the mountains.
> The inner membrane is the mist and clouds.
> The blood-vessels are the rivers.
> The amniotic fluid is the ocean.
>
> *Chhāndogya Upanishad 3:19.1–2*

In the *Bhagavad Gītā,* Kṛishṇa, speaking as the Divine, says more simply that all creation forms from the embryo he places in the womb of *prakṛiti* (primal nature):

> The great *Brahma (i.e. prakṛiti)* is my womb
> in which I place the embryo *(garbha),*
> from which all beings take their birth.
>
> *Bhagavad Gītā 14:3*

Later still, in the *Manu Smṛiti* and the *Purāṇas* (especially the *Brahma* and *Brahmāṇḍa Purāṇas*), it is said that at the beginning of a cycle of the *yugas* (ages), a primal divine seed is deposited by the self-existent *Brahman* in the 'waters' of his first creative expression. From this seed, develops the golden egg *(hiraṇyāṇḍa),* described as resplendent as the sun. From the golden egg emerges the golden embryo *(hiraṇyagarbha),* also identified as *Brahmā,* the creator who then brings the creation into existence. This created cosmos is known as *brahmāṇḍa.*

The use of the term 'waters' is a common metaphor of mystical expression of past ages, especially Judaic and early Near and Middle Eastern mysticism. It refers to the primal creative 'substance' out of which all lower creation is formed. Hence, the allegory of *Genesis* says that "the Spirit of God moved upon the face of the waters."[1] This means that the Spirit – the creative Power of God in the creation – creates the movement or vibration by which the primal power or energy of the Supreme Being is manifested as creation.

Some of the *Upanishads* and later Vedantic texts such as the *Vedāntasāra* relate a more complex and less mythological account of creation.[2] Here, *hiraṇyagarbha* is one of the three stages in the emanative process of creation from *saguṇa Brahman* (*Brahman* with the great attributes), the other two being *avyākṛita* (undifferentiated) and *vishvarūpa* (all-inclusive form), also called *virāṭrūpa* (*lit.* huge or expanded form, the grossly manifested universe) and *vaishvānara* (*lit.* consisting of all men, common to all men, universal, omnipresent).[3]

In the *Upanishads, Brahman* is described as the unchanging Reality that undergoes no change or evolution. All change or evolution belongs to the sphere of *māyā* (illusion). *Brahman* associated with *māyā* is called *Īshvara* (*lit.* Lord). *Īshvara* is described as omnipotent and omniscient, possessing the power to create. *Māyā* at first remains undifferentiated *(avyākṛita),* then becomes differentiated into subtle forms *(hiraṇyagarbha),* and then into gross objects *(virāṭ),* as perceived in this world. These are the three manifestations of *Īshvara.*

The three aspects or stages in the evolution or projection of *Īshvara* into the lower creation are explained in Vedantic texts by the analogy of a seed developing into a tree. *Īshvara,* in its initial projection as undifferentiated *māyā,* is called *avyākṛita.* Here, everything exists in potential, as in a dormant seed that has yet to develop. Everything of the lower creation exists here in seed form as the finest mental essences or energies, just as a tree is present in its seed but that potential has yet to be manifested or realized. This corresponds to the causal *(kāraṇ)* realm.

Hiraṇyagarbha is the second stage in the manifestation of *Īshvara* as the lower creation. Here, a subtly differentiated expression of *māyā* is found, where manifestation may be compared to the swollen state of the seed ready to germinate. This corresponds to the astral or subtle *(sūkshma)* realm.

Īshvara expressed as *māyā* fully differentiated into gross or perceptible objects is called *vishvarūpa, virāṭrūpa* or *vaishvānara,* leading souls in the diverse directions found in the physical universe. This may be compared to the fully grown or fully differentiated stage in the development of the tree. Here, the potential of the seed is fully expressed.

These three aspects of *Brahman* are also reflected in the human *(piṇḍī)* microcosm as the three states of human consciousness: the waking state *(vishva),* the dream state *(taijasa)* and deep dreamless sleep *(prajñā).* Many mystics have referred to the so-called waking consciousness of the physical realm as a deep slumber, where man sleeps, entirely unconscious of the nature of his true Self or of the presence of God within and around him.

Consciousness at the astral *(sūkshma)* level is reflected as the dream state, where the phantoms and images of the mind become immediate reality, just as forms and images are projected in the subtle, illusory astral world. They are fascinating and beguiling, but utterly unstable – a mirage, only, of the higher Reality. Consciousness at the causal *(kāraṇa)* level is reflected in the state of deep, dreamless sleep, where all is seemingly quiescent. Beyond these three states is the fourth state called *turīya,* corresponding to the apparently changeless Reality or the absolute *Brahman.*

According to some Indian *Sants* (Saints), *Brahman* or *Brahm* is not the highest Reality. Nineteenth- and twentieth-century *Sants* have specifically identified *Brahman* with the higher reaches of the region the *Sants* have called *trikuṭī,* also designated the universal mind. Here, *māyā* is so cleverly concealed in its potential and undifferentiated state that the soul believes itself to be wide awake and enlightened, as indeed does man in the physical realm. But, in fact, the soul is still within the realm of the higher mind, separated from its true and eternal self by the limitations of space, time and causality, and still liable to rebirth in the physical realm. What may appear to be the highest and unchanging Reality is actually the most subtle mirage that the mind can produce. It is an imitation of God Himself, its duration and character being so nearly everlasting as to lead its inhabitants to believe they have indeed reached eternity.

Hiraṇyagarbha is also used as epithet of Kṛishṇa.[4]

See also: **avyākṛita**, **Brahman** (2.1), **virāṭrūpa**, **vishvarūpa**.

1. *Genesis* 1:2, *KJV.*
2. Sadānanda, *Vedāntasāra* 91, 111–19; Shankara, *Vivekachūḍāmaṇi* 20.
3. For *avyākṛita,* see *Bṛihadāraṇyaka Upanishad* 1:4.7; for *hiraṇyagarbha,* see *Shvetāshvatara Upanishad* 3:3, 4:12, *Nṛisiṃha Uttara Tāpinīya Upanishad* 1; for *vaishvānara,* see *Māṇḍūkya Upanishad* 3, *Prashna Upanishad 1:7, Bhagavad Gītā* 15:14, *Vedāntasāra* 91; for *virāṭrūpa,* see *Vedāntasāra* 91; for *vishvarūpa,* see *Prashna Upanishad* 1:7, *Bhagavad Gītā* 11:16, *Rām Charit Mānas* 4:21.2, 6:14.
4. *Mahābhārata* 12, *Shāntiparvan* 342:96.

Hod (He) *Lit.* majesty; a quality of God; the eighth of the ten *sefirot.* In the sefirotic system, *Hod* and the seventh *sefirah* of *Neẓaḥ* (Endurance, Eternity), jointly express the full range of God's qualities as the divine Ruler or King.

The divine creative power flows from the level of the Godhead via the ten *sefirot* into the creation. The sefirotic system is a way of expressing the divine qualities acting upon each other and resulting in the various levels of spirituality. At the higher levels, the abundance of divine love flows freely from the fourth *sefirah* of *Ḥesed* (Lovingkindness), but is channelized or limited by the fifth *sefirah* of *Din* (Judgment) before continuing downwards through the lower *sefirot* into the creation.

In the same way, *Neẓaḥ* (Endurance, Eternity) represents the outflowing, 'regal' quality of God as triumphant over time, enduring and eternal, while *Hod* (Majesty) is the quality that channelizes or limits *Neẓaḥ.* The Kabbalists often would say that *Neẓaḥ* and *Hod* are the means by which God governs the world. The limitation arising from the activity of *Hod* on *Neẓaḥ* parallels the action of *Din* on *Ḥesed.* Using a modern metaphor, *Hod* is essentially a lower frequency of *Din.*

See also: **hod** (2.1), **sefirot**.

imkān (A/P) *Lit.* possibility, contingency.

See **dā'irat al-imkān**.

Indralok(a), **Indrapurī** (S/H/Pu), **Indar purī** (Pu) *Lit.* region *(loka)* or city *(purī)* of *Indra;* the heaven over which the god *Indra* is said to preside according to traditional Hindu belief; the heaven or world to which all heroic *kshatriyas* (members of the warrior caste) go after death, according to the *Vishṇu Purāṇa,*[1] *Indra* being the god of the warrior class. *Indra*'s world is also known as *svarga* (paradise), among whose inhabitants are the ravishing *apsarās* (celestial damsels) and sweet-voiced *gandharvas* (celestial musicians).

Indra, Shiva, Brahmā and the other gods of the Hindu pantheon are all traditionally ascribed roles consistent with their being subpowers within the realm of the universal mind. Their realms would thus be a part of the astral or causal heavens and therefore subject to occasional dissolution or *pralaya.* Hence, Guru Arjun says:

> In the realm of *Indra (Indar purī),* death is sure and certain;
> The realm of *Brahmā (Brahm purī)* is not to remain permanent;
> The realm of *Shiva (Shiv purī)* shall perish:
> *Māyā* (illusion) with three qualities (*guṇas,* attributes)
> and the demons shall vanish.
>
> *Guru Arjun, Ādi Granth 237, MMS*

Kabīr also says that even if a soul were to reach *Indraloka* or *Shivaloka* by means of austerities and penances, that soul would still have to be reborn in this world.[2]

See also: **Brahmaloka**, **Indra** (4.2), **Shivaloka**, **Vishṇuloka**.

1. *Vishṇu Purāṇa* 1:6.
2. Kabīr, *Ādi Granth* 692.

inner regions See **heavens**, **mansions**, **regions**.

jabarūt (A/P) *Lit.* power, might, dominion. *'Ālam al-jabarūt* (realm of power) is one of the levels, planes or regions in the hierarchy of the creation, through which the soul passes on its ascent to the Divine.

See also: **'ālam**.

jahannam (A/P) *Lit.* hell; from the Hebrew *Gehinnom* (Gehenna); according to the *Qur'ān*, *jahannam* is a place of permanent suffering for sinners after death:

> The sinners will be in the punishment of hell *(jahannam)*
> to dwell therein (for aye).
>
> *Qur'ān 43:74, AYA*

Islamic tradition describes seven divisions or stages *(ṭibāq)* of hell, souls being sent to the various hells according to the nature of their deeds. Some of these hells are named in the *Qur'ān*, other names stem from Quranic descriptions:

1.	*Jahannam*	A deep pit, burning hell (78:21).
2.	*Laẓá*	A raging fire, a furnace (70:15).
3.	*Ḥuṭamah*	A crushing fire, a fierce fire; a fire that reduces everything to ashes (104:2–7).
4.	*Sa'īr*	A raging fire, "bubbling and sighing" (25:11).
5.	*Saqar*	A scorching fire, "I shall surely roast him in *Saqar*" (74:26).
6.	*Jaḥīm*	A huge hot fire, "you shall surely see *Jaḥīm*" (102:6).

7. *Hāwiyah* A bottomless pit, an abyss, the lowest hell, "a blazing fire" (101:9–11).[1]

The *Qur'ān* alludes to the seven hells as seven gates, one for each category of sinner. *Allāh* 'says' that for those who follow *Iblīs* (the devil):

> Verily, hell *(jahannam)*
> is the promised abode for them all.
> To it are seven gates:
> for each of those gates
> is a (special) class (of sinners) assigned.
>
> *Qur'ān 15:43–44, HQSA*

In common with other religions, heaven and hell are portrayed in vivid terms. The *Qur'ān* speaks of hell as the fire *(al-nār)* and as *al-nār al-jahannam* (the fire of hell), describing it as a place of torture for sinners and unbelievers:

> Fear the fire *(al-nār),*
> whose fuel is men and stones,
> prepared for unbelievers.
>
> *Qur'ān 2:24, KI*

Jahannam is also portrayed as lying in wait, ready to "ambush … transgressors". Once trapped, "they will dwell therein for ages" in extreme discomfort:

> Truly hell *(jahannam)* is as a place of ambush
> for the transgressors.
> A place of destination:
> they will dwell therein for ages.
> Nothing cool shall they taste therein,
> nor any drink, save a boiling fluid,
> and a fluid, dark, murky, intensely cold.
>
> *Qur'ān 78:21–25, HQSA*

It is the 'reward' of sinners on the Day of Judgment. It is a place in which a soul can be said to neither "die nor live":

> Verily, he who comes to the Lord as a sinner,
> (at Judgment), for him is hell *(jahannam):*
> Therein shall he neither die nor live.
>
> *Qur'ān 20:74, HQSA*

There is no unanimity among commentators whether the descriptions in the *Qur'ān* are to be taken literally or figuratively, nor, among those who prefer a figurative interpretation, about its extent. There is the traditional and orthodox view that the descriptions are to be taken literally. The torments of hell are real and physical, the delights of heaven sensuous, as depicted.

The literalist opinion also tends towards the belief that heaven and hell only come into existence on the Day of Judgment. Others say that they have existed from the beginning, but that entry to them will not be determined until the Day of Judgment. Others, notably the Sufis, maintain that entry to heaven or hell is determined on the individual's day of death. Sufis have also sometimes understood hell in a more metaphorical sense, as the state of mind of the sinful person.

See also: **abyss**, **bihisht-u dūzakh**, **Gehenna**, **Hadēs**, **hell**, **naraka**, **Pit**, **Sheol**.

1. *Qur'ān* translations: *KI.*

jambu dvīp(a) (S/H), **jambu dvīp** (H) *Lit.* island-continent *(dvīpa)* of the rose apple *(jambu;* L. *Eugenia jambolana);* the most central of the seven *dvīpas* (island-continents) surrounding the golden mountain, Mount *Meru,* the Indian Olympus, the dwelling place of the gods, especially *Brahmā, Indra* and the other deities. According to Indian mythology, as recounted in the *Purāṇas,* the earth is a flat disc at whose centre is Mount *Meru.* The seven continents were surrounded by seven seas, filled with various substances. On the shores of *jambu dvīpa* stood a huge *jambu* tree, from which the island continent was named. India was understood to be the southern zone of *jambu dvīpa.* The number of continents varies between mythological texts.

The mythological accounts vary from text to text, but according to the *Brahmāṇḍa Purāṇa,* the ruler of *jambu dvīpa,* Āgnīdhra, had nine sons: Nābhi, Hari, Ilāvṛita, Rāmyā, Hiraṇvat, Kuru, Bhadrāshva, Ketumāla and Kimpurusha. These nine sons were appointed to rule over one of the nine regions *(varshas)* into which *jambu dvīpa* was divided, each region being named after the ruling son. After appointing them, Āgnīdhra himself retired to the forest to meditate. The kingship of these realms was then passed from father to son. Āgnīdhra's first son, Nābhi, was succeeded by his son Ṛishabha, who was followed in turn by his son Bharata. This region came to be known as *Bhāratavarsha.*

Indian mystics such as Dariyā Sāhib of Bihar have used *jambu dvīp* to mean this world:

What can the bird (the soul) do,
  when its eyes are lost, its wings torn,
  and it has become lame, with legs broken?
How can it reach its destination?
I am here in this world *(jambu dvīp),* O my Master:
  pray, come to my rescue.
Kindly save me this time,
  my heart is dedicated to your holy feet.

Dariyā Sāhib, Sahasrānī, DSS p.56; cf. DSSB p.204

Speaking of the mission of a Master to this world, Dariyā Sāhib writes in the name of the Lord, speaking here to a Master: "Go, assume an incarnation, and spread your teachings in the world *(jambu dvīp).*"[1] And more fully:

O valiant one, go to the land *(jambu dvīp)* of *Kāl,*
Awaken the souls and bring them back to the ocean of bliss.
When you enter the womb and take human birth,
  then, through you, will people know my secrets.

Dariyā Sāhib, Gyān Dīpak, Chaupaī 757–58, GD p.167; cf. DSSB p.vi

See also: **dvīpa**.

1. Dariyā Sāhib, *Brahm Vivek,* Chaupaī 494, *DG2* p.370.

jannah, al- (A), **jannat** (P) (pl. *jannāt, jannātin) Lit.* the hidden garden; a garden set with trees, a palm grove; thus, paradise, heaven; the commonest term used in the *Qur'ān* for paradise. *Jannah,* from *janna* (to hide, to conceal, to veil), implies that which is covered, veiled or surrounded, an enclosed garden, where beauty and sweet fragrances are contained, and trees and plants grow in verdant abundance, sheltered from storm or wind. The implication of enclosure implies something that is secret and hidden from view, something scarcely imaginable. Spiritual riches beyond description are hidden or enclosed within the body, where they may ripen and bear fruit unseen. Cyril Glassé explains why "gardens" are such an evocative metaphor to desert people:

> The desert is dead, sterile and odourless. To come out of the desert into an oasis is to be overwhelmed by the perfumes of plants and flowers, and the sudden proliferation of life; it is also to be blest with coolness, repose after journeying, and water after thirst. To a desert

people, more than to any other, the planted garden with shade and running water is the most powerfully concrete example by which their imagination may grasp the nature of another, supernatural world.

The *Qur'ān* often speaks of "gardens (of paradise) underneath which rivers run".[1] Deep in the Arabian peninsula are aquifers which carry water under pressure, drop by drop, through porous rock from the mountains of the Red Sea to the Gulf on the other side. There (and in spots across the deserts, as well as on the sea floor of the Gulf itself) these aquifers well up as springs, sometimes warm springs, which create the vast oasis of al-Ḥāsah. The movement of the life-giving water from one end of the peninsula to the other takes as long as ten thousand years, a mysterious, secret presence hidden in the earth.

Cyril Glassé, Concise Encyclopaedia of Islam, CEI pp.206–7

The heavenly realms are likened to gardens throughout Middle Eastern mystical expression. Divine beatitude and spiritual nourishment are symbolized as delicious fruits and sweetmeats, while rivers, fountains or springs flow with Living Water, wine or milk and honey. The *Qur'ān* contains numerous such descriptions:

This is the similitude of paradise *(al-jannah),*
which the godfearing have been promised:
Therein are rivers of water which time cannot corrupt,
rivers of milk unchanging in flavour,
and rivers of wine – a delight to the drinkers,
(and) rivers, too, of honey purified;
And therein for them is every fruit,
and forgiveness from their Lord.

Qur'ān 47:15, KI

Give thou good tidings to those who believe
and do deeds of righteousness,
that for them await gardens *(jannātin)*
underneath which rivers flow;
Whensoever they are provided with fruits therefrom,
they shall say, "This is that wherewithal
we were provided before";
That they shall be given in perfect semblance.

Qur'ān 2:25, KI

God has guarded them (the pious)
  from the evil of that Day (of Judgment),
  and has procured them radiancy and gladness,
  and recompensed them for their patience
  with a garden *(jannah)* and silk;
Therein they shall recline upon couches,
  therein they shall see neither sun nor bitter cold;
Near them shall be its shades,
  and its clusters hung meekly down,
  and there shall be passed around them vessels of silver,
  and goblets of crystal –
  crystal of silver that they have measured very exactly.
And therein they shall be given to drink a cup
  whose mixture is ginger,
  therein a fountain whose name is called *Salsabīl*.
Immortal youths shall go about them;
When thou seest them,
  thou supposest them scattered pearls;
When thou seest them,
  then thou seest bliss and a great kingdom.
Upon them shall be green garments of silk and brocade;
They are adorned with bracelets of silver,
  and their Lord shall give them to drink a pure draught.
Behold, this is a recompense for you,
  and your striving is thanked.

Qur'ān 76:11–22, KI

Those (who repent) – they shall enter paradise *(al-jannah)*,
  and they shall not be wronged anything;
Gardens of Eden *(jannāt al-'Adan)* that the All-Merciful
  promised His servants in the Unseen:
His promise is ever performed.
There they shall hear no idle talk,
  but only "Peace".
There they shall have their provision at dawn and evening.
That is paradise *(al-jannah)*,
  which We shall give as an inheritance
  to those of our servants who are godfearing.

Qur'ān 19:60–63, KI

The *Qur'ān* also speaks of *Allāh*'s own paradise *(jannah)* in a passage where *Allāh* is speaking to the righteous soul of the supreme grace to be bestowed upon it:

> O soul at peace *(al-nafs al-muṭma'innah),*
> return *(irji'ī)* unto thy Lord,
> well pleased (thyself), well pleasing (unto Him)!
> Enter thou among my servants!
> Enter thou my paradise *(jannah)!*
>
> *Qur'ān 89:27–30, KI*

There is no unanimity of understanding regarding the nature of *jannah,* either in Islam as a whole or in Sufism. As the *Qur'ān* describes it, *jannah* is an imperishable dwelling free from all worry and affliction, containing those things that give pleasure in physical life, such as gardens, birds, streams, flowers, fruits, drapery and other delights. These descriptions are variously interpreted.

The traditional interpretation is literal, with an emphasis on the reality of these sensual delights. The descriptions of the *Qur'ān* are amplified in the traditional sayings *(ḥadīth),* to which commentators have added a great deal of their own, exaggerating greatly in order to generate interest among the common people.

In such interpretations, *jannah* is generally located in or above the seventh heaven and below *al-'arsh* (the throne of *Allāh*), and is commonly equated with *firdaws* (paradise) or *jannat al-'Adan* (garden of Eden or garden of eternity), the paradise from which Adam was expelled. Huge dimensions are given in order to create an impression of their vastness or boundlessness, and each part is divided into many (often a hundred) levels. Eight doors are described for entering these different parts. According to one *ḥadīth,* the key to these doors has three teeth: first, faith in unity; second, obedience to God; and third, abstention from all actions forbidden by the *sharī'ah* (Islamic religious law or code). The guests will enter only after the Day of Judgment and the settlement of their accounts. The Prophet will enter first; the poor will precede the rich; Arabic will be the predominant language.

Other interpreters, however, Sufis and philosophers being among them, say that the correct interpretation is metaphorical: that the reality is much higher and finer than the things of this world, and cannot be described in words. They say that things have been described in terms of earthly delights because there is some correspondence to them, and because human beings could not otherwise conceive of them.

There is also a difference of opinion as to whether *jannah* – and hell too – have existed from the beginning or whether they will come into existence on the Day of Judgment with entry being determined at that time. A few, notably Sufis, maintain that everlasting life starts not with the Day of Judgment, but with the death of the individual. The soul will experience those joys which, according to its nature, it can savour and appreciate. Some Sufis have also observed that heaven and hell can be experienced in this life, before physical death.

Ibn Sīnā (Avicenna) and others of his school do not deny the Day of Judgment, but advise that it should be regarded as a lesson to be interpreted metaphorically by the wise man. The highest levels of *jannah* are understood as referring to the highest levels of spiritual attainment, and luxurious living to the inner state of the soul, dwelling as heavenly spirit. Bū 'Alī Sīnā says that the literal meaning of the *Qur'ān* should not be ignored since it is beneficial to those who have lived a godly life, but have no high intellectual or spiritual attainment. But he adds that the blessings of *jannah* are not sensual, but at the level of mind and spirit.

In the *Qur'ān, jannah* occurs by itself and also as a compound term, as in the names of the seven *jannāt* (see below). Paradise is also called by other names, including *firdaws* (paradise), *dār al-khuld* (abode of eternity), *dār al-baqā'* (the everlasting abode) and *dār al-surūr* (the abode of joy). But there is no unanimity as to whether these different terms represent different paradises, different divisions within one paradise, or different attributes of one paradise. It is quite common, however, to speak of *jannāt* (pl.) to mean different paradises or divisions of paradise, arranged systematically in levels. But again, there is no unanimity as to the number of levels.

Following the *Qur'ān,* many commentators have spoken of seven *jannāt* or seven heavens *(sab' samāwāt),* but common reference is also made to eight paradises *(hasht jannat),* as well as the nine heavens (A. *tis' samāwāt,* P. *nuh sipihr*). But perhaps the most common traditional reference is to the seven *jannāt* or seven heavens *(sab' samāwāt).* These are generally listed as:

1. *(Jannat) al-firdaws* (garden of paradise) (23:11).[2]
2. *Jannat al-'Adan* (garden of Eden or garden of eternity) (9:72).
3. *Jannat al-na'īm* (garden of delight) (56:11).
4. *(Jannat) al-khuld* (garden of eternity, paradise) (4:57).
5. *Jannat al-ma'wá* (garden of refuge) (53:15, 79:41).
6. *Dār al-salām* (abode of peace) (6:127).
7. *'Illīyīn* (high, sublime); where the actions of all human beings are recorded (83:18).

When used in the singular, *jannah* means all these paradises together. The nine heavens are the seven, plus the footstool *(kursī)* and throne *(al-'arsh)* of God. These nine heavens are regarded in traditional Islam as comprising the physical heavens, although other names for the various heavens and other systems of classification also exist.

Sufi classifications seek to establish a distinction between the lower heavens for ordinary believers who may have little understanding of spiritual matters, and the higher spiritual levels attained by the Sufi. One such classification, according to Farīd Aḥmad Ṣamdī, describes four levels of *jannah:*[3]

1. *Jannat al-afʿāl* (garden of actions) or *jannat al-ʿawwām* (garden of ordinary people). The heaven where ordinary people reap the reward of their good deeds after death; said to contain the 'choicest eatables and desirables', although the delights are far finer than those available on earth; the lowest of the four paradises; subdivided into eight heavens *(hasht jannat),* named more or less like the seven *jannāt,* other variants included in various lists being *dār al-maqām* (abode of dignity), *dār al-qarār* (abode of tranquillity) and *jannat al-ma'wá* (garden of refuge). The lists of names vary to some extent from one commentator to another.

2. *Jannat al-nafs* (garden of the *nafs*) or *jannat al-wirāthah* (garden of inheritance). The heaven for those who have shown obedience to the Prophet and his commands, earning their place here by right, as a person does an inheritance. This and the two higher heavens can be attained during human life.

3. *Jannat al-ṣifāt* (garden of attributes) or *jannat al-ma'wá* (garden of refuge), also called *jannat al-qalb* (garden of the heart). The spiritual heaven, where God's attributes are manifested; a paradise for those who dwell in the spiritual heart *(qalb).*

4. *Jannat al-Dhāt* (garden of the Essence) or *jannat al-Rūḥ* (garden of the Spirit), also called *jannat al-ʿizzah* (garden of glory), where the unity of the divine Essence is experienced in transcendent and indescribable beauty.

Of these, the first two divisions are for the ordinary, good and pious *mu'min* (faithful, a believer), while the latter two are spiritual stations in the mystic ascent of the Sufi.

Another notable classification is given by Ibn ʿArabī in *al-Futūḥāt al-Makkīyah (The Meccan Revelations),* where he speaks of three *jannāt:*

1. *Jannat al-istithnā'* (garden of exception). For those children who die before reaching adulthood, and also for the weak of intellect who have not received the message of God, but whom God has decided to send there.

2. *Jannat al-wirāthah* (garden of inheritance). For those believers who have lived their lives according to the *sharīʿah* (external religious code), and for those denizens of *jannat al-istithnā'* who will be punished for a while in hell, before coming here.

3. *Jannat al-ʿamal* (garden of deeds). The reward of the virtuous, after death; divided into eight *jannāt,* each having a hundred levels. *ʿAdan* is the highest, its highest level being *ma'wá* (refuge), reserved for the Prophet Muḥammad. Below *ʿAdan* is *firdaws* (paradise). These heavens are concentric and arranged as spheres, one level above the other.

This scheme of Ibn 'Arabī's has been interpreted so as to read metaphorical meanings in the several delights mentioned in descriptions of *jannāt.* These delights are not specifically demarcated as sensory or spiritual, but both aspects have been amalgamated.

Sufis have been foremost in symbolic interpretations of the many heavens. Al-Simnānī, for example, says that the *hasht jannat* (eight heavens) refer to the eight attributes of the Divine: life, hearing, sight, speech, knowledge, power, will and wisdom.[4] Thus, Rūmī speaks of the hearts of the mystics as the receptive ground for the *hasht jannat,* as these divine qualities:

> Ever since the forms of the eight paradises *(hasht jannat)*
> have shone forth,
> they have found the tablets of their (the Sufis') hearts receptive.
> They receive a hundred impressions from the empyrean
> and the starry sphere and the void:
> What impressions? Nay, 'tis the very sight of God.
>
> *Rūmī, Maśnavī I:3498–99, MJR2 p.190*

For the Sufis, *jannah* does not only imply a promise of reward after death. *Jannah* is a realized experience of the reality beyond the physical plane, an experience achieved while still living in this world. *Jannah* refers to all levels of the creation, and to the divine Essence itself:

> In *Ṣūfī* language, *jannat* denotes the level of (God's) manifestations, be it either through the Essence *(Źāt),* the Attributes *(Ṣifāt),* Actions *(Af'āl)* or Signs *(Āśār).*
>
> *Mir'āt-i 'Ushshāq, in TAT p.188, in FNI3 p.164*

Rūzbihān says simply:

> They (the Saints) have said that beholding God is the Saints' heaven *(jannat).*
>
> *Rūzbihān, Mashrab al-Arwāḥ, MAR p.251, in FNI3 p.165*

The eight paradises are also referred to as the *hasht bāgh* (eight gardens), *hasht bustān* (eight gardens), *hasht manẓar* (eight heavens), *hasht khuld* (eight paradises) and *hasht māwá* (eight paradises).

See also: **bihisht-u dūzakh**, **firdaws**, **gardens**, **heavens**, **sab' samāwāt**, **svarga**, **vaikuṇṭha**.

1. *Qur'ān* 2:25.
2. The verse numbers in parentheses refer to the *Qur'ān*.

3. Farīd Aḥmad Ṣamdī, *Iṣṭilāḥāt-i Ṣūfīyah, IS* pp.41–42.
4. Al-Simnānī, in *SAE4* 488:7*ff.*, in *MJR7* p.204.

jhajhrī, jhajhrī dīp, jhajhrī dvīp (H) *Lit.* lattice *(jhajhrī)* island *(dvīp);* a region lying immediately below *sahans dal kanwal* (thousand-petalled lotus); so called because, from there, the light of the thousand-petalled lotus appears as if seen through a sieve or lattice; one of the three subdivisions of *Nirañjan desh* (*i.e.* the astral region) mentioned by the nineteenth-century mystic Swāmī Shiv Dayāl Singh, the others being *shyām kanj* (black lotus) and *set sunn* (white void). Mind and matter, in their most subtle forms, come into being in the region above *sahans dal kanwal,* below which lies *jhajhrī dīp. Jyot Nirañjan* is a name used by Swāmī Shiv Dayāl Singh for the lord of *sahans dal kanwal:*

> The true Lord *(Sat Purush)* manifested
> the two ingredients (mind and matter);
> His name, *Jyot Nirañjan* (Pure Flame), He then assumed.
> These two currents descended and merged into the *jhajhrī dīp.*
>
> *Swāmī Shiv Dayāl Singh, Sār Bachan Poetry 26:1.23–24, SBP p.216*

Swāmī Shiv Dayāl Singh also uses the metaphor of a latticed screen *(jhajhrī)* in various descriptions of the soul's inner journey, as in the ascent from *mahā sunn* (great void) to *bhanwar guphā* (rotating cave), the region on the threshold of eternity:[1]

> Beyond *mahā sunn* the soul peeps through the latticed screen *(jhajhrī);*
> On reaching *bhanwar guphā* she hears the melodious flute.
>
> *Swāmī Shiv Dayāl Singh, Sār Bachan Poetry 27:7.9–10, SBP p.233*

Exemplifying, perhaps, how mystical realities get externalized and literalized, there is a Hindu marriage custom in which the bridegroom is shown a flame through a lattice, which he pierces with his sword before entering the house of the bride. In mystic literature of the East, the soul and the Lord or Master have characteristically been portrayed as the bride and the Bridegroom, or the lover and the Beloved. The lover has to pierce the veil of inner darkness before she can be united with the divine Beloved.

See also: **aṇḍa, sahans dal kanwal, set sunn, shyām kanj**.

1. See also Swāmī Shiv Dayāl Singh, *Sār Bachan Poetry* 6:3, 20:2, 23:1, 24:1, 26:1, 38:8, 41:18, *SBP.*

Kailās(a) (S/H), **Kailāsh** (H) A mountain in the higher Himalayas; mythologically, the fabulous dwelling of *Kuvera* and the paradise of *Shiva.* Of uncertain derivation, some suggest that *Kailāsa* means 'crystalline' or 'icy', from *kelāsa* (crystal), from *ka* (water) + *las* (to shine).[1] Others suggest 'place where beings exist in bliss', from *kaila* (pleasure) + *ās* (to exist).[2] The name has been used by a number of Indian mystics for one of the three 'mountains' or 'peaks' in *trikuṭī,* the highest of the mind regions, the other two being *Meru* (or *Mer*) and *Sumeru* (or *Sumer*).

The three prominences of *trikuṭī* arise when the three streams *(Sat Purush, ādi Shabd* and *Akshar Purush),* which emanate from the highest and nameless region, flow out into the higher confines of *brahmāṇḍa,* coming to the foot (metaphorically) of these three 'peaks' in the highest part of the universal mind. From here arise the three *guṇas* (fundamental attributes) of creation *(rajas),* preservation *(sattva)* and destruction *(tamas)* that permeate and influence all creation below.

These three *guṇas* are personified in Hindu thought as the three gods, *Brahmā* (the creator), *Vishṇu* (the preserver) and *Shiva* (the destroyer). For this reason, through misunderstanding and literalizing the esoteric meaning of the mystics, Mount *Kailāsh* in the Himalayas is believed to be the abode of *Shiva,* and has become a place of pilgrimage.

The nineteenth-century Indian Saint, Swāmī Shiv Dayāl Singh, has described the ascent of the soul through the various regions, referring to these three peaks of *trikuṭī:*

> Pure are the streams, the rivulets and their running.
> Climbing the bridge, the soul crosses the ocean.
> Seeing *Mer, Sumer* and *Kailāsh,*
> the soul reaches a land of immaculate bliss.
> *Swāmī Shiv Dayāl Singh, Sār Bachan Poetry 26:2.15–16, SBP p.227*

Kabīr also writes:

> In the sixth sky is the renowned dwelling place of *Shiva,*
> fanned by *Gaurī* (*Shiva*'s consort);
> There, on Mount *Kailāsh,* where clouds thunder, I rest my head.
> *Kabīr, Shabdāvalī 1, Bhed Bānī 23:15, KSS1 p.69*

Kailāsh is also used in a general sense to refer to heaven.

See also: **guṇa, sahans dal kanwal, trikuṭī**.

1. *e.g. A Dictionary of Hinduism,* James and Margaret Stutley, *DH* p.134.
2. *e.g. A Sanskrit–English Dictionary,* H.H. Wilson, *SED* p.205.

Kāl desh (H) *Lit.* region *(desh)* of *Kāl* (the lord of death); the regions within the administration of *Kāl,* interpreted by some Saints as the negative power; in particular, this world. Swāmī Shiv Dayāl Singh contrasts the realms of *Kāl* with those of *Dayāl* (the Merciful):

> Forgetting her true home,
> the soul *(surat)* has taken *Kāl's* region *(Kāl desh)* as her own.
> *Kāl* has created the three worlds *(trilokī),*
> while *Dayāl* has manifested the true land *(sat lok)* as His own.
> The three worlds are of *Kāl's* domain,
> the fourth region is the realm of *Dayāl.*
>
> *Swāmī Shiv Dayāl Singh, Sār Bachan Poetry 38:11.3–5, SBP p.349*

See also: **Kāl** (6.1).

karam khaṇḍ (Pu) *Lit.* land *(khaṇḍ)* of compassion *(karam);* the land of mercy, the land of grace; used by Guru Nānak for the region beyond *trikuṭī,* the realm of the universal mind or negative power.

See also: **khaṇḍ**.

kawn, al- (A/P) *Lit.* the existent; the manifested world, the cosmos, the universe; derived from *Kun* (Be)!, that which has been brought into existence by the Creative Word, the divine Command "Be! – And it is."[1] *Al-Kawn* is the world of phenomena. *Kawn* also implies generation or growth, as in the expression *kawn wa-fasād,* meaning 'generation and destruction' or 'becoming and decaying'.

See also: **Kun** (3.1).

1. *Qur'ān* 36:82.

kerem (He) *Lit.* vineyard; mystically, a biblical and Middle Eastern metaphor for the heavens or spiritual realms. Speaking ostensibly of Israel, but probably metaphorically of the creation, the prophet Isaiah wrote:

> In that day sing joyously to her,
> the delightful vineyard *(kerem).*
> I, *Yahweh,* am her keeper:
> every moment I water her.
> Lest anyone should hurt her,
> night and day I will watch over her.
>
> *Isaiah 27:2–3; cf. JB, JCL, JPS*

The creation is watered or sustained by *Yahweh* with the Living Water of the creative Power.

In some instances, vineyards also refer both to this physical creation, as well as to the souls here.

See also: **gardens**.

khalq, al- (A/P), **khalaq** (Pu) *Lit.* the created; that which is created; hence, the creation, particularly the physical creation, referring either to mankind or to the physical plane *('ālam al-khalq). Al-Khalq* is what is brought into existence by *al-Amr,* the Command of God. The *Qur'ān* says that God made the creation, that He administers it, and that it will return to Him:

> Surely your Lord is God,
> who created *(khalaqa)* the heavens and the earth in six days,
> then sat Himself upon the Throne,
> directing the affair.
> Intercessor there is none, save after His leave.
> That then is God, your Lord; so serve Him.
> Will you not remember?
>
> To Him shall you return, all together –
> God's promise, in truth.
> He originates creation *(al-khalq),*
> then He brings it back again,
> that He may recompense those who believe,
> and do deeds of righteousness, justly.
> And those who disbelieve –
> for them awaits a draught of boiling water
> and a painful chastisement for their disbelieving.
>
> *Qur'ān 10:3–4, KI*

The creation is created matter, as opposed to the Creator or Ultimate Reality. Ibn 'Arabī, however, observes that *al-Ḥaqq* (Ultimate Reality) is both present in the creation as well as utterly transcending it:

> Reality *(al-Ḥaqq),* of whom transcendence is asserted, is the same as the creation *(khalq)* of whom immanence is asserted, although the Creator is distinguished from the created.
>
> *Ibn 'Arabī, Meccan Revelations, FMA p.106*

See also: **al-Khāliq** (2.1).

khaṇḍ(a) (S/H/Pu) *Lit.* a part, a section, a region; mystically, the regions of creation. According to the Hindu *Purāṇas,* for example, the earth is divided into nine *khaṇḍas* and seven *dvīpas* or *dīps* (islands). The nine *khaṇḍas* are *Bharata, Kiṃnara, Hari, Ilāvṛita, Ramyaka, Hiraṇmaya, Kuru, Bhadrāshva* and *Ketumāla.* However, the names and number of the *khaṇḍas* varies between mythological texts, sometimes only seven being enumerated.

Referring to this system of classification, the nineteenth-century Indian mystic, Swāmī Shiv Dayāl Singh, points out that however the creation is described – it is all created by means of the Word or *Shabd:*

> The *Shabd* is the creator of the three worlds;
> The *Shabd* brought into being *aṇḍ* and *brahmāṇḍ;*
> The *Shabd* has fashioned the seven *dīps* and the nine *khaṇḍas.*
> The *Shabd* produced the three *guṇas* (attributes) and all living beings.
>
> *Swāmī Shiv Dayāl Singh, Sār Bachan Poetry 9:2.1–3, SBP p.88*

Using the same term, Guru Nānak has described the creation as consisting of five main realms or *khaṇḍas.* These are:

1. *Dharam khaṇḍ. Lit.* realm *(khaṇḍ)* of justice *(dharam);* the physical universe or *piṇḍa. Dharam* is always a difficult word to translate since it encompasses more meaning than any one word in English. Within its spread of meaning are included duty, justice, right and appropriate living, righteousness and religion. These are all aspects of living in this world, hence this term.

Guru Nānak says that the souls in *dharam khaṇḍ* are subject to seasons and the passage of time, and are enveloped by matter in its various permutations. Creatures of various forms, shapes and kinds live here, bearing diverse and endless names, all of whom are judged by their actions. This, he says, is God's design for the world:

> (God created) nights, seasons, lunar days, week days,
> wind, water, fire and nether lands.
> In the midst of these, He established the earth
> as a home for the Lord's meditation (*dharamsāl,* spiritual work).
> Therein (He placed) beings of various types and colours:
> various and endless are their names.
> (They are) judged according to their deeds and actions.
> The Lord Himself is true and true His court....
> This (aforesaid) is the moral duty *(dharam)* of *dharam khaṇḍ.*
>
> *Guru Nānak, Ādi Granth 7, MMS*

2. *Gyān khaṇḍ. Lit.* realm *(khaṇḍ)* of knowledge *(gyān);* described as a vast region with many continents, worlds and underworlds, with numerous suns, moons and stars, and inhabited by angels, gods, goddesses and deities, corresponding to the worlds of the mind that lie beyond the eye centre. It is called *gyān khaṇḍ* because the realms of the mind are primarily blissful regions of diversity and activity that the soul and mind perceive with great interest, understanding and knowledge, rather than the deepest love and devotion. Knowledge of this realm also provides deep understanding of how things happen in the physical universe. Guru Nānak writes:

> Now I describe the doings of the realm of knowledge *(gyān khaṇḍ).*
> Good many are winds, waters, fires,
> and good many *Kṛishṇas* and *Shivas.*
> There are many *Brahmās,* who are fashioning forms,
> and many beauties, colours and raiments....
> Numberless are *Indras,* the moons, the suns,
> numberless universes and numberless countries.
> Innumerable there are proficients (*siddhs,* adepts),
> *Gautamas* (enlightened ones), great *yogīs (nāths),*
> and innumerable over innumerable the forms of goddesses.
> Many deities, demons and silent sages,
> and many over many oceans and jewels.
> Numberless, the mines of production, numberless languages,
> and many the dynasties of masters (kings) of men.
> Countless are the men of divine knowledge,
> and countless the servants of God.
> O Nānak, there is no limit to His bounds.
>
> *Guru Nānak, Ādi Granth 7, MMS*

3. *Saram khaṇḍ. Lit.* realm *(khaṇḍ)* of bliss *(saram).* Although the meaning of *saram* is uncertain and variously interpreted, *saram khaṇḍ* is used by Guru Nānak in the *Ādi Granth* for the realm above *gyān khaṇḍ,* corresponding to the higher regions of the mind.

The sound of this region, says Guru Nānak, is full of beauty and attraction. This is a land of indescribable beauty and splendour. All aspects of mind originate from here in fine and subtle form:

> In the domain of knowledge divine *(gyān khaṇḍ),*
> deliberation (*gyān,* knowledge) is greatly resplendent,
> (and the) celestial Strain *(Nād)* resounds there,
> from whom myriads of amusements and joys proceed.
> Beauty is the language of *saram khaṇḍ.*

There, an extremely incomparable make is made
(incomparable, beyond description, is what is forged therein).
The proceedings of that place cannot be described:
if anyone endeavours to describe, he shall afterwards repent.
There inner consciousness, intellect, soul and understanding
are moulded (afresh).
There, the genius of the pious persons
and men of occult powers (*siddhs,* adepts) is moulded (anew).

Guru Nānak, Ādi Granth 7–8, MMS

4. *Karam khaṇḍ. Lit.* land *(khaṇḍ)* of compassion *(karam);* the land of mercy, the land of grace; the spiritual region beyond the mind, but below *sach khaṇḍ;* the land of spirit, love and divine grace, experienced when the soul ascends above the realms of mind and matter. Within the realms of the mind, the prevailing law is that of causality, justice, automatic action and reaction. Beyond that, the prevailing reality is that of love, compassion, forgiveness and grace.

According to Guru Nānak, the sound of *karam khaṇḍ* is full of power and force. Here, duality ends and the soul realizes by experience that it is a drop of pure spirit. Only brave and courageous souls reach here, that is, those devotees who have vanquished the forces of mind and *māyā.* Here, their being is engrossed only by God, and they enjoy unmitigated bliss:

There is spiritual force in the language (*Bāṇī,* Word)
of the realm of grace *(karam khaṇḍ)....*
Very powerful warriors and heroes dwell there:
within them, the might of the pervading Lord remains fully filled.
They who are fully sewn in the Lord's admiration abide there:
their beauty cannot be narrated –
They in whose hearts God abides die not,
and nor are they hoodwinked.
The Saints of various worlds dwell there:
they make merry, that true Lord is in their hearts.

Guru Nānak, Ādi Granth 8, MMS

5. *Sach khaṇḍ.* The realm of truth *(sach);* the realm of real or true existence; the eternal realm; the land of eternal Truth; the soul's true home, also called *sat lok* by some Indian Saints. Guru Nānak says that the formless Lord resides and presides here; from here, He surveys His entire creation within which His Will or Order *(Hukam)* reigns supreme; the glory of this realm of supreme bliss is ineffable, and Guru Nānak says that the wonders of this place are very difficult to describe:

In the realm of truth *(sach khaṇḍ)*
  abides the formless Lord (*Nirankār,* the Formless).
God beholds the creation which He has created,
  and renders them happy when He casts upon the beings
  His merciful glance.
In that realm, there are continents (*khaṇḍ,* regions), worlds (*maṇḍal,* spheres),
  solar systems (*warbhaṇḍ, i.e. brahmaṇḍ,* the universe);
If someone tries to describe them,
  then know that there is no limit or bound of them.
There are universes upon universes, and creations over creations:
  as is the Master's mandate, so are their functions.
The Lord beholds His creation,
  and feels happy by contemplating over it.
O Nānak, to describe (the realm of truth) is hard like iron.

Guru Nānak, Ādi Granth 8, MMS

See also: **sach khaṇḍ** (2.1).

khurshed paya (Pv) *Lit.* heavens *(paya)* of the sun *(khurshed);* the third of the four heavens mentioned in the later Pahlavi literature of Zoroastrianism. Very little is mentioned in the extant writings of Zarathushtra concerning the inner hierarchy of creation. It is possible, however, that some of these teachings have been preserved, though in a somewhat unreliable form, in the Pahlavi literature written perhaps as much as fifteen hundred years later, during the first few centuries CE.

Four heavens are mentioned in Pahlavi writings:

1. *Satar paya,* the star-studded heaven.
2. *Mah paya,* the heavens of the moon.
3. *Khurshed paya,* the heavens of the sun.
4. *Anaghra raochah,* the heavens of boundless light, identified with *garō demāna* (the house of heavenly song) of the *Gāthās,* the dwelling place of *Ahurā.*

While *satar paya* and *mah paya* may perhaps refer to the 'star' and 'moon' regions in the subastral realms, *khurshed paya* is said to be the realm where good deeds dwell. This would locate it as the astral and causal realms, these being the heavens to which those who perform good deeds (especially devotion to God and service to mankind) may go for some while after death.

See also: **havare pishyasū**, **satar paya**.

kshetra (S) *Lit.* field, meadow, land; as in the Buddhist term, *Buddha-kshetra,* the *Buddha*-land or heaven. Terms such as meadows, fields, pastures, gardens and so on have very commonly been used for the heavenly realms, especially in the ancient Middle East.

See also: **gardens, al-jannah**.

kursī, al- (A/P/H) *Lit.* chair, seat, stool, footstool *(kursī);* also, throne; an official position of high rank; a seat of power; in traditional Islamic cosmology, the sphere of the fixed stars, comprising the eighth of nine heavens, the ninth being the throne *(al-'arsh)* of God. The belief in these nine heavens has its origins in the Greek idea that the celestial bodies revolved in fixed, crystalline spheres around the earth. In early Christianity, too, God and His angels were believed to dwell in the 'empyrean' – the highest part of the supposedly spherical heavens.

In Sufism, two terms – *'arsh* and *kursī* – are commonly used for 'throne'. Traditionally, *'arsh* is the throne of God, while *kursī* is a lesser royal seat, the footstool of God. But the terms have been used variously by different writers. Sometimes, *kursī,* which can mean both throne and footstool, appears to refer to some intermediate heaven. In other cases, the 'footstool' of God is clearly located at a very high level, as in the *Qur'ān:*

> His throne *(kursī)* extends
> over the heavens and the earth,
> and He feels no fatigue
> in guarding and preserving them;
> For He is the Most High, the Supreme (in glory).
>
> *Qur'ān 2:255; cf. AYA*

The use of the term 'throne', as a mystic metaphor, has been in common usage in a variety of Middle and Near Eastern spiritual literature, including Zoroastrian, Manichaean, Mandaean and Jewish. It is a part of a family of metaphors in which the divine Presence is seen as the King.

See also: **'arsh** (2.1), **throne** (2.1).

land of the living (He. *erez ḥayyim*) A biblical term for this world, used in the *Psalms, Ezekiel, Isaiah, Jeremiah* and *Job.*[1] However, using the expression in its own way, the medieval Kabbalist text, the *Zohar,* takes the term to mean the heavenly or supernal realms, calling it "the world to come, the world of souls, the world of consolations".[2]

In *Isaiah,* for instance, King Ḥezekiah recounts the story of a severe illness in which he thought he was about to leave this world, the "land of the living":

> I said, I shall not see the Lord,
> the Lord, in the land of the living;
> I shall behold man no more with the inhabitants of the world.
>
> *Isaiah 38:11, JCL*

But in the *Zohar,* the verse is given a spiritual meaning when Rabbi Simeon says:

> "I will not see God." Naturally, one cannot see God, but the expression is explained by the concluding words, " … God, in the land of the living". When souls ascend to the place of the "bundle of life",[3] they feast their eyes on the beams of the refulgent mirror which radiates from the most sublime region. And were the soul not clothed in the resplendency of another (*i.e.* non-fleshly) garment, it would not be able to approach that effulgence.
>
> The esoteric doctrine is that in the same way as the soul has to be clothed in a bodily garment in order to exist in this world, so is she given an ethereal supernal garment wherewith to exist in the other world, and to be enabled to gaze at the effulgence of life radiating from that 'land of the living'.
>
> *Zohar 1:65b–66a, ZSS1 p.216, JCL*

Here, the "refulgent mirror" is a term used for the source of prophecy, regarded as bright for Moses, but dim for others. More generally, it refers to the divine Light within, which contains all knowledge and wisdom.

In another place, the *Zohar* once more uses the "land of the living" for eternity, the "supernal realm":

> Everyone of you is closely attached to the holy King on high: ye are the mighty chieftains of that land which is called 'the land of the living', the princes of which feed on the *manna* of holy dew.
>
> Another then discoursed on the text: "Happy art thou, O land, when thy king is a son of freedom and thy princes eat in due season."[4] … The reference in the verse "happy art thou, O land" is to the supernal realm which has control over all the life above, and is therefore called 'land of the living'. Of this, it is written, "a land which the Lord thy God careth for continually",[5] and again "a land where thou shalt eat bread without scarceness, thou shalt not lack anything in it".[6]
>
> *Zohar 1:95b, ZSS1 p.315, JCL*

And commenting on a verse from *Isaiah,* the *Zohar* again equates the "land of the living" with eternity as the "supernal heaven" or the heavenly Jerusalem:

> Rabbi Simeon continued: "We have expounded the closing words of this verse, 'I will cause thee to ride upon the high places of the earth',[7] to mean the supramundane world, called 'heaven', and God is above this."
>
> Rabbi Abba said that 'the Lord' here means 'heaven', and the high places of the earth the 'land of the living', consisting of Zion and Jerusalem which are above, the supernal heaven and the supernal earth. This, however, is quite in harmony with Rabbi Simeon's interpretation, as it is all one celestial sphere.
>
> *Zohar 2:83a, ZSS3 p.250, JCL*

See also: **land** (2.1).

1. *Ezekiel* 26:20, 32:23–32; *Isaiah* 38:11, 53:8; *Jeremiah* 11:19; *Job* 28:13; *Psalms* 27:13, 52:5, 116:9,17a, 142:5.
2. *Zohar* 1:1b, *ZSS1* p.4, *JCL.*
3. *1 Samuel* 25:29.
4. *Ecclesiastes* 10:17.
5. *Deuteronomy* 11:12.
6. *Deuteronomy* 8:9.
7. *Isaiah* 58:14.

lok(a) (S/H/Pu), **loa** (Pu) *Lit.* region, realm, locality, world, space, sphere, plane; refers either to this world and/or to one or other of the realms of creation, both actual and mythological. In Indian mystic and sacred literature, *lokas* are classified in a number of ways, but are generally said to fall into three main categories:

1. *Devaloka,* heaven (world of the gods); also called *svarga.*
2. *Mṛityuloka* (world of death, the physical world); also called *pṛithvīloka* (world of the earth), *manushyaloka* (world of men) and *bhūloka* or *bhūmiloka* (world of the earth).
3. *Pātālaloka* (worlds below, the nether worlds).

These three *lokas* are referred to in Indian sacred writings as *lokatraya, tribhuvan, triloka,* and by a number of similar names. According to traditional Hindu mythology, these three *lokas* are also further subdivided into fourteen *bhuvans* or *lokas:* seven upper worlds, including the physical or material world, and seven lower or nether worlds.

According to the *Vedāntasāra,* the seven lower *lokas* are, in descending order: *atala, vitala, sutala, rasātala, talātala, mahātala* and *pātāla.*[1] The seven higher *lokas,* as listed, for example, in the *Āruṇeya Upanishad,*[2] are called, in ascending order:

1. *Bhūloka.* The physical realm, inhabited by human beings and other creatures with physical bodies of various kinds.
2. *Bhuvaloka.* The mid-region between the earth and the sun, inhabited by *munis, siddhas* and so on.
3. *Svarloka.* The region between the sun and the pole star, also known as *Indra*'s heaven.
4. *Maharloka.* The region above the pole star, inhabited by highly evolved sages such as Bhṛigu and so on, who survive the destruction of the three worlds below it.
5. *Janaloka.* The region inhabited by immaculately pure souls such as Sanat-Kumāra and so on; the region of delight.
6. *Tapoloka.* The region inhabited by deified beings utterly detached and contented; the world of consciousness and power.
7. *Satyaloka.* The region of truth and existence *(satya)* where the perfected souls rejoice in the bliss of eternal union with the true Being; also called *Brahmaloka.*

Sometimes these seven higher regions are described as earth, sky, heaven, middle region between celestial and spiritual regions, higher celestial regions still subject to rebirth, the spiritual region of the blessed souls not subject to rebirth, and the region of Truth. At other times, only the threefold division of earthly, atmospheric and celestial regions is mentioned.

In a slightly different system of enumeration, the three worlds *(triloka)* are comprised of these two sets of seven *lokas,* plus a further seven *lokas* of *naraka* (hell), which are called: *put* or *pud, avīchi, saṃhāta, tāmisra, ṛijīsha, kudmala* and *kākola.* These variant enumerations of the *lokas* have arisen from several millennia of Hindu culture, where apparent contradictions are tolerated without difficulty.

According to Jain belief, *loka* is a place of happiness and misery, consisting of three parts: *ūrdhva* (upwards, where the gods reside), *madhya* (middle, the physical world) and *adho* (downwards, where the denizens of hell reside). Beyond this *loka* is the transcendent region called *aloka,* which is the region of liberated souls.

See also: **triloka**.

1. Sadānanda, *Vedāntasāra* 2:104.
2. *Āruṇeya Upanishad* 1.

mahā ākāsh (H/Pu) *Lit.* great *(mahā)* heaven *(ākāsh);* great sky; specifically, the 'sky' or upper boundary of *trikuṭī.*

See also: **gagan**, **sky**.

mahā sunn (H) *Lit.* great *(mahā)* void *(sunn),* vacuum or sky; a spiritual region of intense darkness situated above *daswān dwār* (tenth door) and below *bhanwar guphā* (rotating cave). *Mahā sunn* is really one of the great spiritual regions, but is rarely referred to as such by the Saints because their disciples are advised not to dwell upon it, for their own protection. It can be crossed only with the help of one who has travelled that way before, that is – a perfect Master. *Mahā sunn* is generally described as a part of *daswān dwār,* also called *sunn,* rather than a separate region.

All the major realms of creation are bounded by 'veils', 'voids', 'vacuums', 'skies', 'firmaments' or *sunnas.* These are all earthly terms used in the attempt to express the inexpressible. The 'boundary' or 'sky' (spiritually speaking) of the physical universe, for example, is what man perceives as space *(ākāsh).* Even physicists recognize that space is the primary reality of the physical universe within which all else exists. Similarly, there are boundaries to *sahans dal kanwal* (thousand-petalled lotus) and *trikuṭī* (*lit.* three peaks) – the 'sky' of *trikuṭī* being known as *gagan* (heaven) or *mahā ākāsh* (great sky, great heaven).

The nineteenth-century mystic of Agra, Swāmī Shiv Dayāl Singh, identifies the location of *mahā sunn* in his poetry. It borders onto *bhanwar guphā,* which itself lies on the threshold of eternity:

> Beyond the three worlds *(trilokī)* is (the region of) *sunn,*
> and beyond *sunn* lies the *mahā sunn.*
> Across *mahā sunn* is the station
> that has been described as *bhanwar guphā.*
> *Swāmī Shiv Dayāl Singh, Sār Bachan Poetry 26:1.183–84, SBP p.224*

In another poem, he depicts its extent as "seventy *pālangs*" – a *pālang* being an archaic unit of measurement used here as a figure of speech to convey a sense of vastness:

> Hearing this sound (of *daswān dwār*),
> the soul penetrated and crossed *triveṇī,*
> there entering the vestibule of *mahā sunn,*
> where you pick up the secret knowledge.

This great sphere is seventy *pālangs* in circumference,
and in this sphere there is at first pitch darkness *(ghor andherā)*.

Four hidden sounds are heard here,
and the soul hears many new melodies.
How can I describe these wonderful sounds *(jhankārs)?*
I am enraptured upon hearing them.
Here are five egg-shaped regions or worlds,
all full of a variety of creations,
and each permeated and governed by a *Brahm* (ruler or lord).
How can one describe the beauty of these creations?
Each has its own predominating colour,
like green or yellow or even white.
They are quite vast in extent, in comparison with which
the entire universe below *trikuṭī* appears insignificant.

Swāmī Shiv Dayāl Singh, Sār Bachan Poetry 26:3.5–12, SBP pp.227–28

Mahārāj Sāwan Singh also describes this darkness:

Above *daswān dwār* lies *mahā sunn,* a vast void of such utter darkness that the spirit, which is now a glorious thing giving forth the radiance of twelve suns, finds itself overwhelmed by the pitch darkness and cannot pass through it without the benign grace and guidance of the *Satguru* (true Master). In this region, there are many thousands of spirits, each with the light of twelve suns shining round it, yet unable to extricate itself from this region of darkness. But the spirit that crosses it once with the help of the Master is, thereafter, free to do so at will.... It is clear, therefore, that a living Master is the prerequisite for a safe journey to the regions beyond *mahā sunn.*

Mahārāj Sāwan Singh, Discourses on Sant Mat 1, DSM pp.25–26

Mahārāj Charan Singh describes the function of this darkness in his answer to a question:

As long as the soul is with the mind, it is separated from infinity. When you withdraw it from the body, and bring it to the eye centre, it is still attached to the mind. It has not yet merged into the Infinite, and still retains its identity. Even when it leaves the mind, the impressions of the *karmas* are still over the soul, and they keep that soul away from the Infinite....

Between the mind and *sach khaṇḍ* (true land), there are still the impressions of those *karmas* which, of course, cannot pull the soul back to this creation; but those impressions are still with the soul.

That is why, at the time of initiation, it is explained that there is a darkness through which we have to pierce before we can reach *sat lok* (true region), *sach khaṇḍ.*

That darkness exists from the very point of view that unless the soul becomes so pure that it is able to go through that darkness it will not be able to merge back into the Infinite. It is only in the company of the *Shabd* (Word) form of the Master that the soul is able to go through that darkness of *mahā sunn,* as we call it, and merge into the Infinite.

Q. Then how does the soul know without seeing at that time?

A. It is a realization. There is no question of seeing, touching or feeling. The mystics call it direct perception. The soul gets that inner perception. It is a realization. It is very difficult to explain these things intellectually. I am just trying to tell you why, after all the coverings have been removed, the soul still does not go straightaway and merge back into the Lord. After all, when the soul reaches the third stage, it has no coverings. Why is it then separate from the Lord? Because it still has to pierce through that *mahā sunn,* the intense darkness; but it cannot go with its own light. That is why, when the mystics explain the teachings, they always say that without His grace, the soul can never go back to the Father.

Q. When crossing the darkness, is the soul accompanied by the Master?

A. Always.

Q. Then how does the Master appear there?

A. You must have read … that the soul has its own light, but still it is not sufficient to enable it to cross that veil of darkness. Then the Master's light, which is much brighter, and is sufficient to pierce that darkness, has to envelop the soul, so to say, and merge back into the infinite Light. This is just a way of explaining things which really have to be experienced to be realized.

Mahārāj Charan Singh, Thus Saith the Master 418, TSM pp.414–15

See also: **ākāsha** (5.1), **aṇḍa**, **sunn**.

mah paya (Pv) *Lit.* heavens *(paya)* of the moon *(mah);* the second of the four heavens mentioned in the later Pahlavi literature of Zoroastrianism; probably one of the subastral realms.

See also: **chandra**, **khurshed paya**, **satar paya**.

maidān (Pu/H), **maydān** (P) *Lit.* open ground, a large lawn, a large open field, a square, an arena, a battleground, a combat area, a race course, a playground, a plain. Only physical language being available, many mystics have spoken of the inner realms as meadows, fields, pastures, gardens and so on. One such term is *maidān,* as in a description by Swāmī Shiv Dayāl Singh of the eternal realm:

In the fifth region is the fort
with the Emperor's throne.
Know him to be the true Emperor.
The soul advances and sees an open lawn *(maidān)* –
a wondrous city, with marvellous squares,
abounding with golden palaces set amidst pools of nectar,
and girdled by moats filled with ambrosia.

Swāmī Shiv Dayāl Singh, Sār Bachan Poetry 26:5.1–3, SBP p.229

See also: **gardens**, **al-jannah**.

makān (A/P) *Lit.* place, space. *Makān* refers to the visible, sensible world, and *lā-makān* (no place, placeless, spaceless) refers to the infinite realm of Reality. Mystics always point out that although this *makān* may be all that earthbound souls know, nonetheless, it is not their source or home:

You are in space *(makān),*
but your origin is in the spaceless *(lā-makān):*
Close your business here and open it there.
Do not flee to the six directions,
because in directions there is the *shashdarah,*
and the *shashdarah* is mate, mate.

Rūmī, Maśnavī II:612–13; cf. MJR2 p.253

Rūmī says that to go in any outward direction is to go to *shashdarah,* a disastrous position in the game of *nard,* equivalent to checkmate in chess. The direction in which the soul must go to reach *lā-makān* is inward, away from the space of this world.

See also: **lā-makān** (2.1).

malakūt (A/P) *Lit.* kingdom, dominion, government; hence, heaven, heavenly court; a term of Aramaic origin. In Middle Eastern mystical and religious traditions, God is often referred to as the King. Hence, the heavens are His kingdom *(malakūt):*

And thus did We show Abraham
the kingdom *(malakūt)* of the heavens and the earth,
that he might be of those possessing certainty.
Qur'ān 6:75, MGK

Do they see nothing in the government *(malakūt)*
of the heavens and the earth and all that God has created?
(Do they not see) that it may well be
that their term is nigh drawing to an end?
In what message after this will they then believe?
Qur'ān 7:185; cf. AYA

His Command *(Amr),* when He desires a thing,
is to say to it "Be *(Kun)!*" –
And it is.
So glory be to Him in whose hand
is the dominion *(malakūt)* of everything,
and unto whom you shall be returned.
Qur'ān 36:82–83, KI

Malakūt refers to the divine Power within all things, the governance and sustenance of creation from the divine Reality.

As *'ālam al-malakūt* (world of the kingdom), the term is also used by some Sufis for the region just above the physical universe and below *'ālam al-jabarūt* (world of power). Sometimes, however, the names given to these two regions are reversed.

Malakūt is also the name given to a type of *dhikr* (repetition).

See also: **'ālam**, **malakūt** (▸2), **Malkut**.

Malkut (He) *Lit.* kingdom, kingship; the lowest of the ten *sefirot;* also equated with the *Shekhinah* (divine indwelling presence).

See also: **sefirot**.

mānsarovar (H), **mānasarovara** (S) *Lit.* lake *(sarovara)* of mind or spirit *(mānasa);* derived from the Sanskrit *mānasa* meaning spiritual, having to do with mind and spirit, and also (as a noun) mind, heart, soul, thought, wish; a sacred lake and place of pilgrimage in the Himalayas, situated near Mount *Kailāsh.* According to the *Skanda Purāṇa,* it is so-called because "*Brahmā* created it with his mind."[1]

Mystically, *mānsarovar* is the name used by some Indian Saints for a lake, sea or ocean of spiritual energy and consciousness situated above *trikuṭī* (*lit.* three peaks, the highest region of the mind, the universal mind) in *daswān dwār* (tenth door), at the confluence of the three streams of *iḍā, pingalā* and *sushumṇā. Mānsarovar* is also called the lake of nectar and the reservoir of the Water of Life.

When the soul bathes in this lake, it is purified almost entirely of its past impressions and entanglements of mind and *māyā* (illusion), emerging and knowing itself as a pure soul for the first time since it descended into the realms of the mind, aeons before. By this means, it becomes fit to enter the higher realms of the spirit. Mahārāj Sāwan Singh writes:

> By reaching the pool of nectar, the three covers of the soul (gross, astral and causal) and the bondage of the *guṇas* (attributes), mind, *māyā* and the five elements *(tattvas)* are all removed, and the soul becomes pure.
>
> *Mahārāj Sāwan Singh, Philosophy of the Masters 3, PM3 p.27*

Drawn out from the realm of the mind, with neither body nor mind to shackle it, the soul floats forth into a new element where time and space no longer exist, experiencing – in the most intense fashion and by direct perception – all that has been and will be as though it were all 'now'. Here, the universe has no bounds, no limits, and yet it is all eternally present within the soul itself.

It is because the region lying immediately above that of mind and *māyā* still has traces, so to speak, of mental impressions that when the soul reaches here, it is still not completely pure. But before it, lies the lake of spiritual nectar, a reservoir of strength, *mānsarovar,* in which it immerses itself, washing away much of the final residue of *māyā,* and the impression even of the primal desire to be in the lower creation.

As the soul emerges from the lake, it shines in full radiance. Indian mystics have described the soul here as a *haṃsa* or swan, as opposed to a *kāg* or crow – the soul entrapped by mind and *māyā.* From its condition, like that of a black crow, it is transformed into a white and radiant swan. It is in this pool of spiritual refreshment that the newly awakened soul is immersed, rendering it a divine being, filled with transcendent self-knowledge and bliss, recognizing itself as pure soul.

Around the shores of this lake, fountains and streams of spiritual nectar flow through moonlit gardens and orchards where the soul wanders in bliss. The light is of a soft silver brilliance as though twelve thousand moons were shining down from a clear sky. The *surat* (hearing power of the soul) is entranced by the melody of the *Shabd* (the divine Word), which here resembles that of a lute or harp, beguiling it into a divine ecstasy. Untrammelled by either body or mind, it no longer 'feels' or 'guesses' but is, for the first time, completely free. The whole panorama of transmigration and its determining *karma* is clearly beheld. This state in *bhajan* (meditation) is the true *nirvikalpa samādhi,* the *samādhi* of liberation from the wheel of birth and death. The soul also begins to comprehend here, to some degree, why it came down in the first instance – a question raised by everyone, but not answered fully until the soul finally returns to God.

Many mystics have mentioned this reservoir of spirit. In his description of the inner realms, Swāmī Shiv Dayāl Singh describes the ascent of the soul beyond the 'skies' of the astral and causal realm *(ākāsh* and *gagan),* into *daswān dwār,* also called *sunn* (void), which lies beyond the causal realm:

> The soul now goes forward, removing the third veil,
> hearing the sound of *sunn maṇḍal,*
> seeing the brilliant light of *daswān dwār.*
> Leaving behind *gagan* and *ākāsh,*
> the soul bathes in lake *mānsarovar,*
> and joins the group of pure souls *(haṃsas)* there.
> Circling about, the soul ascends to the top of *sunn,*
> where the music of *kingrī* and *sārangī* abounds.
>
> *Swāmī Shiv Dayāl Singh, Sār Bachan Poetry 26:3.1–4, SBP p.227*

Souls who reach these stages will only speak of it to their Master. One such communication is recorded from a letter in the diary of Rāi Sāhib Munshī Rām, secretary to the twentieth-century Master, Mahārāj Sāwan Singh:

> I beg to submit that during my inner journey I have crossed the stars, the sun and the moon many times. Then came the lotus feet of Huzūr. Several times Huzūr appeared during the inner progress, but you went so fast that the soul could not keep pace with you. Your radiant form was so attractive that words cannot express it. Once, instead of a turban, there was some sort of a beautiful crown on your head.
>
> After doing *simran* (repetition) and catching the Sound, the upward journey starts; but due to imperfect *dhyān* (contemplation of the Master within), Huzūr's form does not stay. The soul also does not stay higher up very long, but remains concentrated within the eyes. Through your grace, I give three or more hours both morning and evening to *bhajan* and *simran.*
>
> The light of the first region is white, that of the second red, and that of the third very bright white. I bathed there in the pool *(mānsarovar).* Here Huzūr gives a great deal of *darshan.* Then darkness starts after this. For a long time the soul did not go across it, but then you, Huzūr, came and I then crossed this also. After this, when the

soul flies up, I see thousands of white lights like so many dazzling suns. I cannot now go beyond these. It appears as if there is a short way now to go. The soul then again comes down and stays within the eyes. Even with great effort Huzūr does not appear, and the *dhyān* or inner vision also is not stabilized.

Anon., in WTM2 pp.137–38

See also: **amṛit sar**, **daswān dwār**.

1. *Skanda Purāṇa, Himavat Khaṇḍa* 15, *HV17* p.40.

mansion(s) A residence, a dwelling place, especially one that is large and imposing; mystically, the heavenly regions; a term used in the *King James Version* and a number of subsequent translations of John's gospel. In his farewell speeches, according to the writer of John, Jesus says:

In my Father's house are many mansions:
if it were not so, I would have told you.
I go to prepare a place for you.

And if I go and prepare a place for you,
I will come again and receive you unto myself;
That where I am, there ye may be also.
And whither I go ye know, and the way ye know.

John 14:2–4, KJV

Jesus is telling his disciples that although he is going to leave this world, he is going to receive them in the inner heavens when they either leave this world at death or when they are able to leave their bodies and enter the higher worlds during their spiritual practice. As he says, "Whither I go ye know, and the way ye know."

This interpretation is endorsed by the second-century Bishop of Lyons, Irenaeus. He quotes the "presbyters, the disciples of the apostles" as saying that some souls are worthy of "heaven", some of "paradise" and others of the "city", the heavenly Jerusalem or eternity:

As the presbyters say, then (in the higher state) those who are deemed worthy of an abode in heaven shall go there, others shall enjoy the delights of paradise, and others shall possess the splendour of the city (of God). For everywhere, the Saviour will be seen, according to the worthiness of those who see Him.

Irenaeus, Against Heresies V:36.1; cf. AH2 p.156

Terms such as "heaven" and "paradise" get used variously by different writers, where the intended meaning can, to some extent, be determined from the context. Irenaeus goes on to relate the varying ascent of different souls to Jesus' parable of the Sower, finally indicating that these regions are a part of the "many mansions" of the "Father's house":

> But that there is this distinction between the habitation of those who produce a hundredfold, and that of those who produce sixtyfold, and that of those who produce thirtyfold. For the first will be taken up into the heavens, the second class will dwell in paradise, and the last will inhabit the city (of God).
>
> On this account the Lord said, "In my Father's house are many mansions": for all things belong to God, who supplies all with a suitable dwelling place, even as His word says, that a share is given to all by the Father, according to the worthiness of each one....
>
> The presbyters, the disciples of the apostles, say that this is the gradation and arrangement of those who are saved, and that they advance through steps of this nature; and that, moreover, they ascend through the Spirit to the Son, and through the Son to the Father.
>
> *Irenaeus, Against Heresies V:36.2; cf. AH2 p.156*

The unknown writer of the *Doctrine of Addai the Apostle* is also thinking of the same passage in St John when he asserts that "this King of ours" has "gone to prepare ... blessed mansions." He also adds that God's purpose in creating man is so that he may worship Him:

> Wherefore, as wayfarers and sojourners, who tarry for a night and return early to their homes, so may you yourselves consider concerning this world, that from here you go forth to the places where the Son went to prepare for every one worthy of them. As with kings of countries, their armies go forth before them, and prepare for them a dwelling house for their honour. So this King of ours, behold, he is gone to prepare for his worshippers blessed mansions in which they may dwell.
>
> For it was not in vain God created the children of men; but that they might worship and glorify Him here and there forever. As He passes not away, so those glorifying Him cease not.
>
> *Doctrine of Addai the Apostle, DAA pp.42–43*

Speaking of the inner realms, he also says:

> All the souls of men, which depart from this body, die not; but they live and rise, and have mansions, and a dwelling place of rest, for the

understanding and the intelligence of the soul do not cease, because the Image of God (the *Logos*) is reflected in it, which dies not.

Doctrine of Addai the Apostle; cf. DAA pp.44–45

See also: **heavens**.

manzil (P) (pl. *manāzil*) *Lit.* house, home, abode, place; way station, stage, destination; mystically, a series of stages or stations on the spiritual journey to God. Some Sufis have named the stages *nāsūt* (humanity), *malakūt* (kingdom), *jabarūt* (power) and *lāhūt* (divinity). Some have called them *'ālam al-ajsām* (realm of bodies), *'ālam al-mithāl* (realm of patterns) and *'ālam al-arwāḥ* (realm of spirits). The term *manāzil* conveys the idea that the soul progresses stage by stage; that is, only after achieving *malakūt* does the soul reach *jabarūt,* and so on.

Some Sufis have designated seven stages *(haft manzil),* also called seven houses, resting places or valleys. These have been enumerated by the Persian mystic Farīd al-Dīn 'Aṭṭār in his allegorical story, *The Conference of the Birds.* The allegory describes the spiritual odyssey of a group of birds (souls) back to God. They are led by a hoopoe, who describes the journey that lies ahead:

"Before we reach our goal," the hoopoe said,
"the journey's seven valleys lie ahead;
How far this is, the world has never learned,
for no one who has gone there has returned –
Impatient bird, who would retrace this trail?
there is no messenger to tell the tale;
And they are lost to our concerns below –
how can men tell you what they do not know?

"The first stage is the Valley of the Quest,
then Love's wide valley is our second test;
The third is Insight into Mystery,
the fourth Detachment and Serenity;
The fifth is Unity; the sixth is Awe,
a deep Bewilderment unknown before;
The seventh, Poverty and Nothingness –
and there you are suspended, motionless:
Till you are drawn – the impulse is not yours –
a drop absorbed in seas that have no shores."

'Aṭṭār, Conference of the Birds 3226–33, CBD p.166

See also: **al-marātib al-maḥsūsah** (6.3).

maqām (A/P) (pl. *maqāmāt*) *Lit.* station, rank, position, standing, standpoint; a position or rank or dignity; *maqāmāt* (stations) generally denote different stages attained by the traveller on the mystic path. Each station represents a stage of moral and spiritual discipline in which the individual must become firmly established before further ascent:

> 'Station *(maqām)*' denotes anyone's standing in the way of God, and his fulfilment of the obligations appertaining to that station, and his keeping it until he comprehends its perfection so far as lies in a man's power. It is not permissible that he should quit his station without fulfilling the obligations thereof. Thus, the first station is repentance *(tawbat),* then comes conversion *(inābat),* then renunciation *(zuhd),* then trust in God *(tavakkul),* and so on. It is not permissible that anyone should pretend to conversion without repentance, or to renunciation without conversion, or to trust in God without renunciation.
>
> *Hujwīrī, Kashf al-Maḥjūb XIV:1, KM p.181*

Emphasis is laid on making the attainment of each of the successive stages a permanent spiritual condition. Once a soul has reached a particular *maqām,* it can reach that *maqām* at will:

> In *Ṣūfī* terms, *maqām* is that level which is gained through bearing the pain and difficulties related to its achievement. Once attained, the status is said to be possessed or occupied. The wayfarer's dwelling is his *maqām.*
>
> *Jurjānī, Kitāb al-Ta'rīfāt, KTA p.289, in FNI8 p.266*

Sufi writers differ in their classification of the various stations, but repentance, trust in God and poverty are emphasized by all. According to Farīd Aḥmad Ṣamdī, there are one hundred *maqāmāt* (stations),[1] of which ninety-nine – corresponding to the ninety-nine names of God – are changing states *(talvīn).* As the adept is established at one station, without fear of falling, he ascends to the one above, until he reaches the ninety-ninth. The hundredth stage is that of *tamkīn,* where the soul merges with the Essence.

Talvīn and *tamkīn* are a pair of Sufi technical terms. *Talvīn* refers to changing states or stations on the way to the state of spiritual perfection, denoted by *tamkīn.* This is the ultimate state, also called *maqām-i faqr* (station of poverty or humility) and *maqām-i ghanī* (station of wealth), both meant in a spiritual sense. It is the timeless and spaceless region of the unity of the Absolute where the soul stays forever, rapt in perpetual wonder. Hujwīrī explains the difference between *maqām* and *tamkīn,* the final resting place:

> *Maqām* (station) denotes the perseverance of the seeker in fulfilling his obligation towards the object of his search with strenuous exertion and flawless intention. Everyone who desires God has a station *(maqām),* which, in the beginning of his search, is a means whereby he seeks God. Although the seeker derives some benefit from every station through which he passes, he finally rests in one, because a station and the quest thereof involve contrivance and design *(tarkīb-u ḥīlah),* not conduct and practice *(ravish-u mu'āmalat).*
>
> God hath said: "None of us but hath a certain station."[2] The station of Adam was repentance *(tawbat),* that of Noah was renunciation *(zuhd),* that of Abraham was resignation *(taslīm),* that of Moses was contrition *(inābat),* that of David was sorrow *(ḥuzn),* that of Jesus was hope *(rajā'),* that of John (the Baptist) was fear *(khawf),* and that of our Apostle was praise *(dhikr)....*
>
> *Tamkīn* denotes the residence of spiritual adepts in the abode of perfection and in the highest grade. Those in stations can pass on from their stations, but it is impossible to pass beyond the grade of *tamkīn,* because *maqām* is the grade of the beginners, whereas *tamkīn* is the resting place of adepts; and *maqāmāt* (stations) are stages on the way, whereas *tamkīn* is repose within the shrine. The friends of God are absent (from themselves) on the way and are strangers (to themselves) in the stages: their hearts are in the presence (of God), and in the presence every instrument is evil and every tool is (a token of) absence (from God) and infirmity....
>
> When Moses attained to *tamkīn,* God bade him to put off his shoes and cast away his staff,[3] those being articles of travel, and Moses being in the presence of God. The beginning of love is search, but the end is rest: water flows in the river bed, but when it reaches the ocean it ceases to flow and changes its taste, so that those who desire water avoid it, but those who desire pearls devote themselves to death and fasten the plummet of search to their feet and plunge headlong into the sea that they may either gain the hidden pearl or lose their dear lives.
>
> *Hujwīrī, Kashf al-Maḥjūb XXIV, KM pp.370–72*

In Sufi texts, *maqām,* attained partly through effort and discipline, is distinguished from *ḥāl,* a state that is a gift from God:

> 'State *(ḥāl)*', on the other hand, is something that descends from God into a man's heart, without his being able to repel it when it comes or to attract it when it goes, by his own effort. Accordingly, while the term 'station' denotes the way of the seeker, and his progress in the field of exertion, and his rank before God in proportion to his

> merit, the term 'state' denotes the favour and grace which God bestows upon the heart of His servant, and which are not connected with any mortification on the latter's part. Station belongs to the category of acts, state to the category of gifts. Hence, the man that has a station stands by his own self-mortification, whereas the man that has a state is dead to self and stands by a state which God creates in him.
>
> *Hujwīrī, Kashf al-Maḥjūb XIV:1, KM p.181*

Sufis are not agreed whether a state *(ḥāl)* is a permanent or fleeting spiritual condition. It is more in the latter sense that Rūmī writes:

> The *ḥāl* is like the unveiling of that beauteous bride,
> while the *maqām* is (the king's) being alone with the bride.
> The unveiling is witnessed by the king and by others as well;
> At the time of being alone,
> there is no one except the mighty king.
> The bride unveils before commons and nobles:
> in the bridal chamber the king is alone with the bride.
> There is many a one of the *Ṣūfīs* who enjoys *ḥāl:*
> he among them who has attained to *maqām* is rare.
>
> *Rūmī, Maśnavī I:1435–38; cf. MJR2 p.79*

Rūmī goes on to speak of the journey of the soul from its original oneness with God before the beginning of the creation when it resided in the *maqām-i quds* (station of holiness), descending through the successive layers of creation, and of the journey of return that the soul now undertakes, the journey back up through the successive layers of creation (the *maqāmāt*) to that original oneness:

> He ('Umar) reminded him of the stages *(manāzil'hā)*
> traversed by the soul,
> and he reminded him of the journeys of the spirit,
> and of the time which has ever been void of time,
> and of the station of holiness *(maqām-i quds),*
> which has ever been majestical,
> and of the atmosphere wherein the *Sīmurgh* of the spirit,
> before this (life), has flown and experienced grace,
> every single flight thereof being greater
> than the horizons of this world
> and greater than the hope and greed of the longing lover.
>
> *Rūmī, Maśnavī I:1439–42, MJR2 p.79*

See also: **ḥāl** (▸2), **lā-maqām, maqām** (▸2).

1. Farīd Aḥmad Ṣamdī, *Iṣṭilāḥāt-i Ṣūfīyah, IS* p.127.
2. *Qur'ān* 37:164.
3. *Qur'ān* 20:12.

marātib al-kullīyah, al- (A), **marātib-i kullī** (P) *Lit.* the encompassing *(al-kullīyah)* stages, stations or ranks *(marātib,* sg. *martabah);* the totality of the stages; essentially, the whole of creation; also, the corresponding stations or stages of spiritual development.

Six stages comprise the *marātib al-kullīyah:*

1. *Aḥadīyah* (Oneness) is absolute oneness, all-comprehensive and all-inclusive.
2. *Waḥdah* (Oneness) is the first stirrings within the divine Essence of the consciousness or possibility of existence; associated with *al-Ḥaqīqah al-Muḥammadīyah* (the Reality of Muḥammad).
3. *Waḥdānīyah* (Oneness) is the first expression of the first stirrings of consciousness within the divine Essence; the origin of the divine creative power called the Voice of God, Speech of God, *Kun,* Word, *Logos* and by many other names.
4. *'Ālam al-arwāḥ* (realm of spirits).
5. *'Ālam al-mithāl* (realm of patterns).
6. *'Ālam al-ajsām* (realm of bodies).

These names of the regions of creation also appear in descriptions of the *'ālamīn* (worlds), the *ta'ayyunāt* (entifications, individuations), the *manāzil* (abodes, stages), the *maqām al-tanazzul al-Raḥmānī* (stations in the descent of the Merciful), the *Ḥaḍarāt al-Ilāhīyah al-Khams* (Five Divine Manifestations), and other similar terms. The fourth, fifth and sixth *marātib* – the realms of spirits, of patterns and of bodies – represent the lower end of the creation in all of these listings. The *ta'ayyunāt* depict the highest realms of the creation, including the aspects of eternal and divine Unity: *aḥadīyah, waḥdah* and *wāḥidīyah.*

The *marātib* below that of the absolute, divine Essence *(Dhāt)* are also called the *'ālam al-Insān al-Kāmil* (realm of the Perfect Man). The Perfect Man, as the archetype of creation, encompasses all the *marātib* from the domain of bodies *('ālam al-ajsām)* to *aḥadīyah.*

This parallels descriptions of the Five Divine Manifestations *(al-Ḥaḍarāt al-Ilāhīyah al-Khams),* which consist of the three *'ālamīn (ajsām, mithāl, arwāḥ),* the First Entification *(al-Ta'ayyun al-Awwal),* and the Manifestation of the Perfect Man, which is again seen as encompassing all the other Manifestations.

The *marātib al-kullīyah* (totality of the stages) is also similar in meaning to the *'avālim-i kullī* (totality of the realms). In the latter, the five realms of creation are *lāhūt* (divinity), *jabarūt* (power), *malakūt* (kingdom), *mulk* (*lit.* kingship, the physical universe) and, lastly, *'ālam al-nāsūt* (realm of humanity). The realm of humanity is said to be the all-comprehensive manifestation and the ultimate purpose of creation.

See also: **'ālam**, **All (the)**, **maqām**, **ta'ayyun**, **Totality**.

maṭarata (Md) *Lit.* places of detention; customs houses; a Mandaean term for worlds of purification through which the soul must pass, expiating her evil deeds and impurities, before reaching the worlds of light.[1]

1. *cf.* E.S. Drower, *Secret Adam, SA* p.30.

meadow(s) See **gardens**.

menorah (He) *Lit.* lamp, candelabra; from the Hebrew *ner* (candle), having the same origins as the Arabic *nūr* (light); the oldest Jewish symbol, commonly found in a seven-branched form, often fashioned so that its individual lamps resemble the branches of a tree. In Jewish mystic tradition, the *menorah* is understood as a symbolic representation of the Tree of Life, which is itself a metaphor for the creative Power, the Word that nourishes the soul through its divine light.

Because the branches of a tree spread out at different levels, suggesting a hierarchy of stages with a definite progression from one to the other, the mystics also understood the Tree of Life to represent the inner spiritual journey. Thus, the *menorah,* as a symbol of the Tree of Life, also serves to portray the stages of the spiritual journey, the lights of each inner region being represented by its lamps or candles. The seven-branched *menorah* may also signify the seven heavens of Jewish and Middle Eastern understanding.

During the time of the Kabbalah, the seven branches of the *menorah* became associated with the seven lower *sefirot* or divine emanations through which the divine power is spread into the world. *Tiferet* (Splendour, Mercy) serves as the central axis, symbolizing its role as the harmonizer of *Ḥesed* (Lovingkindness, overflowing love and grace) and *Din* (Justice), and as the axis on which the lower *sefirot* depend.

There is a passage in the Jewish Prayer Book, consisting of an early morning recitation for men as they put on the *tefillin* (phylacteries, boxes containing scriptural passages), which originated as a Kabbalistic commentary by the sixteenth-century Moses Albas. The prayer asks God to spread His "good

Oil" on the seven branches of the *menorah* so that His influence will spread into the creation. This is a symbolically rich image of the divine creative power of the Godhead *(Ayn-Sof)* – represented here as the "good Oil" – being distributed to all levels of the creation:

> And from Your Wisdom, O supreme God,
> emanate upon me (inspire me);
> And from Your Understanding,
> give me Understanding;
> With Your Lovingkindness enlarge me also;
> With Your Might frustrate my enemies;
> And Your good Oil pour on the seven branches of the *menorah*
> to spread Your good influence to Your creation.
> Open Your Hand, and satisfy all life with Your will.
>
> *Jewish Prayer Book; cf. PB p.3, DPB p.8*

This prayer is rich in Kabbalistic references. The "seven branches" represent the seven lower *sefirot,* while "Wisdom", "Understanding", "Lovingkindness" and "Might" are the second, third, fourth and fifth *sefirot.*

The lamp or *menorah* was also used by Jewish mystics as a metaphor for the spiritual teacher.

See also: **menorah** (▸2), **sefirot**, **Tree of Life** (3.1).

midot (He) *Lit.* qualities, attributes, measurements. Early Jewish mystics of the rabbinic period (200 BCE – 400 CE) associated the qualities of God, as described in the Bible, with embodied attributes of God, which they called His *midot.* Six such qualities, for instance, are described in *1 Chronicles:*

> Thine, O Lord, is the Greatness *(Gedulah),* and the Power *(Gevurah),* and the Glory *(Tiferet),* and the Victory *(Neẓaḥ),* and the Majesty *(Hod).* For all that is in the heaven and in the earth is Thine. Thine is the Kingdom *(Mamlakhah, i.e. Malkut)....*
>
> *1 Chronicles 29:11, KJV*

The rabbis associated these qualities with the divine utterances by which God brought the creation into existence, according to the first chapter of *Genesis.* ("And God said, 'Let there be light!'" and so on). These initial utterances or *ma'amarot* (Gk. *logoi*) of God were understood as expressions or embodiments of His attributes, distilled from the unity of God. Hence, a frequently quoted saying of Rav in the third-century *Babylonian Talmud* identifies the divine creative utterances with particular *midot* or attributes:

> Rabbi Zutra bar Tobiah said in the name of Rav: "By ten qualities was the world created: wisdom, understanding, reason, strength, rebuke, power, righteousness, justice, lovingkindness and compassion."
>
> *Babylonian Talmud, Ḥagigah 12a; cf. in MTJM p.74, BLBR p.7:11*

Likewise, in another text from Talmudic times:

> Seven *midot* serve before the throne of glory: wisdom, right and justice, love and mercy, truth and peace.
>
> *Avot de Rabbi Nathan 37, in MTJM p.74*

For some Jewish gnostics of the rabbinic period, the *midot* served the same role as the gnostic *archons* and *aeons,* as emanations of God. Later Jewish mystics identified the *midot* or utterances with the *sefirot* of the Kabbalists – the emanations of the divine power through whose projection and interaction the creation is described as coming into being.

See also: **sefirot**.

mount See **mountains**.

mountains (Native North American) Mystically, the higher realms; probably all cultures have had mystics who have spoken from personal experience of the higher worlds. Though these realms are beyond description in physical terms, it is necessary to use human words if the attempt is made to convey something of the experience. Naturally, such descriptions use images familiar to the speaker and his audience. Thus, the nineteenth-century Lakota Sioux holy man, Ḃlack Elk *(Hehaka Sapa),* speaks of such an experience in terms of the mountains, forests and colours known to him. But he also describes seeing, "in a sacred manner", the "shapes of all things in the spirit". He is seeing the essence or subtle blueprints that are projected outward into lower worlds and into this world:

> I looked ahead and saw the mountains there, with rocks and forests on them, and from the mountains flashed all colours upward to the heavens. Then I was standing on the highest mountain of them all, and round about beneath me was the whole hoop of the world. And while I stood there, I saw more than I can tell, and I understood more than I saw; for I was seeing, in a sacred manner, the shapes of all things in the spirit, and the shape of all shapes as they must live together like one being. And I saw that the sacred hoop of my people

was one of many hoops that made one circle, wide as daylight and as starlight, and in the centre grew one mighty flowering Tree to shelter all the children of one mother and one father. And I saw that it was holy.

Black Elk, in BES pp.42–43

mountain(s), mountains of the Covenant, mountains of God, mountain of myrrh, mountains of radiance, mountain of Yahweh A mountain is a natural upward projection on the earth's surface, generally with a rocky summit; expressions using the term are common references for the inner regions of creation, especially in Judaic, Christian and Islamic literature, as well as other Eastern mystical writings. In particular, the eternal realm itself was known as Mount Zion, the holy mount, the holy mountain, the heavenly Jerusalem, the city of God and so on.

The term is frequently encountered in the Hebrew Bible, where mountains are generally taken to infer the transcendence and eternal changelessness of God. The word *har* (mountain), is from the same root as *ẓur* (rock), which also means mountain in Arabic *(ṭūr). Ẓur* (rock) was another epithet for God in the ancient Hebrew and Middle Eastern literature. In many instances, however, the intended meaning of 'mountains' is that of the higher realms.

Many biblical descriptions concerning the ascent of the prophets speak of particular mountains. These probably allude to the inner ascent of the soul. The most renowned of these incidents must be the ascension of the prophet Moses on Mount Sinai, where he experienced the revelation of God's Commandment or Word.

Likewise, in *1 Kings,* the expression "Ḥoreb, the mountain of God *(har ha-Elohim, Ḥoreb)*"[1] is used to describe the place to which the prophet Elijah travelled for forty days and forty nights to await the "Word of God". Elijah is described as eating a meal provided by an angel, then fasting, and finally climbing the mountain, sitting in a cave, and ultimately experiencing God's Word as a "still small Voice".[2] Though the meaning is unclear, interpreted allegorically, it could mean that Elijah began his spiritual journey in this world; then fasted from this world; and then ascended to the inner realms where he came into contact with the Word of God.

'Ḥoreb' literally means desert, and Mount Ḥoreb – a name that only appears in the Bible – is usually considered to be the same as Mount Sinai. It refers to the mountain in the Sinai desert which – according to the *Exodus* story – Moses ascended in order to receive the revelation of God's Word or Will, after his wanderings with the Israelites. The desert is commonly taken as a metaphor for the material world – a spiritual desert that has to be left behind in order to climb the spiritual mountain within. Geographically,

Mount Sinai is usually identified with one or the other of two hills (Jebel Musa or Jebel Serbal) in the mountainous South Sinai peninsula, 'Jebel' being Arabic for 'hill'.

Another variant of the 'mountain' metaphor is the 'peak of Carmel *(rosh ha-Karmel)*'. Mount Carmel is a mountainous ridge in northwest Israel running from the Samarian hills to the Mediterranean, reaching a height of about 1800 feet. It is the site of another of Elijah's encounters with God, while in an attitude of humility and prayer:

> And Elijah went up to the top of Carmel;
> And he crouched down on the earth,
> and put his face between his knees.
>
> *1 Kings 18:42; cf. KB, KJV*

'Mountain' terms are common in the *Psalms,* where the interpretation is more certain:

> Who has the right to climb the mountain *(har)* of *Yahweh,*
> who the right to stand in His holy place?
> He whose hands are clean, whose heart is pure,
> whose soul does not pay homage to worthless things,
> and who never swears to a lie.
>
> The blessing of *Yahweh* is his,
> and vindication from God his saviour.
> Such are the people who seek Him,
> who seek Your presence, God of Jacob!
>
> *Psalm 24:3–6, JB*

The one who climbs the "mountain of *Yahweh*" and stands in "His holy place" is the one who is pure in heart. The writer is speaking of the inner, mystic ascent. And again:

> Your love, *Yahweh,* reaches to the heavens,
> Your faithfulness to the clouds;
> Your righteousness (holiness) is like the mountains of God,
> Your judgments like the mighty deep.
>
> *Psalm 36:5–6, JB*

Similarly:

> I will lift up mine eyes unto the hills (mountains)
> from whence cometh my help.

My help cometh from the Lord *(Yahweh),*
which made heaven and earth.
Psalm 121:1–2, KJV

Here, the psalmist explains specifically that he is not looking for help from the mountains of this world, but from God.

The metaphor also appears in the *Song of Songs,* a section beginning with the soul's hearing her Beloved as he comes to her:

I hear my Beloved;
See how he comes,
leaping on the mountains,
bounding over the hills.
My Beloved is like a gazelle,
like a young stag.
Song of Songs 2:9–8, JB

The lover "hears" her Beloved – an allusion to the inner Sound. He is the Master of the inner realms – he leaps "on the mountains" and bounds "over the hills" with the agility of one who lives among them – a "young stag" or a "gazelle".

Likewise, the lover alludes to nightly devotion and transport into the heavenly realms within, redolent with the intoxicating 'fragrance' of divine love – the "mountain of myrrh" and the "hill of frankincense":

Before the dawn wind rises,
before the shadows flee,
I will go to the mountain of myrrh,
to the hill of frankincense.
Song of Songs 4:6, JB

There are a great many instances of the same or similar terms in the ancient mystic literature. In the allegorical and apocalyptic biblical *Joel,* for example, a delightful mix of metaphors is encountered. The prophet Joel ben Pethu'el writes:

And it shall come to pass in that day,
that the mountains shall drop down sweet wine,
and the hills shall flow with milk,
and all the streams of Judah shall flow with waters;
And a Fountain shall issue from the house of the Lord,
and shall water the valley of Shittim.
Joel 4:18, JPS

Although commonly understood to be a prophecy of the end of the world, a mystical interpretation of this passage also makes good sense. "Mountains" that "drop down sweet wine" and "hills" that "flow with milk" are metaphors referring to the inner realms of spirituality, while the "streams of Judah" and the "valley of Shittim" refer to the physical realm. The "sweet wine", the "milk", the "waters" and the "Fountain" are all references to the Living Waters of the divine creative power that brings the sweetness of spiritual life to this world.

In early Christian times, the story of the transfiguration of Jesus, in which he is transformed into a being of light, is always described as taking place on a mountain. Reading between the lines, the story is probably a misunderstanding of a meeting with the spiritual form of Jesus on the inner planes. There is no doubt that the term was understood to mean the heavenly realms. In an early Coptic Christian text purporting to describe the death of Jesus' mother, Mary, the writer – credited as a certain Theodosius, Archbishop of Alexandria – relates some of Mary's last words. Looking forward to her departure from this world, she speaks of being "brought … to this holy mountain":

> "Better is a day in your courts than thousands (in this world). I had rather dwell in your courts, my Master." And again, "Your Holy Ghost has brought me to this holy mountain. Therefore, I will go in unto your holy place, and will worship at your temple, O you whom my soul loves." When she had said these things, she was in joy unspeakable, in the place whence grief has fled away.
>
> *Theodosius, Falling Asleep of Mary; cf. CAG pp.115–17*

In the *Book of Revelation,* there is little doubt as to the mystical meaning of the "high mountain", the "great city" and the "holy Jerusalem" when the writer describes how an angel took him to see "the bride, the Lamb's wife". For he is "carried … away in the spirit". The experience is spiritual, not physical:

> "Come hither, I will shew thee the bride, the Lamb's wife."
> And he carried me away in the spirit
> to a great and high mountain,
> and shewed me that great city, the holy Jerusalem,
> descending out of heaven from God,
> having the glory of God:
> And her light was like unto a stone most precious,
> even like a jasper stone, clear as crystal.
>
> *Book of Revelation 21:9–11, KJV*

It is evident that being "carried … away in the spirit to a great and high mountain" is a reference to the inner creation.

Jerome (*c.*347–420) and other early Church fathers say that there was once a *Gospel According to the Hebrews* that closely resembled yet also possessed significant differences from the Greek *Gospel According to Saint Matthew.* It was written in Hebrew characters, in the Aramaic or Hebrew language, and was used by the Nazarenes or Nāṣoraeans, the early Christians of Palestine. The text has long since been lost, and is extant only as a handful of brief citations in the writings of Jerome and others; but in it there is a passage resembling the story in *Revelations,* quoted in the early third century by Origen:

> Even so did my Mother, the Holy Spirit,
> take me by one of my hairs,
> and carry me away to the great mountain Tabor.
> *Gospel of the Hebrews, in Origen: Commentary on John 2:12.87 (on John 1:3); cf. OG p.85*

The Holy Spirit is the "Mother" of the soul who is carried high up into the inner regions, symbolized once again as a high mountain. To which region this refers is unclear, but it is certain that the writer is referring to travel through the inner realms, for the means of transport is the Holy Spirit. Being caught by "one of my hairs" presumably refers to the ease and lightness of touch by which the Holy Spirit carried the soul upwards. Mount Tabor is a mountain in northern Israel, near Nazareth, and is traditionally held to be the mountain where the transfiguration took place.

Elsewhere among the Middle Eastern writings of this period, the inner regions are explicitly referred to simply as "mountains" or as the "mountains of radiance, light and glory",[3] and so on. Mixing a number of common mystic allusions, a Manichaean psalm portrays the inner realms, and particularly the eternal abode, by a variety of metaphors, including "all the holy mountains". They are described as the

> habitation of the blessed,
> fountain that gushes greatness,
> trees of fragrance,
> fountains filled with Life,
> all the holy mountains,
> fields that are green with Life,
> dew of ambrosia.
> *Manichaean Psalm Book, MPB p.136*

Another of these psalms speaks of the Lord's creative 'act' through the Word, referred to by a number of common allusions. Here, the inner realms are again referred to as the "holy mountains":

My Father, … the glad and honoured Light: …
He evoked clouds of brightness,
dropping down the Dew of Life.
He summoned a holy Fire,
giving a sweet burning.
He evoked a Wind and an Air (of the spirit),
breathing the Breath of the Living.
He evoked holy mountains,
sending up fragrant roots.

Psalms of Thomas I, Manichaean Psalm Book; cf. MPB p.203

Likewise, the Master himself, in this case Mār Zaku, one of Mānī's successors, is described as:

O green Mountain where sheep graze.

Manichaean Hymns, MM3 p.865ff., RMP ch, ML p.31; cf. GSR p.87:7.2

The same expression is commonly used in Mandaean literature, as in a poem where the writer addresses these mystic mountains:

To the mountains I say:
"How fragrant are your odours,
how delightful your perfume!
Within you all is full of brightness!"

They reply, "The Being who passed through our midst
has no tangibility or substance;
No substance or tangibility has he,
nor is there any kind of desire in him.
The Being who passed among us,
released some of his vivifying power among us."

Mandaean Prayer Book 157; cf. CPM p.135

The mountains "reply" that the entirely spiritual Word or Saviour who "has no tangibility or substance", passed through them, showering his life-giving power. The image is akin to that of the Beloved in the *Song of Songs,* who "comes leaping on the mountains, bounding over the hills.… like a gazelle, like a young stag".[4] There is nothing worldly about him, nor is there any kind of desire in him.

In another of the Mandaean poems, the poet is writing in the name of the Master. Here again, there is no doubt that the "mountain" is that of the spirit. The wind or spirit that blows off this mountain onto the valley of the world brings life to the world and its "nations" – its people:

I beheld a mountain,
white as the congregation (of pure souls)
that had formed itself on it.
The day on which a wind (spirit) breathes (over it),
nations delight in its perfume.
The day on which the wind (spirit)
bears down upon the valley (of this world),
they are illumined by its radiance.

Mandaean Prayer Book 164; cf. CPM p.142

The Master then requests that a Physician, "a Healer ... for souls, who heals but takes no fee" should be sent to the souls in the "valley":

When standing at my place,
I made a great request, a boon;
I said: "Grant me that from my mountain home,
and from the home of the great company that dwell therein,
there may be (sent) a Healer of souls;
A Healer there may be for souls,
who heals but takes no fee."

As I was standing at my place,
the boon I had asked was granted me,
granted me from my mountain home,
from the home of the great community therein.
I became a Healer for souls!
I became a Healer for souls,
who heals but takes no fee.

Mandaean Prayer Book 164; cf. CPM p.142

The compassionate Master, who saw the need, is deemed suitable for the mission, and is given the divine mandate of Saviour.

In another allegorical poem, the soul is initiated, and then taken up into the "mountain". But the mystic intent is hardly veiled, and the meaning is explicit:

What did your Father do for you, soul,
the great day on which you were
raised up (from death in the body)?

"He took me down to the Jordan (the Living Waters),
planted me (baptized me),
and rose, and stood me upon its bank.

"He broke and gave me (the) Bread (of Life),
blessed the cup, and gave me to drink thereof
(from the Living Waters).
He placed me between his knees,
(he took me under his protection),
and pronounced over me the Name of the mighty Life.

"He passed into the mountain before me,
He cried loudly that I might hear (the Word),
that I might hear he cried loudly,
'If there is strength in thee, soul, come!'

"(And I replied), 'If I climb the mountain, I shall fall,
I shall overturn and perish from the world!'
But I lifted my eyes to heaven,
and my soul waited upon the house of Life.

"I climbed the mountain, and fell not.
I came, and found the life of my Self."

Mandaean Prayer Book 30; cf. CPM pp.24–25

See also: **holy mount** (2.1), **Mount Carmel** (2.1).

1. *1 Kings* 19:8.
2. *1 Kings* 19:12.
3. *Mandaean Prayer Book* 58, *CPM* p.51.
4. *Song of Songs* 2:9–8, *JB*.

mṛityu lok(a) (S/H), **mirt lok** (H/Pu) *Lit.* realm *(lok)* of death *(mṛityu);* this world, where every created thing or being is subject to death or decay; the world of mortals; the world of the dead, the souls in this world being so unconscious that mystics describe them as dead or fast asleep.

See also: **triloka**.

mshunia kūshṭā (Md) *Lit.* truth *(kūshṭā)* + *mshunia,* from the root *tna* (to repeat, to double); a Mandaean term for a sublime other world of truth or reality; a supramundane world of ideal counterparts or subtle patterns that is believed to contain the double *(dmūtha),* the ideal or archetype *(mabda),* of everything in the material world; the world to which pure souls go after the judgment of *Abathur* that follows their death.[1] Writing of this Mandaean belief in the 1930s, E.S. Drower says:

Mshunia kūshṭā is the ideal world of the Mandaeans, peopled by the descendants of *Adam Kasia* and *Hāwa Kasia* (the hidden or mystical Adam and Eve); for, as one priest told me, "Of all things there are two, an actual and its *mabda* (archetype)." Another explained that each individual on earth has his *dmūtha* (double) or likeness in *mshunia kūshṭā,* and at the time of death the earthly individual leaves his earthly body, and assumes the ethereal body of his double.

It is in the latter body that the human soul goes through the pains of purification. As for his double in *mshunia kūshṭā,* at the time of the earthly double's dissolution, he quits the ethereal body which he inhabited for a light-body and, being perfectly pure, he proceeds at once to the worlds of light.

When the human soul *(nishimta)* has completed the cycle of its purification, and the scales of *Abathur Muzania* have proved it to be free of all grossness, it too enters the world of light, and the two are united:

I go towards my likeness
  and my likeness goes towards me;
He embraces me, and holds me close,
  as if I had come out of prison.

Beast, birds, flowers and indeed the whole physical universe have a spiritual counterpart in *mshunia kūshṭā,* and its inhabitants are said to marry and have children, but without pollution in the process. Sometimes they are represented as communicating with their doubles on earth.

E.S. Drower, Mandaeans of Iraq and Iran, MII pp.54–55

"*Mshunia kūshṭā* is reached after purification," continues E.S. Drower, it is "not the final goal". It is a stage in the soul's onward journey to the worlds of light. A Mandaean text describes this ascent of the soul:

And thus, as they depart, set forth and fly into the sky, traversing the road, they behold the gate of mercies which is opened in the midst of *mshunia kūshṭā,* and then they move onwards and sit at the boundary that bounds *mshunia kūshṭā* which no earthly being may cross unless signed with the Sign of the Jordan, having truth *(kūshṭā)* within themselves. So there spirit and soul wait until they are taken up into worlds of light.

And from the day that she (the soul) leaves (the body) until the day that she sets forth, she beholds those forms, trees and souls which dwell in *mshunia kūshṭā....*

> And in that place at each stretch of the way there is a gate through which souls must pass. If the soul be a good one, the gates are opened in a single day, and a glorious light appears from the beginning of the road unto the last of the gates of *mshunia kūshṭā.* She beholds them in light and effulgence, and knows not where she is going until she leaves that place, departing by that gate, (and leaving behind her) the torment of existence there.
>
> And so, as she leaves that place, she assumes a beauteous appearance and is arrayed in fair raiment. And when she puts on that raiment, she remains therein. And there are dwellings *(shkinata)* there, for it *(mshunia kūshṭā)* is called the dwelling of *Abathur:* it is the place in which souls are kept until they depart from it.
>
> And all souls which we have brought from there drink of that Jordan, and pluck and eat of those trees. And they go about freely: in those worlds there is no urinating because the soul's body in that world resembles trees which drink of wind and water, and live. They partake of the fruit, but there is no excrement among them, neither is there any consuming flame or fire which blazes. When they cast incense, their radiance shines forth, and it circles up before them.... And none of the trees that grow there have pip or seed in them, and yet their fruit neither diminishes nor is it of poor quality.
>
> *Thousand and Twelve Questions I:283–85; cf. TTQ pp.189–90*

Twentieth-century Mandaeans had varied ideas as to the whereabouts of *mshunia kūshṭā.* Some believed it to be in the north, divided from the actual world by a high and snowy mountain. Another favourite theory was that "it hangs between heaven and earth, and is invisible to us. Its inhabitants are purer than we are, and we cannot see them." Others believe it to be located on a star.[2]

See also: **shkinta**, **worlds of light**.

1. E.S. Drower, *Secret Adam, SA* pp.35, 39.
2. E.S. Drower, *Mandaeans of Iraq and Iran, MII* p.56.

mumkin (A/P) (pl. *mumkināt) Lit.* possible, potential, contingent; used in the expression *mumkin al-wujūd* (possible being, contingent being, conditional being). 'Possible' or 'conditional' beings are distinguished from *Wājib al-Wujūd,* the Necessary Being, *wājib* meaning necessity. God is the Necessary Being, and all creatures are possible beings. All beings other than God are contingent or conditional, and liable to perish *(fanā');* but God is inherently and necessarily existent.

Mumkin or *mumkināt* and the noun form, *imkāniah* (pl. *imkāniāt*), are used in Sufi metaphysics, especially by Ibn 'Arabī and his followers, for possibilities, potentials, contingencies. The idea, in brief, is that everything exists within God, but as pure undifferentiated potential. In the process of emanating the creation, these 'potentials *(imkāniāt)*' came into existence, though in seed form, in the higher, subtle realms. As the emanative process continued, the *mumkināt* became more and more differentiated or manifested, culminating in the physical universe where differentiation and crystallization reach their peak.

See also: **dā'irat al-imkān**, **Wājib al-Wujūd** (2.2).

narak(a) (S/H/Pu) *Lit.* hell; a place of torment. Hindu texts speak of varying numbers of hells. The *Mārkaṇḍeya Purāṇa* mentions six; the *Manu Smṛiti,* twenty-one; the *Brahmāṇḍa Purāṇa,* twenty-seven; and the *Agni Purāṇa,* twenty-eight. These hells are depicted as lying one above the other, and the warders are described as possessing the faces of cats, owls, jackals, vultures and so on. The *Vishṇu Purāṇa* talks of a number of *narakas* for sinners, including one for those who treat their teachers' wives badly, and another for fathers who eat sweets without offering them to their children! Generally speaking, Hindu lore encompasses seven hells:[1]

1.	*Put* or *Pud*	To which those without children are sent.
2.	*Avīchi*	Where souls await rebirth on earth, after bearing their punishment.
3.	*Saṃhāta*	Where lesser forms of punishment are meted out for minor offences.
4.	*Tāmisra*	Where souls are punished for non-serious crimes. The gloom of hell begins here.
5.	*Ṛijīsha*	Where the inmates are tormented by their conscience, which attacks them in the guise of snakes, wild beasts and so on.
6.	*Kudmala*	A hell situated on the banks of *Vaitaraṇī* river – a river of filth, to be crossed by all those who are sent to the last hell.
7.	*Kākola*	The bottomless pit; a permanent hell of indescribable torture and misery for those who are so wicked they have no hope of rebirth. Souls are roasted and pierced with copper spikes; their flesh is torn to shreds by demons with red hot pincers. When the sufferers are thirsty, they are given

dirty water taken from the *Vaitaraṇī* river. Having no hope of gaining rebirth on earth, they stay until the time of dissolution *(pralaya).* Such details, if anything other than mythological, are presumably intended metaphorically, since there are no physical bodies in hell.

Mystics, speaking in general terms, confirm the existence of hellish zones, often when describing the suffering of souls both in this world as well as in hell. They also say that these hells are not places of eternal torment, for after the prescribed period their inhabitants are reborn either as lower or higher beings, according to their *karma.* Sahajobāī paints a graphic picture of the soul's suffering after death:

> The angels of death *(jam)* shackle and chain him,
> and present him before *Dharam Rāi* (the lord of justice).
> Often, previously, has he appeared (before him), too:
> now, fifty-six types of dread (await him) there.
> Many are the forms of punishment
> and the terrors there, O Sahajo;
> After suffering pain in the fires of hell *(narak),*
> into the (wheel of) eighty-four is he sent to live again.
>
> *Sahajobāī, Bānī, Mṛityu Dashā 94–95, SBB p.27*

Charaṇdās says that human beings suffer in hell "according to their degree of sinfulness":

> There are eighteen hells *(narak);*
> Sinners are sent to these hells *(narak),*
> according to their degree of sinfulness,
> and they also suffer correspondingly.
>
> *Charaṇdās, Bhakti Sāgar, Nasketlīlā Varṇan Dohā 8, SBG p.604*

Like many other mystics, Guru Arjun says that only devotion to *Nām,* the mystic Name, can save the soul:

> By the supreme good fortune, I have received the Name *(Nām)* treasure,
> and so shall not fall into hell *(narak),* O Nānak.
>
> *Guru Arjun, Ādi Granth 915, MMS*

See also: **abyss**, **dūzakh**, **Gehenna**, **Hadēs**, **hell**, **jahannam**, **Pit**, **Sheol**.

1. *cf. Manu Smṛiti* 4:88–90; *Mārkaṇḍeya Purāṇa* 12; *Brahmāṇḍa Purāṇa* 4:2.146–50; *Agni Purāṇa* 352:13.

ñe'eng-güery (G) *Lit.* land *(güery)* of souls *(ñe'eng);* hence, country of the dead; a Guaraní term for the dwelling place of souls who have lived on earth, and who are destined to be reincarnated. At death, a person's *ñe'eng,* or higher soul, may travel to paradise or may go to the *ñe'eng-güery* to await reincarnation. Advanced shamans travel to the *ñe'eng-güery,* where they encounter shamans of the past, who share their wisdom.

See also: **oka-vusú**, **ywy mará ey**.

next world Life after death, the hereafter, the afterlife, the future life; a colloquial expression for existence after the death of the physical body.

See also: **afterlife**.

Neẓaḥ (He) *Lit.* triumph; hence, endurance, eternity; the seventh of the ten *sefirot;* probably derived from the sense of God as triumphant over time – His enduring and eternal being. In the Kabbalistic system of the *sefirot, Neẓaḥ* is paired with *Hod* (Majesty) as the two pillars of God's kingship. These two *sefirot* embody the qualities of divine governance or rulership of the world. The outflowing energy of *Neẓaḥ* is kept within boundaries, moderated and channelized by *Hod.* This parallels the action of *Din* (Judgment), the fifth *sefirah,* which moderates and limits the activity of *Ḥesed* (Loving-kindness), the fourth *sefirah,* but at a lower level.

Divine governance was understood as the process of God's emanation of His Essence into the creation. The further this emanation flows from God, the more diluted it becomes. The *sefirot* serve as conduits for the transmission of this divine grace into creation. The *sefirot* of *Hod* and *Din* were understood as filters that pass along the emanation from *Neẓaḥ* and *Ḥesed* to the *sefirot* below. *Hod* and *Din* are the conduits by which the divine Essence is transmitted from the upper *sefirot* to the lower *sefirot,* especially *Malkhut* (Kingship). They are the means by which divine preservation of the world is assured.[1]

See also: **Hod**, **sefirot**.

1. *cf.* David Ariel, *The Mystic Quest, MQ* p.81.

nihakshar (H) *Lit.* beyond *(nih)* the imperishable *(akshar);* used by Swāmī Shiv Dayāl Singh for the realm or void of great darkness, also called *mahā sunn* (great void). Normally, *nihakshar* means unwritten – literally, 'without *(nih)* letter *(akshar)*'. In this instance, *nihakshar* appears to mean the realm beyond *akshar* (imperishable).

The entire creation of mind and *māyā* (illusion) in the physical, astral and the causal worlds is subject to occasional dissolution, and is hence called *kshar* (perishable). Beyond these three worlds is the realm of *akshar,* also called *daswān dwār* (tenth door) or *sunn* (void). Beyond *akshar,* lies *nihakshar* or *mahā sunn.* Beyond that, on the edge of eternity, is *bhanwar guphā* (rotating cave):

> Ever new is the story of the skies:
> The secrets of *sunn (akshar)* are unfolded.
> I go to *nihakshar* (*i.e. mahā sunn)* and then to *bhanwar guphā,*
> where an entrancing melody is heard.
>
> *Swāmī Shiv Dayāl Singh, Sār Bachan Poetry 6:10.5–6, SBP p.58*

Although the realms of *akshar* and *nihakshar* are called 'imperishable' and 'beyond the imperishable' because they remain intact at the dissolution *(pralaya)* of the worlds below, they are dissolved at a grand dissolution *(mahā pralaya).* Then, only the truly eternal realm, or *sat lok* (true region), and the higher aspects of the Godhead remain.

See also: **akshara** (2.1, 4.1), **kshara** (6.2).

Nirañjan desh, **Nirañjan dhām** (H) *Lit.* region *(desh)* or dwelling *(dhām)* of the unblemished one *(Nirañjan);* the region ruled by *Nirañjan;* specifically, the astral plane or *sahans dal kanwal* (thousand-petalled lotus). Swāmī Shiv Dayāl Singh writes:

> The Master gave it such a cup to drink
> that the humble soul became intoxicated.
> Ardently, it rose to the sky,
> and found *Nirañjan dhām.*
> Ascending further, it opened the door of *bank nāl,*
> and found the *Guru*'s Name.
>
> *Swāmī Shiv Dayāl Singh, Sār Bachan Poetry 36:11.1–3, SBP p.315*

Bank nāl (crooked tunnel) is the 'passageway' leading from *sahans dal kanwal* to the realm above, called *trikuṭī* (*lit.* three peaks).

See also: **Jyot Nirañjan** (4.2).

nuzūl (A/P) *Lit.* descending, alighting; the descent of creation from the Divine; revelation; derived, like many Sufi terms, from a verse in the *Qur'ān* that uses a verb form:

> Has not the time arrived for the believers
> that their hearts in all humility
> should engage in the remembrance of *Allāh* and of the Truth
> which has been revealed *(nazala)* (to them)?
>
> *Qur'ān 57:16, HQSA*

See also: **ta'ayyun**, **tanazzul**.

oka-vusú (AC) *Lit.* paradise; the heavenly paradise of the Paraguayan Avá-Chiripá. In contrast to the earthly paradise *(ywy mará ey),* the *oka-vusú* is located beyond this earth. Pure souls, those without imperfections *(tekó-achy)* are able to enter this celestial paradise. Other souls go to the *ñe'eng-güery* to await rebirth.

See also: **ñe'eng-güery**, **paradise**, **ywy mará ey**.

'olam (He) *Lit.* realm; hence, world, level; hence also, eternity, everlastingness, of old. *'Olam* means 'realm' in the sense of both time (as eternity) and space (as a level or world). Thus, the biblical expression, *me'olam ve'ad 'olam,* commonly translated as 'eternally', literally means 'from realm to realm', and thus 'from eternity to eternity', implying the realm of the spirit that exists outside the human understanding of time and space.

'Olam has also been used in various terms by Jewish mystics to refer to specific inner realms. According to the medieval *Zohar,* the four main realms are, in descending order:

1. *'Olam ha-azilut* (world of emanation) refers to the realm of pure and eternal spirit that lies above all created realms. There, only God exists. This realm is beyond the creation, and is where the divine Unity first bestirs Itself as the 'will to will' to create, the first stirrings of the divine intention to create. Above *'olam ha-azilut* is the concealed or hidden divine Source, the *Ayn-Sof* (limitless, infinite), which is beyond the will (or even the will to will) to emanate or create.

2. *'Olam ha-briah* (world of creation), also called *'olam ha-merkavah* (world of the chariot) in the *Zohar,* is the heavenly region that both early Jewish mystics and later Kabbalists hoped to reach.

3. *'Olam ha-yeẓirah* (world of formation), also described by the Kabbalists as the 'world of divine angels', which refers perhaps to the astral region, a realm of subtle mind and matter.

4. *'Olam ha-'assiah* (world of making, world of actualization), where the subtle forms of *'olam ha-yeẓirah* are crystallized as the physical world, the world of bodies. It is also called the world of *Sama'el,* the devil, since it is here that negative tendencies predominate.

Each of these realms is reflected in the one below, but with its spiritual vibration at a lower intensity – with its divine energy increasingly obscured. In reality, the divine Essence activates and energizes each of the levels equally, but is obscured by layers of decreasing spirituality, so that Its radiance and power seems diminished in the lower realms.

Inclined to interpret the Bible mystically, the Kabbalists appear to have drawn the three latter names of this system from a passage in *Amos:*

> Lo, He that forms *(yoẓer, yeẓirah)* the mountains,
> and creates *(boreh, briah)* the wind,
> and declares to man what is His Thought,
> that makes *('oseh, 'assiah)* the morning darkness,
> and treads upon the high places of the earth:
> The Lord *(Yahweh),* the God of Hosts, is His name.
>
> *Amos 4:13, KB*

In Middle Eastern mysticism, "mountains" are commonly used metaphorically for the higher realms, here related to the process of 'formation *(yeẓirah)*'. All lower realms are formed out of the energy patterns or archetypes of the higher regions, just as physical objects or events first arise as ideas in the minds of those involved.

Likewise, 'creation *(briah)*' is the process that gives rise to breath or "wind *(ruaḥ)*", a word that also means spirit, although the meaning of spirit varies according to the understanding of the user.

The last of the three, 'making *('assiah)*', refers to the creative process that gives rise to the physical universe. In the passage from *Amos,* this is related to the "morning darkness", the period before dawn, understood, perhaps, by the Kabbalists as an allusion to the beginning of physical light.

The conclusion of this extract then identifies *Yahweh* as the "God of Hosts", of all the heavenly powers and regions. He is the one who walks upon the "high places" of the earth – the mountains – another allusion to the higher realms.

There is a significant passage in the *Zohar* that discusses the meaning of "creation *(briah)*" and "making *('assiah)*":

> Rabbi Tanḥum began by quoting: "Thus says God, the Lord who created the heavens, and stretched them forth...."[1] When the Holy One, blessed be He, created His worlds, He created them from Nothing, and brought them into actuality, and made substance out of them; and you find the word *bara* ('He created', hence *briah*) used always of (the) Something *(Yesh)* that He created from Nothing *(Ayin)*, and brought into actuality."
>
> Rav Ḥisda said: "Were the heavens really created from Nothing? Were they not created from the light above?"
>
> Rabbi Tanḥum said: "It is so. The body of the heavens was created from Nothing, but their form from Something substantive.... So you find 'creation' used of the heavens, and subsequently 'making'. 'Creation *(briah)*': "Who created the heavens", that is, from Nothing. 'Making *('assiah)*': "To Him that made the heavens"[2] – from Something substantive, from the light above.
>
> > Zohar Ḥadash (Bereshit) 17b, Midrash ha-Ne'elam, WZ2 pp.572–73

Some Kabbalists used the symbolism of the ten *sefirot* (emanations) to describe the process of creation throughout all realms, the entire process being repeated at progressively lower levels. Each set of *sefirot* are thus a reflection at a lower level of the set above. According to this system, each of the realms of *aẓilut, briah, yeẓirah* and *'assiah* consists of all ten *sefirot* vibrating at decreasing intensities. Thus, for example, looking from the realm of spirit downwards, the lowest *sefirah* of *malkut* in *'olam ha-aẓilut* becomes the top of *'olam ha-briah,* the realm below. The sixteenth-century Moses Cordovero described the creation in this manner:

> The existence stemming from God, extending to the lowest point, is divided into four divisions. The first is *aẓilut* (emanation), namely, the ten emanated *sefirot,* through which spreads the light of *Ayn-Sof* (the Infinite, the transcendent Godhead).
>
> The second is the realm of the throne of glory, called *briah* (creation). The light of the ten *sefirot* spreads through it – called here the *sefirot* of creation. Thus, the light of *Ayn-Sof* clothes itself in them through the medium of emanated light.
>
> The third realm comprises ten bands of angels and the celestial palaces. The light of the ten *sefirot* spreads also through them, through the light of the ten *sefirot* of creation. This realm is called *yeẓirah* (formation), and as the *sefirot* spread through them, they are called the ten *sefirot* of formation....
>
> The fourth realm is the heavens and the entire material world. This is called *'assiah* (actualization), and it includes ten heavens. The light of the *sefirot* spreads through them, and they are called the ten *sefirot* of actualization. Here, holiness pervades physical matter.

> So these four are called *azilut, briah, yezirah, ʻassiah:* emanation, creation, formation, actualization. Their acronym is *ABiYA*. Emanation transcends creation; creation transcends formation; formation transcends actualization. All four divisions are found in each one, since the degrees descend from cause to caused.
>
> *Moses Cordovero, Or Neʻerav, ONC 6:5.52a–b, in EKH pp.48–49*

Other Kabbalists allocated the ten *sefirot* between all four of these realms. The upper three *sefirot* of *Keter, Ḥokhmah* and *Binah* were placed in *azilut;* the next triad in *briah;* the next triad in *yezirah;* and the lowest *sefirah* of *malkut* (kingdom) was placed at the gateway to the physical plane, *ʻassiah.* Originally, however, the system of the *sefirot* was applied solely to the divine activity within *ʻolam ha-azilut* – the realm of pure spirituality.

The general principle of creation as the reflection of higher worlds in the ones below is discussed in the *Zohar:*

> Rabbi Isaac and Rabbi Judah were sitting together one night and studying *Torah.* Rabbi Isaac said to Rabbi Judah: "We have learned that when the Holy One, blessed be He, created the world, He constructed the lower world on the pattern of the upper world. One parallels the other in everything, and this is His glory both above and below."
>
> *Zohar 1:205b, WZ2 p.733*

See also: **ʻālam**, **aṇḍa**, **ʻolam** (2.1), **ʻolam ha-azilut**, **regions**.

1. *Isaiah* 42:5.
2. *Psalm* 136:5.

ʻolam ha-ʻassiah (He) *Lit.* world or realm *(ʻolam)* of making *(ʻassiah);* realm of actualization; a Kabbalist term for the physical universe.

Of the four realms in this terminology, *ʻassiah* is the lowest, where matter predominates and where the creative Power or Word is veiled. It is also described as corresponding to the level of *Sama'el,* the evil angel or the devil.

According to Rabbi Isaac Luria, the realm of *ʻassiah* was originally non-physical and existed at a higher, more subtle level. But after Adam's sin in the garden of Eden, *ʻassiah* fell to the physical level (symbolized by Adam's banishment from the garden). Consequently, the regions higher up also fell by one rung, so to speak. *ʻAssiah* thus became the realm of the *kelipot,* the 'husks', Isaac Luria's term for the coverings of matter that isolate the soul from its source of spiritual light. Although mystics have generally agreed that the *Genesis* story of the garden of Eden is to be interpreted allegorically, different interpreters have ascribed different inner stages to the garden itself.

See also: **'olam**.

'olam ha-aẓilut (He) *Lit.* world or realm *('olam)* of emanation *(aẓilut),* possibly derived from the root *eẓel* (beside, next to), implying 'next to God'. The term *'olam ha-aẓilut* comes from a system of Kabbalist classification that saw the heavenly regions as divided into four main realms. In this system, *aẓilut* is the highest realm, next to (or sometimes including) the Godhead. Over the centuries, different writers and mystics have used the term in slightly different ways.

According to the *Zohar,* for instance, *'olam ha-aẓilut* refers to the first three *sefirot* of *Keter, Ḥokhmah* and *Binah.* But in the fourth-century *Sefer Yeẓirah (Book of Formation), 'olam ha-aẓilut* corresponds to the realm from which the ten *sefirot* first emanated, together with the archetype or 'idea' of the twenty-two letters of the Hebrew alphabet. The ten *sefirot* (emanations) and the twenty-two archetypal letters were considered to comprise the "thirty-two paths to Wisdom" – the thirty-two methods of uniting with the divine Will or Source.

In another Kabbalistic description, originating with Rabbi Isaac Luria, *'olam ha-aẓilut* is also said to correspond to the *Adam Kadmon,* the Primal Man, whose 'body' was used symbolically to describe the configuration and emanation of the *sefirot.*

See also: **'olam**.

'olam ha-ba (He) *Lit.* world *('olam)* to come *(ha-ba);* heaven; a commonly used term in Judaism for life after death. According to the rabbis of the *Talmud,* the souls of the righteous ascended to *'olam ha-ba* where they enjoyed the splendour of God's presence. It is also called the garden of Eden.

Mystically, the term *'olam ha-ba* is also interpreted by the medieval Jewish mystic, Rabbi Abraham Abulafia, to mean the ecstasy of meditation, when the soul experiences the nature of life after death. This relates to death during life or to dying while living during the practice of meditation. Abulafia understood it as corresponding to the prophetic state that was attained by Moses and other prophets, as described in the Bible.

An extension of this is the interpretation of the term that would translate it as "'the world that is coming' – constantly coming, constantly flowing, a timeless dimension of reality available right here and now, if one is receptive".[1]

1. Daniel Matt, *Essential Kabbalah, EKH* p.1.

'olam ha-briah (He) *Lit.* world or realm *('olam)* of creation *(briah);* According to the Kabbalists, *briah* is the region directly below that of *'olam ha-aẓilut* (world of emanation).

In the *Zohar, 'olam ha-briah* is also called *'olam ha-merkavah,* the realm of the chariot or throne of glory, a reference to the inner palaces or seven *hekhalot* regarded as the spiritual goal by Jewish *Hekhalot* mystics of antiquity. It also corresponds to the 'supernal garden of Eden', a metaphor for the spiritual regions, used by the Jewish mystics.

See also: **'olam**.

'olam ha-merkavah (He). *Lit.* world or realm *('olam)* of the chariot *(merkavah).*

See also: **merkavah** (▸2), **'olam ha-briah**.

'olam ha-yeẓirah (He) *Lit.* world *('olam)* of formation *(yeẓirah).* According to Kabbalist cosmogony, *'olam ha-yeẓirah* is the third world or realm below the highest *'olam* of *aẓilut* (world of emanation). In the *Zohar,* it is said to be the abode of the angels, led by *Metatron,* the chief archangel. It probably corresponds to the astral realm in more modern terminology, and is the level directly above the physical world.

See also: **'olam**.

orchard See **gardens, nut orchard** (6.2), **pardes**.

outer darkness Hell; also, the physical universe; an early Judaic and Christian term. The gnostic author of the *Gospel of Philip* explains his understanding of Jesus' use of the term in a passage where he talks of the inner and the outer man; the inner man being the soul, the outer man, the physical body. He is referring to the soul incarnate in this world when he speaks of

> the inner and the outer and what is outside the outer.
>
> *Gospel of Philip 68, NHS20 pp.176–77*

What lies "outside the outer" is the physical universe itself, in which the physical body lives. He then adds:

> Because of this, the Lord (Jesus) called corruption, "the outer darkness": there is not another outside of it.
>
> *Gospel of Philip 68; cf. NHS20 pp.176–77*

The physical universe is the lowest or outermost region of creation: "There is not another outside of it." Corruption is another term commonly used for this world in the sense that everything here is impermanent and changing, tending towards destruction, decay and death. It is also the world where nothing is what it seems to be. Everything is fraudulent, illusory and corrupt.

There is corroboration of this interpretation of "outer darkness" in a number of places in the allied literature of the period. The early-third-century Christian teacher, Origen, suggests that it refers to life in "this coarse and earthly body" beyond "the reach of any light of understanding":

> The 'outer darkness' too is, in my judgment, not to be understood as a place with a murky atmosphere and no light at all, but rather as a description of those who through their immersion in the darkness of deep ignorance have become separated from the reach of any light of understanding.... Perhaps, the 'gloom and darkness' should be taken to mean this coarse and earthly body.
>
> *Origen, On First Principles II:10.8; cf. OFP p.145, WO1 p.144*

This understanding brings the meaning of some of Jesus' parables into sharper focus. In the parable of the wedding feast, when all the poor people are invited to come in off the street, there is one who arrives without a "wedding garment". And not only is he refused entry, but is bound "hand and foot" and "cast ... into outer darkness":

> And when the king came in to see the guests,
> he saw there a man which had not on a wedding garment:
> And he saith unto him,
> "Friend, how camest thou in hither
> not having a wedding garment?"
> And he was speechless.
>
> Then said the king to the servants,
> "Bind him hand and foot, and take him away,
> and cast him into outer darkness;
> There shall be weeping and gnashing of teeth."
>
> *Matthew 22:11–13, KJV*

This seemingly harsh treatment is actually a statement of the reality as described by mystics. The king (the Lord or Master) invites everyone to a wedding feast – to mystic union with the Lord. All people in this world are invited by virtue of their having a human form. The human form itself is an invitation to seek God, something unavailable to other forms of life here. But the garment that all souls require in order to consummate this divine marriage is that of the soul's true spiritual purity. This must be sufficiently in evidence at the time of death, otherwise the soul is sent back into this world, into "outer darkness", where there is a great deal of suffering and misery of all kinds – "There shall be weeping and gnashing of teeth."

The same expression is used by Jesus in the parable of the servants who are entrusted with a certain number of "talents", or sums of money. Two of the servants increase the wealth assigned to them, but the third simply hides it, doing nothing profitable with it. The wealth with which they are entrusted is the human form, given to all human beings – servants of the Lord – at the time of their birth. Some make use of this wealth for its true purpose of seeking God, while others do nothing profitable with it. Hence, the lord says to the servant who makes a profit:

> Well done, good and faithful servant;
> Thou hast been faithful over a few things,
> I will make thee ruler over many things:
> Enter thou into the joy of thy Lord.
>
> *Matthew 25:23, KJV*

He is taken back to God, while concerning the other, he says:

> Cast ye the unprofitable servant into outer darkness:
> there shall be weeping and gnashing of teeth.
>
> *Matthew 25:30, KJV*

He is returned to this world of outer darkness.

It is worth observing that the expression, "the outer darkness", is a favourite of whoever compiled and edited Matthew's gospel. The same parables in Luke and Mark do not use this phrase. It is therefore possible that Jesus never used the term at all, and that the gospel compiler has given these parables an apocalyptic touch of his own.

See also: **hell, Pit, Sheol**.

pad(a) (S/H/Pu) *Lit.* place, abode, home; region, station, stage; state, status, position, rank, office; used extensively in Indian mystic literature to refer to the various realms of creation, almost always with a qualifying adjective, as for instance, *sat pad* (true home), *mukti pad* (the place of liberation), *asat pada* (realm of untruth, this world), *pūraṇ pad* (perfect abode), *uttam pad* (supreme abode) and so on.

paradise A term derived from the Greek, *paradeisos,* in turn derived from the Persian, *paridaiza,* meaning 'an enclosure', hence, 'an enclosed garden'. Thus, in the *Septuagint,* the early Greek translation of the Bible (*c.*300 BCE), the 'garden of Eden' is translated as the 'paradise of delight'.

'Paradise' is used variously in mystic literature. Sometimes, it refers to the heavenly regions to which good souls hope to go after death. At other times, it refers to eternity.

See also: **bihisht-u dūzakh**, **firdaws**, **gardens**, **heavens**, **jahannam**, **mansions**, **oka-vusú**, **pardes**, **sab' samāwāt**, **svarga**, **vaikuṇṭha**, **ywy mará ey**.

paraloka (S), **parlok** (H/Pu) *Lit.* the other *(par)* world *(lok);* the next world, the hereafter, the beyond, heaven; the future state; the life following the present one; a common Indian expression for the hereafter. It is the manner in which this life is lived that determines where the soul goes after death. Speaking metaphorically of man's selfish existence, Nāmdev says:

> O sinner, by highway robbery and others' house-breaking,
> thou fillest thy belly.
> Thou hast practised the ignorance,
> wherewith infamy shall go with thee to the beyond *(parlok).*
>
> *Parmanaṇd, Ādi Granth 1253, MMS*

But Sūrdās puts the other side of the picture. Those who are truly devoted to the Lord are already in "heaven *(parlok)*":

> Seeing the Lord's vision, they are freed of sin,
> and obtain all the things.
> Gazing on the Lord's beauteous face,
> they have nothing to do with any other affair.
> Forsaking the sable and beauteous Lord,
> he who desires anything else is like a leech on the body of a leper.
> Sūrdās, the Lord has taken my soul in His hand,
> and has blessed me with this heaven *(parlok)* of His.
>
> *Sūrdās, Ādi Granth 1253, MMS*

See also: **afterlife**, **al-ākhirah**.

parbrahm (H), **pārbrahm** (Pu) *Lit.* beyond *(par, pār) Brahm;* in the terminology of Swāmī Shiv Dayāl Singh and some other Indian Saints, the realm above *trikuṭī* or *Brahm,* the universal mind; also called *daswān dwār* (tenth door) and *sunn* (void), where the soul becomes free from all coverings of mind and body:

> Two stages below *sat lok* (true realm) is the region of *sunn* or *daswān dwār,* where the *surat* (soul) made its first stop in its descent from *sat lok,* and thence came down into *brahmāṇḍ* and *piṇḍ* (the physical universe).… When the soul reaches this region, after freeing itself from the five *tattvas* (elements), the three *guṇas* (attributes), and the three bodies – gross, subtle and causal, then it becomes fit for *bhakti* (devotion) of the Lord, and from here, with the force of divine love, proceeds to *sat lok,* and then to the *Rādhā Swāmī* region.… In this region also, groups of *haṃsas* (*lit.* swans, pure souls) dwell in bliss and all manner of delights, and live on the water of immortality.… This is also called the *pārbrahm* region.
>
> *Swāmī Shiv Dayāl Singh, Sār Bachan Prose 1:13, SB pp.10–11*

Mahārāj Sāwan Singh describes the experience of the soul in *pārbrahm:*

> *Pārbrahm* is the shrine where the spirit has a bath of purification and becomes immaculate. It has now transcended the three bodies – physical, astral and causal – and is neither black nor white. Its light is now the light of twelve suns. This sounds incredible to us in this world where the light of one sun is enough to dazzle us with its glare. Actually, however, on this material plane the soul is like an incandescent lamp thickly wrapped in several coarse covers, which create an impression of darkness. In *pārbrahm,* the *ātman* (soul) is without any coverings and is, therefore, radiant and effulgent.
>
> *Mahārāj Sāwan Singh, Discourses on Sant Mat 1, DSM p.24*

Pārbrahm has also been used to include *mahā sunn* (great void), a vast expanse of great darkness lying between *daswān dwār* and *bhanwar guphā* (rotating cave), the realm on the edge of eternity. Speaking of *achint dīp* (carefree island) and *sahaj dīp* (peaceful island) as realms within *mahā sunn,* Kabīr writes:

> In *parbrahm,* there is an eight-petalled lotus;
> To the right is one with twelve petals,
>   where *achint (dīp)* is situated;
> To the left is the ten-petalled *sahaj (dīp);*
> Thus are these lotuses.
>
> There are five *Brahms,* encased in eggs,
>   and all five are called *nihacchar* (beyond the imperishable);

Four regions are hidden there,
  where prisoners (souls) dwell, exiled by the Lord.
Kabīr, Shabdāvalī 1, Bhed Bānī 22:20–21, KSS1 p.66

Pārbrahm also has a general sense as transcendent, common in descriptions of God, a usage in which it frequently appears in the *Ādi Granth.*

See also: **pārbrahm** (2.1).

pardah-'i ẓulmat (P) *Lit.* the veil *(pardah)* of darkness *(ẓulmat);* in Sufi terminology, a region of great darkness in which the water of life *(Āb-i Ḥayāt)* is to be found. Some Indian mystics have also described a similar region, generally known as *mahā sunn,* which the soul has to cross on its spiritual journey.

See also: **mahā sunn**.

pardes (P/He) *Lit.* orchard. Like gardens, meadows, pastures and other similar terms, *pardes* was used by Jewish mystics for the inner regions. The word is derived from the old Persian *(paridaiza),* through the Greek (*paradeisos,* paradise), having the original meaning of an enclosed area of land and, hence, an enclosed garden or orchard.

The sole biblical occurrence of *pardes* is in the *Song of Songs,* where the lover is describing the Beloved:

Your shoots form an orchard *(pardes)* of pomegranate trees,
  the rarest essences are yours:
Nard and saffron,
  calamus and cinnamon,
  with all the incense-bearing trees;
Myrrh and aloes,
  with the subtlest odours.
Fountain that makes the gardens fertile,
  well of living water,
  streams flowing down from Lebanon.
Song of Songs 4:13–15, JB

The Beloved is being described using a number of terms that were also used for the creative Power, including the Tree of Life, the Fragrance, the Living Water and so on. Using the symbolism of worldly love, the divine Beloved is being depicted as the creative Power itself.

Indicating the mystical interpretation given to both *pardes* and the *Song of Songs,* the phrase "orchard of pomegranates" was used by Moses Cordovero as the title of his book, *Pardes Rimmonim,* summarizing and methodically explaining the teachings of the Kabbalah.

Pardes, as a term for the spiritual realms traversed during the inner journey, is well known to students of Jewish mysticism through a Talmudic *midrash* (interpretive story) that was used to warn people of the dangers of trying to enter the inner realms unprepared:

> Four men entered the garden *(pardes):* Ben Azzai, Ben Zoma, Aḥer (Abuyah), and Rabbi Akiva.... Ben Azzai glimpsed and died.... Ben Zoma looked and became demented.... Aḥer cut the shoots.... Rabbi Akiva merged in peace.
>
> *Babylonian Talmud, Ḥagigah 14b*

The story relates the experience of four rabbis who set out upon the inner spiritual journey, and is symbolic. The account continues with Rabbi Akiva warning the other sages not to be deceived by a vision of shining marble plates, which may appear to be water; they are an illusion that guards the gate of the sixth palace within, encountered by the soul prior to entering the seventh palace where the Lord in His glory sits on His throne.

Rabbi Akiva is portrayed in the story as having entered in peace and returned in peace. The verse from *Song of Songs* is quoted in relationship to him: "The King has brought me to his chambers,"[1] where the "chambers" are interpreted as the inner realms.

Ben Azzai, it is said, "glimpsed and died", illustrating the line from the *Psalms:* "Precious in the sight of the Lord is the death of His saints."[2] Although it is commonly interpreted to mean that Ben Azzai died a physical death as a result of the intensity of his spiritual experience, it may actually mean that he attained union with God. As many mystics have said, for the soul to attain union with the Divine, it is necessary to 'die while living' – to pass through the experience of death while still living in the body.

The third sage, Ben Zoma, went insane, since he could not integrate the spiritual life with the material. Perhaps he became confused by the vision of the marble plates.

The fourth, Elisha ben Abuyah, who suffered from doubt and confusion, perceived an inner duality in creation and subsequently lost his faith in God. To "cut the shoots" is an obscure expression, variously interpreted. Some say it means that he cut himself off from the one God of his tradition, and thus withered spiritually, like the cut shoots of a plant. His experience is described in the *Sefer Hekhalot (Book of the Chambers),* where it is said that he saw the angel *Metatron* sitting on the throne of glory, surrounded by the divine powers of all nations. Thinking mistakenly that *Metatron* was a power equal to God himself, he declared, "There are two powers in heaven." Looking at the celestial realms from the human level, Elisha made the error of assuming that the power whom he had first encountered in his inner ascent was the Lord of the entire creation. In fact, he was only an intermediate lord or ruler. Elisha did not understand that his experience did not contradict his understanding of one God.

Pardes has also been understood as a symbol of the *Torah,* the Hebrew Bible, which was believed to be the Tree of Life or the way back to God, containing many hints of the true inner teaching. Jewish mystics even used the word *pardes* as a mnemonic for the four levels on which the *Torah* could be understood. As generally understood, P stands for *pshat,* or the literal level. R stands for *remez,* the level of allusion, hint or allegory. D stands for *drash,* the level of interpretation based on legend, symbolism and *aggadah* (Talmudic homilies). S stands for *sod,* the secret or esoteric, mystical meaning of the *Torah* as the Tree of Life, the inner spiritual journey back to God. Only a rare few would ever be taught the highest *(sod)* level of meaning.

Some of the mystics understood the *sod* level to be the path of permutation and combination of the letters of the *Torah* to reveal hidden, holy 'names' of God. Through concentration on these names, they would have ecstatic experiences and inner visions of higher realms, which they described as entering *pardes.*

See also: **gardens**, **Torah** (3.1).

1. *Song of Songs* 1:4.
2. *Psalm* 116:15.

pasture(s) See **gardens**.

pātāl(a), **pātāl(a) lok(a)** (S/H/Pu) *Lit.* place *(lok)* of *pātāla,* the name of one of the seven nether regions, described as being 'below' the earth and populated by serpents *(nāgas)* and demons; sometimes, the collective name of all seven; the subterranean regions; the third of the three worlds *(triloka)* of heaven *(devaloka),* earth *(mṛityuloka)* and the nether worlds *(pātālaloka),* according to Hindu mythology. The seven nether regions, in descending order, as described in the *Vedāntasāra* are:[1]

1.	*Atala*	The abode of *yakshas* (nature spirits).
2.	*Vitala*	The abode of an underworld people.
3.	*Sutala*	The domain of Mahābalī, previously, by virtue of his

		goodness, ruler of the three worlds *(triloka),* but tricked by *Vishṇu* into losing everything but the reign of one of the nether worlds.
4.	*Rasātala*	The abode of the *asuras* (giant demons), *daityas* (demons), *dānavas* (titans).
5.	*Talātala*	The abode of *rākshasas* (ogres).
6.	*Mahātala*	The abode of the *pretas* (ghosts).
7.	*Pātāla*	The abode of the king of cobras, *Vāsuki.*

This list also appears in the *Padma Purāṇa,* though in a slightly different order, and is the largely accepted one. There are other variations, however. The *Shiva Purāṇa* lists eight nether regions, for example, while the *Vishṇu Purāṇa* omits *rasātala* and *talātala,* and includes *nitala* and *gabhastimat.*[2]

Each region is said have its own ruler and to be tens of thousands of *yojans* in depth, a *yojan* being a traditional measure of distance, of uncertain length, but generally reckoned to be between four and eighteen miles. The ruler of *pātāla* is *Vāsuki,* king of cobras. Guru Nānak speaks of hundreds of thousands of *pātālas* (nether regions).[3] The *talas* are subterranean regions and should not be confused with the seven hells *(narakas).* According to one legend, Ṛishi Nārada visited *pātāla* and declared that its splendour far exceeded that of *Indra*'s paradise.[4]

See also: **loka**.

1. Sadānanda, *Vedāntasāra* 2:104.
2. *Vishṇu Purāṇa* 2:5.2.
3. Guru Nānak, *Ādi Granth* 6.
4. *Vishṇu Purāṇa* 2:5.

physical universe See **regions**.

piṇḍ(a) (S/H/Pu) *Lit.* clod, lump; the physical and material universe; the lowest of the regions of mind and matter; the realm of coarse matter; also, the physical body, especially of human beings. Specifically, *piṇḍa* is comprised of the gross and subtle realms of being, up to and including the eye centre, as well as the 'linkage' above that (the 'sky' of the body) leading into the lower astral realm *(aṇḍa). Piṇḍa* includes the gross physical body and the universe perceived through its gross senses, as well as the subtle physical body with its microcosmic centres or *chakras* that permit entry into the subtle physical world. The *chakras* also provide the energy blueprint or matrix by which the gross body is formed and organized. Though actually the lowest centre in *aṇḍa,* the individual human mind (the *antaḥkaraṇa*) is also an integral aspect of *piṇḍa.* Most psychic phenomena are also subtle aspects of *piṇḍa.*

According to Indian mystics, *piṇḍa* is the lowest realm of creation. Here, hidden mind energies are so crystallized as to appear as solid forms – the mind being the architect of all form, motion and change in this world. The underlying creative energy, however, is the vibration of the divine Music, observable in matter through its incessant movement and vibration – from the motions of the stars and planets down to the constant whirling of energies at the subatomic level. Nothing can exist without this primal force within it as its fundamental ground of being.

Physical matter and the physical universe exist by virtue of the *karma* and the minds of all the souls inhabiting this realm. In a very real way, through the interwoven fabric of mind and *karma,* all souls in *piṇḍa* have jointly 'thought' the universe into existence. To each creature, human or otherwise, the world consists of the sensory impressions it receives. Yet these sensory impressions are incommunicable and subjectively experienced entirely within the mind. No person, for example, can ever convey to someone else even his or her experience of the colour red. Likewise, with all other sensory experiences. In fact, the physical universe, so apparently solid and real is only an experience in consciousness, shared by the minds of all its inhabitants, human and otherwise.

All physically incarnate souls are thus 'shareholders' in the physical creation. The shareholding is represented by the *karma* of the individual, and this *karma* consists of the impressions stored within the mind, expressing themselves outwardly as the world each individual feels that it inhabits. The fundamental ground of the physical universe only appears to be matter or substance. Actually, it is one of 'being'. The supreme source of being is the Divine, and everything exists within His Being. Substance or matter is an aspect of being. Life or being does not arise out of matter or substance, matter arises out of being. Physical substance is really only sensory experiences within the mind – the being – of individual creatures.

See also: **aṇḍa**, **chidākāsha** (5.1).

piṇḍī (S/H/Pu) *Lit.* relating to *piṇḍa;* pertaining to the physical universe.

Pit, pit of destruction, pit of fire, pit of ignorance, pit of no forgiveness, pits
The Pit was a common Middle Eastern expression in ancient times, found particularly in Judaism, Christianity, Manichaeism and allied literature. In

the Bible, the Pit usually connotes death in general, which was understood as a kind of hell. It conveys the sense of punishment, and is where the souls of sinners went, while those who were righteous or repentant would be forgiven and saved by God. The Pit (He. *Shaḥat* or *Baur*) was used synonymously with *Sheol,* the abode of the dead in Judaism.

The prophet Isaiah, for example, recounts a song to God by the Israelite King Ḥezekiah after a period of recovery from a serious illness of which he thought he would die. Here, the "Pit" means death:

Lord, my heart will live for You,
my spirit will live for You alone.
You will cure me and give me life,
my suffering will turn to health.

It is You who have kept my soul
from the Pit *(Shaḥat)* of nothingness;
You have thrust all my sins
behind Your back.

For *Sheol* does not praise You,
death does not extol You;
Those who go down to the Pit *(Baur)*
do not go on trusting in Your faithfulness.

The living, the living are the ones who praise You,
as I do today.
Fathers tell their sons
about Your faithfulness.

Isaiah 38:17–19, JB

The term was used by many of the other biblical prophets, as also in the *Psalms:*

Bless *Yahweh,* my soul,
bless His Holy Name, all that is in me!
Bless *Yahweh,* my soul,
and remember all His kindnesses:
in forgiving all your offences,
in curing all your diseases,
in redeeming your life from the Pit *(Shaḥat),*
in crowning you with love and tenderness,
in filling your years with prosperity,
in renewing your youth like an eagle's.

Psalm 103:1–5, JB

In some later Judaic writings, it seems possible from the context that the Pit refers to this world, even to repeated reincarnation, death and rebirth. In places, the term seems to be used with intentional ambiguity, since reincarnation was not always an acceptable doctrine at that time. The fellow disciples of the writer and later followers of the same mystic path would have understood the allusions clearly, while others would have interpreted things according to their own beliefs, saving the writer from persecution, and helping the literature to remain in circulation.

The term is found in the mystic psalms from the Dead Sea Scrolls, documents where all other aspects of the mystic path of the Word are clearly described. Little is known of the writer of these psalms, but they are usually attributed to the *Ẓaddik,* the Teacher of Righteousness, mentioned elsewhere in the Dead Sea Scrolls. Mystics have often written in guarded or metaphorical language because they realized that political or religious authorities might perceive them as a threat to the established order. These psalms were written in turbulent times, and the Teacher of Righteousness did, in the end, meet his death by execution. Writing in guarded metaphorical language was thus a practical necessity rather than a mere literary fancy.

In passages where it is unclear whether he is referring to this world or hell as the "pit", he writes:

> I thank Thee, O Lord,
> for Thou hast placed my soul
> in the bundle of the living;
> And hast hedged me about,
> against all the snares of the Pit.
> *Thanksgiving Hymns X:20–25 (7), CDSS p.257*

And:

> And the gates of hell shall open
> on all the works of vanity;
> And the doors of the Pit shall close
> on the conceivers of wickedness;
> And the everlasting bars shall be bolted
> on all the spirits of naught.
> *Thanksgiving Hymns XI:15–20 (9), CDSS p.260*

But elsewhere in these psalms, the meaning is actually more clearly that of deliverance or redemption from the Pit of this world and its birth and death. In one instance, the writer says that he has already been lifted up from the "pit" to the "everlasting Height". And he speaks explicitly of man, a "creature of clay", being given the "everlasting destiny" of salvation through "Thy

Name", though he has "stood in the realm of wickedness" – meaning this world, not some other hell:

I thank Thee, O Lord,
  for Thou hast redeemed my soul from the Pit;
And from the hell of *Abaddon,*
  Thou hast raised me up to everlasting Height.

I walk on limitless level ground,
  and I know there is hope for him
  whom Thou hast shaped from dust
  for the everlasting Council.
Thou hast cleansed a perverse spirit of great sin
  that it may stand with the host of the holy ones,
  and that it may enter into community
  with the congregation of the sons of heaven.
Thou hast allotted to man an everlasting destiny
  amidst the spirits of knowledge,
  that he may praise Thy Name in a common rejoicing
  and recount Thy marvels before all Thy works.

And yet I, a creature of clay,
  what am I?
Kneaded with water,
  what is my worth and my might?
For I have stood in the realm of wickedness,
  and my lot was with the damned;
The soul of the poor one was carried away
  in the midst of great tribulation.
Miseries of torment dogged my steps,
  while all the snares of the Pit were opened,
  and the lures of wickedness were set up,
  and the nets of the damned (were spread) on the waters;
While all the arrows of the Pit
  flew out without cease,
  and striking, left no hope;
While the rope beat down in judgment,
  and a destiny of wrath fell upon the abandoned,
  and a venting of fury upon the cunning.
It was a time of the wrath of all *Belial* (Satan),
  and the bonds of death tightened without any escape.

Thanksgiving Hymns XI:15–30 (10), CDSS p.261

Another psalm is equally explicit. It is this world that is the "pit of no forgiveness" – where all desires and deeds are recompensed – and from which the devotee seeks salvation through God's mercies:

> I have no fleshly refuge,
>   and Thy servant has no righteous deeds
>   to deliver him from the Pit of no forgiveness.
> But I lean on the abundance of Thy mercies
>   and hope for the greatness of Thy grace;
> That Thou wilt bring salvation to flower
>   and the branch to growth,
>   providing refuge in Thy strength
>   and raising up my heart.
>
> *Thanksgiving Hymns XV:15–20 (15), CDSS p.276*

During the first few centuries CE, there seems to have been a window in which people felt more able to write openly, as in some of the gnostic and other Greek writings, although there was still considerable opposition to esoteric teachings, and many continued to resort to allegory as a means of expressing whatever they wanted to say. In the Manichaean writings, for example, there is little doubt that the pit referred to this world as the realm of birth and death. In a long Parthian hymn concerning the horrors of transmigration, the devotee sends out a plea for help, which is ultimately answered by the Saviour. Here, this world is also described as the "dark valley":

> Who will willingly save me from the pit of destruction,
>   and from the dark valley where all is harshness?
> Where all is anguish and the stab of death.
>
> Helper and friend is there none therein,
>   never to eternity is there safety there.
> It is all full of darkness and fume-filled fog;
> It is all full of wrath and there is no pity there;
> All who enter are pierced by wounds.
>
> *Manichaean Hymns, Huwīdagmān V:1–4, MHCP pp.86–87*

The "wounds" by which all are "pierced" are the sins that no one who takes birth in this world can escape. In another part of this hymn cycle, it is the bodies themselves that are described as the "pits and prisons":

> Who will release me from all the pits and prisons,
>   in which are gathered lusts that are not pleasing? …

Who will lead me beyond rebirths, and free me from them all,
and from all the waves, in which there is no rest?

Manichaean Hymns, Huwīdagmān IVa:1, 5, MHCP pp.80–83

In the Manichaean Chinese texts from Chinese Turkestan, in a section petitioning Jesus for release from the cycle of birth and death, the writer says that he is presently "living in the pit of fire", meaning this world. Consequently, he begs to be liberated from bondage to the "devils and spirits" of the mind and to be taken to the eternal realm:

I petition only that Jesus will have mercy,
and liberate me from the bondage of all devils and spirits.
I am now living in the pit of fire:
quickly guide me into the peace
of the clean and pure land!

Manichaean Hymns, LSMH p.179:35

Mystics who have taught reincarnation have all described this world in a similar manner. The Indian Farīd writes:

The lonesome bride (soul) writhes in the world-well (pit):
she has neither a mate nor a friend.

Farīd, Ādi Granth 794, MMS

And likewise Guru Arjun:

Abandoning the Lord to do aught else:
that is to fall into the well (pit) of vice.
My soul (*man,* mind) is bewitched by the thirst of the Lord's vision,
and my Lord has pulled me out of hell *(narak).*

Guru Arjun, Ādi Granth 1227, MMS

See also: **abyss**, **Gehenna**, **Hadēs**, **hell**, **outer darkness**, **Sheol**.

pitṛilok(a) (S/H), **pitri lok**, **pitar lok** (Pu) *Lit.* realm *(lok)* of the fathers *(pitṛi);* realm of the ancestors; a heavenly realm, lower than paradise where, according to the Hindu tradition, man's ancestors reside.

See also: **pitṛipūjā** (▸2).

pitṛiyān(a) (S/H) *Lit.* path or way *(yāna)* of the fathers *(pitṛi);* way of the ancestors; the *Upanishads* speak of two distinct paths along which the dead are believed to travel after leaving the body. One is the path of the fathers *(pitṛiyāna)* and the other, the path of the gods *(devayāna).* Those practising Vedic rituals, sacrifices, charity, penance and so on, travel the path of the fathers *(pitṛiyāna)* and, according to their good *karma,* go to the heavenly *chandraloka* (realm of the moon), *svarloka* (realm of heaven) or *pitṛiloka* (realm of the ancestors). In the latter case, they are dependent on their descendants for sustenance, through the regular performance of *shrāddha* (offerings of food). Having experienced the fruits of their good deeds, they then return to this world under the further influence of their *karma.*

Those who have followed the way of enlightenment, and have faithfully practised truthfulness and meditation, travel the path of the gods *(devayāna)* and reach *Brahmaloka,* whence there is no return to the world.

Those who have lived badly and are badly tarnished by sins go to one of the lesser hells where they are punished for shorter or longer periods until their sins are expiated. Then they are reborn on earth as outcasts or as animals.[1]

Those who have committed unpardonable sins face eternal damnation and are consigned to the lowest of the hells till the end of time.

It is significant that the *Upanishads,* departing from earlier Vedic ritualism, speak of a higher knowledge leading to liberation, previously unknown to the *Brāhmaṇas.*[2]

See also: **pitṛipūjā** (▸2).

1. *Bṛihadāraṇyaka Upanishad* 6:2.1*ff.; Chhāndogya Upanishad* 5:10.1*ff.*
2. *Bṛihadāraṇyaka Upanishad* 6:2.8; *Chhāndogya Upanishad* 5:3.7.

Pleroma (Gk) *Lit.* a filling up, fullness; fullness of deity, divine fullness. A Greek term referring to a kind of vast created, yet eternal, archetype or blueprint of the spiritual regions or higher *aeons,* postulated by some gnostic schools (especially that of Valentinus) of the early Christian period; often called the 'divine *Pleroma*'.

The concept embodies the creative principle of reflective projection described by many mystics, as in the Hermetic axiom: "As above, so below". It means that all creation takes place by emanation or projection of the higher into the lower. What is found in the lower is a reflection of a more subtle essence and pattern existing in the higher. Lower realms are thus always within the orbit or sphere of the higher and, ultimately, everything is within the orbit of God, nothing being outside of Him. The *Pleroma* is the first and highest eternal blueprint for the remainder of the spiritual creation.

According to this system, the *Pleroma* is the primal emanation of the Lord, consisting of an *ogdoad,* a set of eight pairs of divine entities, together with a similarly composed *decad* (ten such pairs), and a *duodecad* (twelve such pairs). It was thus considered that the *Pleroma* was composed of thirty pairs of divine entities from which the rest of the creation was formed.

There were variants on the basic pattern, however, and in one description of the system, in the *Tripartite Tractate,* only an initial trinity is conceived. This trinity comprises the Father, who originally existed entirely on His own as the supreme One, and His two first emanations – the Son, and a mystic archetype of the Church.

The term is sometimes used in the plural where it refers to the sources or archetypes of particular areas of creation, as in the *Gospel of Truth:*

> Therefore, all the emanations of the Father are *pleromas;*
> And the Root of all His emanations
> is in the One who made them all grow up in Himself.
> He assigned them their destinies.
> Each one is then manifest.
>
> *Gospel of Truth 41, NHS22 pp.114–15*

In the gnostic description of the creative process, something goes wrong, perhaps by divine design (the descriptions vary), and a 'deficiency' or a 'descent' is formed due to the activities of certain powers within the *Pleroma.* Essentially, this 'deficiency' is ruled over by a negative creative force or demiurge who creates a series of lower worlds as copies of the realms within the *Pleroma,* the lowest of these being the world of matter, the physical universe. In these systems, the 'gnostic myth' of the soul's salvation takes the form of the Saviour restoring the 'deficiency' to the *Pleroma:*

> The Son of God, Rheginos, was Son of Man. He embraced them both, possessing the humanity and the divinity, so that on the one hand he might vanquish death through his being Son of God, and that on the other, through the Son of Man, the restoration to the *Pleroma* might occur.
>
> *Treatise on the Resurrection 44, NHS22 pp.148–49*

Different gnostic writers offered variations on the theme, and while certain similarities of principle are evident in relationship to the descriptions of Indian and other mystics, it would be unwise to draw anything but the broadest of parallels. However, it seems clear that the negative power or *Kāl* of some Indian descriptions bears clear resemblances to the demiurge of the gnostic systems, while the role of the Saviour in rescuing the soul from the 'deficiency' parallels that of the *Satguru* of the Indian systems and the *Murshid* or *Pīr* of the Sufis.

See also: **aeons**, **All (the)**, **Totality**.

Prayāg(a) (S/H), **Pirāg** (Pu) *Lit.* a place of sacrifice *(yagya, yajña);* a pilgrimage place; the ancient name of the city, now known as Allahabad, situated on the banks of the confluence of the three rivers, the Ganges, the Yamunā and the now dried up and possibly legendary Sarasvatī. This confluence is considered a holy place, honoured with the title *Tīrtharāja* (king of pilgrimage sites), and understood to have been the sacrificial altar of *Brahmā.* According to Indian mythology, it was here that *Brahmā* prepared his first *ashvamedha yajña* (horse sacrifice) to celebrate the recovery of the lost *Vedas.* Bathing in its waters is said to wash away many sins. Every twelve years, devotees gather at Allahabad from all parts of India for the *Kumbh Melā,* a kind of spiritual festival or fair.

These three rivers and their confluence have been used by mystics as symbols to represent two 'places' in the inner realms – the lower in *sahans dal kanwal* (thousand-petalled lotus) and the higher in the spiritual regions above the level of the universal mind. At these confluences, three streams of creative energy *(iḍā, pingalā* and *sushmanā* or *sukhmanā)* meet, the lower being a reflection of the higher. Speaking of the higher confluence as Prayāg, Beṇī Jī says:

> *Iṛā, pingulā* and *sukhmanā:*
> these three abide in one place.
> Prayāg (Pirāg) is there, where the three streams … meet:
> My mind bathes at that place.
> O Saints, the immaculate Lord abides there:
> going to the *Guru,* some rare one understands this.
>
> *Beṇī Jī, Ādi Granth 974, MMS*

Prayāg is also called *triveṇī* (*lit.* three braids, three rivers).

See also: **triveṇī.**

principality A realm presided over by a prince; mystically, part of a family of metaphors, found especially in Judaic and early Christian mystical writings, drawn from the administration and rule of worldly kingdoms, and used to describe the administration of the inner hierarchy of creation. All regions in creation have rulers or centres of power, as does – by reflection – the administration of this world. Esoterically, therefore, a principality is a realm or region governed by an appropriate power, ruler or *archon.*

Paul, for example, in his letter to the Colossians, says that "all things created, that are in heaven and that are in earth, visible and invisible", have been created by the Son, by which he means the Word or *Logos.* And among these created things are the many powers, principalities, thrones, dominions and so on of this and the higher worlds:

By him (the Son) were all things created, that are in heaven,
and that are in earth, visible and invisible,
whether they be thrones or dominions,
or principalities or powers:
All things were created by him and for him:
And he is before all things,
and by him all things consist.

Colossians 1:16–17, KJV

Similarly, in *Ephesians,* he writes that God has

set him (Jesus) at His own right hand in the heavenly places,
far above all principality and power,
and might and dominion, and every name that is named,
not only in this world,
but also in that which is to come.

Ephesians 1:20–21, KJV

Likewise in the *Acts of John,* John speaks of these powers, principalities and authorities as all being subject to God:

Upon You who are the only God do I call …
to whom the power of all principalities is subjected,
to whom all authority bows.

Acts of John 79; cf. ANT p.248

See also: **archon** (4.2), **dominions**, **powers** (4.2), **sovereignty**.

puhup dvīp, **puhup dīp** (H) *Lit.* flower *(puhup)* island *(dvīp);* one of the realms of creation as described by Dariyā Sāhib, Kabīr and other mystics. In this context, *dīp* is a corruption of *dvīp* meaning island, not *dīp* meaning a lamp or lighthouse. Descriptions of *puhup dvīp* identify it as either *daswān dwār* (tenth door) or *bhanwar guphā* (rotating cave), regions beyond those of the mind. Kabīr writes:

In its upward flight, encompassed by the sound of joy,
the soul enters *puhup dīp.*
Bound by the strings of love,
it goes forward and takes hold of the Saint.

Kabīr, Shabdāvalī 2, Mangal 6:4, KSS2 p.92

With deep affection inspired by love,
the bride-soul advances.
Entering *puhup dīp,*
it merges into the all-encompassing fragrance.

Kabīr, Shabdāvalī 2, Nirakh Prabodh kī Ramainī 1:4, KSS2 p.108

From the land of mortals *(mirt lok),*
pure souls (*haṃsas, lit.* swans) ascend;
To *puhup dīp,* they proceed.
In *amb dīp* (island of water, *mānsarovar*), they remember (their real self):
then only will they see that (eternal) land.

Kabīr, Shabdāvalī 1, Bhed Bānī 27:2, KSS1 pp.70–71

See also: **dvīpa**.

qudrah (A), **qudrat** (P/Pu) *Lit.* omnipotence, power, authority, strength, potency, capacity; God's omnipotent power and grandeur; hence, the creation or nature as a display of divine power; the wonderful character and nature of creation. The term has been commonly used by mystics to express the grandeur and omnipotence of God:

Infinite is the Creator
who manifests Himself through His omnipotence *(qudrat):*
The created one has no power before Him.
Creating the creatures, He Himself reaches (gives) them sustenance:
His writ runs over all.

Guru Nānak, Ādi Granth 1042, MMS

Firstly God created light and then, by His omnipotence *(qudrat),*
made all the mortals.
From the one Light has welled up the entire universe:
then who is good and who is bad?

Kabīr, Ādi Granth 1349, MMS

Qudrah is also a name for the archangel *'Izrā'īl,* the angel of death, for it is said that none can resist him. The name is derived from his epithet, 'Captain of the divine Decree *(qaḍā')*'.

See also: **qaḍā'** (6.3), **qadar** (6.3).

realm(s) See **regions**.

region of commixture See **regions**.

region(s) A large, indefinite expanse of space, often geographical; mystically, a term commonly used for the realms or regions of the creation, including the inner regions or heavens, as well as the physical universe.

According to a great many mystics, God is the one supreme power, and everything else is formed from Him as a projection or emanation. In the hierarchy of creation, everything below is a reflection of what lies above or deeper within. Similarly, what is above is contained in what is below. The Lord is within everything, and everything is actually His play, His show, His projection or emanation. He is enfolded within everything; He is what gives it existence. From His point of view the creation is a simple and completely ordered affair. It is simply the ramifications of one creative Power. From the point of view of a soul within the creation, it is a multilevel, multidimensional, intricately complex, interwoven affair that is fundamentally beyond comprehension.

Mystics of all ages and cultures have said that there are other regions in the creation in addition to the physical universe perceived by the five human senses. Most religions have preserved this teaching, though normally in a general and unspecific fashion, sometimes mythological. Probably all religions, for example, speak of both heaven and hell, although their location is usually unspecified.

Mystics say that everything lies within man. There is a Sufi saying: "The universe is a great Man, and the Man is a little universe *(al-'ālamu insānun kabīrun wa-al-insānu 'ālamun saghīrun)*."[1] Man is the epitome or microcosm of creation. He is a unit of 'being', so to speak, in the great Being of God, and in this unit of being the entire creation is reflected and may therefore be contacted. Indeed, since God is pure Being, the creation itself, including the physical universe, is comprised of being, rather than substance. But since it requires some degree of mystical perception to understand how everything can exist within oneself, mystic teachings have commonly become distorted in the popular and religious mind.

The more outward the tendencies of an individual's mind, then the more difficult it will be for him or her to comprehend that vast realms or planes of creation are accessible to one who focuses his attention within himself. It is not surprising, therefore, that in many religions of the world, the heavens have been described as if they existed in concentric, physical spheres, around the earth, stretching out among the stars. The idea is possibly Greek in origin, but is encountered in gnosticism, in early Christianity and Islam, as well as in Indian sacred literature and religious belief. It is also to be found in Zoroastrian and Judaic belief of ancient times.

The situation is further confounded by the fact that mystics must necessarily describe the inner regions by means of physical language. Hence, the realms or planes that are crossed as the soul leaves the body have been called the regions of the moon, and the nature of the inner light encountered in these realms has been likened to that of the stars, the sun and the moon. These regions have hence been called the star, the sun and the moon regions. But this has nothing to do with the outer stars, the outer sun or the outer moon, other than that of some resemblance in the character of the light seen there. It is simply that the inner realms are regions of light and sound, experienced mentally and spiritually, and hence the only way to describe them is by reference to the lights and sounds of the physical universe.

The physical universe itself is described as the realm or region of dense matter and crystallized physical forms lying at the foot of creation, where mind in its grossest form is the predominant power. However, the mind here remains largely unrecognized, concealed within the forms of physical matter. It is the realm in which the soul, under the influence of the mind's attractions and tendencies, takes birth in successive bodies, together with corresponding destinies, both of which accurately reflect the character of the individual physical mind. The material universe is often referred to by early Middle Eastern mystics, including Jesus, as the prison and the dungeon, as well as the outer darkness, the Pit and even hell.

Immediately 'above' the physical universe – 'above' in consciousness or being, not space – lies the astral realm or region. It is a world of the greater mind – beguiling, fascinating and mostly blissful. The heavens that are the object of most religious aspiration are located here. It is a region of great subtlety of mind and mental energies when compared to the physical universe. Here, the inclinations and subtle desires of the mind are immediately manifested as astral forms. The subtle, materio-mental energies of the astral region projected from above, act as blueprints for the physical universe.

There are degrees of subtlety and purity within the astral realm, and souls automatically find their own level, according to their own mental propensities. The lowest subastral areas include the hells described by mystics and by many religions. It is here that the hellish tendencies that dominate individuals during their lifetime become a subtle reality for them, as in dreams and nightmares. Similarly, purer minds find a place in an astral heaven. After some time, souls again take birth in the physical universe, according to the physical attachments, tendencies and entanglements of their minds.

Above the astral region lies the causal realm, the highest region of the greater mind, the region of the universal mind, the source of the mind. It is the origin of all illusion – the complex web of diversity, multiplicity and the seeming causality spun by the universal mind out of the oneness of the creative Power. The causal region is a blissfully intoxicating realm comprising the finest mental essences or energies, these being the seed or blueprint forms of time, space, causation and duality as experienced in dense, crystallized manifestation in the physical universe.

The physical, astral and causal regions have been depicted in various ways in the world's mystical traditions. In Vedantic descriptions, they are known as *sthūl* (gross – physical), *sūkshma* (subtle – astral) and *kāraṇ* (causal). In Buddhism, the physical universe is *kāmaloka,* the realm *(loka)* of desire *(kāma),* the field of the five senses. The plane of invisible or subtle forms is known as *rūpaloka* (world of form). Above that is *arūpaloka,* the formless world.

These three regions or realms also constitute one interpretation of the Indian term, *triloka* (three realms). This expression is found in the Manichaean Chinese texts from Chinese Turkestan, which use Indian, Judaic, Christian, Greek, Chinese and Zoroastrian terminology. In one passage, the disciple prays to the Master to release souls from the "sea of birth and death" who are "scattered in the three realms":

> All the hindered or unhindered bodies
> and (light)-natures (souls)
> have long been in misery, sunk into the sea of birth and death,
> their limbs and articulations scattered in the three realms.
> Pray gather and restore them,
> to soar above the myriad things.
>
> Never again cut them off
> from the stream of the right Law (the Word);
> Never again throw them into the devils' mouths;
> But bestow great opportunity and compassionate power,
> and, pray, reanimate the universally suffering light-natures.
>
> *Manichaean Hymns; cf. LSMH p.180:52–53*

These "three realms" are the Vedantic or Buddhist *triloka,* for while within these regions, souls remain prone to birth and death. The "myriad things", the ten thousand things *(wàn wù)* of Taoism, is a specific reference to the multiplicity that characterizes these realms. The greater mind takes the oneness of the Word and divides it into time, space, duality, causation and all the ten thousand things. In Indian terminology, the illusion thus created is called *māyā.*

The three worlds, vast as they may be, are small by comparison with what lies beyond them. Above the realms of the mind are regions of more refined spirituality, where the soul knows itself as pure soul, untrammelled by the coverings of the mind, beyond the reach of *karma,* birth and death. Above that lies the purely spiritual and eternal region of God, which has been given many names at different times. This is the origin and true home of the soul.

In early Christian gnostic terminology, the astral and causal realms were sometimes described as the 'regions of the midst', the 'way of the midst', the 'region of commixture', the 'region of righteousness (spirituality) which is mixed', and so on, since they are essentially regions where mind and spirit are mixed. But references are generally few because such details were usually kept secret, given only to initiates of those schools who taught about them.

The writer of the *Pistis Sophia* has no such inhibitions, however, and at one place in this narrative, Mary Magdalene asks Jesus, "Who compels men until they commit sin?" It is a good question, and Jesus explains that a human being is comprised of the creative "Power", the "soul", and the "counterfeit spirit" (the mind), all three being bound together in a physical body. The "soul," he says, is either dragged down by the "counterfeit spirit" or upwards by the Word. Of these three elements in human constitution, Jesus says:

> Each one of them perceives according to its nature. The Power perceives in order to seek the light of the Height. The soul, on the other hand, perceives in order to seek the region of righteousness which is mixed, which is the region of commixture. The counterfeit spirit, however, seeks all evil and desires and all sins. The body does not itself perceive anything, unless its material substance receives power (from the soul and mind).
>
> *Pistis Sophia 282:111; cf. PS pp.564–65, PSGG p.235*

He says that the soul, associated with the mind, yearns only for the more spiritual atmosphere of the "region of righteousness which is mixed" even though they are still within the domain of the negative power. But the "counterfeit spirit … seeks all evil and desires and all sins". It is only interested in the body and the things of this world.

At other places in the *Pistis Sophia,* the writer (in the name of Jesus) speaks of the "region of the *archons* of the way of the midst".[2] From the context, it is clear that these regions are those through which the soul passes on its upward ascent, and where the debt of sins has not yet been paid off.

There are many places in mystic literature where the inner heavenly regions are described, the idea being to inspire the soul to relinquish attachment to this world and strive to reach the higher regions of the spirit. In one of the Manichaean texts, for instance, translated from the Parthian, and unfortunately full of lacunae, the writer describes the beauty and joy of eternity, and of the souls who dwell there. The description employs allusion, analogy and inference, since these realms and experiences are literally out of this world, indescribable in mortal language:

Their fragrant garlands are sacred and immortal:
  their bodies are full of living pure drops.
All with one mind praise one another:
  they bless one another with living blessings,
  and become blessed forevermore.

In my mind, when I recalled this place,
  I wept (inwardly) in (silent) yearning, saying:
"Who will save me from the terrors and fears of this world?
  Who will take me up to that happy realm,
  so that joy shall be mine,
  (abiding) in union with all who dwell there?"

Manichaean Hymns, Huwīdagmān Vc:1–4; cf. MHCP pp.92–93, ML p.85

And:

All their dwelling places are magnificent …
  for they are happy in the Light and know no pain.
All who enter there, stay for eternity,
  neither blows nor torture ever come upon them.
The garments which they wear, none has made by hand.
[They are ever clean and bright;]
  nothing of the earth is in them,
  (*lit.* no ants are in them)….
Their verdant garlands never fade,
  and they are wreathed brightly, in numberless colours.
Heaviness and weariness do not exist in their bodies,
  and paralysis does not affect any of their limbs.
Heavy sleep never overtakes their souls,
  and deceptive dreams and delusions are unknown among them….
Hunger and anguish are not known in that land….

The waters of all its lakes give out a wondrous fragrance.
Floods and drowning are never known among them….
Their walk is quicker by far than lightning.
In the bodies they possess, there is no sickness….
Fear and terror do not exist in those places,
  and … in those lands there is no destruction….
Within and without, it is full of brightness.
All the gardens give out fragrance, …
  stones and thorns are never found there….

Everyone who ascends up to their (own true) land,
and who has that experience,
will praise His manifestation (His creative Power),
lauded and beneficent.

None is among them who has a dark shadow:
all the bodies and forms in that land are radiant.
Precious are they, [with forms that are free from injury]:
feebleness and old age do not affect their limbs.
They are joyous, uttering wonderful praises:
they continually do reverence to the exalted and beneficent One.
All is filled with happiness and sweet delightful song....
The dwellings are all splendid, and fear is unknown therein....

The barking of dogs, the call of birds, confusing and
troublesome evil howling – they are not heard in that land.
From all darkness and fog, [they are completely free] ...
there is nothing of that sort within those pure abodes.
Full of light is their living self (soul);
Ever in gladness and purity loving each other,
they are very beautiful....
No living self (soul) dies among them.

Manichaean Hymns, Huwīdagmān I:6ff.; cf. MHCP pp.66–77, ML pp.81–82

Likewise, the fourth-century Christian, generally known as Aphrahat the Persian sage, whose writings were well known in the Syriac language of Eastern Christianity, writes inspiringly of the "mansions of the saints", the "saints" being the devotees of early Christianity:

In that place they shall forget this world.
There they have no want,
and they shall love one another with an abundant love.
In their bodies there shall be no heaviness,
and lightly shall they fly "as doves to their windows".[3]
In their thoughts, they shall not remember wickedness at all,
nor shall anything of uncleanness arise in their heart.
In that place there shall be no natural desire,
for there they shall be weaned from all appetites.
There shall not arise in their heart anger or lasciviousness,
also they shall remove from them all things that engender sins.
Fervent in their heart will be the love of each other,
and hatred will not be fixed within them at all.

They shall have no need there to build houses,
  for they shall abide in light, in the mansions of the saints.
They shall have no need of woven raiment,
  for they shall be clothed in eternal light.
They shall have no need of food,
  for they shall recline at His table and be nurtured forever.
The air of that region is pleasant and glorious,
  and its light shines out, and is goodly and gladsome.
Planted there are beautiful trees,
  whose fruits fail not, and whose leaves fall not.
Their boughs are glorious, their perfume delightful,
  and of their taste no soul shall grow weary forever.
Spacious is the region, nor is it limited:
  yet its inhabitants shall see its distance
  even as that which is near.
There the inheritance shall not be divided,
  and no man shall say to his fellow:
  "This is mine and that is thine."
They shall not be bound there in the desire of covetousness,
  nor shall they go astray there concerning recollection (of God).
There a man shall not love his neighbour with special reverence,
  but abundantly shall they all love one another,
  after one fashion.
They shall not marry wives there, nor shall they beget children,
  nor shall there the male be distinguished from the female;
But all shall be sons of their Father who is in heaven,
  as the prophet said:
"Is there not one Father of us all?
Is there not one God who created us?"[4]

Aphrahat the Persian Sage, Demonstrations XXII:12, HEDA pp.405–6

See also: **'ālam**, **dwelling place** (2.1), **dwellings**, **heavens**, **loka**, **mansions**, **mountains**, **'olam**, **paradise**.

1. In R.A. Nicholson, *Commentary on Maśnavī* IV:521 (heading), *MJR4* p.301, *MJR8* p.138.
2. *e.g. Pistis Sophia* 113, *PSGG* p.244.
3. *Isaiah* 60:8.
4. *Malachi* 2:10.

regions of the midst See **regions**.

room(s) Rooms, chambers, bedchambers and particularly bridal chambers are common expressions for the inner realms, especially in biblical and ancient Middle Eastern texts, as in the biblical book of the prophet Amos:

> It is He (God)
> that builds His upper chambers in the heavens,
> and has founded His stairway in the earth.
>
> *Amos 9:6, KB*

Similarly, in the *Song of Songs,* the soul – referring to the divine Beloved as the "King" – says that she has been taken into the King's "rooms":

> The King has taken me into His rooms.
>
> *Song of Songs 1:4, JB*

Likewise, she speaks of her love and yearning as a "perfume" that reaches the "room" of the "King". "Nard" is the aromatic herb, spikenard:

> While the King rests in his own room,
> my nard yields its perfume.
>
> *Song of Songs 1:12, JB*

The Christian mystic, Bernard of Clairvaux comments on this passage:

> The bedroom of the King is to be sought in the mystery of divine contemplation.
>
> *Bernard of Clairvaux, On the Song of Songs 23:9, WBC2 p.33*

Since the Christian gospels contain much that is a literalization and externalization of mystic allegory, it is possible that the last supper, which Jesus is said to have eaten with his disciples in an "upper room", was actually meant mystically. At this supper, the disciples were fed with the Bread of Life, the Living Wine and the Living Water – all terms used for the Word of God – in the inner realms, in the "large upper room". Jesus, it may be recalled, according to the story told in Mark, tells two of his disciples to go to a certain house, and prepare it for their Passover meal. Jesus says:

> And he will shew you a large upper room
> furnished and prepared:
> There make ready for us.
>
> *Mark 14:15, KJV*

See also: **bride chambers** (▸2), **Bridegroom** (▸2).

rukmiṇī nāl, rukmiṇī surang (H) *Lit.* bright or radiant *(rukmiṇī)* tunnel *(nāl, surang);* by extension, *rukmiṇī* also means 'adorned with gold', being derived from *rukma* ('what is bright or radiant', hence, an ornament of gold); *Rukmiṇī* is also the name of Kṛishṇa's wife.

Rukmiṇī nāl and *rukmiṇī surang* are terms for a tunnel, passageway or valve lying between *mahā sunn* (great void, great darkness) and *bhanwar guphā* (rotating cave), such terms being used metaphorically for places of spiritual contraction in which all the energies of the soul have to be focused and concentrated with great love in order to proceed to the next higher plane.

In a poem describing the inner realms, Swāmī Shiv Dayāl Singh indicates that this 'tunnel' is encountered after the soul has risen above *trikuṭī* (*lit.* three peaks, the highest realm of the mind), bathed in the 'lake' of *mānsarovar,* crossed the realm of *daswān dwār* (tenth door), and been guided through the region of great darkness, the *mahā sunn.* He continues:

> The soul then made ready for the fourth stage.
> Catching the Sound,
> it crossed the pass above the *haṃsnī nāl,*
> and entered the *rukmiṇī nāl.*
> It beheld an impressive passageway,
> seeing which the *surat* (power to hear)
> and the *nirat* (power to see) were both reassured
> (to find an upward path).
> On the right side there were bright islands,
> and on the left were innumerable continents
> covered with palaces made of pearls,
> their top stories made of rubies,
> and studded with emeralds and diamonds.
> This innermost secret I have described:
> only the bold spirit (*lit.* soldier-Saint) can experience it.
> The soul then beheld the mountain of *bhanwar guphā,*
> approaching which it heard the sound of *sohang.*
>
> *Swāmī Shiv Dayāl Singh, Sār Bachan Poetry 26:4.1–7, SBP p.228*

See also: **haṃsnī nāl.**

sab' samāwāt A/P), **sab'a samāwāt** (A) *Lit.* seven *(sab, sab'a)* heights *(samāwāt);* the seven skies, the seven heavens, the seven firmaments. According to the *Qur'ān,* there are seven heavens, one above the other:

> He who created the seven heavens *(sab'a samāwāt)*
> one above another *(ṭibāqan):*

No want of proportion wilt thou see
in the creation of the Most Gracious.
So turn thy vision (look) again:
seest thou any flaw?

Qur'ān 67:3, HQSA

It is He who has created for you
all things that are on earth;
Then He turned to the heaven
and made them into seven firmaments *(sab'a samāwāt).*
And of all things He has perfect knowledge.

Qur'ān 2:29; cf. AYA

The *Qur'ān* does not say whether these seven heavens are to be understood spiritually or physically, and commentators have interpreted them both ways. Interpreted as external, the seven heavens are the spheres of the five planets (wandering stars) known to ancient astronomy, plus the sun and the moon, all regarded as part of a geocentric universe. Beyond these lay the sphere of the fixed stars, also known as God's footstool *(al-kursī),* and the black backdrop to all the heavenly spheres, the empyrean, also called God's throne *(al-'arsh).* But it is only the most literal interpretations that actually consider the seven heavens to be physically concentric with the earth.

Mystically, these spheres are taken as symbols of the inner reality and the hierarchy of creation, with the empyrean symbolizing the divine ocean of Being. The seven heavens, along with the two further heavens, make up what are also referred to in Islam as the nine heavens (A. *tis' samāwāt,* P. *nuh sipihr*).

The *Qur'ān* also mentions fourteen strata *(chahārdah ṭabaq):* seven heavens and seven nether worlds, "of the earth", all arrayed around the divine "Command" or Word:

Allāh is He who created the seven firmaments *(sab'a samāwāt),*
and of the earth a similar number.
Through the midst of them (all) descends His Command:
That you may know that *Allāh* has power over all things,
and that *Allāh* comprehends all things in (His) knowledge.

Qur'ān 65:12; cf. AYA

This principle of reflection and infusion of the higher in the lower through the stages of reality is an integral part of Sufi teaching. Thus, each of the subtle centres in the body *(laṭā'if)* is regarded as a reflection of one of the levels of heaven.

See also: **heavens**, **al-jannah**, **ṭabaq**, **T'iēn**.

sahaj achint, **sahaj dvīp** (H), **sahaj dīp** (H/Pu) *Lit.* carefree *(achint)* peace *(sahaj)* or island *(dvīp)* of peace *(sahaj);* a realm lying above *daswān dwār* (tenth door) within *mahā sunn,* the great 'void' or darkness. This realm is described by Kabīr in a poem in which he gives a complete description of all the *chakras* and centres, both higher and lower, that lie within the human body:

> The abyss of *mahā sunn* is like an ocean, perilous and awesome:
> without a perfect Master no one can find a way through.
> Tigers, lions and snakes abound there, attacking (the passers-by).
> There is the realm of *sahaj achint.*
>
> *Kabīr, Shabdāvalī 1, Bhed Bānī 22:19, KSS1 p.66*

Dariyā Sāhib of Bihar also speaks of a region he calls *sahaj dvīp,* which possibly refers to the same realm,[1] though he is not explicit.

See also: **aṇḍa**, **dvīpa**.

1. See *DSSB* p.92 (n.4).

sahans dal kanwal (H/Pu), **sahasra dal(a) kamal(a)** (S/H) *Lit.* thousand *(sahans, sahasra)* -petalled *(dal)* lotus *(kamal, kanwal);* an appellation of the first spiritual region or astral plane lying above the six *chakras* of *piṇḍa;* so named because of its central radiance, surrounded by one thousand unimaginably beautiful and transcendent lights; also called *sahasrāra* (thousand-spoked).

Sahans dal kanwal is the central powerhouse and energy crossroads of the astral level of consciousness, the origins of whose thousand lights or energies can be traced from the divine Source. Beginning from above, in the undifferentiated oneness of *anāmī desh,* the highest region of all, the *Shabd* (Word) moves downward in its creative urge, becoming increasingly divided. From *Anāmī* flow the three energy currents, powers or divisions of *Sat Purush* (true Being), *ādi Shabd* (primal Word) and *Akshar Purush* (imperishable Being). These three then flow out into the higher confines of *brahmāṇḍa,* thence to the foot of the three prominences or mountains *(Meru, Sumeru* and *Kailāsh)* whose shining peaks give this region its name – *trikuṭī.*

Some Indian mystics[1] have called the controlling power or lord of *trikuṭī, Kāl* or *Brahm,* with his receptive counterpart of *māyā,* the power of concealment, illusion and projection into lower planes. At this cosmic stage, *māyā* appears to be undivided, ineffably and deceptively beautiful. But from then on, *māyā* begins to multiply, imposing forms, divisions and names upon the *Shabd,* slowly diffusing and hiding it, until the isolation from its origin is complete.

In *trikuṭī,* the first three currents are joined by these last two, *Kāl* and *māyā,* making five in all. Through the garment of illusion that *māyā* begins to weave around them, creating the first appearances of time, space and causation, a sense of separateness and division is increasingly felt, and the three primal currents assume the three attributes or *guṇas* of creation, preservation and dissolution.

These eight currents in *trikuṭī* (the primal three, plus *Kāl, māyā* and the three *guṇas*) now give rise to, or diversify into, the subtlest or seed form of the five *tattvas* (elemental conditions of matter). These highly subtle forms of the *tattvas* are like seeds, for they possess within them the unexpressed potential of all that lies below in the creative hierarchy. The first five currents (the primal three, plus *Kāl* and *māyā*) interacting with the five *tattvas* also result in the twenty-five *prakṛitis,* subtle mind currents or energies that are ultimately reflected in the physical form.

Each of the eight currents in *trikuṭī* attracts and absorbs the subtle forms of the five *tattvas,* making forty energy currents in all. Like spinning flames of energy or petals of a flower chalice, they assume a lotus-like shape.

The forty energy currents interacting on each of the twenty-five *prakṛitis,* each carrying its own attributes, colours and sounds – all throbbing and glowing with astral effulgence and energy – make, in all, one thousand flame-shaped currents. This, with one central flame, constitutes what is called *sahans dal kanwal.*

In simple terms, it can be said that the thousand energy currents comprising *sahans dal kanwal* come into being from the intermingling and interaction of the more primal or subtle energy currents situated at higher or more inward levels. It is all one Power – the *Shabd* – but by the time it has reached *sahans dal kanwal,* it has diversified into one thousand primary currents or flames.

This energy crossroads is the great powerhouse of the astral world, sometimes described as a mountain of light. Each of these flame-shaped jets is the energy or power responsible for the existence of a portion of the physical plane or *piṇḍa,* drawing its life from that celestial source. Astral energies on earth, however, are very weak dilutions of these thousand streams of power, far less subtle and volatile, and with a greatly limited range.

Through the subastral regions below *sahans dal kanwal,* these thousand currents continue to act separately and in innumerable permutations and combinations, slowly diminishing in effulgence and energy as they interact, but nevertheless presenting a spectacle of breathtaking beguilement and splendour, vividly dancing and whirling in endless displays.

As matter condenses further and further on them as they move, they slowly stultify and sink until they approach and are drawn down into the physical universe of *piṇḍa.* Like a grand and tragic opera drawing to its close, the eternal music of the Life Stream, the *Shabd,* is hushed. The diffused and muted currents now enter the sphere of the human mind and body, or even the minds and bodies of lower creatures.

Just as an electric current, after it leaves the main powerhouse, has to be stepped down at transforming stations so that it can be used for domestic consumption, so does the great main current of the *Shabd* undergo a change at these localities, becoming clothed in the coverings and crystallizations of the various regions through which it passes.

Through the outward tendencies of the creative process, the mind has so effectively associated the *Shabd* with time, space, relativity, *māyā,* causation, creation, preservation, destruction, the pairs of opposites, and all the attributes of the human mind and body, that the encumbered soul (the *jīva*) cannot find its way back through the mass of subtle and intricate threads of relationship that bind it to the physical plane. Only a perfect and unencumbered soul, straight from the soul's own country, the eternal realm of *sach khaṇḍ* (true region), can cut through these threads, restoring the *jīva*'s inner sight and hearing, permitting it to find its way back to its original home.

Looking upward, from the human point of view, an aspirant reaches *sahans dal kanwal* after leaving the body and crossing the inner starry sky, the sun and the moon regions, and entering the astral realm. At the centre of this region, as its central powerhouse, lies *sahans dal kanwal.*

This centre is also called the Thousand-headed Serpent *(Shesha Nāga)* on whose head, according to Hindu mythology, the whole world rests, a symbolic allusion to the fact that all lower creation is sustained and administered from here.

The light of *sahans dal kanwal* is like that of a flame *(jyoti),* hence the deity of this region, *Nirañjan,* is called *jyoti-svarūp Bhagvān* (flame-shaped Lord) or *Jyoti Nirañjan.* The melody of the Sound Current is heard in this region like that of a deep resounding bell.

Many Saints and yogis have written of this region. Kabīr calls it *sahas dal kanwal:*

> Hear the sound of the gong and conch:
> The divine Music flows out ceaselessly
> from the refulgent thousand-petalled lotus *(sahas dal kanwal).*
> There behold the creator (of all below).
>
> *Kabīr, Shabdāvalī 1, Bhed Bānī 22:12, KSS1 p.66*

Swāmī Shiv Dayāl Singh frequently speaks of it, calling it *sahans dal kanwal.* To reach this region, he says, the attention must first be focused at the eye centre, and then taken up:

I will focus the attention at the eye centre,
and enter *sahans dal kanwal.*
Swāmī Shiv Dayāl Singh, Sār Bachan Poetry 8:6.14, SBP p.78

After *sahans dal kanwal,* the soul rises to *trikuṭī* (*lit.* three peaks, the highest realm of the mind) and beyond, to *daswān dwār* (tenth door) or *sunn* (void):

From *sahans dal kanwal* to *trikuṭī,* I ascended,
and then opened the tenth door *(daswān dwār).*
Beyond the region of *sunn,* situated in utter darkness,
is the realm of *mahā sunn* (great void), crossing which,
I have seen the radiant glory of *bhanwar guphā* (rotating cave).
Swāmī Shiv Dayāl Singh, Sār Bachan Poetry 6:21.21–22, SBP pp.67–68

Dariyā Sāhib calls this centre the *sahasra kamal,* and speaks of the bliss and "great delight" of the souls who witness it:

There, you will find a resounding melody
emanating from the primal Word *(mūl Shabd).*
Merge yourself into that melody.
There, the thousand-petalled lotus *(sahasra kamal)* blooms,
but the primal Source is above this unutterable lotus.
From the thousand-petalled lotus,
there arises a unique fragrance,
enjoying which, souls are rapt in great delight.
Dariyā Sāhib, Dariyā Sāgar, Chaupaī 168–70, DG2 p.17; cf. DSSB p.284

See also: **sahasrāra** (5.1).

1. *i.e.* Swāmī Shiv Dayāl Singh and his successors.

samā', al- (A/P) (pl. *samāwāt*) *Lit.* the highest part, the uppermost part; hence, sky, firmament, heaven; also, in Arabic, a height and, thus, roof. In the *Qur'ān,* it means the physical heavens:

(It is He) who has made the earth your couch,
and the heavens *(al-samā')* your canopy;
And sent down rain from the heavens;
And brought forth therewith
fruits for your sustenance;
Then set not up rivals unto *Allāh,*
when ye know (the truth).
Qur'ān 2:22, HQSA

Heaven as a "canopy" suggests it to be a source of protection for the earth: that the clouds, the sun, the moon, the stars, the planets, and the various weather and atmospheric conditions have a protective part to play. The *Qur'ān* also speaks of seven heavens *(sab' samāwāt)* in the hierarchy of creation.

See also: **sab' samāwāt, sky, T'iēn**.

saram khaṇḍ (Pu) *Lit.* realm *(khaṇḍ)* of bliss *(saram)*. Although the meaning of *saram* itself is uncertain, *saram khaṇḍ* is used by Guru Nānak in the *Ādi Granth* for the realm above *gyān khaṇḍ* (*lit.* realm of knowledge, the astral realm). It is hence equivalent to the causal realm, also called *trikuṭī* (*lit.* three peaks) by other Indian Saints. Others have translated *saram* to mean 'spiritual effort'.

See also: **khaṇḍ**.

sarovar(a) (S/H/Pu), **saras** (H) *Lit.* a lake, a reservoir, a very large pond or expanse of water; used metaphorically in a number of ways in Indian mystic literature. Both the Name of God and the *Guru* are described as a lake of divine nectar, the world is depicted as a stormy lake, the body as a lake to be filled with the divine Water of Life, and so on.

The term is also used as *mānsarovar,* for the 'reservoir' of spirit in which the soul 'bathes' on reaching *daswān dwār.*

See also: **mānsarovar**.

satar paya (Pv) *Lit.* star-studded *(satar)* heaven *(paya);* the first of the four heavens mentioned in the later Pahlavi literature of Zoroastrianism. As the soul and mind rise up out of the body in meditation, they first experience flashes of light within, like that of the stars at night, and later on like that of the clear and steady light of the moon. These are the subastral regions of the stars and the moon (though unconnected with the outer stars and moon), that are located on the inner journey between the physical realm and the true astral domains.

Satar paya possibly relates to this starry region in the subastral worlds. In the Pahlavi literature, this realm is called the place 'where good thoughts dwell'. This gives confirmation to the suggestion, since it is in this realm that the *antaḥkaraṇ* of Indian terminology is located, also known as the 'instrument' of human thought.

Similarly, the second heaven of the Pahlavi literature, *mah paya* (the heavens of the moon), is said to be the realm 'where good words dwell'. The subastral regions of the stars and the moon are closely related, as are words and thoughts. It is possible, therefore, that *satar paya* and *mah paya* relate to the star and moon regions mentioned by Indian and Sufi mystics. Alternatively, they may be just a general way of depicting the light of the astral realms. They may also have been understood in a literal sense as external, physical heavens, according to the understanding of ancient cosmology.

See also: **khurshed paya, tārā**.

sefirot (He) (sg. *sefirah*) *Lit.* emanations, spheres, levels; the successive divine emanations; divine qualities or aspects; the divine utterances, names or lights, through which the creation took place; a teaching central to the Kabbalah.

The derivation of the word *sefirot* has not been determined with any certainty. Contemporary scholars derive it from the Hebrew for 'numbers' or 'ciphers *(misparim)*'; the Hebrew root *sfr* means both 'to recount' (as in a story) or 'to count', suggesting the successive stages of emanation of the creation. The term may also come from the Greek *sphaira,* meaning sphere, level, layer, plane or region. Others trace it to the Hebrew *sappir* (sapphire), a biblical term representing the beauty and radiance of the divine Light. Derived in this way, the term *sefirot* would imply that the creation took place through the radiance of light.

The actual term *sefirot* first appears in the fourth-century *Sefer Yeẓirah (Book of Formation),* but did not come into common usage until many centuries later. The teaching of the *sefirot* arose during the rabbinic period (200 BCE – 400 CE), when the rabbis described the creation in terms of ten divine attributes: wisdom, understanding, reason, strength, rebuke, might, righteousness, judgment, lovingkindness and compassion. These qualities were understood as God's 'instruments' or 'utterances'.

In the eleventh century, Solomon ibn Gebirol (also known as Avicebron) wrote in his *Mekor Ḥayyim (Fountain of Life)* that the creation took place through a series of emanations from the primal divine Light. He, however, did not use the term *sefirot* in his descriptions. It was only in the twelfth century that the term *sefirot* was linked with the description, and came into common use. Over time, the system was then embellished with more and more complex symbolism and elaboration.

The description of the ten *sefirot* as emanations of the divine Will by which the creation took place was based upon an interpretation of the ten utterances (H. *ma'amarot,* Gk. *logoi*) of God that were instrumental in the process of creation, according to a mystical interpretation of *Genesis.* In the first chapter, the phrase, "And God said", followed by "Let there be light!" and so on, is repeated ten times as God creates and arranges the various aspects of the creation.

The Kabbalah explains that the primal divine will, energy or Light, in its purity and unity, needed to be stepped down and channelled in order for the process of creation to take place. The sixteenth-century Kabbalist, Moses Cordovero, provides an overview of the emanation of the *sefirot* in his *Pardes Rimmonim (Orchard of Pomegranates):*

> In the beginning, *Ayn-Sof* (the Infinite One) emanated ten *sefirot,* which are of its essence, united with it. It and they are entirely one. There is no change or division in the Emanator that would justify saying it is divided into parts in these various *sefirot.* Division and change do not apply to it, only to the external *sefirot.*
>
> To help you conceive this, imagine water flowing through vessels of different colours: white, red, green and so forth. As the water spreads through those vessels, it appears to change into the colours of the vessels, although the water is devoid of all colour. The change in colour does not affect the water itself, just our perception of the water. So it is with the *sefirot.* They are vessels, known, for example, as *Ḥesed, Gevurah* and *Tiferet,* each coloured according to its function, white, red and green, respectively, while the light of the Emanator – their Essence – is the water, having no colour at all. This Essence does not change; it only appears to change as it flows through the vessels.
>
> Better yet, imagine a ray of sunlight shining through a stained-glass window of ten different colours. The sunlight possesses no colour at all, but appears to change hue as it passes through the different colours of glass. Coloured light radiates through the window. The light has not essentially changed, though so it seems to the viewer. Just so with the *sefirot.* The light that clothes itself in the vessels of the *sefirot* is the Essence, like the ray of sunlight. That Essence does not change colour at all, neither judgment nor compassion, neither right nor left. Yet by emanating through the *sefirot* – the variegated stained glass – judgment or compassion prevails.
>
> *Moses Cordovero, Pardes Rimmonim, PRC 4:4.17d–18a, in EKH p.38*

The emanation and activity of the *sefirot* is to be understood as an interrelated step-by-step process. The first and most subtle step, according to the sixteenth-century Rabbi Isaac Luria, was the withdrawal of the Godhead into itself in a process called *ẓimẓum* (contraction). Thus, the topmost *sefirah* of *Keter* (Crown) was projected from the Godhead, the *Ayn-Sof,* which is self-contained and transcendent. *Keter* is actually at the same level as the Godhead, but embodies within it the subtle and unexpressed will to create (sometimes called 'the will to will to create'), whereas the *Ayn-Sof* is totally aloof. *Keter* is also called *Ayin,* meaning Nothing, since it is purely spiritual, without substance. The relationship of the *Ayn-Sof* to the *sefirot,* particularly to *Keter,* is described by Moses Cordovero:

> Furthermore, you should know that *Ayn-Sof* emanated its *sefirot,* through which its actions are performed. They serve as vessels for the actions deriving from *Ayn-Sof* in the world of separation and below. In fact, its existence and essence spread through them....
>
> *Ayn-Sof* is not identical with *Keter,* as many have thought. Rather, *Ayn-Sof* is the Cause of *Keter; Keter* is caused by *Ayn-Sof,* Cause of causes. *Ayn-Sof* is the primal Cause of all that exists; there is no cause higher than it. *Keter* is the first to derive from it. From *Keter* the rest of emanation is drawn forth. This does not contradict the fact that *Keter* is counted as one of the *sefirot.* It is reckoned as one of the ten, considered similar to the emanated ones. On account of its loftiness, however, *Keter* does not reveal itself in the emanated totality of ten. The decad is kept complete by including *Da'at* (Knowledge) in place of *Keter....*
>
> At the very beginning, *Ayn-Sof* emanated the subtle emanation, namely, ten *sefirot* – noetic forms – from its essence, uniting with it. It and they together constitute a complete union.
>
> *Moses Cordovero, Or Ne'erav, ONC 6:1.42b, 43b–44a, in EKH pp.39–40*

From *Keter* emanates the second *sefirah* of *Ḥokhmah,* Wisdom – the divine Will itself. It is the divine creative power, identical with the Word, *Logos,* the Holy Name, the Voice of God, and known by a great many other names. Wisdom is also called *Reshit* (Beginning) and *Yesh* (Something), since it represents the first manifestation of the divine will. It is from *Ḥokhmah* that the creation begins. In projecting the divine will, *Ḥokhmah* acts upon the third *sefirah* of *Binah* (Understanding). Kabbalists use the image of *Ḥokhmah* planting a seed in the womb of *Binah.*

Binah is the 'receptacle' where the primal 'intention' of *Ḥokhmah* is expressed. *Ḥokhmah* and *Binah* are often called the 'father and mother' of the other *sefirot,* as *Binah* is the mother who gives birth to the actual design or plan for the creation. Through their synthesizing interaction they produce a 'son' – an additional or 'shadow' *sefirah* called *Da'at* (Knowledge). Etymologically, *da'at* means attachment or union. It represents the higher or divine knowledge produced by the union of *Ḥokhmah* with *Binah,* and contains within it the 'idea' or subtle blueprint of the entire creation below. *Binah,* through *Da'at,* gives birth to the lower seven *sefirot* through whose activity the creation will come into being.

The next three *sefirot* are *Ḥesed* (Lovingkindness, Grace, Love, Mercy), *Din* (Judgment, also called *Gevurah* – Might) and *Tiferet* (Splendour, Beauty). *Ḥesed* represents the totally unlimited and unqualified outpouring of divine love. The creation, however, is finite, and cannot contain the infinitude of *Ḥesed. Din* therefore acts to restrain and channel the flow of *Ḥesed,* so that it might be absorbed into the creation. The activity of *Din* mirrors that of the original *ẓimẓum,* or contraction of the *Ayn-Sof,* but at a lower intensity. Because of its limiting activity, *Din* contains the potential for evil in the creation.

Tiferet is the mediating quality necessary for the qualities of *Din* and *Ḥesed* to synthesize and harmonize. It is associated with the divine name *Yahweh,* and is also called *Raḥamim* (Mercy, Merciful), since it sustains the entire creation through its harmonizing activity. Through it, equilibrium is maintained among all the lower *sefirot. Tiferet* stands in relation to *Ḥesed* and *Din* in much the same way as *Da'at* stands in relation to *Ḥokhmah* and *Binah.*

The next three lower *sefirot* are receptacles and channels for the energy or divine will, released by the *sefirot* above them. They are: *Neẓaḥ* (Endurance, Victory), *Hod* (Glory) and *Yesod* (Foundation). *Neẓaḥ,* as Endurance, gives *Ḥesed* the strength to flow into the creation. *Hod,* as a lower vibration of *Din,* seeks to preserve the divine majesty and prevent it from flowing unrestrained. *Yesod* blends all the preceding *sefirot,* and receives their light. It is called the foundation of the creation, symbolized in the Kabbalah by the *phallus,* since the divine creative power flows through it.

Malkut (Kingship, Sovereignty) is the lowest of the *sefirot.* It receives the outpouring of divine energy or light from *Yesod,* and channels it into the physical creation, making the physical creation possible. It represents the divine presence manifested in the creation, and is associated with the *Shekhinah* (the divine presence in creation).

In the system of the *sefirot, Malkut* is considered to be the lower mother of the revealed world, just as *Binah* is the upper mother of the concealed world. The activity of the *sefirot* is thus completed. *Malkut* is the link between the *Ayn-Sof,* the supreme transcendent Godhead, and the physical plane. It represents the final channelling of the uncontrolled, limitless, infinite divine Light into the material realm.

Just as *Tiferet* harmonizes the activity of *Ḥesed* and *Din,* so *Malkut* harmonizes the activity of the *sefirot* above her. She is also *Tiferet*'s lover, but their relationship is not always harmonious. To the Kabbalists, the tension between them is a symbolic way of representing what they understood as 'masculine' and 'feminine', or the potential for active and passive principles within the divine Unity. The goal of the Kabbalists was to bring these divine forces into harmony.

The medieval *Zohar* describes the original emanation of the creation through light, at the level of *Binah:*

> Come and see. When the Holy One, blessed be He, wished to create the world, He brought forth a single hidden light *(Binah),* so that from this light all the revealed lights (the lower *sefirot*) would emerge and shine, and so that from this light the other lights (the *sefirot*) would emerge, extend themselves, and be formed; and this was the upper world. This light extended itself again, and made the artisan (*Binah,* from whom the other *sefirot* emanated), the light that does not shine, and the lower world *(Malkut)* was made. And because it is a light that does not shine, it sought to link itself with the realms below, and through the link below to receive illumination through the link above.
>
> *Zohar 1:156a–156b, WZ2 p.574*

Overlapping with the idea of the *sefirot* was the description of the *'olamot* (sg. *'olam*), the worlds or realms of the creation, corresponding (in modern terminology) to the spiritual, causal, astral and physical planes. To begin with, the entire activity of the *sefirot* was ascribed to *'olam ha-aẓilut* (world of emanation, the spiritual plane). But later Kabbalists divided the activities of the *sefirot* among the realms, with the first triad of *Keter, Ḥokhmah* and *Binah* ascribed to *'olam ha-aẓilut; Ḥesed, Din* and *Tiferet* to *'olam ha-briah* (realm of creation, probably the causal plane); *Neẓaḥ, Hod* and *Yesod* to *'olam ha-yeẓirah* (realm of formation, corresponding to the astral plane); and *Malkut* to the level of *'olam ha-'assiah* (realm of making, the physical plane). Later, other Kabbalists posited hierarchies of several layers of ten *sefirot,* sometimes even up to forty layers, each one reflecting the one above, but at a lower intensity.

The principle demonstrated here is: "As above, so below." The *Zohar* says that the designs for all the worlds were sketched within the *sefirot,* so to speak, and then served as patterns for the lower creation:

> He made this world to match the world above, and whatever exists above has its counterpart below.
>
> *Zohar 2:20a, Midrash ha-Ne'elam, WZ2 p.569*

The sefirotic system was also used as a meditational device or path by Jewish mystics, like Abraham Abulafia and many others, who realized that intellectual knowledge of the *sefirot* was less important than the actual spiritual practice of meditation that could lead to union with the Godhead. The mystics taught that the *sefirot* corresponded to the successive stages of the inner journey in meditation. They often used the metaphor of the Tree of Life and its ascending branches to describe the successive levels of the *sefirot,* upon which the devotee was to meditate in order to rise spiritually, and eventually unite his soul with the highest level.

The model of the *sefirot* was also used to explain many other Kabbalist ideas. The three parts of the soul *(neshamah, ruaḥ* and *nefesh),* for example, are generally viewed in the *Zohar* as corresponding to and representing the qualities of *Binah, Tiferet* and *Malkut,* respectively. Similarly, the Bible was understood symbolically as possessing hidden esoteric mysteries, with every word and even every letter given an esoteric meaning. Thus, biblical events and personalities were viewed as corresponding to different *sefirot,* embodying their qualities. Not only was the *Genesis* account of creation understood as the emanation of the *sefirot,* but biblical stories of the patriarchs were also understood not as stories of real people, but as cosmic dramas concerning the divine powers embodied by the *sefirot.* Abraham was seen as representing *Ḥesed,* for instance, Isaac as *Din,* Jacob as *Tiferet,* Joseph as *Yesod,* and so on.

The *sefirot* were also understood to correspond to and represent the various descriptive names of God that appear in the Bible. Each name was felt to pertain to a different divine quality or aspect, embodied by a particular *sefirah.* The names are: *Ehyeh, Yah, Yahweh* (vocalized as *Elohim*), *El, Elohim, Yahweh ẓeva'ot, Elohim ẓeva'ot, Shaddai* and *Adonai.* In the *Zohar, Ehyeh* (meaning, 'I will be') corresponds to *Keter,* the source of emanation. *Yahweh* (meaning, 'I was, am and will be') represents *Tiferet,* the axis around which the other *sefirot* rotate. *Adonai* (meaning 'Lord') corresponds to *Malkut* (Kingship), and to the divine presence active within the creation – the *Shekhinah.*

See also: **Pleroma**, **Tree of Life** (3.1).

set sunn, **set kanwal** (H) *Lit.* white *(set)* void *(sunn)* or emptiness; white *(set)* lotus *(kanwal);* luminous void or lotus; a 'void' or 'sky' in the upper part of *sahans dal kanwal,* the thousand-petalled lotus; the highest of the three regions within *sahans dal kanwal,* the lowest being *jhajhrī dīp* (lattice island), above which is *shyām kanj* (*lit.* black lotus). *Set sunn* or *set kanwal* is reached by passing through a subtle 'channel' (the *sushumṇā*), leading upwards from the central flame *(jyoti)* of *sahans dal kanwal.*

From *set sunn,* the ascending soul is drawn into the *bank nāl* (crooked tunnel) – a 'passageway' leading into the causal realm *(trikuṭī)* above. The administrative centre here is said to be like a lotus with sixteen petals, referring to sixteen major functional aspects. This centre is reflected in the sixteen-petalled *kaṇṭha chakra* (throat centre) in the physical body, and is itself a reflection of a corresponding centre in *mahā sunn* (great void).

Swāmī Shiv Dayāl Singh describes the ascent of the soul through the "flame" of *sahans dal kanwal,* into *set sunn,* and from there, through the *bank nāl,* into *trikuṭī:*

Draw your senses, mind and soul within,
and by ascending to the (inner) sky
meet the Word form of the Master *(Shabd Guru).*
Listen constantly to the unstruck Sound *(anhad Bānī),*
and behold the wondrous flame.
Pierce the flame, and merge in the *(set) sunn,*
and through the *sushumṇā,* enter the *bank nāl.*
Beyond *bank nāl* listen to the melody of *trikuṭī.*

Swāmī Shiv Dayāl Singh, Sār Bachan Poetry 23:1.74–77, SBP p.200

Set sunn has also been used by Swāmī Shiv Dayāl Singh as a name for the realm of *sunn* or *daswān dwār* (tenth door), the first spiritual realm lying above *trikuṭī.* In one of his poems, he writes of the soul's ascent through *shyām kanj,* through the *bank nāl* (crooked tunnel) into *trikuṭī,* on into *"set sunn",* and through *mahā sunn* (great void) into *bhanwar guphā* (rotating cave), and thence to the eternity of *sach khaṇḍ* (true region):

My soul ascended to the black lotus *(shyām kanj),*
to the *Guru* do I pay obeisance;
I entered the crooked tunnel *(bank nāl),*
I broke open the adamantine door of *trikuṭī;*
In the white void *(set sunn),* I became a pure soul,
I proceeded further, beholding *mahā sunn.*
I heard the melodies of the flute *(muralī)* in *(bhanwar) guphā;*
In the true region *(sach khaṇḍ),*
there rose the strains of the *bīn (vīṇā).*

Swāmī Shiv Dayāl Singh, Sār Bachan Poetry 34:13.15–21, SBP p.290

Kabīr also uses *set sunn* for the realm beyond *trikuṭī:*

A (true) *sādh* (holy man) is he who conquers this fort *(i.e. trikuṭī).*
Going beyond the nine manifested doors to the tenth,
he opens the tenth, which had been locked.
Further on is the white void *(set sunn),* O brother:
bathe there in *mānsarovar.*

Kabīr, Shabdāvalī 1, Bhed Bānī 22:16–17, KSS1 p.66

See also: **sahans dal kanwal**, **sunn**.

seven heavens See **heavens**.

shāh rag (P/H/U) *Lit.* principal *(shāh)* vein *(rag);* main vein; thus, royal vein; specifically, the jugular vein; derived from the Persian, probably owing its origins to a verse in the *Qur'ān:*

> It was We who created man,
> and We know what suggestions his soul makes to him:
> For We are nearer *(naḥnu aqrabu)* to him
> than his jugular vein *(ḥabl al-warīd).*
>
> *Qur'ān 50:16, HQSA*

A number of mystics have alluded to this verse, changing the term from "jugular vein *(ḥabl al-warīd)*" to the "royal vein *(shāh rag)*". Thus, Bulleh Shāh:

> Nearer than the *shāh rag* is God to be found:
> over nothing have people been raising such a turmoil
> (in search of God).
>
> *Bulleh Shāh, Kullīyāt 100, KBS p.221, SBSU p.92; cf. BS p.81*

And:

> When our eyes met, I lost my senses:
> now I have found how close You are.
> Nearer than the *shāh rag* is the Lord.
>
> *Bulleh Shāh, Kullīyāt 37, KBS p.63, SBSU p.273; cf. BS p.82*

Similarly, Sulṭān Bāhū writes:

> Look within, and you will find God
> nearer than the royal vein *(shāh rag).*
> He is in me and I in Him, O Bāhū:
> Not only distance from Him,
> but even nearness to Him,
> is now meaningless!
>
> *Sulṭān Bāhū, Bait 194, SBU p.367; cf. SBE (193) pp.360–61*

Alluding specifically to the verse in the *Qur'ān,* though not using the term *shāh rag,* Bulleh Shāh also says:

> You have written,
> "We are nearer to you *(naḥnu aqrabu)* (than the jugular vein)."
> You have given the lesson,
> "I am with you."

You have ordained,
  "Know me within yourself."
Why then have You put on this veil?
Bulleh Shāh, Kullīyāt 75, KBS p.155, SBSU p.92; cf. BS p.81

Similarly, also alluding to the inner Music as the means of knowing God:

He (God) played on the flute the notes
  of "*naḥnu aqrabu* (we are nearer to you)",
  and gave the call, "Know me within yourself."
Bulleh Shāh, Kullīyāt 156, KBS p.335, SBSU p.92; cf. BS p.81

And, likewise, Sulṭān Bāhū:

Whoever realizes the oneness of God,
  makes progress on his spiritual journey;
He finds (the meaning of)
  "We are nearer *(naḥnu aqrabu)* (than the jugular vein),"
  and puts an end to all tribulations.
Sulṭān Bāhū, Bait 170, SBU p.361; cf. SBE (169) pp.344–45

Like Bāhū, other mystics have extended the sense to mean that God is to be found by 'passing through' the *shāh rag*. In this sense, the term is used for the central pathway, known to Indian mystics as the *sushumṇā, sushmanā* or *sukhmanā,* that leads upwards from the eye centre, tracing the mystic Word to its divine source with God. Metaphorically, this 'pathway' has been described as a fine or narrow pathway, but in essence it refers to the path of the Sound Current upon which the soul ascends rapidly back to God, as in a lift shaft. Mystically, this is the true path of the Saints. Hence, mystics have said that half the spiritual journey is covered when the soul reaches the eye centre and, leaving the physical body, begins the inner ascent.

Tulsī Sāhib of Hāthras, in one of his poems written for the Muslim seeker, Shaykh Taqī, also describes the *shāh rag* as the path to God, the divine "Friend" and "Beloved":

Why do you wander (in vain)
  in search of the Friend?
The path to the Beloved
  lies through (*lit.* in) the royal vein *(shāh rag).*
O Taqī, devote yourself to the perfect Master
  with patience and steadfastness.
He will give you the knowledge
  to enter the royal vein *(shāh rag).*

> A few days' practice will open your inner ear,
> and your journey to reach *Allāh* the great
> will become smooth.
> This is Tulsī's call: heed it O practitioner,
> and act on it.
> The *Kun* of the *Qur'ān* leads on to *Allāh* the great.
>
> *Tulsī Sāhib, in Santon kī Bānī, Ghazal vv.6–9, SKB pp.303–4*

Although the *shāh rag* of the Sufis is the same as the *sushumṇā* of Indian mystics, it is not to be confused with the *sushumṇā nāḍī* of the yogis. The latter is a reflection of the higher pathway, manifested in the human body as the central *nāḍī* running down the spine. It is the *nāḍī* up which the consciousness ascends in practices such as *prāṇāyāma,* which attempt to awaken the individual to awareness of the *kuṇḍalinī,* the power of the *prāṇas* within the body.

Sheol (He) The abode of the dead, the nether world, the underworld, hell, the Pit; a common term in Hebrew, Aramaic and Syriac, whose etymology is unknown; a biblical metaphor for death, punishment and despair, as well as for the material world and punishment. *Sheol* also appears in such expressions as *ḥevlei Sheol* (bonds of *Sheol*), generally translated as 'the sorrows of hell'. *Sheol* has a traditionally accepted meaning as a place bereft of God's influence and, figuratively, as a place of exile or extreme degradation in sin. The bonds *(ḥavelim)* of this physical world are the desires and attachments that keep the soul in a state of spiritual death.

In the earliest parts of the Bible, in keeping with the cultural beliefs and mythology of those times, *Sheol* is understood as a kind of nether world, a physical underworld beneath the ground. Hence, a story in *Numbers* in which Moses is instructed by God to invoke the divine punishment on a group of men who had challenged Moses' authority as leader:

> And Moses said, "Hereby you shall know that the Lord has sent me to do all these works; for I have not done them of my own mind. If these men die the common death of all men, or if they are visited by the fate of all men, then the Lord has not sent me. But if the Lord creates a new thing, and the earth opens her mouth, and swallows them up, with all that belongs to them, and they go down alive into *Sheol,* then you shall understand that these men have provoked the Lord."
>
> And it came to pass, as he finished speaking all these words, that the ground split beneath them. And the earth opened her mouth, and swallowed them up, and their houses, and all the men who belonged to Koraḥ, and all their goods. They, and all that belonged to them,

> went down alive into *Sheol,* and the earth closed upon them; and they perished from among the congregation.
>
> *Numbers 16:28–33, JCL*

Sheol is portrayed somewhat similarly in *Ezekiel,* where the prophet is speaking of the death of Pharaoh and the Egyptians. They will all go down into *Sheol,* he says, although – unlike *Numbers* – the method of entry is not described.[1]

Again, in the *Psalms,* though written some centuries later, when a psalmist thanks God for not sending his soul to *Sheol,* it seems he has something very frightening in mind, whether or not he understands *Sheol* literally:

> I have set the Lord always before me:
> because He is at my right hand, I shall not be moved.
> Therefore my heart is glad, and my glory rejoices,
> my flesh also dwells secure.
> For You will not abandon my soul to *Sheol,*
> nor will You suffer Your pious one to see the Pit.
> You will show me the path of life;
> In Your presence is fullness of joy;
> At Your right hand there are pleasures for evermore.
>
> *Psalm 16:8–11, JCL*

The understanding of *Sheol* as a dark nether world seems to have survived until the last two or three centuries BCE. After that, with the development of the idea of individual retribution after death, the portrayal of *Sheol* began to change. Souls awaiting the resurrection were believed to go to a multi-level *Sheol.* According to some descriptions, the lower levels were reserved for the torment of the wicked, while the righteous enjoyed bliss in the upper levels.[2] In other accounts, *Sheol* is replaced by *Gehinnom* (Gehenna) as the place of torment for the damned. The good, on the other hand, enjoy the delights of paradise, either immediately after death or at the resurrection.[3]

The idea continued to develop, and by the time of the Kabbalah, during the Middle Ages, *Sheol* had become a level in *Gehinnom,* where evil spirits dwelt, awaiting the opportunity to take control over the souls of the righteous:

> As soon as the Sabbath ends, there ascends from the *Gehinnom,* from the grade called *Sheol,* a party of evil spirits who strive to mingle among the seed of Israel, and to obtain power over them. But when the children of Israel perform the ceremonies of the myrtle and the cup of blessing, and recite the separation prayer (to commemorate the end of the Sabbath), that evil spirit departs to his place in *Sheol.*
>
> *Zohar 1:17b, ZSS1 p.74, JCL*

Further, according to the *Zohar,* sentence to *Sheol* is not permanent. There is still hope for those who repent, the writer quoting *Job* as his authority:

> The wicked who had never given a thought to repentance go down to *Sheol,* and never come out from thence, as it is written of them, "As the cloud is consumed and vanisheth away, so he that goeth down to *Sheol* shall come up no more."[4] But, concerning those others who had intended to repent, it says, "The Lord killeth and maketh alive; He bringeth down to *Sheol* and bringeth up."[5]
>
> *Zohar 2:150b, ZSS4 p.27, JCL*

In common with other terms for hell, there are places where *Sheol* is used metaphorically, to mean this world, where everyone faces death. Thus, in the early Christian *Odes of Solomon,* the writer speaks of being "brought up out of the depths of *Sheol*":

> The Lord is my hope,
> I shall not be ashamed of Him....
> And He brought me up out of the depths of *Sheol,*
> and from the mouth of death, He drew me.
> And I laid low my enemies,
> and He supported me by His grace....
>
> And the Lord overthrew my enemies by His Word,
> and they became like the chaff,
> which the wind carries away.
> And I gave praise to the Most High,
> because He had magnified His servant
> and the son of His handmaid.
>
> *Odes of Solomon 29:1, 4–5, 10–11*

Among the Nestorian writings, notable for their use of mystic metaphors, it is the Medicine of Life, the Word, that brings up souls "who are dying" in *Sheol,* having "taken up … abode" there "on account of your sins". Again, this seems to be a reference to life and death in this world:

> Behold, the Medicine of Life,
> which descended from on high....
> Put forth now your hands, O you who are dying,
> and have taken up your abode in *Sheol*
> on account of your sins.

Take and be forgiven, and attain unto life,
  and reign with Christ, and sing and say:
"Alleluia, this is the Bread of which
  if any man shall eat he shall escape hell."

Nestorian Liturgy; cf. NR2 p.167, MEM p.137

The passage speaks specifically of men eating Bread and escaping from *Sheol* – not a *Sheol* they are going to, but one they are already in – that is, this world.

It was perhaps confusion over the meaning of *Sheol,* hell and other similar terms that led Christians in the second century, long after the death of Jesus, to develop the belief that he had gone down to hell and brought up all those who were there. The metaphorical meaning of this otherwise odd scenario becomes clear when it is understood that the hell to which Jesus came was this world. It is the spiritually dead who live in this world whom he is said to have saved. This is evident in the *Acts of Thomas,* where Judas Thomas says:

You descended into *Sheol* with mighty power,
  and the dead saw you and became alive....
You ascended with great glory,
  and took up with you
  all who sought refuge with you,
  and in your footsteps, all your redeemed followed;
And you brought them into your fold,
  and joined them with your sheep.

Acts of Thomas 156; cf. AAA p.288, ANT p.432

See also: **abyss**, **dūzakh**, **Gehenna**, **Hadēs**, **hell**, **ḥevlei Sheol** (6.3), **jahannam**, **naraka**, **outer darkness**, **Pit**.

1. *Ezekiel* 31:16–17.
2. *e.g. 4 Ezra* 7:36–37.
3. "Eschatology", in *Encyclopedia Judaica, EJCD.*
4. *Job* 7:9.
5. *1 Samuel* 2:6.

Shivaloka, **Shivapurī** (S), **Shiv lok**, **Shiv purī** (H/Pu) *Lit.* region *(lok)* or city *(purī)* of *Shiva; Shiva*'s abode; *Shiva*'s heaven; usually identified with Mount *Kailāsh* in the Himalayas, the scene of *Shiva*'s austerities. According to Hindu belief, many deities have their own particular heavenly realm over which they rule, and to which their devotees hope to go at death.

In Hindu mythology, *Shiva* quarrels with many of the gods, cutting off *Brahmā*'s fifth head, for instance, for which he was obliged to become a perpetually wandering ascetic and a haunter of cemeteries. Eventually, however, he acquired a heaven of his own, on Mount *Kailāsh.*

See also: **Brahmaloka**, **Indraloka**, **Shiva** (4.2), **Vishṇuloka**.

shkinta (Md) (pl. *shkinata*) *Lit.* dwelling, habitation; esoterically, an inner region; a Mandaean term for the higher dwelling places of the soul within the creative hierarchy. In later Mandaean religion, the sacred cult or priestly huts used for baptism came to be known as *shkinata.*

See also: **dwellings**, **habitations**.

shoot See **branch**.

shūnya (S/H) See **sunn**.

shyām kanj (H) *Lit.* black *(shyām)* lotus *(kanj);* one of the three parts of *sahans dal kanwal* (thousand-petalled lotus), the astral plane, as described by Swāmī Shiv Dayāl Singh. *Shyām kanj* is the central part; below it lies *jhajhrī dīp* (lattice island), and above it is *set sunn* (white void) or *set kanwal* (white lotus). Speaking of the soul's ascent from *shyām kanj* to *set kanwal,* and thence through the *bank nāl* (crooked tunnel) into *trikuṭī* whose boundary 'sky' is known as *gagan,* he writes:

> The Master has initiated the humble ones
> into *surat Shabd yoga.*
> He instructs them to open the door to *gagan,*
> and concentrate on *shyām kanj.*
> The mind is then stabilized in *set kanwal:*
> the flame *(jyoti)* appears to lead on to *(set) sunn.*
>
> Leave both black and white lotuses,
> and fix your mind on the third lotus *(tīsrā dal).*
> This is the doorway to the *bank nāl.*
> There you will lose all consciousness of your body.
>
> *Swāmī Shiv Dayāl Singh, Sār Bachan Poetry 34:1.6–10, SBP p.281*

Speaking poetically of the steady progress and purification of the soul, he says:

The hearth was washed in *shyām kanj,*
and the flame *(jyot)* was lit in *sahans dal kanwal.*
Swāmī Shiv Dayāl Singh, Sār Bachan Poetry 42:2.4, SBP p.387

See also: **jhajhrī dīp**, **sahans dal kanwal**, **set sunn**.

Sidrat al-muntahá, al- (A), **Sidrah-i muntahā** (P) *Lit.* the Lote Tree *(Sidrah)* of the limit *(muntahá);* the Lote Tree of the uttermost limit or the farthest bourne. A tree said to stand as a sign at the peak of the seventh heaven, marking the beginning of the gulf that stands between the creation and the absolute Being of God. This final chasm is marked by the Lote Tree of the uttermost limit. The use of the lote tree (jujube) as a symbol in this context is because lote trees grow as the last, scrubby patches of vegetation bordering the vast expanse of unbroken desert.

According to Islamic tradition, the four rivers of paradise, depicted in *Genesis*[1] as flowing out of Eden, run from the base of this tree. Similar motifs appear in Sumerian mythology of the fourth millennium BCE. This tree is also said to be in the seventh heaven with its root in the sixth. In the account of Muḥammad's vision of God, he sees the Lote Tree "shrouded" in mystery. The vision of the Lote Tree is thus associated with the revelation of the Prophet. The *Qur'ān* says that the second of the two occasions when Muḥammad saw Gabriel *(Jabra'īl)* appear in visible form was near the "Lote Tree of the uttermost limit":

Then he approached and came closer,
and was at a distance
of but two bow lengths or (even) nearer;
So did *(Allāh)* convey
the inspiration (revelation) to His Servant –
(conveyed) what He (meant) to convey.
The (Prophet's mind and) heart
in no way falsified that which he saw.
Will you then dispute with him concerning what he saw?
For indeed he saw him *(Jabra'īl)* at a second descent,
near the Lote Tree of the uttermost limit *(Sidrat al-muntahá):*
Near it is the garden of refuge *(jannat al-ma'wá).*
Behold, the Lote Tree *(Sidrah)* was shrouded
(in mystery unspeakable)!
Qur'ān 53:8–16; cf. AYA

Because of this story, the *Sidrah* is often depicted in Islam as the heavenly mansion of the angel *Jabra'īl.* It is both his dwelling place and the limit beyond which he cannot go. Traditional accounts describe *Jabra'īl* turning back, saying he would be burnt if he went a hair's breadth further, while the Prophet goes on to "two bow lengths" from the presence of God, or "nearer".

Among the Sufis, the *Sidrah* served as a general image for the higher spiritual heavens, sometimes the highest, sometimes of a lower station. Thus Ḥāfiẓ says of the soul:

> When the bird of the heart flies away,
> its dwelling will be on the *Sidrah* tree.
> *Ḥāfiẓ, Dīvān, DHM (465:3) p.418, DIH p.349; cf. DHWC (465:3) p.772*

And:

> I am that bird whose cry, dawn and dusk,
> reaches the (lofty) *Sidrah* tree.
> *Ḥāfiẓ, Dīvān; cf. DHA p.166; DHM (371:6) p.347, DIH p.292; cf. DHWC (377:8) p.651*

Rūmī similarly portrays the soul as a "bough of the *Sidrah*" whose "origin … is the seventh heaven", and the *nafs* (worldly mind) as "firewood" whose source is the "fire and smoke" of this world. The eye of this world cannot distinguish between the two, he says, only the "eye of the heart" can see the difference. By "heart" here Rūmī means the soul – the spiritual heart of one's being:

> Know the bough of the *Sidrah* from the firewood,
> though both are green, O youth.
> The origin of that bough is the seventh heaven,
> the origin of this bough is from fire and smoke.
> To sense perception, they are similar in appearance,
> for the eye and habit of sense perception is seeing falsely;
> But that difference is manifest
> to the eye of the heart:
> Exert yourself, advance towards the heart
> with the exertion of one whose means are small.
> *Rūmī, Maśnavī V:1100–3; cf. MJR6 pp.67–68*

In another instance, Rūmī uses the image of the *Sidrah* in a way that seems to place it at a more specific spiritual level in the higher regions, not merely as a general image of a high spiritual stage. He relates the story of Daqūqī's vision of the seven *Abdāl* (Saints). In this vision, they appear to him as candles, then as men, then as trees, but as trees that reach beyond the *Sidrah* and even beyond the void that is beyond the *Sidrah.* The implication is that it is possible for man to progress spiritually, beyond the *Sidrah* that 'marks the limit', and beyond the void as well:

> Then each man assumed the shape of a tree:
> my eye was happy in their greenery.
> On account of the denseness of the leaves,
> no boughs were visible;
> The leaves, too, had become scant
> on account of the plenteous fruit.
> Every tree had thrown its boughs above the *Sidrah:*
> What of the *Sidrah?*
> They had reached beyond the void.
>
> *Rūmī, Maśnavī III:2003–5, MJR4 p.112*

Possibly, the "void" beyond the *Sidrah* is what some Indian mystics have called the *mahā sunn* (*lit.* great void), a realm of such depth and darkness that is is impossible for the soul to cross it without the help and company of a perfect Saint. *Mahā sunn* lies high up in the spiritual realms, the last great barrier before the region lying on the threshold of eternity. Or perhaps Rūmī is referring to the region beyond which the *nafs,* the mind, can no longer draw the soul down. Either way, the *Sidrah* would mark a definitive limit on the ascent of the soul.

Ibn 'Arabī says that the *Sidrah* is a tree in the seventh heaven, and identifies it with *al-Rūḥ al-A'ẓam* (the Greatest Spirit), the first emanation or entification of the Absolute.[2]

See also: **Gabriel** (4.2), **al-Mi'rāj** (▸2), **sab' samāwāt**, **Tree of Life** (3.1).

1. *Genesis* 2:10–14.
2. Ibn 'Arabī, *Tafsīr,* in *MJR7* p.86.

sitārah (P) *Lit.* star; one of the seven spheres comprising the visible world in traditional Islamic cosmology; more generally, in a mystical context, the inner heavens.

See also: **akhtar**, **tārā**.

sky, **skies** The expanse extending upwards from the horizon on all sides; that which lies above, from which light comes, appearing as an ultimate boundary that (at least until modern times) cannot be reached; mystically, the inner heavens, especially in the Manichaean writings, as in a psalm where the writer speaks of leaving "this body upon the earth" on hearing the inner sound of the "trumpet":

Save me, O blessed Christ,
  Saviour of holy souls.
I will pass up into the skies,
  and leave this body upon the earth.
The trumpet sounds I hear:
  they are calling me up to the immortals.

Manichaean Psalm Book CCLXI; cf. MPB p.75

And, speaking of the inner door or third eye by which the soul leaves the body:

Open to us the passage of the vaults of the skies,
  and walk before us to the joy of your kingdom,
  O Glorious One.

Manichaean Psalm Book CCXL; cf. MPB p.41

And again, this time indicating that the inner doorway or "gates" have been opened so that the soul may go within and meet the light form of the Saviour, "his glorious likeness of light":

The gates of the skies have opened before me
  through the rays of my Saviour
  and his glorious likeness of light.
I have left the garment (body) upon the earth,
  the senility of diseases that was with me;
The immortal robe I have put upon me.
Ferry me across to the sun and the moon,
  O ferryboat of light that is at peace.

Manichaean Psalm Book CCLXIV, MPB p.81

See also: **firmament**, **heavens**, **sab' samāwāt**.

so'ham (S/H), **sohang** (Pu) *Lit.* He *(sah)* + I *(aham);* I am He; one of the fundamental precepts of the *Upanishads*[1] and subsequently of *Advaita Vedānta,* expressing the identity of *ātman* and *Brahman,* and having the same meaning as the Upanishadic sayings, "Thou art That,"[2] and "I am *Brahman.*"[3]

The expression appears in both the *Bṛihadāraṇyaka* and the *Īshāvāsya Upanishads* as an invocation to "Truth", personified and symbolized in the writer's mind as the "Sun":

The face of Truth is obscured by a golden disc.
Unveil it, O Nourisher, so that I whose nature is the Truth,
may see it!
O Nourisher! O lone Traveller! O Controller!
O Sun! O Offspring of *Prajāpati* (Lord of creatures)!
Gather in Your rays, withdraw Your light,
for I would see that most blessed form of Yours.
Whoever is the Being dwelling there, I am He *(so'ham).*

Bṛihadāraṇyaka Upanishad 5:15.1–2, Īshāvāsya Upanishad 15–16

Later mystics have understood *sohang* as the soul's joyful cry (metaphorically) of ecstatic realization of kinship with the Creator when it reaches the threshold of the divine eternity. It is here that the soul ('I') really begins to experience that its reality is the same as that of the indescribable Lord ('He'). It is at this stage that the soul begins to truly know God, and to understand that "what You are, the same am I." It learns that it is a drop of the same divine Essence that constitutes the ocean of Spirit, the divine immensity of God.

Sohang is also a name used for the lord or ruler of the region that lies on the shores of eternity, as well as for that region itself. This realm, also known as *bhanwar guphā* (rotating cave), is designated the fourth major spiritual region in the descriptions of a number of Indian Saints. It is a realm filled with the longing of separation from God and the promise of union with the great ocean of spiritual love. It is a region of self-identification of the soul with the Divine, pervaded by a sense of the immanence of the divine presence, filled with the hope of merging into Him.

Swāmī Shiv Dayāl Singh specifies the location of *sohang* as lying beyond *mahā sunn* (great void):

Listen to the sound of *sunn,*
and thereby act upon the teachings of the Saints.
From there, proceed and enter *mahā sunn;*
Beyond that you will see the region of *sohang.*

Swāmī Shiv Dayāl Singh, Sār Bachan Poetry 20:16.4–5, SBP p.164

He also calls the lord of this region, "*Sohang*". Having described the eternal realm of *sat lok* (true region), he says:

From that region came into being the creation of *bhanwar guphā,*
the lord of which is *Sohang.*

Swāmī Shiv Dayāl Singh, Sār Bachan Poetry 23:1.38, SBP p.198

Speaking of the soul's realization of its true nature on entering this realm, Bulleh Shāh writes:

You are the embodiment of bliss and unceasing consciousness:
O Bullah, that is what the four *Vedas* proclaim....
O Bullah, recognize your own true self:
you are everlasting bliss, you are resplendent light....
O Bullah, know yourself and behold:
the light of *sohang* ever swings round you....
O Bullah, take care and recognize yourself!
you are immortal – why do you cling to the body?

Bulleh Shāh, Kullīyāt, Sī-ḥarfī a, ḍ, k, w, KBS pp.389–95, SBSU pp.27–28; cf. BS pp.34–35

Likewise, Guru Nānak writes that he who realizes through the power of the Word that 'He is I' is completely contented:

He who recognizes God within himself (*sohang,* 'He is I')
and is pierced through with His Name (*Shabd,* Word) is satisfied.

Guru Nānak, Ādi Granth 60, MMS

The sound of this region, likened to the poignant notes of the flute, is sometimes called the *sohang Shabd* (the word or sound of *sohang*), and is heard as the soul glimpses the light of eternity. The expression could refer generally to the music of this region, also called *sohang,* or it could indicate that the notes here are distantly reminiscent of the intonation of the word *'sohang',* or that the consciousness of the soul that hears the sound of this region is imbued with the understanding that "I am He," and longs to experience the fulfilment of that ultimate mystic promise:

The soul then beheld the mountain of *bhanwar guphā,*
approaching which it heard the sound *(shabd)* of *sohang.*
There the piercing melody of the flute arises,
and the soul sees the intense radiance of the white sun.

Swāmī Shiv Dayāl Singh, Sār Bachan Poetry 26:4.7–8, SBP p.228

Hence, Paltū describes the ecstasy of the divine longing experienced on the threshold of complete divine union, where the soul hears the *sohang Shabd:*

The flute rings in the sky,
and my soul goes into ecstasy.
My soul has gone into ecstasy,
and has made its home in the eighth palace,
from where the sound *(shabd)* of *sohang* arises,
and in which my soul is immersed.

Paltū, Bānī 1, Kuṇḍalī 170:1–2, PSB1 p.72

See also: **bhanwar guphā**, **sohang** (▸2).

1. *Bṛihadāraṇyaka Upanishad* 5:15.1; *Īshāvāsya Upanishad* 15.
2. *Chhāndogya Upanishad* 6:8.7.
3. *Bṛihadāraṇyaka Upanishad* 1:4.10.

solah dal kamal (H) *Lit.* lotus *(kamal)* of sixteen *(solah)* petals *(dal);* sixteen-petalled lotuses or centres are found in *brahmāṇḍa* (at the top of *mahā sunn*), in *aṇḍa* (in *set sunn*) and in *piṇḍa* (at the throat *chakra*).

See also: **aṇḍa**, **solah dal kamal** (5.1).

sovereignty A land or province under the rule of a sovereign; mystically, the inner realms, used interchangeably with 'principality'; commonly found in early Christianity. Speaking of the Saviour as a manifestation of the Word, the gnostic writer of the *Trimorphic Protennoia,* for example, says that the sovereignties and powers (the rulers of the sovereignties) all derive their existence from the Word, although the powers themselves are unaware of this:

> I (the Word) dwell within all the sovereignties and powers
> and within the angels,
> and in every movement that exists in all matter....
> And none of them (the powers) knew me,
> although it is I who work in them.
> Rather they thought that the All was created by them
> since they are ignorant, not knowing their Root,
> the place in which they grew.
>
> *Trimorphic Protennoia 47:19–22, 24–28, NHS28 pp.426–27*

See also: **dominions**, **principality**.

sukhmanā, **sukhmanā nāṛī** (Pu) See **sushumṇā**.

sunn (H/Pu), **shūnya** (S/H) *Lit.* zero, empty, vacant, nonexistent, vacuum, void; used by mystics for the 'gateways', 'valves', 'skies' or 'thresholds' that exist within the dynamic process of creation. The creative hierarchy is not, so to speak, a smooth, linear progression of one realm after another, each of increasing density or materiality in the descent from the divine Source. The system is far more complex, incapable of adequate description in words or by any human means. The physical universe, for example, is created out of the space within which it exists. This space is known as the *ākāsha tattva.* And this space also acts as a barrier to the perception of the souls who dwell here, in that they are not only unable to *see* beyond it, but the majority also come to believe that there *is* nothing beyond it.

Moreover, what appears to man as external space, filled with matter or substance, is actually an aspect of being and is reflected within the microcosm of man himself. Thus, another aspect of the *ākāsha tattva* is that it comprises the inner 'sky' of the body that must be pierced with great effort before the soul can leave the physical body, and consequently, the physical domain.

The creation is projected from within in an outward 'direction', outward not in space, but in being. The means of exit from any realm is to focus the attention within: to pass through the gateway, the valve or the sky that bounds that region and out of which it is created, and to enter the realm beyond.

It is these 'skies' or 'gateways' that mystics have described as *sunnas.* One meaning of the term is void or nothingness, for these areas of creation appear as such when observed from below. Physicists, for example, especially of the past, have often described space as a vacuum – empty or void. More modern considerations, however, suggest that far from being a 'nothing', space is a seething formative ocean of energy and activity within which all other physical matter and forces are formed like bubbles on an ocean. Space is thus the ocean of potential energy out of which the manifold forms of the physical creation come into being. The same is true of the other *sunnas* in the hierarchy of creation. As Mahārāj Charan Singh wrote in a letter:

> What you have asked about the *sunnas* is more of an academic than practical nature. The word *sunn* is a Prakrit (vernacular) formation of the Sanskrit word *shūnya,* which means a void or emptiness. They are, however, far from being mere voids, and to one who has not completed his spiritual journey, it is not only of no use but may even be of some risk to dabble in the lower *sunnas.* The Master gives us knowledge and information only about those *sunnas* which are helpful in our journey upward. It is only after having reached *sach khaṇḍ* (true region) that the *abhyāsī* (practitioner) may be allowed to see and go about anywhere, for then there is no chance of his being misled.
>
> *Mahārāj Charan Singh, Light on Sant Mat 237, LOSM p.262*

At the physical level, it is unseen processes of the mind that whip up the physical creation into such a plethora of ever shifting forms and patterns. This is a part of the outworking of the karmic process. Behind or within everything, however, is the primal energy or power of the ever vibrating Sound Current.

There are numerous such *sunnas* in the creation. Tulsī Sāhib writes in his *Ghaṭ Rāmāyaṇ* that there are twenty-two such 'gateways' in all that the soul has to encounter and pass through on its ascent, and he has given names to all of them.[1] Each one bears resemblances to the others and, without a perfect guide, the lower may easily be mistaken for one that is higher. Further, a number of regions have come to be called *sunn,* with or without another qualifying name. This can sometimes be confusing, though the particular meaning can usually be determined from the context. *Sunn* on its own, for example, is commonly used as an appellation of the third spiritual region, also called *daswān dwār* (tenth door) or *pārbrahm* (beyond *Brahm*). This is the spiritual region lying immediately above the regions of the mind, where the soul on its return journey to God first knows itself as a pure soul.

Speaking of the soul as it rises up from *sahans dal kanwal* (thousand-petalled lotus), Swāmī Shiv Dayāl Singh identifies the location of *sunn* as above *trikuṭī* (*lit.* three peaks, the highest region of the mind). *Mānsarovar* is described as a 'lake' of spirituality in *daswān dwār.* Above that is the realm of *bhanwar guphā* (rotating cave), lying on the threshold of eternity, reached after traversing *mahā sunn* (great void):

> Push your way through *bank nāl* (crooked tunnel),
> and establish your seat in *trikuṭī.*
> Soaring through the void of *sunn,* my brother,
> your soul will bathe in lake *mānsarovar.*
> Cross the dark square of *mahā sunn,*
> and go on to dwell in *bhanwar guphā.*
>
> *Swāmī Shiv Dayāl Singh, Sār Bachan Poetry 19:18.14–16, SBP p.153*

Swāmī Shiv Dayāl Singh also calls this region *sunn pad* (stage of *sunn*) and *sunn maṇḍal* (orbit of *sunn*). Identifying *sunn maṇḍal* with the realm above both *ākāsh* (here meaning the 'sky' of *sahans dal kanwal*) and *gagan* (the 'sky' of *trikuṭī*), he says:

> The soul now goes forward, removing the third veil,
> hearing the sound of *sunn maṇḍal,*
> seeing the brilliant light of *daswān dwār.*
> Leaving behind *gagan* and *ākāsh,*
> the soul bathes in lake *mānsarovar,*
> and joins the group of pure souls (*haṃsas, lit.* swans) there.
> Circling about, the soul ascends to the top of *sunn,*
> where the music of *kingrī* and *sārangī* abounds.
>
> *Swāmī Shiv Dayāl Singh, Sār Bachan Poetry 26:3.1–4, SBP p.227*

Kabīr writes that the ruler of this realm is *akshar Brahm* (imperishable *Brahm*).[2]

Situated above *daswān dwār* is the greatest *sunn* of all, named *mahā sunn* by a number of mystics. Its 'purpose' in creation is to act as a 'roadblock', preventing the souls in the realms below from immediately flying back to God. This aptly highlights the role of these *sunnas* in the lower realms of creation. They are, so to speak, the prison walls of each region. Not only are they difficult to pass through, but it is also difficult to see that there is anything beyond them. Clearly, this helps to maintain order within the creation, preventing the souls from going anywhere they please, and protecting them from entry into 'high velocity' areas that would be too much for their present state of understanding and capacity to appreciate. The passage through these gateways or creative skies is through the narrowing of the attention within, focusing or concentrating the mind and soul, and ridding it of all attraction to the levels below.

Though *mahā sunn* is called the great void or the great darkness, the last *sunn* of all is eternity itself, also called *sach khaṇḍ* and various other names. The eternal realm is a *sunn* in the sense that it is the ultimate 'space' or 'realm' out of which all lower 'spaces' or 'realms' emanate. Just as physical space interpenetrates all parts of the physical universe, so does *sach khaṇḍ,* the eternal realm, pervade and interpenetrate all parts of the entire creation. God is everywhere and within everything. Eternity is here, right now. It is not far off, but only appears so because the attention or consciousness, in its present condition, is not capable of fixing upon it.

It is in this sense that Guru Nānak writes how everything is contained within the divine *sunn:*

> Within us is God (*sunn,* void) without us is God *(sunn),*
>   and God *(sunn)* alone is filling the three worlds *(tribhavaṇ).*
> The man who realizes the Lord in the fourth state (*sunn,* void),
>   him vice and virtue affect not.
> He who knows the mystery of God *(sunn)*
>   who is pervading all the hearts is himself
>   the manifestation of the primal, immaculate and bright Lord.
> The mortal who is imbued with the immaculate Name:
>   he himself, O Nānak, is the Lord Creator.
>
> *Yogīs* say:
> "Everyone utters of God *(sunn),*
>   the dispassionate God *(sunn).*
> Whence is the immortal Lord *(sunn)* obtained?
> Of what kind are they who are imbued with the imperishable Lord?"

The *Guru* says:
"They are like Him, from whom they have emanated.
They transmigrate not, nor do they come and go.
It is through the *Guru,* O Nānak,
that the imperishable Lord is obtained by instructing the mind."
Guru Nānak, Ādi Granth 943, MMS

Guru Nānak also speaks of the divine eternity as *sunn maṇḍal:*

The detached soul, night and day, remains absorbed in one God,
and obtains an abode in *sunn maṇḍal.*
The true *Guru* has shown me the limitless,
unseen and the darling, primal Lord.
Guru Nānak, Ādi Granth 436, MMS

Sunn is also used in the sense of 'emptiness' or 'void' in reference to a high state of spiritual consciousness, as in the yogic term, *sunn samādhi;* it is an emptiness of everything except God.

See also: **akshara**, **mahā sunn**, **sunn samādhi** (▸2).

1. Tulsī Sāhib, *Ghaṭ Rāmāyaṇ* 1, *Chaupaī, Sunnan ke Nām, GR1* p.53.
2. Kabīr, *Shabdāvalī* 1, *Bhed Bānī* 22, *KSS1* p.66.

sūrya lok(a) (S/H) *Lit.* region *(lok)* of the sun *(sūrya);* the sun world; a term from Hindu mythology; a region or world around the sun, regarded as a heaven of which the sun is ruler; mystically, one of the subastral regions.

See also: **chandra**, **tārā maṇḍal**.

sushumṇā (S/H), **sushumṇā nāḍī** (S), **sushumṇā nāṛī**, **sushmanā**, **sushman** (H), **sukhman**, **sukhmanā**, **sukhmanā nāṛī** (Pu) *Lit.* duct or channel *(nāḍī, nāṛī)* of *sushumṇā;* the central path starting from the rectal centre *(mūlādhāra chakra),* and leading upwards through the eye centre into and through the higher spiritual regions.

Like *iḍā* and *pingalā,* the other two primary *nāḍīs* with which it is associated, no certain derivation can be ascribed to the word. *Sushmanā* and *sukhmanā* both come from the Sanskrit, *sushumṇā,* which has tentatively been derived as most *(sa)* gracious *(sumna). Sumna,* however, is a rare word, and the derivation is probably fanciful. *Sukhmanā,* the vernacular form of *sushumṇā,* arises from the common Punjabi change of 'sh' to 'kh', as in *purush* (being) to *purakh.* By coincidence, *sukhmanā* also yields the meaning 'peace *(sukh)* of mind *(manas)*', and is often translated in that sense, although this is unlikely to be the meaning originally intended.

The *sushumṇā* described in yogic and tantric texts is a reflection within the physical body of the higher *sushumṇā* lying above the eyes. In the body, it is the central *nāḍī* running up the spine, linking and providing energy to the six *chakras* (centres of *prāṇa* or life energy). At the base of the *sushumṇā,* in the *mūlādhāra chakra* (rectal centre) lies the *kuṇḍalinī,* described as guarding the entrance to the *sushumṇā.*

The *sushumṇā* is the central of three *nāḍīs,* the other two being *iḍā* and *pingalā.* It is the means of ascent through the *chakras* in the yogic practice of *prāṇāyāma* (control of the *prāṇa*):

> Lock the throat (in *khecharī mudrā*) and retain the breath. Then the *prāṇa* will rise straight, just as a snake struck with a stick becomes straight.
>
> The *kuṇḍalinī shakti* will immediately become straight, and the two *(iḍā* and *pingalā)* will become lifeless, as the *shakti* (energy) enters *sushumṇā....*
>
> This middle *nāḍī (sushumṇā)* becomes straight by the *yogī*'s persistent practice of *āsanas* (postures), *prāṇāyāma* and *mudrās* (yogic exercises).
>
> *Haṭha Yoga Pradīpikā 3:11–12, 117; cf. HYP pp.29–30, 45*

These three *nāḍīs* are commonly symbolized as the sacred rivers of the Ganges *(iḍā),* the Yamunā *(pingalā)* and the legendary Sarasvatī *(sushumṇā).*

Within the realms of the mind, these three currents are reflections of the three *guṇas* of harmony, activity and inertia. Their prototypes or subtlest essences, however, arise from eternity itself, and at various points in their downward descent they form areas of confluence, called by mystics *triveṇī* or Prayāg, named from the meeting of the three Indian rivers in the city of Allahabad. The upward path for the ascending soul always lies in the centre path, the *sushumṇā.*

The term has been used by a number of Saints in descriptions of the spiritual ascent of the soul above the eyes. Kabīr, for instance, writes of the soul's ascent through the 'sky' of the body. After this, he continues, the soul who is following the Sound Current finds and takes to the *sushumṇā.* By means of this central highway, the soul ascends to the *triveṇī* encountered in the astral realm, and then rises higher. Here, as in many other places, *pingalā* and *iḍā* are symbolized as the sun and moon:

Bring the sun *(i.e. pingalā)* and moon *(i.e. iḍā)* together at one point,
  and fix your attention in the *sushmanā.*
Merge your attention in *triveṇī,*
  and then go beyond.

Kabīr, Shabdāvalī 1, Bhed Bānī 22:11, KSS1 p.66

And:

Finding the *sukhmanā,* the soul became pure,
  proceeding further, it ascended the (inner) sky.

Swāmī Shiv Dayāl Singh, Sār Bachan Poetry 5:3.8, SBP p.45

Dariyā Sāhib of Bihar speaks in a similar manner. Here, the "blooming flower" is *sahans dal kanwal* (thousand-petalled lotus) and the "mountain peak" is *trikuṭī* (*lit.* three peaks, universal mind). In this instance, the "sun and moon" probably refer to the light seen by the soul on its ascent through the subastral regions:

The sun and moon come into view,
  then both set as the soul rises.
Rising to the mountain peak,
  you find the *sushumṇā.*
Iḍā and *pingalā* flow below,
  from the blooming flower emanates sweet fragrance;
With the manifestation of love,
  the lotus is filled with nectar.
There lies the fruit of spiritual practice,
  the foundation of spiritual ascent.
And there, too, blooms the thousand-petalled lotus.

Dariyā Sāhib, Gyān Dīpak, DYD pp.312–13, GD pp.227–28; cf. DSSB p.65

This royal highway of the soul leads on past *trikuṭī* and the regions of the mind, through the regions of spirit, to eternity itself. Guru Nānak speaks of this divine home of the soul as the *sunn maṇḍal* (realm of void). To reach there, he advises listening to the sound that comes from the central path of the *sukhman:*

Hear thou the music of *sukhman,*
  and be attuned to *sunn maṇḍal.*
Reflecting on the ineffable Discourse
  (*akath Kathā,* unspoken language) of God,
  man's desire is dissolved in the very mind
  (the desires of the mind are dissolved).

Guru Nānak, Ādi Granth 1291, MMS

Further underlining the meaning of *sukhmanā* as the central inner path is its association by Beṇī Jī with *iḍā* and *pingalā,* when he writes of the confluence of these three currents at Prayāg, above the regions of mind and *māyā:*

> *Iṛā, pingulā* and *sukhmanā:*
> these three abide in one place.
> Prayāg (Pirāg) is there, where the three streams … meet:
> My mind bathes at that place.
> O Saints, the immaculate Lord abides there:
> going to the *Guru,* some rare one understands this.
>
> *Beṇī Jī, Ādi Granth 974, MMS*

See also: **triveṇī**.

svarg(a), **svarg(a) lok(a)** (S/H/Pu) *Lit.* region *(loka)* of heaven or paradise *(svarga);* in general, heaven or paradise, or one of its subdivisions; specifically, the paradise of *Indra,* the ruler of the gods, according to Hindu mythology; of uncertain derivation, possibly from *svar* (light, heaven) and *gam* (to go), thus, 'going' or 'leading to the light' or 'leading to heaven'. In post-Vedic mythology, *Indra, Kuvera* and other gods each have their own paradise *(svarga)* or region *(loka)* situated on one or other of the mythologized mountains of the Himalayas. The Himalayas being in the north, the *Shatapatha Brāhmaṇa*[1] hence describes the doorway to *svarga* as lying to the northeast. Seven such *svargas* are sometimes enumerated: *Brahmaloka, Vishṇuloka* or *vaikuṇṭha, goloka* (Kṛishṇa's paradise), *Kailās* (*Shiva*'s paradise), *svarga* or *svarloka (Indra*'s paradise, *Indraloka), alakā* (*Kuvera*'s paradise) and the paradises of solar, lunar and other deities. Beyond *svarga* lies *apavarga* (heaven or heavens above *svarga; lit.* completion, liberation from birth and death), of which there are also said to be seven.

Souls leaving the physical plane after death go where their minds take them: the law of the mind – of *karma* or cause and effect – is inexorable. A life of purity and good deeds cleanses the mind, automatically making the soul fit for one of the astral or subastral spheres or heavens. A life of selfishness, greed, anger and bad deeds arises from and leaves the mind in an impure state, which is reflected in the hellish place to which the soul proceeds. Sooner or later, however, all souls who have not attained liberation return to the physical realm due to the attractions of their own minds, though a soul descending from *svarga* will first incarnate as a human being rather than one of the lower species.

Thus, the *Bhagavad Gītā* says that those who live religious lives go to heaven for a certain period of time, but after the harvest of their "good deeds" has been reaped, they return to the round of birth and death. In this context, "good deeds" includes the practice of religious observances:

Those well versed in the *Vedas,* cleansed of their sins
by the performance of sacrificial rites,
accompanied by drinking the blessed *soma* juice,
pray for the attainment of heaven *(svarga).*
Having reached the heaven of *Indra,*
attainable by such meritorious practices,
they enjoy the supernal and celestial pleasures of heaven.

Having, for a long time, enjoyed these varied pleasures
of the heavenly realms *(svargaloka),*
when the merit of their good deeds is exhausted,
they re-enter the world of men.
Thus, ridden with desire *(kāma),*
those who practise religious rites
endure repeated coming and going.

Bhagavad Gītā 9:20–21; cf. BGT

In a dialogue between King Subāhu and the wise *brāhmaṇ,* Jaimini, the *Padma Purāṇa* provides a detailed inventory of the kinds of deeds that lead to hell and to heaven:

Now learn from me about those who go to heaven *(svarga).*
Those who follow religion, practising truth, penance,
forgiveness, charity or study (of the *Vedas*) go to heaven *(svarga).*
Those high-minded ones who are engaged in sacrifices,
and exclusively devoted to the worship of deities,
as well as those who approve of these, go to heaven *(svarga).*
The pure who are exclusively devoted to *Vishṇu,*
reciting and singing (hymns) to *Vishṇu* in a pure place
go to heaven *(svarga).*

Padma Purāṇa 2:96.20b–23; cf. PP4 p.1256

The *Padma Purāṇa* then continues at length, enumerating many other good qualities that will ensure a place in *svarga.* Individuals destined for *svarga* include those who do no harm; who look to the welfare of all; who never speak ill of others, even their enemies; who are friendly to their enemies; who are free from greed and jealousy; who keep good company; who give clothes to the needy; who build wells and reservoirs; who avoid sleeping by day; who respectfully serve their parents; who have many sons; and who protect, like their own sons, insects that bite the body, such as lice, bugs and gadflies!

From the mystics' viewpoint, the various heavens that lie within the realms of the mind and the sphere of birth and death stand in the way of the ascending soul. Mahārāj Sāwan Singh writes:

> Just as on the physical plane there are continents and countries with their different types of populations, the same is the case on the astral plane. One such place is the heaven inhabited by houris. Mohammedans call it *bihisht* and Hindus call it *svarg* – there is a difference in name, but the place is the same. The place is subject to karmic law and transmigration. It is not a permanent abode, and is not worth living in, but a place to be shunned, a design of the negative power to prevent the soul from going up. The whole astral plane is subject to the five passions, the same as the physical plane.
>
> *Mahārāj Sāwan Singh, Spiritual Gems 198, SG p.316*

Paradise is therefore to be transcended, for God is to be found beyond all the heavens:

> Far beyond the paradises *(svargas)* and heavens *(apavargas),* He abides,
> where there is neither air nor water, nor sun nor moon,
> where there is neither night nor day.
> The *Vedas* know not the mysteries of that land,
> where *Brahmā* and *Vishṇu,* the learned and the holy have no access.
> Paltū, the slave, says:
> He is One – One without a second:
> there is no other king or queen.
>
> *Paltū, Bānī 2, Rekhtā 75, PSB2 p.28*

See also: **bihisht-u dūzakh**, **heavens**, **T'iēn**, **vaikuṇṭha**.

1. *Shatapatha Brāhmaṇa* 6:6.2.4.

ta'ayyun (A/P) (pl. *ta'ayyunāt*) *Lit.* specification, individualization; the formation of specific, singular items; the creation of specific entities, hence, 'entification'. *Ta'ayyun* is often translated as 'entification', a word coined by scholars that conveys the sense of *ta'ayyun* better than any other available. God is said to create the creation through a process of *ta'ayyun.* In descriptions of the creative process, *ta'ayyun* is paired with *tanazzul* (descent, devolution).

The one Lord, who is the only Reality and beside whom there is no other, descends from the level of *al-Dhāt* (Essence) through many planes of consciousness to the physical level, and in the process He 'entifies' Himself. That is, He becomes specific 'entities' or 'entifications' *(ta'ayyunāt)* at the various planes of consciousness that make up creation. 'Entification' thus means the process of creation through the extension of the divine Being, resulting in the creation of particular 'entities' that comprise the different levels of creation.

The First Entification *(al-Ta'ayyun al-Awwal),* descending from the level of the Essence, is that aspect or part of the Godhead who speaks the divine Creative Word, "Be *(Kun)!*", to the creation. In other words, the vast undifferentiated Essence of God, who is a Oneness that is all-encompassing, becomes the One from whom the many forms of creation arise. The First Entification of 'God the formless Essence' is thus 'God the Creator' and also 'God the Merciful'. Both presuppose the existence of a creation. God the Creator implies that there is something already created; God the Merciful implies that there is something over which to exercise His mercy. The First Entification *(al-Ta'ayyun al-Awwal)* is also what may be called the personal God, because it is He who has created and continually sustains and cares for His creation. The First Entification is also called the Great Isthmus *(Barzakh),* because it borders the 'sea' of creation and the 'sea' of Oneness like a narrow strip of land that is embraced and encompassed by the two 'seas' on either side.

The First Entification is also called the First Cause. That is, the unmanifested Essence of God *(al-Dhāt)* cannot even be termed the 'cause'. The absolute formless Oneness that is God's Essence 'entifies' into the personal God, who is the actual 'cause' of creation. And the first thing brought into being by this First Cause is the Second Entification *(al-Ta'ayyun al-Thānī),* or the 'First Caused'. This Second Entification or First Caused is the *'Aql al-Awwal,* the Primal Intelligence or Mind of God. Essentially, the First Caused is the divine creative power out of whom the entire creation actually proceeds, as a series of descending firmaments, heavens or regions. It is also called the *Kun,* the *Kalām Allāh,* the *Āvāz-i Khudā* and so on.

The First Entification or First Cause is also known as the Most Holy Emanation *(al-Fayḍ al-Aqdas),* while the Second Entification or First Caused is called the Holy Emanation *(al-Fayḍ al-Muqaddas).*

There are clear parallels to this description in other traditions. In Kabbalistic terms, the Essence is *Ayn-Sof;* the First Cause or Entification is *Keter* (Crown), and the First Caused or Second Entification is *Ḥokhmah* (Wisdom), the creative Power. In Indian terminology, the Essence is *Anāmī* (the Nameless), the First Cause or personal God is *Sat Purush* (true Lord), and the First Caused is *Shabd,* the creative Sound or Word. Some gnostic descriptions also speak of similar phases of the Godhead.

The Sufis often described the creation as the Five Divine Manifestations *(al-Ḥaḍarāt al-Ilāhīyah al-Khams).* The first of these five is *al-Ta'ayyun al-Awwal* (the First Entification). Then there are the three grand divisions of the creation, termed the world of spirits *('ālam al-arwāḥ),* the world of patterns *('ālam al-mithāl)* and the world of bodies *('ālam al-ajsām).* Finally, the fifth Divine Manifestation is the all-encompassing Manifestation, the Perfect Man *(al-Insān al-Kāmil),* the macrocosmic Man. The Perfect Man is called the all-encompassing manifestation because his consciousness includes and embraces all levels of the creation.

Some Sufis differentiated the First Entification into three distinct planes of consciousness above the origin of the creative Power and below the level of the formless Essence. They describe the creation as comprised of seven *ta'ayyunāt* (entifications) – or six, if *al-Dhāt* (the Essence) is excluded. Of these seven planes of consciousness or regions, the first three descending from *al-Dhāt* are all *tanzīh,* or imperceptible, indescribable, beyond comparison with anything else. These *tanzīh* (imperceptible) *ta'ayyunāt* are:

1. *Dhāt.*
2. *Aḥadīyah.*
3. *Waḥdah.*
4. *Waḥdānīyah* or *wāḥidīyah.*

Although *aḥadīyah, waḥdah, waḥdānīyah* and *wāḥidīyah* all translate into English as 'oneness', there are subtle distinctions between them. *Wāḥid* is the number 'one'. Just as the number 'one' leads to the thought of two, three and many, out of *wāḥidīyah* (oneness) comes the creative Power that creates manyness.

Waḥdah, the level of unity above *wāḥidīyah* is sometimes called the 'self-existent God'. The distinction is sometimes made that *waḥdah* is the unity that excludes all multiplicity, while *wāḥidīyah* or *waḥdānīyah* is the unity that includes all multiplicity. That is, God, as the speaker of the word "Be!" is meaningless unless there is also that which is brought into existence by His Speech. His Speech implies and includes a hearer. God, as the Beloved, is meaningless unless He also manifests as lover.

Aḥad (from *aḥadīyah*) also means 'one', but not the number one. It denotes a 'one' that is all-comprehensive and all-inclusive. In it, all things are contained, and all things are one. *Aḥadīyah* denotes a oneness that may not be describable in English – or, perhaps in any language.

As 'Ināyat Khān describes it, first in descent came *aḥadīyah,* which was eternal consciousness. But there was nothing of which this divine Essence was conscious. The next 'entification *(ta'ayyun)*' in the descent was *waḥdah,* which comprised the consciousness of existence. In this plane of unity, God is conscious of His own existence. Out of this came the next level in descent, *waḥdānīyah,* the plane of unity from which the *Logos* emanates. It is from here that the divine Word, "Be *(Kun)!*", originates, by which God creates and sustains the creation. In this level of unity is the ultimate origin of all duality: of God the Creator and His creation, or God the merciful and that over which He exercises His mercy:

> A consciousness arose out of the Absolute, the consciousness of Existence. There was nothing of which the Absolute could be conscious, except Existence. This stage is called *vaḥdat.* Out of this

> consciousness of existence a sense developed, a sense 'that I exist'. It was a development of the consciousness of existence. It was this development which formed the First Ego ('Entification'), the *Logos,* which is termed *vaḥdānīyah* by the Sufis.
>
> *'Ināyat Khān, Sufi Message, SMIK1 p.111*

Interestingly, Indian mystics have also said that above the plane where the Creative Word *(Shabd)* originates are three levels: *alakh, agam* and *anāmī.* These levels are similarly said to be completely indescribable, other than by epithets such as limitless and nameless. The description of the Essence 'entifying' at each plane of consciousness in the descent into creation also seems to parallel the descriptions of Indian mystics, as well as the gnostics and others, that each level of the creation has a 'ruler'.

While many Sufis used the term *al-Dhāt* (the Essence) for that which is beyond any 'entification', Ibn 'Arabī and his followers used the term *Wujūd* (Being), while 'Irāqī calls it 'Love'. In his book, *Divine Flashes,* 'Irāqī says that in creating the creation, Love manifests as Beloved and lover, so that Love may see itself in the mirrors of Beloved and lover. But the Reality beyond all *ta'ayyunāt* (entifications) is the boundless unity of Love itself, in which there is no distinction between lover and Beloved:

> Know that in each of the 'flashes', we make allusion to a reality purified of all entification. Call it Amorousness *(Ḥubb)* or Love *('Ishq),* let us not quarrel over words. We here recount the nature of its degrees and phases, its journey through stages.... 'Lover' and 'Beloved' are derived from 'Love', but Love upon its mighty throne is purified of all entification *(ta'ayyun)* in the sanctuary of its Reality, too holy to be touched by inwardness or outwardness. Thus, that it might manifest its perfection (a perfection identical both with its own Essence and its own Attributes), it showed itself to itself in the looking glass of lover and Beloved. It displayed its own loveliness to its own eyes, and became viewer and Viewed; the names 'lover' and 'Beloved', the attributes of seeker and Sought, then appeared:
>
> When Love revealed the outward to the inward,
> It made the lover's fame;
> When it embellished the inward with the outward,
> It made known the Beloved's name.
> Other than that Essence, not one atom existed;
> When it manifested itself,
> these 'others' came to life.
> O Thou whose outward is 'lover',
> whose inward is 'Beloved'!

Who has ever seen the Sought
  become the seeker?[1]

'Irāqī, Divine Flashes 1, DF pp.72–73

Below *waḥdānīyah,* the level at which the creative Power originates, are three *ta'ayyunāt* (entifications) that are called *tashbīh* (perceptible, capable of some description). These fifth, sixth and seventh *ta'ayyunāt,* taken together, comprise the creation, the *arbāb,* that which is cherished and sustained by *al-Rabb,* the Lord:

5.	*'Ālam al-arwāḥ*	world of spirits.
6.	*'Ālam al-mithāl*	world of patterns.
7.	*'Ālam al-ajsām*	world of bodies.

First in descent below the origin of the creative Power are the realms of spirit *('ālam al-arwāḥ),* where the spirit is without any covering or any body, and functions without any tool, vehicle or faculty of perception other than itself. Then comes the realm wherein lies the hidden forces that shape the physical world, the realm of patterns *('ālam al-mithāl).* The final stage of descent is where the soul is clothed with a physical body *('ālam al-ajsām).*

Sufi terminology is not also used consistently by different writers. Thus, 'Ināyat Khān provides a variant of the terms for these last three *ta'ayyunāt,* listing the perceptible planes as:[2]

5.	*'Ālam al-arwāḥ*	world of spirits.
6.	*'Ālam al-ajsām*	world of bodies.
7.	*'Ālam al-insān*	world of human beings.

He thereby equates the *'ālam al-ajsām* with the realm of subtle patterns and prototypes, and the *'ālam al-insān* with the physical plane. Human beings lie at the foot of creation. Yet, in their essence, they are all one with God; they are the final *ta'ayyun* (entification, individualization) of the Divine. All mystics have stressed this simple and fundamental truth. Rūmī writes that at the level of absolute Being the illusion of 'I' and 'we' does not exist:

Simple we were and all one substance:
  we were all without head and without foot yonder.
We were one substance, like the sun:
  we were knotless and pure, like water.
When that goodly Light took form,
  it became many in number like the shadows of a battlement.

Rūmī, Maśnavī I:686–88, MJR2 p.39

The question naturally arises, therefore, as to why God should have 'entified' Himself in this way. Rūmī explains that God invented the "I" and "we" in order to play the game of worshipping Himself. Addressing God and the Creative Word, he writes:

> You whose soul is free from 'we' and 'I',
> You who are the subtle essence
> of the spirit in man and woman;
> When man and woman become one,
> You are that One;
> When the units are eliminated,
> You are that (Unity).
> You contrived this 'I' and 'we'
> in order that You might
> play the game of worship with Yourself –
> That all 'I's' and 'you's' should become one soul,
> and should at last be submerged in the Beloved.
> All this is true; so come, then, O Creative Word,
> You who transcend "Come" and speech!
>
> *Rūmī, Maśnavī I:1785–89; cf. MJR2 pp.97–98*

Like colourless light divided into colours by a prism, individual is divided from individual; indeed, individual may even be in "conflict" with individual, though their source is one:

> Since colourlessness (pure Unity)
> became the captive of colour (physical manifestation),
> a Moses came into conflict with a Moses.
> When you attain unto the colourlessness,
> which you once possessed,
> Moses and Pharaoh are at peace.
> If it occurs to you to ask questions about this mystery,
> (I reply), how should the world of colour
> be devoid of contradiction?
>
> *Rūmī, Maśnavī I:2467–69; cf. MJR2 p.134*

However, merely asserting a belief in the oneness of all souls is insufficient. As long as the soul's attention functions at the level of the physical plane, there will be division and separation. The purpose of the "prophets" is to lead souls to the level where they actually are one with each other and one with the Divine:

Like the hunter who catches a shadow –
how can a shadow become his property?
The man has tightly grasped the shadow of a bird.
The bird on the branch of the tree
is fallen into amazement, thinking,
"I wonder who this crack-brained fellow is laughing at?
Here's folly for you, here's a rotten cause!"

And if you say that the part is united with the whole,
then eat thorns: for the thorn is united with the rose.
Except from one point of view,
the part is not united with the whole:
Otherwise, indeed, the mission of the prophets would be vain,
for the prophets only exist
in order to unite the part with the whole:
How, then, would the prophets unite them,
if the part and whole were already one body?

Rūmī, Maśnavī I:2808–13; cf. MJR2 pp.153–54

In these passages, Rūmī is saying that the purpose in the *ta'ayyun* (entification) of the Divine is for souls to play the game of love and worship with Himself, and to realize thereby their own essential divinity.

1. 'Aṭṭār, in *DF* p.73.
2. 'Ināyat Khān, *Sufi Message, SMIK5* p.25.

ṭabaq (A/P) (pl. *ṭibāq, aṭbāq*), **ṭabaqat** (A), **ṭabqah** (P), **tabaq** (Pu/H) *Lit.* stratum, layer, level; a stratum of earth, a stratum of air, a stratum of society and so on; thus, the heavens, inner or outer, expressing the idea that the realms of the creation are arrayed like strata, one above the other. The *Qur'ān* speaks of "seven heavens, in levels *(ṭibāqan)*",[1] as well as "seven heavens, and of the earth a similar number".[2] This has given rise to the tradition of the fourteen realms or stages in creation.

The *Qur'ān* does not say whether these stages or heavens are material or spiritual, though it does indicate, without additional explanation, that the soul travels from one stage to another:

I call to witness the ruddy glow of sunset,
and the night and what it envelops,
and the moon when it is at the full:
You shall surely travel from stage *(ṭabaq)* to stage *(ṭabaq)*.

Qur'ān 84:16–19

North Indian Sufis have hence coined the Punjabi-Arabic combination *chawdah tabaq* (fourteen realms), and have been explicit as to where these realms are to be found:

All fourteen realms *(chawdah ṭabaq)* are within your heart,
O Bāhū, if only you knew how to peep within!

Sulṭān Bāhū, Bait 113, SBU p.346, SBE (112) pp.306–7

And:

I have, at last, grasped the beginning and the end:
The whole spectacle of past, present and future
has passed before my eyes.
Within my heart are fourteen realms *(chawdah ṭabaq):*
chambers of light ablaze with the profusion of God's radiance.
Those who have not realized God will wander,
homeless in this world, destitute in the next.

Sulṭān Bāhū, Bait 8, SBU p.8; cf. SBE (7) pp.232–33

Sulṭān Bāhū also says that the "fourteen realms" are within the orbit of the *"Kalmah",* the Creative Word or Speech of God:

You will only know the marvel of *Kalmah*
when it has opened the window of your heart.
Lovers practise *Kalmah* within their hearts,
lit by the Master's radiance.
All fourteen realms *(chawdah ṭabaq)* are within the *Kalmah* –
how can the ignorant comprehend this secret?
As for me, my Master initiated me into the *Kalmah.*
Since then I have dedicated my soul only to him.

Sulṭān Bāhū, Bait 145, SBU p.354, SBE (144) pp.328–29

In a poem addressed to a Muslim seeker, Shaykh Taqī, Tulsī Sāhib says that the divine "Beloved" as well as the "fourteen realms *(chawdah tabaq)*" are within:

Listen, O Taqī, seek not your Beloved in the world outside:
behold the splendour of your Beloved within your own self.
In the pupil of your eye is a mole (the third eye),
within which is hidden the entire mystery;
Look within and see what lies
beyond this dark curtain.
The secret of the fourteen realms *(chawdah tabaq)*
will be disclosed to you, for sure.

Tulsī Sāhib, in Santon kī Bānī, Ghazal vv.1–3, SKB p.304

See also: **heavens, sab‘ samāwāt, regions**.

1. *Qur’ān* 67:3.
2. *Qur’ān* 65:12, *AYA*.

tanazzul (A/P) (pl. *tanazzulāt*) *Lit.* a descent; a sending down, a devolution. In Sufism, the process by which the absolute Being manifests the creation includes both *tanazzul* (descent) and *ta‘ayyun* (‘entification’, the creation of entities or regions). Through them all, creating and sustaining them, runs the divine creative power or Command. In the *Qur’ān,* the term is used in verb form:

> *Allāh* is He who created the seven firmaments *(sab‘a samāwāt)*
> and of the earth a similar number.
> Through the midst of them (all) descends *(yatanazzalu)* His Command:
> That you may know that *Allāh* has power over all things,
> and that *Allāh* comprehends all things in (His) knowledge.
>
> *Qur’ān 65:12; cf. AYA*

See also: **ta‘ayyun**.

tārā, tārā maṇḍal (H/Pu) *Lit.* star *(tārā);* the sphere *(maṇḍal)* of the star *(tārā);* the realm of the stars, the star region; used mystically in descriptions of the ascent from the body into the inner regions. As the soul and mind leave the body, they collect together or focus at the eye centre, and then move progressively inwards through the ‘sky’ of the body until they reach the astral world. As this concentration and transition slowly comes about, the seeing power *(nirat)* of the soul is awakened.

Because it is not yet accustomed to seeing inside clearly, the attention wavers and the soul sees the inner light like stars or flashes of light across a dark sky. As concentration improves, the *nirat* becomes used to seeing within. As a result, the light becomes steady and, in time, bright like the sun. It is also circular, as if the soul is passing through a tunnel that is illuminated at the far end. After the sunlike light, it becomes like that of the moon: circular, cool and steady. The soul passes through this light, and enters the threshold of the astral worlds.

This kind of experience has been described by some of those who have had what modern researchers have called near-death experiences or out-of-the-body experiences. Sometimes, the soul is met by a being, an ‘angel’, who after conversing in the direct mind-to-mind manner that is natural to that plane, sends the soul back into this world. In the case of a disciple of a perfect

Master, it is here that they are met by the radiant, astral form of their Master. The astral body itself is so called because it glistens and sparkles with radiance as if sprinkled with 'star dust'.

Mahārāj Sāwan Singh describes this preliminary ascent in a letter to a disciple:

> When the concentration is complete, it will appear as if you are separate from the body and the body is a corpse of someone else. The starry sky will appear in time. Fix your attention in the bright star and continue repetition as before. When the star is approached, it will burst, and the attention will penetrate through it. The starry sky has been crossed. In the same manner, the sun and the moon in succession will be crossed by the attention doing repetition all the time. After crossing the moon region, the Master's radiant form will be visible. Fix your attention in that, and hand yourself over to the Master.
>
> *Mahārāj Sāwan Singh, Spiritual Gems 87, SG p.119*

> When, by repetition of the names with attention fixed in the eye focus, you have become unconscious of the body below the eyes, then your attention will catch the Sound Current. Select the sound resembling the church bell and discard all other sounds. Then slowly your soul will leave the body and collect in the eyes and become strong. Then fix your attention in the biggest star, so much that you forget everything else except the Sound and the star. Then this star will burst, and you will see what is within it and beyond.
>
> After crossing the star you will have to cross the sun and the moon. Then you will see the form of the Master. When that form becomes steady it will reply. This form will reply to all of your inquiries, and guide you to higher stages. I do not wish you to stop at the appearance of the stars, but wish to take you higher up. These stars are of the first sky only, and Hindu philosophers have spoken of seven skies. You will also see other skies.
>
> *Mahārāj Sāwan Singh, Spiritual Gems 38, SG pp.68–69*

He also speaks of 'stars' in the regions beyond the initial ascent from the body:

> After crossing the flames of *sahans dal kanwal* and going through considerable spiritual journey, you will reach the second sky, with its stars and moons and suns, which lies below *trikuṭī*. Crossing this sky you will enter a crooked tunnel … then you enter the *Brahm* stage, which is so strange and wonderful!
>
> *Mahārāj Sāwan Singh, Spiritual Gems 50, SG p.77*

Swāmī Shiv Dayāl Singh also describes the same experience:

At the eye centre my consciousness was inverted –
  leading up, towards the thousand-petalled lotus.
Then, leaving the mind behind, I ascended with the soul.
When *Jyoti Nirañjan,* the lord of light, revealed his form,
  I was elated beyond measure, unable to speak.
I heard the bell and conch sound;
I saw the sun, the moon and the star *(tārā)* (within).
The door to *bank nāl* (crooked tunnel) was then opened
  through which my soul ascended to *trikuṭī,*
  where I made contact with the *Guru*'s Word *(Shabd).*

Swāmī Shiv Dayāl Singh, Sār Bachan Poetry 5:5.6–9, SBP p.48

The two primary characteristics of the inner realms are those of sound and light, and mystics have no alternative but to use the terms of this world to describe them. They therefore speak of suns, moons and stars, and utilize any other images that convey a sense of light in order to provide some inkling of what these realms are like.

See also: **chandra**.

tashbīh (A/P) *Lit.* simile, comparison, allegory; the identification of the only Being by comparison (*e.g.* He is like this or like that); also, distinguishable, perceptible, capable of being described by some analogy. In theological discussions, *tashbīh* refers to the belief that God is immanent, and is present in every particle of the creation. *Tashbīh* implies God's manifestation in the world. The concept that all things are signs of His presence, that all creation points to Him is *tashbīh.*

'Ināyat Khān uses the term *tashbīh* to designate the three lower realms of the creation, and *tanzīh* (imperceptible) for the three higher levels, *al-Dhāt* (the Essence) being the seventh and highest level.[1] The *tashbīh* planes of the creation include everything below the origin of the Creative Word which brings the creation into existence. The *tashbīh* planes are (in order of descent): *'ālam al-arwāḥ* (world of spirits), *'ālam al-mithāl* (world of patterns) and *'ālam al-ajsām* (world of bodies).

Mystics have often said that the subtle realms cannot be described because there is nothing in this visible world to which they can be compared. Words are simply too limited a means of communication. However, many mystics have nonetheless attempted descriptions of the subtle planes, comparing the sounds to various musical instruments, comparing the landscapes to gardens, rivers and so on. Their purpose is to give encouragement to struggling human beings to rise above the material world, to provide assurance that there are better worlds, and to describe some landmarks on the way that deepen the confidence of the ascending soul that it is following the right path. But mystics have all said that the realms beyond the origin of the Creative Word are utterly impossible to describe or compare, other than with such vague epithets as 'no-place *(lā-makān)*'.

See also: **ta'ayyun, tanzīh** (2.2).

1. 'Ināyat Khān, *Sufi Message, SMIK1* pp.111–12, *SMIK5* pp.25–26.

three realms, three worlds See **loka, regions, triloka**.

T'iēn (Tiān) (C) *Lit.* Sky, Heaven; hence, divine Spirit, divine Principle, natural Law. Before the emergence of Taoism, *Shàng Tì* (Lord on High), a tribal anthropomorphic God, was regarded as the Creator. With the coming of Taoism in the sixth century BCE, *Shàng Tì* was replaced by the broader, more inclusive term *T'iēn. T'iēn* is generally used to denote that which is heavenly or divine, under whose will or jurisdiction the celestial deities as well as the earthly plane operate.

T'iēn is often combined with *Tào,* as *T'iēn Tào,* to denote its intrinsically divine nature. However, Lǎo Tzu clearly indicates that there is an ascending natural order:

> Man emulates Earth;
> Earth emulates Heaven *(T'iēn);*
> Heaven emulates *Tào;*
> And *Tào* emulates that which is natural to It.
>
> *Lǎo Tzu, Tào Té Chīng 25, LTTN p.142*

"Natural to It" infers that which is self-existent: *Tào* is of Itself what It is, emulating or reflecting nothing. *Tào* is formless and transcendent, governing Heaven, Earth and man through the enduring cosmic Law. The existence of *T'iēn,* like everything else, is dependent on *Tào.*

In common parlance, *T'iēn* is interchangeable with *T'iēn mìng* (the mandate or will of Heaven), implying the eternal principles or natural laws that govern the world of man. In this sense, *T'iēn* is commonly interpreted as nature or even fate, since everything happens by the will of Heaven. Thus, Chuāng Tzu writes:

Life and death are fated *(mìng)* –
constant as the succession of dark and dawn,
a matter of Heaven *(T'iēn)*.
There are some things which man can do nothing about –
all are a matter of the nature of creatures.

Chuāng Tzu 6, CTW p.80

Other allied terms include *T'iēn shàng* (Heaven above), which refers to the transcendent, and *T'iēn hsià* (under Heaven), a common Chinese term for the physical world. *T'iēn Tì* (Heaven and Earth), on the other hand, refers to the entire cosmos.

T'iēn t'áng (hall or palace of Heaven) is used in religious Taoism, indicating the highest reach of the human spirit, a state of paradise which exists within man. According to most schools of Taoism, the spirit's journey home begins in each person's brain at a place called *shàng tān t'ién*, the highest energy or spirit centre located behind and between the two eyes. It is believed that nine compartments exist within the human brain, corresponding to nine spiritual palaces called *chiŭ kūng*. Each is thought to be inhabited by a deity *(shén)*. At the centre of the brain is a palace called *nì huán*, a transliteration of the Buddhist term *nirvāṇa*. It is the seat of the highest deity, and is the spirit's ultimate dwelling place as one with *Tào*.

See also: **heavens**, **sab' samāwāt**, **Shàng Tì** (2.1), **sky**, **Tào** (2.2).

Tiferet (He) *Lit.* splendour, beauty; the sixth of the ten *sefirot;* the divine quality or harmonizing principle between the masculine (outflowing, abundant) and feminine (inflowing, confining, limiting) energies represented by the *sefirot* of *Ḥesed* (Lovingkindness, Abundant Love) and *Din* (Judgment). The harmonious relationship of all the lower *sefirot* is considered to depend on the activity of *Tiferet*. *Tiferet* also corresponds to the patriarch Jacob and the name of God, *Yahweh*.

See also: **sefirot**.

timir khaṇḍ (H) *Lit.* region *(khaṇḍ)* of darkness *(timir);* a name used by Swāmī Shiv Dayāl Singh for the region of intense darkness, also called *mahā sunn* (great void), that Indian mystics have said is located between the two main spiritual realms that lie above the universal mind and below eternity:

How can I describe the depth of this region of darkness *(timir khaṇḍ)?*
My soul descended billions of *jojans,* but could not plumb its depth.

> So, considering further exploration unnecessary, the soul of this mystic returned, and resumed its onward journey, according to the Master's instructions. Such is the vast expanse of *mahā sunn*.
>
> *Swāmī Shiv Dayāl Singh, Sār Bachan Poetry, Bachan 21, Hidāyat Nāmā, SBP p.174*

A *jojan* or *yojan* is a traditional measure of distance, of uncertain length, generally reckoned to be between four and eighteen miles. Swāmī Shiv Dayāl Singh is simply expressing the vastness of this realm.

See also: **mahā sunn**.

Totality, Totalities A gnostic term found largely in Coptic texts, meaning the entire hierarchy of creation. The Totality was the entire creation, while the Totalities were the realms or *aeons* comprising the creation. All realms were created by God. Hence, the *Tripartite Tractate* says:

> As for the Totalities, He is the One who begot them and created them. He is without beginning and without end.
>
> *Tripartite Tractate 52, NHS22 pp.192–93*

And:

> The Father, in accordance with His exalted position over the Totalities, being an unknown and incomprehensible One, has such greatness and magnitude that if He had revealed Himself suddenly, quickly, to all the exalted ones among the *aeons* who had come forth from Him, they would have perished. Therefore, He withheld His power and His inexhaustibility within that in which He is.
>
> *Tripartite Tractate 64–65, NHS22 pp.212–15*

The Totalities or realms of creation were considered to exist within God, as His extension or emanation, rather than being something "cast off from" or exterior to Him:

> The emanation of the Totalities, which exist from the One who exists, did not occur according to a separation from one another, as something cast off from the One who begets them. Rather, their begetting is like a process of extension, as the Father extends Himself to those whom He loves, so that those who have come forth from Him might become Him as well.
>
> *Tripartite Tractate 73, NHS22 pp.228–29*

And:

> As for the incomprehensible, inconceivable One, the Father, the perfect One, the One who made the Totality, within Him is the Totality, and of Him the Totality has need.
>
> *Gospel of Truth 18, NHS22 pp.84–85*

See also: **aeons**, **All (the)**, **Pleroma**.

trikuṭī (H/Pu) *Lit.* three *(tri)* peaks *(kūṭa);* the second spiritual region counting from the bottom up, according to the description of many Indian Saints, including Kabīr, Charaṇdās, Tukārām, Swāmī Shiv Dayāl Singh and the *Gurus* whose writings appear in the *Ādi Granth;* the mental or causal region; the highest realm of the mind, the universal mind; the origin of all aspects of the mind, including time, space, causality, *karma,* duality, birth and death, and so on.

Trikuṭī receives its name from the three peaks, prominences, mountains or fountainheads of energy *(Meru, Sumeru* and *Kailāsh)* that form its highest part. Indian mystics over the last several centuries have called this realm *trikuṭī.* These three peaks are formed from above by three currents flowing into this region. These peaks are also the origin of the three *guṇas* below, which prevail in all regions of the mind.

Mahārāj Sāwan Singh describes this region in letters to Western disciples. "Mind is derived from *trikuṭī,*"[1] he says. It is the source of all mind and mind energies, but in a highly refined and subtle form:

> In *trikuṭī,* the *nij man* (innermost or causal mind) or *Brahm* or the universal mind covers the spirit. The forms here are made of very pure *māyā* (illusion), so much so that a majority of the seekers have failed to see here the spirit apart from *māyā* or mind, and therefore considered *Brahm* as all-pervading.
>
> *Mahārāj Sāwan Singh, Spiritual Gems 20, SG p.27*

At the level of the universal mind are to be found the seed forms, the subtle essences, energies or patterns of all that lies below in the causal, astral and physical regions:

> The *nij* mind *(man)* is as a drop of the second stage, *trikuṭī,* and in it lies the seed of all creation below *trikuṭī.*
>
> *Mahārāj Sāwan Singh, Spiritual Gems 165, SG p.269*

The ruler of *trikuṭī* is the negative power, which some Saints have identified with *Kāl* (*lit.* time), the lord of death in Indian mythology. In this sense,

Kāl is also equated with *Brahm* or *Brahman,* the absolute Reality of the *Upanishads:*

> *Kāl* is not only the lord of this physical world but of all the worlds below and above and surrounding it, up to *trikuṭī.* His technical Hindu name is *Brahm.* He rules over *trikuṭī* and *sahans dal kanwal* and all the regions below them. He is with every creature in the shape of mind!
>
> *Mahārāj Sāwan Singh, Spiritual Gems 120, SG p.177*

Mind is the architect of the multiplicity and diversity that characterizes the causal, astral and physical realms. By means of this diversity, the mind spins the web of illusion over the reality of pure spirit. Oneness or wholeness is seemingly split thereby into manyness, bringing into being the consequent illusions of time and causation, which have their origins in *trikuṭī.* As a result, from the perspective of the physical universe, the primary law of creation appears to be cause and effect, or *karma.* This is the means by which *Kāl* keeps his allotment of souls confined within his domain:

> From *trikuṭī* down to the vegetable kingdom is the sphere of *Kāl,* in which are rotating all the souls according to their *karma.* The ruler of the circle is *Kāl (Brahm),* who wishes to confine all these souls to his own domain, taking care not to let them go out of his own sphere, so that the latter may not become depopulated.
>
> *Mahārāj Sāwan Singh, Spiritual Gems 140, SG p.200*

Over the course of many lifetimes, souls accumulate a great deal of *karma* that cannot all be paid off in just a few lifetimes. This excess *karma* is 'stored' or 'recorded', so to speak, at the top of *trikuṭī:*

> The reserve actions are stored at the top of *trikuṭī,* and only when a spirit has crossed the third mind or *trikuṭī* is it said to be free from all *karma.* Below this, the spirit suffers from the ills of *karma.*
>
> *Mahārāj Sāwan Singh, Spiritual Gems 20, SG p.31*

Hence, liberation of the soul from birth and death and freedom from the effects of *karma,* time, causation and all the illusions of the mind are only possible when the soul rises above *trikuṭī:*

> Once *trikuṭī* has been crossed (this will only be when all karmic accounts are settled), the soul never goes back into transmigration. It will go up to merge in its origin.
>
> *Mahārāj Sāwan Singh, Spiritual Gems 20, SG p.33*

Paraphrasing Swāmī Shiv Dayāl Singh, Julian Johnson writes of this region:

> Now, my dear companion, prepare to enter the second stage, and behold *trikuṭī,* the abode of the *Guru,* where the sound of *Onkār* is heard perpetually resounding. You go up (to the top of *sahans dal kanwal*) and open a gate and enter *bank nāl* (crooked tunnel), passing on to the other end of it. Then you cross high and low hills. Now the vision appears to be reversed, and one sees as if from the opposite side of the veil which he has penetrated. Looking upward, he passes into a fortlike region which he enters, and becomes master of it. He reigns there as lord of that region. Here the soul becomes adorned with the attributes of devotion and faith. Here the seed of all *karma* is burned, destroyed. You will see thick dark clouds, from which peals of thunder constantly resound. When rising above these dark clouds, behold, the entire sphere is red, with the beautiful red sun in the centre imparting its colour to everything.
>
> This is where the *Guru* really gives *Nām* (the Name), for the Master's *Shabd rūp* (Word form) is here.... Here, you will see the red four-petalled lotus spoken of by the Saints, the details and colours becoming visible as one comes nearer to it. Here, the bell and conch sounds are left behind and the sound of *mardang* (drum) is heard.
>
> After that, the soul resumes its upward journey. Now comes the sound of a huge drum, beaten incessantly. Here, the soul has grasped the Primal Current, from which all creation emanates. Innumerable suns and moons are seen here and many kinds of skies, filled with stars. The soul here realizes its complete separation from *piṇḍa* (the physical universe), and rises to the upper *brahmāṇḍa,* as if intoxicated with joy. He sees and traverses deserts and mountains and gardens. In the gardens are flowers arranged in artistic designs and groups everywhere. Canals and rivulets of transparent water are flowing in abundance. Then he approaches an ocean, which he crosses by means of a bridge. He then beholds the three mountains or prominences called *Mer, Sumer* and *Kailāsh* (from which the region is named). After this, he passes on to a region of the most unalloyed delight.
>
> *Julian Johnson, With a Great Master in India 14; cf. WGMI pp.190–91*

Among the other Saints who have used the term, Tukārām speaks of the "peak of *trikuṭī*" as the realm where the "highest knowledge" is attained, beyond "good and bad *karma*", and beyond the "three *guṇas*":

> At the peak of *trikuṭī,* I received
>   the rare gift of the Lord's grace, effortlessly.

Now I have cast off my load of worldly desires,
together with my good and bad *karma.*
I am beyond the turmoil of the three *guṇas,*
and am sure I have to beg no more.
For attainment of the highest knowledge,
fulfils all desires.

Tukārām, Gāthā 426, STG p.76

In the *Ādi Granth,* Guru Rāmdās says that through the guidance of the Master the doors locked by deception are opened, and the doubt and fear inherent in the realms of *trikuṭī* are dispelled.[2] And Guru Nānak writes that by coming to dwell in the all-pervading Lord, seeing Him everywhere, the soul is released from *trikuṭī.*[3]

See also: **aṇḍa**, **sahans dal kanwal**.

1. Mahārāj Sāwan Singh, *Spiritual Gems* 25, *SG* p.50.
2. Guru Rāmdās, *Ādi Granth* 986.
3. Guru Nānak, *Ādi Granth* 220; see also Kabīr, *Ādi Granth* 857, 1123.

trilok(a), **trilokī** (S/H/Pu), **tribhuvan** (S/H), **tīn lok**, **tirlokī** (H/Pu), **bhūmitraya**, **jagat-traya**, **lokatraya** (S), **tiloka** (Pa), **tribhavaṇ**, **tribhuvaṇ** (Pu) *Lit.* three *(tri, traya, tīn)* worlds *(loka, bhuvan, bhūmi, jagat);* the three worlds of traditional Hindu thought, regarded as comprising all created worlds. They are:

1. *Bhūloka* or *bhūmiloka* (world of the earth), the world of men, the physical universe; also called *mṛityuloka* (world of death), *manushyaloka* (world of men) and *pṛithvīloka* (world of the earth).
2. *Pātālaloka* (world below), the nether worlds.
3. *Devaloka* (world of the gods), the heavenly worlds; also called *svarga* (heaven) or *svarloka* (paradise).

Devaloka and *pātālaloka* are further subdivided into seven heavens and seven nether worlds, but the nether worlds are not to be construed as the antithesis of the heavenly realms. Some mythological accounts describe their bliss and light.

Descriptions of *triloka* vary throughout Indian literature. In some cases, the three worlds are those of the earth *(bhūloka* or *bhūmiloka),* the atmosphere *(bhuvaloka)* and the sky *(svarloka).* Thus, *pātālaloka* is replaced by *bhuvaloka* (world of the atmosphere), an intermediate region inhabited by *munis* and *siddhas* (sages) of the past, and *devaloka* by *svarloka.* In other cases, the intermediate *loka* is identified as *pitṛiloka,* the world of the ancestors. Hence, the *Bṛihadāraṇyaka Upanishad:*

> Verily, there are three worlds *(lokatraya):*
> the world of men,
> the world of the ancestors,
> and the world of the gods *(devaloka).*
> The world of men *(manushyaloka)* can only be obtained through a son,
> and by no other rite;
> The world of the ancestors *(pitṛiloka)* through rites;
> And the world of the gods *(devaloka)* through *gnosis (vidyā).*
> The world of the gods *(devaloka)* is the best of the worlds.
> Therefore, they praise *gnosis (vidyā).*
>
> *Bṛihadāraṇyaka Upanishad 1:5.16*

Being largely mythological, the account makes no attempt to identify the location of these three worlds. However, the reaching of *devaloka* "through *gnosis*", through mystic knowledge *(vidyā)* or experience, does identify the heavenly worlds as inner regions. In the *Bhagavad Gītā,* Kṛishṇa, a personification of the Supreme Being, is said by Kṛishṇa's disciple, Arjuna, to be greater than and to pervade all the "three worlds":

> O high-souled One!
> All the three worlds *(lokatraya)* tremble with fear
> at the sight of that wondrous, awe-inspiring form of Yours –
> The one Existence filling all space between heaven and earth,
> and all other places, too....
>
> You are the father of the world –
> of all that moves and is unmoving.
> You are the object of its worship,
> the most venerable of its Teachers.
> In all the three worlds *(lokatraya),*
> there is none equal to you, much less one greater,
> O You of incomparable power!
>
> *Bhagavad Gītā 11:20, 43; cf. BGT*

In the *Bhāgavata Purāṇa,* in a passage where Ṛishi Vyāsa is addressing Ṛishi Nārada, there is again an indication, as in the *Bṛihadāraṇyaka Upanishad,* that the three worlds lie within:

> Like the sun, you travel
> everywhere throughout the three worlds *(triloka);*

> And, moving within all like the *prāṇa* (subtle life energy),
> you can enter the inner spaces of everyone.
>
> *Bhāgavata Purāṇa 1:5.7*

Later texts are more definitive. The *Shiva Saṃhitā,* speaking of the bodily *chakras* and their conquest through the yogic practice of *prāṇāyāma,* indicates that the human body is a microcosm of the three worlds. "All beings" in these worlds also have a part to play, by reflection, in bodily processes:

> All beings that exist in the three worlds *(triloka)*
> are also to be found in the body;
> Surrounding the *Meru* (spinal axis),
> they are engaged in their respective functions.
>
> *Shiva Saṃhitā 2:4; cf. SSV p.16*

Success in this yogic practice thereby gives the yogi access to the three worlds, through the gateway of this bodily microcosm:

> The mighty *yogī* having attained, through *prāṇāyāma,*
> the eight kinds of psychic power,
> and having crossed the ocean of vice and virtue (this world),
> moves about freely in the three worlds *(triloka).*
>
> *Shiva Saṃhitā 3:52; cf. SSV p.32*

Such a yogi, continues this text, "obtains immortality" and "is worshipped even by the gods".[1] In fact, the writer adds, "There is no greater secret than this throughout the three worlds *(triloka).*"[2]

Buddhist teachings also speak of the three worlds, *tiloka* in the Pali language. The physical universe is *kāmaloka,* the realm *(loka)* of desire *(kāma),* the field of the five senses. The plane of hidden or subtle forms is known as *rūpaloka* (world of form). Above that is *arūpaloka,* the formless world. Emphasizing the inner location of these worlds, *rūpa* and *arūpaloka* are understood to correspond to particular *jhanas,* planes of meditation reached in Buddhist contemplation.

This Buddhist definition of the three worlds corresponds closely to that of *Vedānta,* which also speaks of three worlds: the *sthūla* (physical), *sūkshma* (subtle, astral) and *kāraṇa* (causal) planes. Hence, the *Vedāntasāra* states:

> Taken as a whole, the gross *(sthūla),* subtle *(sūkshma)* and causal *(kāraṇa)* worlds *(prapañcha)* make a vast universe, just as smaller forests, taken together, make a vast forest, or a group of smaller lakes makes a vast expanse of water.
>
> *Sadānanda, Vedāntasāra 2:118*

Some later Western writers, notably the theosophist Annie Besant (1847–1933), have identified the gross, subtle and causal planes of *Vedānta* with the traditional Indian *triloka*. By "mental plane", in this context, she means the causal plane:

> The physical, astral and mental planes are 'the three worlds' through which lies the pilgrimage of the soul, again and again repeated. In these three worlds revolves the wheel of human life, and souls are bound to that wheel throughout their evolution, and are carried by it to each of these three worlds in turn....
>
> To the three worlds ... is confined the life of the Thinker (man, as a mental being), while he is treading the earlier stages of human evolution. A time will come in the evolution of humanity when its feet will enter loftier realms, and reincarnation will be of the past. But while the wheel of birth and death is turning, and man is bound thereon by desires that pertain to the three worlds, his life is led in these three regions.
>
> *Annie Besant, The Ancient Wisdom, AW pp.188, 192*

Though this identification of the three worlds with the physical, astral and causal realms is not unlikely, it is not definitively confirmed by any early Indian literature, nor even by the well-known early Vedantic philosophers, Shankara and Rāmānuja. Indeed, Shankara, commenting on the *Bhagavad Gītā,* says that *lokatraya* refers to *bhūloka, bhuvaloka* and *svarloka.*[3] Rāmānuja, on the other hand, in his commentary on the *Bhagavad Gītā,* says that *lokatraya* means the unconscious (inanimate matter), the conscious associated with the unconscious (animated matter, life forms), and the disembodied pure consciousness (liberated, pure soul).[4] However, although speaking of a multitude of worlds both above and below us, he says that *lokatraya* also means the three kinds of gods and incorporeal beings – the malicious, benevolent and indifferent – from among *Brahmā,* the lesser deities, the demons, the *pitṛis* (ancestors), the *siddhas* (adepts), the *gandharvas* (celestial musicians), the *yakshas* (nature spirits) and the *rākshasas* (ogres).[5] It is clear, then, that the term had no precise definition.

Some later Indian Saints have pointed out that the three worlds lie within the domain of the negative power or universal mind, whose highest realm they have called *trikuṭī* (*lit.* three peaks). Referring to this negative power as *Onkār Purush,* Swāmī Shiv Dayāl Singh specifically identifies the highest point in the three worlds as *trikuṭī. Sunn* (void) is the realm immediately above *trikuṭī:*

From there *(sunn)* was created the region of *trikuṭī*,
which is in the domain of *Onkār Purush*....
This is the station *(maqām)* of the *Vedas* and the scriptures;
This place is the origin of *trilokī*.

Swāmī Shiv Dayāl Singh, Sār Bachan Poetry 23:1.40–42, SBP p.198

Elsewhere, Swāmī Shiv Dayāl Singh commonly speaks of *piṇḍa* (the physical universe), *sahans dal kanwal* (*lit.* thousand-petalled lotus) and *trikuṭī* as the three main regions of the mind. These are equivalent to the physical, astral and causal realms. He also depicts the negative power and ruler of the *trilokī* as *Kāl*, the mythological lord of death in Indian tradition:

O soul, you have forgotten your (real) country,
and have accepted this land of *Kāl (Kāl desh)* as your own.
Kāl created all these three worlds *(trilokī)*:
the merciful One *(Dayāl)* made *sat lok*.
The three worlds *(tīn lok)* are the prison of *Kāl*:
the fourth is the abode of *Dayāl*.
Kāl deceived the soul,
and prevented everyone from reaching the fourth.

Swāmī Shiv Dayāl Singh, Sār Bachan Poetry 38:11.3–6, SBP p.349

Swāmī Shiv Dayāl Singh also writes that it is the creative Power, the *Shabd* (Word), which has made and which sustains the multifaceted diversity and illusion *(māyā)* of the three worlds:

Shabd has created the three worlds *(trilokī)*:
from *Shabd* has *māyā* proliferated.

Swāmī Shiv Dayāl Singh, Sār Bachan Poetry 9:2.1, SBP p.88

Without any specific identification, many Indian mystics have also portrayed the three worlds as a place of the soul's bondage, emphasizing that the way of escape from these worlds is through the *Nām* (Name, creative Power) of a Master:

I can think of no other door:
If man wanders through the three worlds *(tribhavaṇ)*,
even then he understands naught.
The true *Guru* is the banker who possesses the Name *(Nām)* treasure:
this gem *(ratan)* of the Lord's Name is obtained from him.

Guru Arjun, Ādi Granth 1078, MMS

Likewise, Guru Nānak:

> Imbued with the Name *(Nām),*
> the mortal gains knowledge of the three worlds *(tribhavaṇ).*
> Nānak, imbued with the Name *(Nām),* one attains eternal peace.
>
> *Guru Nānak, Ādi Granth 941, MMS*

And Gharībdās:

> The merciful One *(Dayāl)* cast a divine look:
> The true Master – the all-wise Saint,
> blessed and accepted the souls lost in *tirlokī.*
>
> *Gharībdās, in Sant Bānī Sangrah 1, Binaya 25, SBS1 p.181*

See also: **loka**.

1. *Shiva Saṃhitā* 4:38, 5:40.
2. *Shiva Saṃhitā* 5:140.
3. Shankara, *Commentary on Bhagavad Gītā* 15:17, in *EBB* p.382.
4. Rāmānuja, *Commentary on Bhagavad Gītā* 15:17, in *EBB* pp.382–83.
5. Rāmānuja, *Commentary on Bhagavad Gītā* 11:20, in *EBB* p.382.

triveṇī (S/H), **tribeṇī** (H/Pu) *Lit.* three *(tri)* braids *(veṇī);* triple braids; a place near Allahabad where the three rivers of the Ganges (Gangā), the Jumna (Yamunā) and the now dried up and possibly legendary Sarasvatī join together; also called Prayāg and *sangam;* mystically, a name used by Indian mystics for two places in the inner regions where there is a confluence of three primary creative currents, the lower of the two being a reflection of the higher.

Ascending from the body, the three currents of *iḍā, pingalā* and *sushumṇā* come together in *sahans dal kanwal,* the central powerhouse of the astral zones. These three currents are aspects of the three *guṇas* (attributes), and are found in the body as the primary *nāḍīs* or channels of energy running within the spinal area of every human being. Speaking of this lower *triveṇī,* reached – as the writer has earlier described – after awakening the *kuṇḍalinī* and rising up through the *chakras,* the *Shiva Saṃhitā* says:

> Between the Ganges and the Yamunā flows this Sarasvatī: by bathing at their junction, the fortunate one obtains salvation.
>
> We have said before that the *iḍā* is the Ganges and the *pingalā* is the daughter of the sun (the Yamunā). In the middle, the *sushumṇā* is the Sarasvatī; the place where all three join is most inaccessible.

He who bathes his mind at the junction of the white *(iḍā)* and the black *(pingalā)* becomes free of all sins, and reaches the eternal *Brahma*....

He who bathes just once at this sacred place enjoys heavenly bliss; his manifold sins are burned, and he becomes a pure-minded *yogī*.

Pure or impure, whatever his state may be, by washing at this mystic place, he becomes truly holy.

At the time of death let him bathe himself in the water of this *triveṇī:* he who dies thinking of this, immediately reaches salvation.

Shiva Saṃhitā 5:132–134, 137–39; cf. SSV pp.74–75

Also speaking of the lower *triveṇī* in *sahans dal kanwal,* Kabīr writes of the ascent of the soul as it leaves the body by concentration of the attention between the two eyes, and rises within:

Close your eyes, your ears and your mouth,
and listen to the *anhad* (unstruck) *Shabd*
with the sound of the cricket *(jhīngur).*
When the two eyes become one,
then you will see a flowered garden.

Bring the sun *(i.e. iḍā)* and moon *(i.e. pingalā)* together at one point,
and fix your attention in the *sushman.*
Merge your attention in *triveṇī,* and then go beyond.
Crossing to that land, be forever free from illusion.

Kabīr, Shabdāvalī 1, Bhed Bānī 22:10–11, KSS1 p.66

Higher up, these three currents emanate from *trikuṭī* as the three *guṇas.* Above *trikuṭī,* they again merge together in the higher spiritual realms. This is the higher *triveṇī.*

Looking down from above, three primary energy currents flow out from the highest realm of the nameless Lord, *Anāmī Purush.* These are the powers or divisions of *Sat Purush, Akshar Purush* and *ādi Shabd.* Pouring out into the higher confines of the universal mind, they come to the foot of the three 'peaks', 'prominences' or 'mountains' of *Meru, Sumeru* and *Kailāsh,* whose shining summits give this region its Indian name of *trikuṭī.* These three primary currents give rise to the three peaks, from which, in turn, emanate the three *guṇas,* providing the underlying fabric and pattern of all creation that lies below in the causal, astral and physical planes. Thus, Swāmī Shiv Dayāl Singh, writing of the ascent of the soul beyond *trikuṭī,* locates *triveṇī* at the top of *sunn,* also called *daswān dwār,* on the borders of *mahā sunn:*

The soul now goes forward, removing the third veil,
hearing the sound of *sunn maṇḍal,*
seeing the brilliant light of *daswān dwār.*
Leaving behind *gagan* and *ākāsh,*
the soul bathes in lake *mānsarovar,*
and joins the group of pure souls (*haṃsas, lit.* swans) there.
Circling about, the soul ascends to the top of *sunn,*
where the music of *kingrī* and *sārangī* abounds.
Hearing this sound,
it penetrates and crosses *triveṇī,*
entering the vestibule of *mahā sunn.*

Swāmī Shiv Dayāl Singh, Sār Bachan Poetry 26:3.1–6, SBP p.227

Charaṇdās, on the other hand, locates *triveṇī* in *bhanwar guphā.* It can be reached, he says, through the hearing *(surat)* and seeing *(nirat)* faculties of the soul:

Triveṇī is located in *bhanwar guphā:*
reach there with the help of *surat* and *nirat;*
Through *yoga,* immerse yourself in it,
and from a crow be turned into a swan (*haṃsa,* pure soul).

Charaṇdās, Bānī 1, Shabd 4:6–7, CDB1 p.48

See also: **Prayāg**, **sahans dal kanwal**, **sushumṇā**.

vaikuṇṭh(a) (S/H), **baikuṇṭh** (H/Pu) *Lit.* paradise, heaven; *Vishṇu*'s heaven, where his devotees go after death. According to Indian mythology, *vaikuṇṭha* is located on Mount *Meru.* Flowing through it is the river Ganges, whose source is sometimes said to be *Vishṇu*'s foot. In Vedic times, *vaikuṇṭha* was an epithet of *Indra,* some hymns in the *Ṛig Veda,* for example, referring to him as *Indra-vaikuṇṭha.*[1]

Mystics have pointed out that the heavenly realms, *vaikuṇṭh* included, are a temporary reward for lives well led. After that souls are reborn:

> Now take the souls inhabiting the higher regions of subtle matter. They are as much subject to pain, pleasure and passion as the souls in the world of gross matter. Those whose *karma* is worst are made to suffer in the region of hell; others whose *karma* is a little better are made to wander as ghosts and evil spirits; those whose *karma* is still better reside in *dev lok* or *pitṛi lok;* while still higher souls enjoy themselves in paradise. Those still purer reside in *baikuṇṭh;* while the souls of incarnations, prophets of higher degrees and *yogīs* rest

> themselves in the region of *Brahm (trikuṭī).* There they enjoy the pleasures of that region for a very long period of time, but in the end they, too, after running their course, have to be born in this material world.
>
> *Mahārāj Sāwan Singh, Spiritual Gems 140, SG pp.200*

See also: **bihisht-u dūzakh**, **heavens**, **svarga**, **T'iēn**.

1. *e.g. Ṛig Veda* 10:47–50.

veil, **curtain** (He. *pargod, vilon;* Gk. *katapetasma*) A cosmic veil or curtain concealing the glory of God's throne from the hosts of angels is an image appearing in the *aggadah* (rabbinic anecdotal texts) as far back as the second century CE, and in the Jewish *Hekhalot* literature. Woven into this cosmic veil, according to the symbolism of the apocryphal *3 Enoch* (C5th or C6th CE), are the images of all souls, along with their actions and all the events that will ever take place in the creation, including the final Day of Judgment – the 'end of days' or 'messianic period' as it is called in Jewish writings. It is, so to speak, a heavenly blueprint of all earthly history, as preordained by God. The idea of such a veil assumes a pre-existent reality that gradually unfolds itself in the realm of time.

According to the revelational story of *3 Enoch,* Rabbi Ishmael is taken on a trip through the seven heavens by the angel *Metatron.* The angel says to the rabbi:

> Come and I will show you the curtain *(vilon)* of the omnipresent One, which is spread before the Holy One, blessed be He, and on which are printed all the generations of the world and all their deeds, whether done or to be done, till the last generation.
>
> *3 Enoch 45:1, OTP1 p.296*

The veil indicates the transcendence of the Supreme Being beyond the realm of time, and that all events of the past, present and future are contained in and known to Him. The veil separates the supreme Godhead, the Source, from His creation. It prevents those not spiritually worthy from ascending to or perceiving this highest level of spirituality. The angels in the hierarchy of creation represent particularized or differentiated projections of His divine Unity, and thus they, too, are unable to ascend to the supreme realm.

In this revelation, and in some other texts too, the first heaven is named *vilon* (curtain, veil), derived from the Latin, *velum* (curtain). The same word is also used for a door curtain. Its purpose seems to be to obscure the heavenly realms from human vision. Hence, in the *Midrash,* it says:

> The Holy One, blessed be He, created seven heavens. The lowest of them is called 'curtain *(vilon)*', and it is like a curtain *(vilon)* drawn across the doorway of a house, so that those within can see those without, but those without cannot see those within.
>
> *Midrash 'Aseret ha-Dibrot, BM1 p.63ff., in OTP1 p.269 (n.f to 3 Enoch 17:5)*

Other texts describe the curtain in different ways. In one *midrash,* "curtain" is the first of the seven heavens or "firmaments" that, when drawn, is retracted into a "sheath" or covering:

> Resh Lakish said: "There are seven firmaments: curtain *(vilon),* expanse, grinders, habitation, dwelling, depository and heavy clouds. Curtain *(vilon):* It serves no purpose whatever except that it enters its sheath in the morning and comes out of its sheath in the evening, thus renewing daily the work of creation. Expanse: where the sun, moon, stars and planets are fixed. Grinder: where millstones stand and grind *manna* for the righteous. Habitation: ... etc."
>
> *Babylonian Talmud, Ḥagigah 12b–13a, 'Ein Ya'akov ad. loc., in BLBR p.511:66*

There are also varying and colourful traditions concerning the *pargod,* also meaning veil or curtain. Some take it to be a curtain that prevents the ministering angels from seeing the Glory,[1] while others hold that "the seven angels that were created first" continue their ministry inside the *pargod.*[2]

A similar idea appears in some of the gnostic texts of the early Christian period, especially the *Bruce* and *Askew* Codices. The *First Book of Jeu* and the *Pistis Sophia* both mention the "veils *(katapetasma)*" encountered as the soul ascends through the various heavenly *aeons* or realms.[3] The *Pistis Sophia* also speaks of the "veil of the treasury of Light" in the thirteenth (and highest) *aeon*[4] and the "veil of the First Mystery of the Only One, the Ineffable".[5] Similarly, the *Second Book of Jeu,* describing a complex hierarchy of realms and rulers, says that "veils are drawn before" the "invisible God" who dwells in the "twelfth *aeon*", because of the "many gods ... who ... are great *archons* (rulers, lords)" who also dwell there, serving the "invisible God".[6] This conception of the veil drawn between God and the angelic hosts is similar to the use of the term in Jewish *Hekhalot* literature, which comes from a similar era to the gnostic texts.

A variant of the same essential idea also appears in the revelational *Hypostasis of the Archons,* a text from the Nag Hammadi codices, where an angel explains allegorically to Norea how Satan came into existence. First, a "shadow" or darkness appears beneath the veil that separates the higher realms from the lower. Then, that "shadow became matter":

> A veil *(katapetasma)* exists between the world above and the realms that are below; and Shadow came into being beneath the veil *(katapetasma);* and that Shadow became matter.
>
> *Hypostasis of the Archons 94:22, NHS20 pp.252–53*

From Shadow, a changing form is then projected in "matter", and it "became an arrogant beast resembling a lion" – the "lion" being a common epithet of Satan.

See also: **al-ḥijāb** (6.2), **Sama'el** (6.1), **sunn**.

1. *Targum of Job* 26:9.
2. *Massekhet Hekhalot* 7, in "Kabbalah", *Encyclopedia Judaica, EJCD.*
3. *First Book of Jeu* 83–92:33–40, *BC* pp.92–111; *Pistis Sophia* 1, 14, 29, 84, 86, 93, 125, 128, 130, 140, 148, *PS* pp.2–3, 46–47, 82–83, etc.
4. *Pistis Sophia* 41–46:29–31, *PS* pp.82–93.
5. *Pistis Sophia* 223:95, *PS* pp.446–47.
6. *Second Book of Jeu* 133:52, *BC* pp.194–95.

vibhūti (S/H), **vibhūtī** (Pu) *Lit.* penetrating, pervading; abundant, plentiful; mighty, powerful; excellence, dignity, majesty, glory, greatness, magnificence, splendour; plenty, abundance; hence, opulence, wealth, riches, fortune; also, manifestation of might and power; hence, supernatural, superhuman or divine power.

The term is used a number of times in chapters ten and eleven of the *Bhagavad Gītā,* which describe all aspects of the creation as the glorious and divine manifestation *(vibhūti)* of the divine being of Kṛishṇa, personified as an incarnation of the Supreme Being, *Brahman.* Kṛishṇa is talking to his friend and disciple, Arjuna:

> He who knows the true nature
> of these divine manifestations *(vibhūti)* and powers of mine
> is steady in unwavering communion with me:
> Of this, there is no doubt.
>
> *Bhagavad Gītā 10:7*

And:

> O scorcher of enemies!
> To my divine manifestations *(vibhūti),* there is no end;
> What I have described are but a few, as examples.

Know this: whatever is endowed with great glory *(vibhūti),*
attractiveness and vitality –
Reflects a fragment of my splendour.

Bhagavad Gītā 10:40–41; cf. BGB, BGT

Vibhūti is also the name given to the three horizontal stripes of cow dung ash painted by Shaivites on their foreheads as a reminder of the three powerful bonds that rule mankind. These are ego *(anava), karma* (action, hence, cause and effect) and *māyā* (illusion). They also signify the Shaivite belief in the power of *Shiva* to bestow his grace, and release man from these bonds. *Vibhūti* is also a name for *Lakshmī,* the goddess of wealth.

virāṭ (S/H) *Lit.* vast, huge, enormous, gigantic, massive, large, bulky; also, imposing, splendid; hence, universal, macrocosmic; the term is used in *Vedānta* for that form of *Brahman* (absolute Reality) that is manifested in the physical *(sthūla)* creation. According to the *Upanishads,* the entire creation is a manifestation of *Brahman,* split and divided by *māyā,* the power of concealment, illusion and reflection into lower planes. According to *Advaita* (non-dualistic) *Vedānta, māyā* at first remains unmanifested, then becomes subtly manifested, and finally manifests itself in gross forms. These can be compared to:

1. The seed or causal stage where everything is in potential and nothing is manifest. This relates to *Brahman* in association with undifferentiated *māyā,* and is called *Īshvara* (Lord) or *avyākṛita.* It is the Vedantic conception of God existing prior to actual creation, but possessed of the power of creation.

2. The swollen and germinating stage of the seed, where manifestation or actualization of potential is beginning to take place. This relates to *Brahman,* apparently divided by subtly differentiated *māyā,* and is called *hiraṇyagarbha.* In this aspect, *Brahman* is the totality of all subtle essences, ready to spring into complete manifestation.

3. The stage when it is fully differentiated into a tree or plant. Here, *Brahman* is possessed of *māyā* differentiated fully into the vast *(virāṭ)* creation, that is, into perceptible objects, and is called *virāṭ* or *virāṭrūpa* (vast form). This aspect of *Brahman* is the totality of all gross objects, the entire manifested universe.

See also: **avyākṛita**, **hiraṇyagarbha**, **vishvarūpa**.

virāṭ purush(a), **virāṭrūp(a)** (S/H), **virāṭ-svarūpa Bhagavān** (S), **virāṭ-svarūp Bhagvān** (H) *Lit.* huge *(virāṭ)* form *(rūp)* or being *(purush);* the Lord *(Bhagavān)* possessed of universal, cosmic or macrocosmic form *(virāṭ-svarūpa).* These terms refer to the Supreme Being in universal or macrocosmic form, encompassing the entire creation.

See also: **virāṭ**.

Vishṇu-dhām(a), **Vishṇulok(a)**, **Vishṇupurī** (S/H/Pu) *Lit.* home *(dhām),* region *(lok)* or city *(purī)* of *Vishṇu,* one of the Hindu trinity *(trimūrti)* and a major deity; the abode of *Vishṇu;* the region or heaven of *Vishṇu;* variously located by the *Purāṇas* and similar mythological texts. The *Kūrma Purāṇa,* for example, identifies it with *Brahmaloka;* the *Shiva Purāṇa* places it above *Brahmaloka;* and in both it is located below *Rudraloka.* In the *Mahābhārata* and many other texts, *Vishṇu*'s heaven is identified with *vaikuṇṭh.*[1]

See also: **Brahmaloka**, **Indraloka**, **Shivaloka**, **Vishṇu** (4.2).

1. *Mahābhārata, Bhishmaparvan* 9:15, 21.

vishvarūp(a) (S/H) *Lit.* all- *(vishva)* formed *(rūpa);* of all-inclusive form, of universal form; hence, omnipresent, existing everywhere. The idea of the all-inclusive form of the One is exemplified in a long passage in the *Bhagavad Gītā,* where Kṛishṇa, as the personification of *Brahman,* identifies himself with all aspects of the creation, higher and lower. Speaking to his companion and disciple, Arjuna, he says:

"My mighty forms are indeed divine,
 and of course I shall tell you
 what they are in essence.
My total extent has no end.

"I am the Reality that abides
 in the soul of all creatures;
And, of all creatures,
 I am the beginning, middle and end.

"Of the gods of heaven, I am *Vishṇu,*
 of lights, the brilliant sun.
I am the leading storm god.
I am the moon among the stars.

"Of sacred scriptures, I am the *Book of Songs.*
I am king of the celestial race.
I am the mind presiding over the senses.
Of all that evolved, I am awareness.

"I am *Shiva* among the terrifying gods,
lord of wealth among elves and goblins.
Of the radiant gods, I am fire,
of mountain peaks, *Meru....*

"Of the great seers, I am the greatest, Bhṛigu,
of speech, the one supreme, subtle Sound,
of sacrifices, the offering of whispered chants,
of mountain ranges, Himalaya,

"Of all trees, the sacred fig tree,
of divine seers, Nārada,
of the heavenly musicians, *Chitraratha,*
of perfect wise men, the sage Kapila....

"Of every world brought forth,
I am beginning, middle and end.
I am that knowledge that affects the self,
the true subject of learned debaters.

"I am the A of the alphabet,
in grammar the compound of perfect balance.
I alone am imperishable time,
and I turn everywhere sustaining the world.

"I am death that snatches all,
and the birth of all yet to be born.
Of feminine names: glory, fortune, divine speech,
memory, prudence, constancy, patience.

"In ritual, I am the perfect chant,
and the perfectly scanned verse.
I am the first of months
among seasons the spring....

"I am Kṛishṇa of the Vṛishṇis (a Hindu clan),
Arjuna of the Pāṇḍavas!
Of saintly hermits, I am Vyāsa,
of seers, Ushanas.

"I am the justice stern masters mete,
the statecraft of leaders who desire victory;
I am the silence of mysteries,
the wisdom of the wise.

"I am all that is,
the nucleus of any being.
Nothing moving or unmoving
could exist without me.

"To my divine manifestations,
there is no end;
What I have described are but a few,
as examples.
Know this: whatever is endowed with great glory,
attractiveness and vitality –
Reflects a fragment of my splendour.

"But there is no need to know everything!
I have spread out this entire world,
and continue to support it
with one fraction of myself....

"Open your eyes and see
my hundreds, my thousands of forms,
in all their variety, heavenly splendour,
in all their colours and semblances....

"Here in my body, in one place,
now, the whole world –
All that moves and does not move –
and whatever else you want to see.

"Of course, with the ordinary eye
you cannot see me.
I give you divine vision.
Behold my absolute power!"

Bhagavad Gītā 10:19–23, 25–26, 32–35, 37–42, 11:5, 7–8; cf. BGB

Hearing all this, Arjuna asks to be shown it is so. At this request, Kṛishṇa appears, granting Arjuna a vision of the entire wonder and majesty of the Supreme Being. He opens Arjuna's divine eye, which can behold the supreme Godhead, its unity, the One in the Many and the Many in the One. Arjuna sees the supreme form of the infinite Godhead, in whom are all wonders of existence, who is an infinite and luminous mass of energy and light, the supreme Immutable, the imperishable guardian of eternal laws, the everlasting and self-existent Soul of existence:

Then and there, Arjuna saw
the entire world unified,
yet divided manifold,
embodied in the God of gods.

Bewildered and enraptured,
Arjuna, the pursuer of wealth,
bowed his head to the God,
joined his palms, and said:

"Master! Within You I see the gods,
and all classes of beings,
the Creator on His lotus seat,
and all seers and divine serpents.

"Far and near, I see You without limit,
reaching, containing everything,
and with innumerable mouths and eyes.
I see no end to You, no middle and no beginning –
O universal Lord and form of all *(vishvarūpa)!* …

"In my understanding, You are the supreme imperishable One,
the essence of all knowledge;
You are the ultimate refuge of the universe;
You are the perennial guardian of the eternal Law;
You are the ancient Being.

"There is no telling
what is beginning, middle or end in You.
Your power is infinite.
Your arms reach infinitely far.
Sun and moon are Your eyes.
This is how I see You.
Your mouth is a flaming sacrificial fire.
You burn up the world with Your radiance."

Bhagavad Gītā 11:13–16, 18–19; cf. BGB

This divine presence encompassing all parts of His creation is God's *vishvarūpa* – His universal form.

See also: **virāṭ**, **virāṭrūpa**.

water(s) Water or waters is encountered as an esoteric term in a number of ancient Judaic, Christian, gnostic and other Middle Eastern writings, where it usually means one of two things. When its context is that of the Living Water, the Water of Life, the eternal Fountain and so on, it refers to the Creative Word. Alternatively, it is a way of speaking generally of the Lord's creative force or Spirit, the 'spiritual substance' or 'essence' of God, so to speak, often in the context of the higher realms of creation or some aspect of them. It is probably in this second context that it is meant in the *Genesis* creation myth, where it says that the "Spirit of God" (the creative Power) "moved upon the face of the waters":

> In the beginning, God created the heaven and the earth:
> And the earth was without form, and void,
> and darkness was upon the face of the deep.
> And the Spirit of God moved upon the face of the waters,
> and God said, "Let there be light!": and there was light.
>
> And God saw the light, that it was good:
> and God divided the light from the darkness.
>
> And God called the light: Day!
> and the darkness he called: Night!
> And the evening and the morning were the first day.
>
> And God said, "Let there be a firmament
> in the midst of the waters,
> and let it divide the waters from the waters."
> And God made the firmament,
> and divided the waters which were under the firmament
> from the waters which were above the firmament:
> And it was so.
> And God called the firmament: Heaven!
> And the evening and the morning were the second day.
>
> *Genesis 1:1–8, KJV*

Since the processes of creation are impossible to describe or understand in human language, mystics have commonly resorted to myths or allegories.

Moreover, there is no guarantee that the *Genesis* account is as it was first penned by someone who knew what he was talking about. Most scholars agree that *Genesis,* like so many other biblical documents, is an edited compilation of previously separate writings.

Taking a general meaning, therefore, the creation is said to have been created by the "Spirit of God", the Creative Word. As it says, "God said" – He manifested everything by means of His Word. The "light" or "Day" represents the higher realms, perhaps, while the "darkness" or "Night" signifies this world. The two are separated by a "firmament", a veil or 'sky' of which there are many in the hierarchy of created realms, separating the lower from the higher, the darkness from the light.

The lower "waters" of this world are thereby divided from the "waters" of heaven. These "waters" represent the 'primordial substance', the spiritual essence, which is moulded by God to form the creation. They are, in effect, His own Being out of which He forms creation.

The *Genesis* story is echoed in the Mandaean writings, where the "waters" are explicitly said to be the "Living Waters", the "Banner" being another metaphor for the creative Power:

> Let *Yawar*'s (God's) radiance shine forth....
> The brightness of the Banner has shone forth
> over the Living Waters!
> It shone forth:
> the waters dance towards its radiance
> and the radiance towards the waters.
> Waters and radiance are intermingled, are interlaced,
> and its brightness inspires the *'uthras* (pure beings)
> in their *shkinata* (inner realms), immeasurably.
>
> *Mandaean Prayer Book 342; cf. CPM p.238*

Genesis was well known in the ancient Middle East among Jews, Christians and, later, among Muslims, and echoes of the *Genesis* myth are found in many places, where the regions or subdivisions of the regions themselves are depicted as the "waters". The gnostic tractate *Zostrianos,* for example, which purports to describe the various inner realms or *aeons,* depicts each of these *aeons* with its own array of powers, which it calls "waters",[1] "lights",[2] "powers",[3] "angels",[4] "glories"[5] and so on.

Likewise, describing the fate of the soul after death, the *Pistis Sophia* speaks of souls being taken to some realm or "sphere", according to the way they have lived:

> The ministers of the sphere take it forth to a water that is below the sphere.
>
> *Pistis Sophia 374:144, PS pp.748–49; cf. PSGG p.316*

The origin of the world from 'primeval waters' is not an uncommon theme. In Indian mythology, *Brahman* (the absolute Reality) is said to bring the creation into being by depositing a seed in the 'primeval waters', which develops into a golden egg *(hiraṇyāṇḍa),* and thence into the creation. In a later variant of the same myth, *Vishṇu,* the supreme Creator, rests on a couch formed from the coils of the cosmic serpent *Ananta* or *Shesh Nāg,* who floats upon the 'primeval waters'. At the start of every age, *Vishṇu* awakens, bringing the creation into being, dissolving it again at the end of the cycle.

See also: **air**, **Living Water** (3.1), **Water of Life** (3.1), **Waters** (3.1).

1. *Zostrianos* 5, 15, 17, 22, 48, 55, *NHS31.*
2. *Zostrianos* 6, 29, 48, 51, 53, 62, 74, 119–21, 126–28, *NHS31.*
3. *Zostrianos* 4, 6–8, 11, 14, 20, 25, 29, 32, 34, 40, 46, 48, 53, 55, 58, 63, 65–66, 74, 85, 113, 115, 121, 124, *NHS31.*
4. *Zostrianos* 4, 6, 19, 28, 30, 34–35, 47–48, 51, 55, 95, 113, 130, *NHS31.*
5. *Zostrianos* 4–6, 24, 46–47, 52–55, 62–63, 86, 120–25, *NHS31.*

way of the midst See **regions**.

world(s) of light The higher regions, mentioned by many traditions; specifically, a Mandaean term for the heavenly realms lying beyond the purgatories *(maṭarata)* and the intermediate realm of *mshunia kūshṭā* (world of archetypes, patterns or likenesses), entered only when the soul has been purified:

> In the world of light there is nothing save devotional prayer *(rahmia)* and praises, because the soul is delivered, has risen, and is firmly established in the worlds of light.... In worlds of light, there are no filthy mysteries in the body: you cannot live as you did when dwelling on earth.
>
> *Thousand and Twelve Questions I:287–88; cf. TTQ p.191*

The term commonly appears in Mandaean invocations to the Divine, the First Life:

> In the name of the great first other-worldly Life! From the sublime worlds of light that are above all works, may there be healing, victory, strength, soundness, speech and hearing, joy of heart, and forgiving of sins for me.
>
> *Mandaean Invocation; cf. CPM p.1, TTQ (II:44) p.210*

The worlds of light are contrasted with the worlds of darkness, meaning the material world. The two worlds are separate, yet closely intertwined. When the soul comes to the darkness of the body, it takes the *rūha* (spirit) as companion. Here, the *rūha* refers to the carnal nature or lower mind:

> The worlds of darkness and the worlds of light are body and counterpart (complements) of one another. Neither can remove from or approach the other, nor can one distinguish either from its partner; moreover each derives strength from the other....
>
> When the soul came from worlds of light and fell into the body, there came with her some of all the mysteries that exist in the world of light, some of its radiance and its light, some of its sincerity, some of its unity, its order, its peacefulness and its truth; some of all that there is in the realm of light came to bear her company, to delight her, to purify her and to surround her in order that she may commune with them, and that there may be for her that which will aid her against the evils and temptations of the earth.
>
> And the evil spirit *(rūha bishta)* came with her, accompanied by all the mysteries that exist in darkness; and in the body she introduced song, frivolity, dancing, deceit and falsehood, excitement and lust, lying and witchcraft, violence and perversion, which accompany the spirit in the body of Adam so that the soul should not dominate her (the spirit). For spirit *(rūha)* and soul are distinct from one another, and I (*Yawar*, God) placed strife between them.
>
> *Thousand and Twelve Questions II:47ff.: cf. TTQ pp.213, 215–16*

Mandaean literature speaks of a great many "worlds of light", created by the primal divine Being:

> Then the great mighty Intelligence *(Mānā)* planned and created
> vast and pure worlds of light.
> Jordans He deployed, He made *shkinata* (dwellings, realms),
> installed *'uthras* (pure beings) and appointed *ashgandia* (envoys).
> Chief of these *ashgandia* before Him was *Adakas,*
> the 'great Word' is his name.
>
> *Mandaean Prayer Book 379, CPM p.293*

Mandaean poems speak of varying numbers of such worlds. There are "sixty worlds of light", "three hundred and sixty worlds of light", "three hundred and sixty-six mighty celestial worlds of light" and "a thousand thousand and eight hundred and eighty-eight thousand myriads of mighty and celestial worlds of light".[1] The intention seems to be to convey the impression of a large number.

See also: **mshunia kūshṭā**, **shkinta**, **worlds of darkness** (6.2).

1. *Mandaean Prayer Book* 334, 374, 379, *CPM* pp.234, 268, 295, 298, 303.

Yesod (He) *Lit.* Foundation; the ninth of the ten *sefirot;* the axis that brings the lower *sefirot* of *Neẓaḥ* (Triumph, Eternity) and *Hod* (Majesty, Glory) into harmony.

See **sefirot**.

yeẓirah (He) *Lit.* formation.

See **'olam ha-yeẓirah**.

ywy mará ey (G) *Lit.* land *(ywy)* without *(mará)* evil *(ey);* an earthly paradise, according to the Guaraní of Paraguay, located to the east, across the great primeval sea *(pará guazú rapytá).* A paradise of plenty, and a land free of anxiety and death, the *ywy mará ey* can be reached only by the living. Immortality is considered possible in this land, where life is lived under the protection of Saviours who have achieved *agüyjé* or spiritual perfection.

Miguel Alberto Bartolomé, who lived several months with the Avá-Chiripá subgroup of the Paraguayan Guaraní in 1968 and 1969, describes the "immense exercise in spiritual endeavour"[1] that these people believe is necessary to reach the land without evil. A strict vegetarian diet and "special techniques of concentration extending over the hours of sleep as well as periods of consciousness"[2] render a person fit for travel to the *ywy mará ey.* These practices free the soul from imperfections *(tekó-achy),* and the body from physical weight, creating the spiritual perfection that allows a person to fly over the great primeval sea to the *ywy mará ey.* The Chiripá chief, Avá-Nembiará, explains:

> Our ancestor departed in life without dying, and left no trail for us to follow. It is he who thunders in the east, he who departed with our human body and, while he who went away dances, we too shall dance. Long ago the chief danced, and his feet did not touch the Earth. This is why, in order to dance, we must not eat meat but only those things which *Nanderú* (the Creator) has commanded us.
>
> *Avá-Nembiará, in SAC p.119*

This somewhat enigmatic passage must be interpreted in light of the beliefs surrounding the *ywy mará ey.* Avá-Nembiará presumably refers to a highly developed *paí guazú* or shaman who had achieved spiritual perfection and had thus been able to travel to the land without evil. It is unclear how to take the statement that this shaman left no trail to follow, since the techniques of concentration and obedience to spiritual commands are presumably the keys to following the shaman to this land. Perhaps he means that the passage of a soul to the realms of the spirit leaves no physical track that can be followed. It is also difficult to imagine in what sense the shaman departed "with our human body", unless the speaker means the shaman left taking with him some claim on the body.

Dancing is probably a metaphor for spiritual effort and spiritual experience. Dancing without the feet touching the Earth clearly implies something other than literal, bodily dancing. In order to "dance" in this way, says Avá-Nembiará, a person has to avoid eating meat and to obey God's (*Nanderú's*) commands.

Many Guaraní, however, understood the *ywy mará ey* not as a spiritual dwelling, but as a literal geographical location. Mass migrations of Guaraní seeking this paradise are recorded from as early as 1515. Dancing and singing, the Guaraní followed their prophets in a tragic quest for a physical paradise to the east. Those who did not perish from war or disease made it to the eastern sea. There they danced, expecting to levitate across the sea or walk on dry land through the parted waters.

Just as Christ's teaching about the kingdom of heaven has been interpreted as an earthly kingdom presided over by Christ as an earthly king, so have many of the Guaraní interpreted the *ywy mará ey* as an earthly paradise. But why would spiritual perfection attained by intense inner concentration be a prerequisite for reaching a physical paradise? The spiritual efforts needed to attain this land without evil are meaningful only when the *ywy mará ey* is understood as an inner reality rather than an earthly region.

Mystics of other times and places have taught that spiritual exercises in concentration, along with a moral life and vegetarian diet, can release the soul to travel to regions of spiritual peace and bliss. Death of the body is not required for this spiritual journey; rather, the soul can depart the living body, and later return, causing no harm at all to the individual. It is perhaps to this reality that the *ywy mará ey* actually refers.

See also: **ñe'eng-güery**, **paradise**, **oka-vusú**.

1. Miguel Bartolomé, *Shamanism Among the Avá-Chiripá, SAC* p.117.
2. Miguel Bartolomé, *Shamanism Among the Avá-Chiripá, SAC* p.117.

Ẓe'ir Anpin (Am) *Lit.* small *(ẓe'ir)* face *(anpin);* the Short-faced One; idiomatically, the Impatient One. In Kabbalist descriptions of the divine Being and the hierarchy of His powers or aspects, *Ẓe'ir Anpin* represents the level or realm of judgment. He is contrasted with *Arikh Anpin* (the Long-faced One, the compassionate One), who signifies the level of mercy. The level of *Ẓe'ir Anpin* is transient and subject to change, hence his name – the Impatient One. *Arikh Anpin* is long-suffering, eternal and not subject to change. He represents the highest spiritual level of divine mercy and love. In general terms, *Arikh Anpin* is thus the Supreme Being; *Ẓe'ir Anpin* is the creation.

Ẓe'ir Anpin is used in the Kabbalah to refer to the *sefirot* (divine emanations) from the second *sefirah* of *Ḥokhmah* (Wisdom) down to *Malkut* (Kingship), the lowest *sefirah.* The level of the aloof and transcendent Godhead (comprising *Ayn-Sof* and the first *sefirah* of *Keter*) is called *Arikh Anpin.*

The process of creation was understood as taking place from *Ḥokhmah,* which represents the beginning of the potential for emanation, down to *Malkut,* which is the conduit for the Creative Word to reach the physical creation. Since all realms of creation are subject to change, however subtle, they are called *Ẓe'ir Anpin.*

See also: **Arikh Anpin** (2.1).

4.2 Deities, Rulers, Archons and Angels

Mystics who have taught openly of the higher realms have often indicated that each region has its own 'ruler'. In this world, a ruler is one whose mind affects the lives and destinies of those in his dominion. This arises from the *karma* or destiny of both the ruler and the ruled. In fact, all people are 'rulers', great or small, within the sphere and context of their own destinies. Their 'kingdoms' of influence extend through their families, their employment, their friends, associates and so on. Within this complex web, each person is both ruler and ruled. But the key factor is that the influence arises from the mind or consciousness of the individual. Once a soul has left this world, it no longer exerts the same influence.

The same principle applies to the rulers of the higher realms. The Lord is the ocean of being and consciousness that encompasses all. Consequently, He is the supreme ruler of all. His creation is organized through substations of His one supreme consciousness. These substations are His rulers, great or small, whose sphere of influence extends through everything that flows through them. So powerful, magnificent and full of light and glory are these rulers that souls who encounter these focus points of the Lord's power often mistake them for the highest Lord Himself, for they are the source and administration centre of all creation which lies below them.

Perhaps it is this mystic reality, overlain by the accretions of ancient religion, mythology and folklore, which underlies the pantheon of deities that characterize Hinduism and the polytheistic religions of ancient Greece, Rome, Egypt, Mesopotamia and so on. Likewise, the angels and archangels of Judaism, Christianity and Islam may be a way of explaining how God's power is expressed at various centres in creation, and how divine inspiration is brought to human beings. The *archons* of the gnostics and of St Paul are undoubtedly an expression of this ancient teaching.

Even so, in many cases, the deities are clearly more mythological than mystical in character, but are included here because in many traditions religious mythology forms much of the background to the way in which mystical teachings are expressed. In some instances, the stories related of these deities may have originally been intended allegorically, and it is from a literalization of these myths that the deities have found their way into religion. Plato (*c.*427–347 BCE),[1] Clement of Alexandria (*c.*150–215 CE),[2] the unknown writer of the early Christian *Clementine Homilies,*[3] Bishop Hippolytus of Rome (*fl.*210–236 CE),[4] the twelfth-century Archbishop Eustathius of Thessalonica,[5] and others have all indicated, for example, that the Greek gods and their exploits were commonly understood allegorically.

The present section covers the less mythological and legendary aspects of these deities, rulers and angels. Devils, demons, ghosts, spirits and messengers of death are also included. Since it is difficult to discuss the rulers separately from their regions, more information concerning these rulers will also be found in other sections, especially 6.1. The particular ruler known to different religions by a variety of names, and who is deemed responsible for the negativity and the imprisonment of souls in the lower spheres of creation, is so significant that fuller coverage is deferred to Volume 6.

KEY ENTRIES: **angels, gods, rulers.**

1. Plato, *Republic* 2:378d–e.
2. Clement of Alexandria, *Miscellanies* V:4, 9.
3. *Clementine Homilies* IV:24.
4. Hippolytus, *Refutation of All Heresies* V:2–3, VI:14.
5. Eustathius, *Commentary on Homer's Odyssey.*

Agni (S/H) *Lit.* fire; thus, sacrificial fire; the Vedic deity of fire; a major deity of Vedic times, more hymns being addressed to *Agni* in the *Ṛig Veda* than to any other god; regarded as a source of health and material welfare; depicted as an unrelenting opponent of darkness and evil. Viewed as the mediator between gods and men, *Agni*'s help was invoked to ensure that sacrificial offerings made to gods did indeed reach them. No one was considered more suitable than *Agni* for this purpose since flames on the altar always tended to rise with the aroma of burnt offerings, symbolizing the ascent of the offering itself to the propitiated gods. For this reason, *Agni* is also known by the epithet, *Havyavāhana* (conveyor of oblations).

In the *Ṛig Veda, Agni* is deemed greater than other gods:

> You, O *Agni,* are *Indra,* the hero of heroes;
> You are *Vishṇu* of the mighty stride, adorable.
> You, O *Brahmanaspati,* are *Brahman* who knows power;
> You, O Sustainer, tend us with wisdom.
>
> You, O *Agni,* are King *Varuṇa* whose law stands fast;
> You as *Mitra,* wonderworker, are adorable;
> You are *Aryaman,* lord of heroes, encircling all.
>
> *Ṛig Veda 2:1.3–4, CV p.35*

He is also regarded as a source of material health and welfare:

> O *Agni,* bounteous Lord,
> grant us wealth with heroic strength –
> Most lofty, very glorious, rich in offspring,
> free from disease and full of vigour.
>
> *Ṛig Veda 3:16.3, MV p.236*

> May *Agni* carry us through all our trouble and grief,
> as in a boat across the river.
>
> *Ṛig Veda 1:99, MV p.244*

In the *Yajur Veda, Agni* is again the support of man:

> O *Agni,* you are the body's guard, guard my body;
> You are the giver of life, give me life;
> Giver of lustre are you, give me lustre.
> O *Agni,* supply what is wanting in my body.
>
> *Yajur Veda 3:17; cf. MV p.225*

O lustrous *Agni,* you are splendid among gods:
may I be bright with lustre among men.
Yajur Veda 8:38; cf. MV p.224

O *Agni* of exhaustless strength, pervading all:
protect me from the lightning flash.
Protect me from bondage, from defect in worship,
and from food injurious to health.
Yajur Veda 2:20, MV p.229

There is more to *Agni,* however, than a deity invoked for human support and the fulfilment of worldly aspirations. In the *Kena Upanishad, Agni* represents the power of the Divine on the material plane. He is the heat and flame of the motive force in matter that has formed the universe, in the same way that, as a *tattva* (elemental condition of matter), *agni* is the energy that provides impetus and driving force, at both the physical and mental levels.

Agni also has a mystical aspect. In the *Ṛig Veda,* he is not only considered greater than the gods, but he becomes a symbol of immortality, of the force of the divine will, of transcendence and immanence, of universal lordship, hidden yet manifest. One of his epithets in the *Ṛig Veda* is *Vaishvānara:* "he who belongs to all men", "he who is dear to all men", he who is "dwelling with, present with, common to or benefiting all men",[1] by virtue of his light, inner and outer. It is this *Agni* who is invoked in the well-known hymn, *Agni Vaishvānara.* The writer, seeking the "steady light" within, calls upon *Agni,* the shepherd of immortality, to illumine his mind. As a result, the sage is rendered speechless by an ecstatic experience that transcends his faculties:

A steady light is set for men to gaze on,
of all the moving things, the swiftest Mind!
All spirits divine with but one thought and intention
proceed unerring toward that unique splendour.

My hearing fades away, my eyes grow dim.
The light that dwells within my heart grows brighter.
Far roams my mind, its confines overleaping.
What shall I utter, what my mind envisage?

In fear and trembling, all the gods hailed you,
O lord, when you abode amidst the darkness.
O universal lord, accord us your grace.
May the Immortal now bestow his grace upon us!
Agni Vaishvānara, Ṛig Veda 6:9.5–7, VE p.332

According to Indian mythology, in the quest for immortality even the gods (who were originally mortal) have to struggle, like man. In an account in the *Shatapatha Brāhmaṇa,* depicting the struggle between the gods *(devas)* and demons *(asuras)* for the immortal Fire *(Agni),* the esoteric dimension is highlighted by the victory of the gods who establish the immortal Fire in their "inmost self":

> The gods and the *asuras,* both of whom were offspring of *Prajāpati* (lord of creatures), were striving between themselves. Both sides were destitute of spirit because they were mortal, and he who is mortal has no spirit. Among these two groups of mortal beings one, *Agni,* was immortal, and it was through him, the immortal, that they both had their being.
>
> Now, whichever of the gods was slain by the *asuras* was in very truth slain irrevocably. And so the gods became inferior. They continued worshipping and practising fervent concentration, however, in the hope of overcoming their enemies who were likewise mortal. Their gaze then fell upon the immortal sacred *Agni.*
>
> "Come," they said, "let us establish this immortality in our inmost self! When we have placed that immortality in our inmost self and have become immortal and unconquerable, we shall defeat our enemies who are neither immortal nor unconquerable." …
>
> So the gods established that fire in their inmost self and, having established that immortality in their inmost self and become immortal and unconquerable, they defeated their mortal and conquerable enemies.
>
> *Shatapatha Brāhmaṇa 2:2.2.8–10, 14, VE p.383*

In the *Īshāvāsya Upanishad, Agni* is again represented as a mystical power. He is the divine will or force of consciousness, containing within himself all the gods and all the worlds. He is the immortal Essence in all things, knowing and remembering everything. He leads men to heaven as a reward for their good deeds:

> An immortal Life is the Breath of things,
>   but this body ends in ashes.
> *Om!* O mind, remember!
> That which was done, remember!
>
> O *Agni,* who knows all manifested things,
>   lead us by the good path to felicity.
> You know all our deeds:
>   remove from us the wayward attraction of sin.

> In the words of our prayers,
> we submit to you completely.
> *Īshāvāsya Upanishad 17–18*

See also: **tattva** (5.1).

1. R.T.H. Griffith, *Hymns of the Ṛgveda* 1, *HRV1* pp.339, 362, 136.

angel of death (He. *mal'akh ha-mavet,* A. *mal'ak al-mawt*) The being who dispenses death; also called *'Izrā'īl* in Muslim and *'Azra'el* in Jewish legend. The Hebrew and Arabic translate as the angel *(mal'akh, mal'ak)* of death *(mavet, mawt).*

The existence of an angel of death as a distinct being whose function is to bring about human death evolved in later, post-biblical Judaism. *Mot* or *Mavet,* a deity who dispensed death, did however exist in pre-Judaic Canaanite religion. These names were then inherited by Judaism, and used as terms for death in a generic, non-personalized sense. In the Bible, it is God Himself who has control over man's death, and although He assigns a variety of messengers or angels to implement His decisions, there are no specific personified beings or deities representing 'death' in the same sense as the Canaanite deity.

The idea of an angel of death was combined with the popular folk belief in demons of the ancient Near East. Later, in the European countries where the Jews resided, he was identified with folk beliefs in ogres and such creatures. In the *Talmud* of the rabbinic period (200 BCE – 400 CE), the angel of death was identified with Satan and man's own evil inclination:

> Rabbi Simeon ben Lakish said: "Satan, impulse to evil and angel of death – all three are the same thing."
> *Babylonian Talmud, Batra 16a, in BLBR p.537:15*

Jewish folklore contains many stories of human confrontations with the angel of death, sometimes as attempts to thwart his intentions. In one such legend, the angel of death is cheated by the weasel and the fox, who fool him into thinking that their reflection in the sea is their real selves. The angel of death attacks the reflection, permitting the fox and the weasel to escape. Such folklore is also the origin of the Jewish custom of changing the name of a sick child, so that the angel of death will be fooled and be unable to find him.

In other legends, the angel of death is unhindered. A story in the *Talmud* describes how his mission is accomplished:

> It is said of the angel of death that he is full of eyes (being, so to speak, everywhere). Accordingly, when a sick man is about to die,

> the angel of death stands over the man's pillow, in his hand a drawn sword, a drop of gall hanging from its tip. When the sick man sees him, he trembles and opens his mouth (in terror). Just then, the angel of death drops the gall into his mouth, and from it he dies – from it, his corpse begins to emit a stench, and his face turns green.
>
> *Babylonian Talmud, 'Avodah Zarah 20b, in BLBR p.581:59*

There is also a tradition that the angel of death is not without a sense of compassion, appeals to which can successfully be made. This may be the origin of the prayer directed to God that is recited on the Ten Days of Repentance prior to the Day of Atonement *(Yom Kippur)* appealing for a reversal of the sentence of death.

There is a story in the *Talmud* about the angel of death that is also found, with slight variation, in the spiritual literature of other traditions, including Rūmī's *Maśnavī.*[1] Its message is that death is predestined and nothing can be done to avoid it:

> Two Cushites stood in the presence of King Solomon – "Elihoreph and Ahijah, sons of Shisha, who were (Solomon's) scribes".[2] One day, observing that the angel of death looked distressed, Solomon asked him, "Why are you distressed?" The angel of death replied, "Because the two Cushites seated here are about to be summoned by me." So (to thwart the angel of death) Solomon had spirits take charge of the two and convey them to the city of Luz (a city where people become immortal). But as soon as they reached its wall, they died. The following day, Solomon observed that the angel of death was cheerful. When Solomon asked him, "Why are you so cheerful?" he replied, "You sent them to the very place where they were to be summoned by me."
>
> At that, Solomon spoke up, saying, "A man's feet are responsible for him. They lead him to the place where he is about to be summoned."
>
> *Babylonian Talmud, Sukkot 53a, in BLBR p.583:73*

See also: **'Izrā'īl**, **Yama** (6.1), **yamadūta**.

1. Rūmī, *Maśnavī* I:956–70.
2. *1 Kings* 4:3.

angel(s) (He. *mal'akh,* pl. *mal'akhim;* A. *malak;* P. *firishtah*) A class of spiritual beings attendant upon God or dwelling in the heavenly regions, sometimes carrying out the task of a messenger or intermediary between God and man, sometimes performing other 'administrative' functions in the heavenly realms.

The existence of angelic beings in the higher regions is accepted not only by mystics, but also by most religions, though there is a diversity of opinion as to their nature and function. In Judaism, Christianity and Islam, the terminology and concepts concerning angels can often be traced back to Zoroastrian and earlier Babylonian religions, though the roles assigned to particular angels by the various religions differ to some extent.

Angels are generally regarded as the creation of the supreme Father. In the gnostic tractate, the *Sophia of Jesus Christ,* while identifying God's creative Power with "Christ", the writer says:

> Now First-begotten is called 'Christ'.
> Since he has authority from his Father,
> he created a multitude of angels without number
> for retinue from spirit and light.
>
> *Sophia of Jesus Christ 104–5, NHS27 pp.107–9*

Likewise, in the *Trimorphic Protennoia,* God is said to dwell within all realms, "powers" and "angels":

> I (the Word) dwell within all the sovereignties and powers,
> and within the angels,
> and in every movement that exists in all matter.
>
> *Trimorphic Protennoia 47:19–22, NHS28 pp.426–27*

Modern conceptions of angels are often influenced by their passage through time and by religious doctrine. But, in simple terms, just as human beings are souls in human form who populate the physical world, so too are angels souls in the inner regions, populating their respective heavens:

> The soul, which is a ray of the divine sun in one sphere, the sphere in which it does not touch any earthly being, is called *mal'ak,* or angel.... In other words every soul is an angel before it touches the earthly plane.
>
> *'Ināyat Khān, Sufi Message, SMIK1 p.115*

Angels are often depicted as messengers. In the Bible, they are regarded as bringing the Voice of God to the prophets. In post-biblical Jewish literature, they convey the prayers of the devotees to God. In gnostic literature, certain beings are also described as rulers, lords or *archons* of particular realms or subrealms, these being the centres of consciousness or being through which the creation is manifested. On the inward ascent, some of these lords may seem so full of light and glory that they can be mistaken for the supreme Lord Himself, more particularly since all of creation below appears to be manifested from them.

There are many descriptions in the world's mystic and religious literature of human contact with angels. Sometimes this is described as taking place after the soul has left the body either in a spontaneous and uncontrolled inner experience, or after dedicated spiritual practice of some kind that has purified the mind sufficiently for the devotee to enter the astral region, the first in the hierarchy of heavenly realms. The medieval Christian mystic of Italy, Angela of Foligno (1248–1309), writes of one of her many experiences:

> I was filled with joy and gladness because of the presence of the angels, and if I had not myself beheld them, I should never have believed that angels were so pleasing, or that they could have filled the soul with so much joy.
>
> *Angela of Foligno, Book of Divine Consolation III, BDC p.224*

Based on a study of Christian and Judaic literature, medieval angelologists identified nine kinds of angel: *serafim,* cherubim, thrones, dominions, virtues, powers, principalities, archangels and angels, the classification including both angelic beings as well as regions of creation. Judaism also speaks of the *nefillim* (*lit.* fallen ones, fallen angels), *ḥayyot* (*lit.* creatures, also called cherubim), *ofanim* (*lit.* wheels), *galgalim* (*lit.* wheels) and some others.

In the Hebrew Bible, the general term used for angels is *mal'akh* (emissary), their role being that of divine emissaries, conveying God's message to human beings. The term is also used in the Bible for human agents or messengers, although by post-biblical times *mal'akh* was only applied to superhuman messengers. Other biblical terms used for divine beings or angels are *elohim* (generally translated as God or gods), *benei elohim* and *benei elim* (sons of gods), *kedoshim* (holy ones), and sometimes simply 'man'. In *Daniel,* they are also called the wakeful ones or watchers.[1] Angels, however, make relatively few appearances in the Hebrew Bible, except to the later prophets, Ezekiel, Zechariah and Daniel.

Sometimes, no distinction is made in biblical texts between God and His messenger. This is why a number of interpreters have described angels as embodiments or extensions of the divine Power or Will. Thus, the Babylonian sage Sa'adia (*c.*882–942) and the *Ḥasidei Ashkenaz* (devotees of Germany) described the divine creative power depicted in the Bible in terms of light and glory as an angel.

In fact, most of the Jewish mystics and philosophers from the time of the *Hekhalot* (second century BCE) understood some of the biblical angels as embodiments or personifications of the emanations of the divine Light, as expressions of divine qualities. In the Kabbalah, these qualities were symbolized in the system of the *sefirot,* the emanations of the divine qualities.

Angels are rarely named in the Hebrew Bible, among the most notable being Gabriel and Michael, in *Daniel.* The majority of the angels' names used in the *Hekhalot* and Kabbalist literature are therefore later inventions, often contrived from a combination of Greek and Hebrew. Many angelic names, for instance, end in the Hebrew *El* (God). Also, while biblical angels intercede with humanity on behalf of the Divine, the angels mentioned in this later literature are only active in the heavenly realms.

In the *Merkavah* spiritual practices indicated in the *Hekhalot* texts, the angels' role is twofold: firstly, to pray and to convey human prayers to God; secondly, to protect the soul on the spiritual journey through their realms, something brought about by the seeker's invocation of their names.

Generally, the angels are categorized as angels of love and angels of judgment – alluding to the duality of God's manifestation in the lower creation. In the Kabbalah, this was referred to as the interplay of the 'positive' and 'negative' *sefirot.* These two categories of angel are also called the pillar of mercy and the pillar of judgment, which emanate from God and sustain the universe.

The hierarchy of angels is headed by a group of archangels or holy angels. Some of the Jewish texts describe seven such angels, some eight,[2] and some four – their names and duties differing from text to text. The seven are: *Uri'el,* who leads the angelic host and guards the underworld *(Sheol); Rapha'el,* who is in charge of the spirits of human beings; *Ragu'el,* who takes revenge on the world of lights; Michael, who watches over Israel; *Sari'el,* whose duties are not defined; Gabriel, who rules paradise; *Jeremi'el*[3] who, according to the *Apocalypse of Elijah* (probably originating in the first few centuries CE), guards the souls of the underworld.[4] These seven angels are always in the proximity of God and are the ones always called upon to carry out tasks of special significance for world history, such as the punishment of the fallen angels, etc.[5] But lists of angels and their roles vary. In one of the Dead Sea Scrolls, the War Scroll, for instance, two angels of prime importance are described: the Prince of Light and the Angel of Darkness, the two being in perpetual conflict.

Related to the group of seven angels is a group of four known as the 'angels of the Presence'. In *Enoch,* they are: Michael, Gabriel, *Rapha'el* and *Phenu'el.* These four are considered to be among the cherubim, interpreted as 'those who are near to God' and who carry His throne. Their function is to carry out the divine will in creation, acting – so to speak – as God's executive agents.

One of the most significant angels discussed in rabbinic literature is *Metatron,* who at times seems to be like the gnostic Demiurge (Gk. *Demi-*

ourgos, lit. craftsman), corresponding to the creator of the lower realms of creation, subordinate to the supreme Creator. Other important angels in rabbinic literature include *Sandalfon* and *Surya.*

Islamic beliefs concerning angels are drawn largely from Judaism. According to the allegorical story of creation in the book of *Genesis,* retold in the *Qur'ān,* God commanded the angels to bow down before Adam. By this is meant that man is superior to the angels, and that although the angels inhabit the subtle realms closer to God, they are not constituted in such a way that they can gain the knowledge that man can realize. Man is a complete microcosm of the creation and has been given the potential to realize God. Souls in angelic form do not have that privilege.

Adam's superiority over the angels is symbolized by his knowledge of their names and of the names of all other created things, something that was denied to the angels. In Islamic thought, the true name of something is the thing itself on a higher plane. Adam, who symbolizes man, knows these subtle names or patterns because his inner being is one with the supreme divine Intelligence *('Aql)* or Spirit. In religious and occult lore, to know the name of any being or creature is to have power over it. Thus, man's knowledge of the names of the angels again refers to the fact that man can know things that the angels cannot. According to Islamic tradition, when Muḥammad ascended to the heavenly realms in the company of the angel Gabriel, there came a point when Gabriel could advance no further, leaving Muḥammad to go on alone into the presence of God. The story again indicates man's superiority over the angels.

In Islamic angelology, the hierarchy of angels is headed by four archangels: *Jabra'īl* (Gabriel), the angel of revelation; *Mīkhā'īl* (Michael), the creative and beneficent angel; *Isrāfīl,* the angel of resurrection, the blast from whose horn or trumpet is said to be the force that will bring the creation to an end; and *'Izrā'īl,* the angel of death. Among some Sufi orders, these four archangels are each associated with one of the *laṭā'if* (subtle energy centres) in the body. They are also called the four *ḥamalat al-'arsh* – 'bearers of the throne' or 'bearers of the sky'.

In Islam, as in Judaism, *Shayṭān* or *Iblīs* is the angel who disobeyed God. In some accounts, he is an angel who is downgraded to a *jinn* for his disobedience. According to the *Qur'ān,* angels are made of light and regarded as superior to the *jinn,* who are made of fire.[6]

Ibn Mājah, an Islamic traditionalist (824–887 CE), says of angels:

> It is believed that angels are of a simple substance, created of light, endowed with life, speech and reason; and that the differences between them, the *jinn* and *Shayṭān,* is a difference of species. Know that the angels are sanctified from carnal desire and the disturbance of anger; they never disobey God in what He hath commanded them,

> but do what they are commanded. Their food is the celebration of His glory; their drink is the proclaiming of His holiness; their conversation, the commemoration of God, whose Name be exalted; their pleasure is His worship; and they are created in different forms and with different powers.
>
> *Ibn Mājah, in CEI p.43*

Some mystics have taught that there is an administrative hierarchy in creation. In the past, this teaching has generally been kept secret or described only in allegory or by veiled hints. Hence, the teachings that have become familiar to people are a mixture of the more definitive mystic explanations, together with literal interpretations of allegorical descriptions and religious mythology from indeterminate sources. The result is not something that lends itself to easy analysis or understanding, and in general it can only be said that there are rulers or administrators of the higher realms, together with a host of subpowers through which the Lord's will is manifested in creation.

See also: **mal'ak**.

1. *Daniel* 4:13, 17, 23.
2. *1 Enoch* 20:1–8.
3. *4 Ezra* 4:38.
4. *Apocalypse of Elijah, AE* p.10; see also *Sefer Eliyahu, SE.*
5. "Angels and Angelology", in *Encyclopedia Judaica, EJCD.*
6. *Qur'ān* 15:27, 55:15.

apsarā (S/H) *Lit.* going or moving (from the root *sri*) in water *(ap);* one of a class of mythological, celestial damsels dwelling in various heavens, especially the paradise *(svarga)* ruled by *Indra.* According to the *Vishṇu Purāṇa,* the *apsarās* came into being at the 'churning of the ocean', at the time of creation: "Troops of *apsarās,* the nymphs of heaven, were then produced, of surpassing loveliness, endowed with beauty and with taste."[1] Being excellent dancers, *apsarās* are portrayed as female counterparts to the *gandharvas* (celestial musicians). They have magical powers, and are able to assume any form at will. The most well known *apsarās* in Indian mythology are *Menakā, Urvashī, Rambhā, Tilottamā, Alambushā* and *Pramlochā,* about whom a number of stories are told.

Indian mythology contains accounts of *Indra*'s sending one of the *apsarās* to earth, generally to distract a *ṛishi* (sage, ascetic) whose practice of austerities had made him a threat to *Indra*'s lordship of heaven. Using the anglicized term, peri (fairy) for the *apsarās,* 'Ināyat Khān interprets the meaning of another of these myths:

> There is an old story from India.... The Hindu paradise is called *Indra lok,* where the god *Indra* is king, and where there are peris, the angels or fairies whose task is to dance before *Indra.* There was one fairy from *Indra lok* who descended to earth and loved an earthly being. By the power of her magic, she brought this earthly being to paradise; but when this became known to *Indra,* she was cast out of paradise, and the lovers were separated.
>
> This legend is symbolic of the human soul. Originally the peri, who represents the soul, belonged to *Indra lok,* the kingdom of God, the sphere full of peace, joy and happiness. Life there is nothing but joy; it is a dance. Life and love come from God, and raise every soul till it dances. In its pure condition the soul is joy, and when it is without joy, its natural condition is changed; then it depends upon the names and forms of the earth, and is deprived of the dance of the soul, and therein lies the whole tragedy of life. The wrath of *Indra* symbolizes the breach of the law that the highest love must be for God alone. It is natural that the soul is attached to the spirit, and that the true joy of every soul lies in the realization of the divine spirit.
>
> *'Ināyat Khān, Sufi Message, SMIK8 p.330*

See also: **Indra**.

1. *Vishṇu Purāṇa* 1:9, *VP* p.65.

archon (Gk) (pl. *archontes*) *Lit.* ruler; the nine chief magistrates of ancient Athens. Mystically, the term has been commonly used, especially in gnostic texts, for the rulers of the inner realms in the hierarchy of creation, particularly within the realm of the negative power, the creator-god of the physical universe and some of the heavenly worlds. In the various texts, translators have either left the term as it is or rendered it as 'rulers', 'governors', 'authorities' or by other such terms. In the *Pistis Sophia,* the term appears innumerable times. Speaking, for example, of the point in the ascent of the soul when it rises above the *archons,* Jesus says:

> And, in that moment, it (the soul) becomes a great outpouring of light, shining exceedingly. And the retributive receivers (angels of death) that have brought it forth from the body are afraid at the light of that soul, and they fall upon their faces. And in that moment, that soul becomes a great outpouring of light and becomes entirely winged with light, and penetrates all the regions of the *archons* and all their orders of light, until it goes to the region of its kingdom.
>
> *Pistis Sophia 287:112; cf. PS pp.574–75, PSGG p.239*

And again:

> When you come forth from the body and go to the Height, and reach the place of the *archons,* then all the *archons* will be put to shame before you, because you are (have come from) the dregs of their matter, and you have (now) become light more pure than all of them.
>
> *Pistis Sophia 252:100; cf. PS pp.504–5, PSGG p.209*

See also: **authority**, **dominions** (4.1), **powers**, **sovereignty** (4.1).

arwāḥ (A), **arvāḥ** (P) (sg. *rūḥ*) *Lit.* spirits, angels. *'Ālam al-arwāḥ* (world of spirits) is regarded as one of the seven heavens, levels of existence or planes of consciousness between the divine and the human levels; many Sufis equate *arwāḥ* with angels.

See also: **'ālam al-arwāḥ** (4.1), **angels**, **al-Ḥaḍarāt al-Ilāhīyah al-Khams** (4.1), **rūḥ** (5.1), **ta'ayyun** (4.1), **'uthras**.

Ashṭāngī (S/H) *Lit.* one with eight *(ashṭ)* parts *(anga);* the goddess with eight arms; an alternative name for the Hindu goddess *Durgā;* esoterically, the deity or controlling power of the *kaṇṭha* or throat centre *(chakra).* The arms of a god or goddess, like the petals on a lotus, signify the number of functional aspects possessed by the centre ruled by the deity. The symbolism, however, like Indian mythology itself, is rarely consistent, and in this instance the *kaṇṭha chakra* has sixteen petals, double the number of arms on the goddess.

See also: **Durgā**.

asur(a) (S/H/Pu) *Lit.* lord; to begin with, a deity, a divine being; later, an enemy of the gods, especially of the *suras,* possessing magical powers; finally, a demon; often identified in Indian mythology with the *daityas* and *dānavas,* giant offspring of Kashyapa and the goddess *Diti* and the chaos-hag *Danu,* respectively. Rulers and tribes opposed to the Aryan-speaking influx into India, as well as evil people, especially leaders, real or mythological, were also dubbed *asuras.* In early Ṛig Vedic times, an *asura* is a god:

> Let the merciful and helpful *asura,*
> the good leader with golden hands, come towards us.

Routing the demons and sorcerers,
the god to whom we sing has taken his place
against the evening.

Ṛig Veda 1:35.10

As the name for a god, *asura* often has a higher status than a *deva,* and the term was applied to *Varuṇa, Rudra, Agni, Mitra, Indra* and other major deities. *Rudra,* for example, was invoked as the "*asura* of the mighty heaven",[1] while *Varuṇa* was petitioned as intercessor for man: "Wise *asura,* king of wide dominion, loosen the bonds of the sins we have committed."[2]

In the later parts of the *Ṛig Veda,* the *asuras* undergo a transformation, becoming enemies of the gods, and finally demons, possessing magical powers and skills in metal craft, a significant talent in ancient times. This is the way they appear in subsequent Hindu texts such as the *Atharva Veda,* the *Purāṇas* and also the *Bhagavad Gītā,* where Kṛishṇa associates them with *rākshasas* (ogres):

Foolish men, with no understanding of my higher nature
as the supreme Lord of all that exists,
disregard my manifestation in the human form.
Futile are the hopes, futile the works,
and futile the knowledge of these men
of distorted understanding,
who are deluded by their cruel, proud
and passionate nature,
characteristic of *rākshasas* and *asuras.*

Bhagavad Gītā 9:11–12; cf. BGT

The origin of the name is uncertain. The Sanskrit *asura* is equivalent to the Avestan *ahurā,* as in the Zoroastrian name of God, *Ahurā Mazdā.* But this does not explain how the negative connotation originated. In the past, some scholars have suggested that *asura* is derived from the Assyrian god, *Ashur,* the derogatory connotation stemming from hostility between the Assyrians and Aryan-speaking peoples before the latter spread into India. But that leaves its initial positive sense in the *Ṛig Veda* unexplained. Others have proposed that the *asuras* are so-called because they came into being out of the breath *(asu)* of the Vedic deity, *Prajāpati* (lord of creatures). But this ignores the Avestan origins of the name.

Asura is also the negative form of *sura,* semidivine beings inhabiting *svarga* (paradise). Thus, an *a-sura* would be an antigod or a demon. More reasonably, bearing in mind its early Avestan origin, the original term could have been *asura,* from which the name *sura* was derived.

The *Taittirīya Saṃhitā* classifies evil beings into three categories – the *asuras,* the *rākshasas* and the *pishāchas.* The *asuras* are the enemies of the gods *(devas),* the *rākshasas* of men, and the *pishāchas* of the dead. The categories, however, are not clearly defined, nor are these beings entirely evil. The *rākshasas* have a semidivine nature. They display their baser passions towards gods and men, but among themselves show great virtue in their conduct.

The *asuras* bear resemblance to the Titans of Greek mythology. Their persistent efforts to obtain *Amṛita* (Water of Immortality) are echoed in the struggles of the Titans to obtain fire (light) from Mount Olympus.

In some myths, the *asuras* are ordained by fate to play a malevolent role in a particular situation, the consequence of actions in a past life. Thus, *Jaya* has to incarnate on earth to expiate a past mistake. Given the choice between three incarnations as an enemy of *Vishṇu* or seven incarnations as his friend, he chooses the former. Coming as Hiraṇyakashipu, Rāvaṇa and Shishupāla, he is slain by *Vishṇu* in his *avatār* forms of Narasiṃha, Rāmachandra and Kṛishṇa, respectively. The myth exemplifies expiation and forgiveness, for it is asserted in the *Purāṇas* that an *asura* can only achieve liberation if killed by *Vishṇu.*

Even in later mythology, *asuras* are not always entirely demonic. Legends are related concerning the liberation of *asuras* with good qualities, like Prahlāda (a devotee of *Vishṇu*) and Mahābalī (a good and generous king). Both attained liberation by being slain by one of the incarnations of *Vishṇu.*

In common parlance, however, the *asuras* are understood as demons. Hence, in the *Ādi Granth,* the term is used generally for the 'demon' or 'demons' within man:

> Without the *Guru,* man obtains not God's mansion,
> nor does he attain to His Name.
> Search for and obtain such true *Guru*
> through whom thou mayest gain that true Lord.
> He who slays his evil passion (*asur,* demon) abides in peace:
> whatever pleases Him, that comes to pass.
>
> *Guru Amardās, Ādi Granth 30, MMS*

And, using the name of *Rām,* the epic hero and demon slayer of the *Rāmāyaṇa,* as a name for God:

> My Lord *(Rām)* is the destroyer of demons *(asur):*
> my Beloved Lord *(Rām)* pervades all the hearts.
> Though ever with us, the unseeable Lord is not at all seen:
> by dwelling upon the writ of the supreme *Guru,* He is known.
>
> *Guru Nānak, Ādi Granth 1028, MMS*

See also: **sura**.

1. *Ṛig Veda* 2:1.6.
2. *Ṛig Veda* 1:24.14.

authority A person or group having the power to control, judge or limit the actions of others; mystically, part of a family of metaphors drawn from the rule and administration of this world, and used to describe the administration of the inner hierarchy of creation. In this context, an authority, power or throne is a centre or focus of administration in the inner hierarchy.

See also: **archon**, **dominions** (4.1), **powers**, **sovereignty** (4.1).

Azrael (A/P) An anglicization of *'Azrā'īl,* also called *'Izrā'īl;* the messenger of death in Judaism and Islam; also, the name of the subtle centre *(laṭīfah)* located in the throat.

See also: **'Izrā'īl**.

benei elohim, **benei elim** (He) *Lit.* sons *(benei)* of gods *(elohim, elim),* sons of God, *elohim* meaning either 'gods' or 'God', depending on the context; biblical terms sometimes used for the supernatural beings more generally called *mal'akhim* (angels). The name appears, for example, in a passage from *Genesis,* which the author relates as an episode in the build-up of wickedness that led to the deluge:

> When men had begun to be plentiful on the earth, and daughters had been born to them, the sons of God *(benei Elohim),* looking at the daughters of men, saw they were pleasing, so they married as many as they chose. *Yahweh* said, "My spirit must not for ever be disgraced in man, for he is but flesh; his life shall last no more than a hundred and twenty years." The *nefillim* (fallen angels) were on the earth at that time (and even afterwards) when the sons of God *(benei Elohim)* resorted to the daughters of man, and had children by them. These are the heroes of days gone by, the famous men.
>
> *Genesis 6:1–4, JB*

Benei elohim is also used on occasion for the sons of human judges and rulers, *elohim* sometimes meaning 'judges'. This ambiguity gave rise to differences among the early rabbis over the interpretation of the *Genesis* story of the *nefillim* (fallen angels). Many rabbis interpreted the 'sons of God' to mean distinguished people in this context, rather than angels, and some modern translations of the Bible convey that sense.

As supernatural beings or angels, the *benei Elohim* also appear in *Job:*

> Now there was a day when the sons of God *(benei Elohim)* came to present themselves before the Lord, and Satan came also among them. And the Lord said to Satan, "Where are you coming from?"
>
> Then Satan answered the Lord, and said, "From going to and fro in the earth, and from walking up and down in it."
>
> *Job 1:6–7, JCL*

The story continues with Satan's temptation of Job, and is one of Satan's earliest biblical appearances.

See also: **angels**, **mal'akh**, **nefillim**.

bhūt(a) (S/H/Pu) *Lit.* something which has come into being – divine, human, animal or inanimate; something manifest; hence, the five elements or *tattvas,* subtle or gross; the mental and spiritual aspects of a person that survive bodily death; also, a spirit, a devil, a demon, a ghost, an imp, an elemental, particularly of a malignant kind. In its earliest uses, as in the *Shatapatha Brāhmaṇa,*[1] a *bhūta* denotes any living being, even vegetable, as created by *Prajāpati* (lord of creatures). In later texts, *bhūtas* become "ghosts, spirit bands, goblins, serpent spirits, vampires and the like"[2] – not to be confused with the *asuras* (demons), *yakshas* (nature spirits) and *rākshasas* (ogres).

According to the *Vishṇu Purāṇa, bhūtas* are malignant fiends and eaters of flesh.[3] The *Manu Smṛiti* calls them spirits that roam about by day and night, to whom a sacrificial and propitiatory offering should be made in the morning and evening.[4] Later, the malevolent qualities of the *bhūtas* became assimilated with those of particular *pretas* (spirits), such as those who have met with violent deaths or who have died without receiving the benefit of the correct funeral rites.

Like the so-called vampires and witches of medieval Europe, *bhūtas* were blamed for every domestic calamity, including acts of revenge by neighbours with a grudge, as well as events arising from unknown causes, such as contaminated wells, blighted crops, diseased livestock, and the death of children though sickness. In the *Sushruta Saṃhitā, bhūtas* are said to be the cause of skin diseases, chronic fever, epilepsy and insanity.[5] Because – it is said – *bhūtas* cast no shadow, their presence is not always evident, so that it is necessary to burn turmeric frequently – a deterrent they greatly fear.[6]

Mystics have always said that a truly spiritual person will be unaffected by spirits, real or imaginary, benevolent or evil. Swāmī Shiv Dayāl Singh writes:

> I focused my attention in His devotion.
> Every nerve of my body resounded with the Melody.
> Listening to the *Shabd,*
> the soul penetrated the music of the void *(sunn),*
> vanquishing ghosts *(bhūt)* and evil spirits (on the way).
> *Swāmī Shiv Dayāl Singh, Sār Bachan Poetry 9:10.4–5, SBP p.94*

He also describes wicked people as devils or demons:

> What shall I say now? I have already said enough:
> a single word is all a true seeker needs to understand.
> The shameless and the wicked, enamoured of the world –
> what do they know?
> They are like devils *(bhūt)* and animals.
> *Swāmī Shiv Dayāl Singh, Sār Bachan Poetry 17:1.19–20, SBP p.132*

See also: **ghost**, **preta**.

1. *Shatapatha Brāhmaṇa* 7:4.2.12.
2. "Bhūta(s)", in *A Dictionary of Hinduism, DH* p.47.
3. *Vishṇu Purāṇa* 1:5.
4. *Manu Smṛiti* 3:90.
5. *Sushruta Saṃhitā* 2.
6. "Bhūta(s)", in *A Dictionary of Hinduism, DH* p.47.

Brahmā (S/H/Pu) The creator-god and the first deity of the sacred Hindu trinity or *trimūrti, Vishṇu* (the preserver) and *Shiva* (the destroyer) being the other two; derived from the root *brih* (to make, to form, to grow, to expand).

Brahmā is to be distinguished from *Brahman,* the absolute Reality of the *Upanishads* and the *Vedas.* In fact, the Hindu triad are sometimes described as the 'sons' of *Brahman,* in the sense that they are emanations from *Brahman. Brahmā* is the power or deity that presides over the creation of this universe. *Brahman* is the all-knowing, all-seeing, all-pervading transcendent Absolute, the supreme Self of the *Upanishads.*

In the *Muṇḍaka Upanishad, Brahmā* is the first of the gods, endowing Atharvan (his eldest son) with knowledge of the Absolute *(Brahman):*

Brahmā the creator of the universe,
 and guardian of the world,
 arose as the first among the gods *(devas).*
To Atharvan, his eldest son,
 he disclosed the knowledge of *Brahman,*
 the root of all knowledge.

Muṇḍaka Upanishad 1:1.1

The origin of *Brahmā* is the subject of various myths. According to the *Manu Smṛiti,* the self-existent One, *Brahman,* was at first cloaked in darkness. First He created the 'waters', the primal ground of being, depositing in them a seed, which became a golden egg *(hiraṇyāṇḍa).* From within the egg, He came forth as *Brahmā,* the creator of the universe.[1] In another myth, *Brahmā* is born from a lotus that springs from the naval of *Vishṇu.* The *Rāmāyaṇa,* on the other hand, says that *Brahmā* came into being out of *ākāsha* (void).

Brahmā is depicted as red in colour, with four bearded heads and four arms. In his four hands, he holds (respectively) a water jug, a bow, a sceptre and the *Vedas.* He is mounted on a *haṃsa,* a milk-white swan or goose, a mythical bird symbolizing purity. *Brahmā*'s chief consort is *Sarasvatī,* the goddess of wisdom and science, the Minerva of Hinduism. His dwelling place is called *Brahmaloka, Brahmapurī* or *satyaloka,* the highest heaven of *triloka,* according to the Hindus.

Although *Brahmā* appears in Indian mythology, and many temples have an image of him, he is not the object of great devotion or worship. There is only one well-known temple in India dedicated to him, at Pushkar, near Ajmer, in Rajasthan. His importance as a deity probably declined as a result of the growing popularity of Vaishnavism and Shaivism, and the struggle for supremacy between these two sects, both of whom belittled *Brahmā.* The Vaishnavites (worshippers of *Vishṇu*) asserted that *Brahmā* is inferior to *Vishṇu,* since he was born from a lotus that sprang from *Vishṇu*'s navel. The Shaivites (worshippers of *Shiva*) maintain that *Brahmā* is inferior to *Shiva* because – according to another myth – *Brahmā* originally had five heads, but was powerless to prevent *Shiva* from cutting off one of them in a fit of anger, after *Brahmā*'s refusal to acknowledge *Shiva*'s superiority. In Shaivism, *Brahmā* is represented as *Shiva*'s charioteer.

Hindu thought sees these three primary deities or powers as personifications of the three *guṇas,* the primary attributes of creation within the mind worlds. Although the particular *guṇas* assigned to the three are sometimes switched around, *Brahmā* is generally regarded as an embodiment of *rajas,* the *guṇa* of ceaseless creative activity. 'Ināyat Khān observes:

> The Hindus were the earliest to form the conception of the three aspects of divinity, which were *trimūrti: Brahmā* the creator, *Vishṇu*

> the sustainer and *Shiva* the destroyer. These three powers keep the whole universe in balance, and they are active in everything in the world. *Brahmā* was represented with four arms which signifies that besides the physical arms, there are mental arms which are necessary in the scheme of creation.
>
> *'Ināyat Khān, Sufi Message, SMIK9 p.206*

In reflected form, *Brahmā* is also the presiding deity at the *svādhishṭhāna chakra,* the procreative centre in *piṇḍa.*

Because of the reverence paid to these three deities in Hinduism, many Indian mystics have gone out of their way to point out the real place they occupy in the economy of creation. Although mystics have agreed that these deities personify the three *guṇas,* they have gone on to observe that, as such, these deities exist to serve the creation, not to be worshipped. They perform their functions for Hindu, Christian and Muslim alike, whether or not anyone believes in them, understands what they are or worships them. They derive their power from the supreme Lord, paying worship to Him:

> *Brahmās* and *Shivas (Rudra)* worship Thee:
> Thou art the death (vanquisher) of Death *(kāl kā Kāl).*
> O immaculate Lord, everyone begs of Thee.
>
> *Guru Rāmdās, Ādi Granth 1403, MMS*

They are also within the realm of *māyā:*

> I have thought about *Brahmā, Vishṇu (Bishan)* and *Shiva (Mahesh):*
> They are bound down by the three dispositions (*guṇas,* attributes),
> so, salvation (*mukat,* liberation) remains far from them.
>
> *Guru Amardās, Ādi Granth 1049, MMS*

Mystics have also said that the positions occupied by these deities are not permanently allocated to any soul, but are earned by thousands of years of austerities or other religious practices. Mahārāj Sāwan Singh used to say that the 'offices' of these deities have been occupied by thousands of souls and and will be occupied by thousands more in the future. Hence, the mystic Sahajobāī writes:

> Even if you attain the status of *Indra*
> or obtain the lifespan of *Brahmā,*
> even then you will have to face death some day.
> Everyone passes away.
>
> *Sahajobāī, Bānī, Nām 3, SBB p.30*

See also: **Brahmaloka** (4.1), **guṇa** (5.2), **Vishṇu** (4.1), **Shiva** (4.1)

1. *Manu Smṛiti* 1:9.

cherubim (He. *keruvim,* sg. *keruv*) Winged celestial beings; angels, often taking the role of intercessors or guardians. Originating in Babylonian mythology, the word is probably derived from the Akkadian *karibu* meaning 'an intercessor'. The *karibu* were generally depicted as half-human, half-animal deities who guarded the approach to temples and palaces.

In the *Genesis* story of Adam and Eve, a myth with significant antecedents in Babylonian mythology, the cherubim are set as guardians at the entrance to the garden of Eden after Adam and Eve have been cast out. In *Exodus,* they appear as ornamentation and guardians upon the ark built by Moses to house God's 'testimony' – the Ten Commandments. Whether any allegorical meaning is intended in this description is uncertain.

In the prophet Ezekiel's account of his vision of the heavenly throne, the cherubim seem to represent beings who exist either in the heavenly regions or are physical manifestations of divine power. At the beginning of the vision, they are called *ḥayyot* (living creatures), but are subsequently called cherubim *(keruvim).* They carry the throne on which the Lord sits, and the beating of their wings is like "the Voice of the almighty God when He speaks":

> Then I looked, and behold, in the firmament that was above the head of the *keruvim* appeared over them something like a sapphire stone, in appearance like the shape of a throne. And he spoke to the man clothed with linen, and said, "Go in between the wheels, under the *keruv,* and fill your hand with coals of fire from between the *keruvim,* and scatter them over the city." And he went in before my eyes. And the *keruvim* stood on the right side of the house when the man went in; and the cloud (of the Lord's glory and presence) filled the inner court.
>
> Then the glory of the Lord went up from the *keruv,* and stood over the threshold of the house; and the house was filled with the cloud, and the court was full of the brightness of the Lord's glory. And the sound of the wings of the *keruvim* was heard even in the outer court, like the Voice of the almighty God when He speaks.
>
> *Ezekiel 10:1–5, JCL*

Ezekiel also sees the "glory" (light) of the Lord rising from above the threshold of the house, and standing over the *keruvim.* It is unclear whether this passage is purely imaginative or has some allegorical or metaphorical significance. Either way, it is certain that the earlier Babylonian cherubim have been transformed by their absorption into ancient Judaism.

In the historical books of the Hebrew Bible, the cherubim have become a part of the heavenly host or hierarchy of angels, powers and realms, subject to the supreme Lord, as in *2 Kings:*

> And Ḥezekiah prayed before the Lord, and said, "O Lord God of Israel who sittest upon the cherubim, Thou art the God, even Thou alone, of all the kingdoms of the earth; Thou hast made heaven and earth."
>
> *2 Kings 19:15, KB*

In gnostic literature, the cherubim are sometimes used as a symbol for negative tendencies, or worldly desires and obsessions. In later Christianity, they become plump, winged and human-like angels, often depicted as infants.

In Judaic and early Christian angelology, the cherubim are regarded as the highest form of angel, subordinate only to God. The *Apocryphon of John* represents God as transcendent, who emanates His essence as light.[1] The four *ḥayyot* or cherubim depicted as supporting God's throne are understood on the symbolic level as the bearers of His light in the process of emanation.

The cherubim were associated in the Jewish gnostic literature with the four archangels known as the 'angels of the Presence' (of God). The ninth-century Saʿadia Gaʾon described the first emanation of the divine Light, the divine creative power, as the special cherub or angel of God.

The medieval Jewish philosopher, Moses Maimonides, who interpreted all angels as incorporeal intelligences, understood the throne to be identical with God's Essence, a manifestation of the divine glory *(kavod),* and the *keruvim* as stages in the emanation of that glory.

An interesting comment is made by Kabbalist Rabbi Aryeh Kaplan concerning the portrayal of the cherubs as two infants with wings. It is, he says, symbolic of man's ability to transcend his earthly form and "fly on the wings of his soul, soaring through the highest spiritual universes. This concept was embodied in the very shape of the cherubs, and by meditating on them, a person could indeed fly with his own spiritual wings."[2]

According to *Exodus,* a picture of two cherubs facing each other was used on the front of the ark of the covenant,[3] which was placed in the holy of holies in the Temple. Kaplan says that the image was intended to symbolize the cherubs of the spiritual realms. Their facing each other, with a space between, signified the opening to the spiritual dimension:

> The cherubs on the ark were meant to be a counterpart of the cherubs on high, and thus, in a sense, the space between these two forms was seen as an opening into the spiritual realms. In concentrating his

thoughts between the cherubs on the ark, the prophet was also able to pass between the angelic cherubs, and then ascend on the path of the Tree of Life. Conversely, when God's message was sent to the prophet, it would also follow this same path, first passing through the spiritual cherubs, and then through the ones on the ark. The space between the cherubs was therefore the source of all prophetic inspiration.

Aryeh Kaplan, Meditation and the Bible, MBAK p.59[4]

These meditation practices focusing on the cherubs were probably inspired by the Bible's description of Moses hearing the Lord's 'voice' speaking from between the two *keruvim:*

And when Moses went into the Tent of Meeting to speak with Him (God), then he heard the voice of one speaking to him from the covering that was upon the ark of testimony, from between the two *keruvim;* and He spoke to him.

Numbers 7:89, JCL

1. *Apocryphon of John* 9, 20, 22–23.
2. Aryeh Kaplan, *Meditation and the Bible, MBAK* p.58.
3. *Exodus* 25:18–22, 26:1,31, 36:8,35, 37:7–9.
4. See Baḥya ibn Pekuda, Moses Naḥmanides, Hirsch, Ẓioni and *Midrash ha-Gadol,* on *Exodus* 25:18; *Tanḥuma, va-Yekhel* 7; Moses Maimonides, *Moreh Nebukhim (Guide for the Perplexed)* 3:45; *Zohar* 1:32b.

dev(a) (S/H/Pu), **devatā** (S/H), **deo** (Pu) *Lit.* shining one; a celestial being; a god, a deity, a divine being, particularly male, generally applied to the many lesser gods of the Hindu pantheon; an angel; also, an idol; also, a king, a prince; a title of honour used in addressing a king; derived from the same root as the Latin *div* (divine); among the ancient Persians, the word (as *daeva*) came to mean demon.

In the Vedic dictionary, *Nirukta,*[1] it is said that deities are of three kinds: those with anthropomorphic form, those with no anthropomorphic form and those who, though really non-anthropomorphic, may assume various forms to carry out a specific purpose or activity.

Hindu mythology relates stories of the wars and struggles between the *devas* (shining ones) and the *asuras* (the dark ones, demons). According to the epic Hindu legend, the *Mahābhārata, devas* can be recognized when appearing to mortals, because they neither sweat nor blink their eyes, nor do their feet touch the ground. They are shadowless like *bhūtas* (ghosts), and they wear flowery adornments that never wilt or fade.

In the *Vedas,* numerous deities are depicted, inhabiting the three worlds of the earth, the atmosphere and the sky. Large numbers of Vedic hymns are addressed to *Agni, Vāyu, Sūrya, Varuṇa, Indra* and many other gods. The *Ṛig Veda* refers to thirty-three gods,[2] a number repeated in the *Shatapatha Brāhmaṇa,*[3] where it is said that they consist of eight *vasus,* eleven *rudras,* twelve *ādityas, Dyaus* (the sky god) and *Pṛithvī* (the earth goddess). To this, *Prajāpati* (lord of creatures) is added as the thirty-fourth. At the present time, Hindu tradition speaks of thirty-three crores (330 millions) of *devas,* ruled over by *Indra,* probably an extension of the thirty-three gods of the *Ṛig Veda.* Many of these are personifications of natural forces.

For many Hindus, the innumerable gods are regarded as manifestations of a single divine Reality. Although the origins of Hindu polytheism are complex, the idea that the gods are aspects of a single Reality does occur quite early in Hindu tradition. In fact, the oldest text of all, the *Ṛig Veda* (*c.*1500 BCE) says:

> He is One, sages call Him by many names.
>
> *Ṛig Veda 1:164.46, MV p.65*

Later, in the early *Upanishads,* an underlying Reality *(Brahman)* is described that is common to all the gods. In the *Bṛihadāraṇyaka Upanishad,* Shākalya asks the sage Yājñavalkya how many gods there are. He answers that there are as many gods as there are in the sacred scriptures, three thousand, three hundred and six. When pressed, he answers that there are thirty-three gods, then six, then three, then two, then one and a half, and finally one. That is, all the gods are manifestations of the one Reality.[4]

The *Muṇḍaka Upanishad* also articulates the idea that there is one Absolute that generates the innumerable forms of the cosmos, including the gods:

> As a spider spins out its thread,
>   and then draws it in again;
> As plants sprout up from the earth;
> As hair grows on the head and body of a living man;
> So do all things in the universe arise from the Imperishable.
>
> *Muṇḍaka Upanishad 1:1.7*

By the time of the later *Upanishads,* a theism has developed in which the Lord *(Bhagavān)* is a personal Being, not simply an abstract Absolute. Thus, *Vishṇu* emerges as the supreme Lord in the *Mahānārāyaṇa Upanishad* and in the *Bhagavad Gītā,* while *Shiva* becomes important with the *Shvetāshvatara Upanishad.* The *Devī* (Goddess) tradition developed somewhat later.

There are a number of specific Hindu traditions that regard their own deity as the Supreme, identified with the absolute Reality *(Brahman).* Thus,

Vaishnavites regard *Vishṇu* as the Absolute; Shaivites revere *Shiva;* and *Shāktas* revere *Devī,* each tradition regarding other deities as lower manifestations. The non-dual or *Advaita Vedānta* tradition maintains that all the deities are ultimately identical with the One, though the theistic traditions tend to maintain some distinction between them, and between the self and God. Indeed, there has been a rigorous debate within Hindu theologies concerning whether there is anything outside the One. The monistic traditions maintain that there is nothing outside the One, while the theistic traditions, in varying degrees, argue for difference and plurality.

All areas of creation are administered by beings. The one divine Source is the Supreme Being and everything else is manifested through the apparent division of this one Being. Even creatures of the physical realm – human beings and others – have administration over the field of their own *karma.* Each is effectively the deity of its own tiny area of creation. Similarly, in the inner hierarchy, all areas of creation are administered – indeed come into existence and are maintained – through conscious beings. These beings are the various so-called gods and goddesses, the male and female powers, the *devas* and *devīs* of Hinduism.

Generally, the metaphysical speculation of the various schools does not appeal to the common man, and many Hindus are unconcerned whether or not there is one Supreme Being with *Agni, Vāyu, Varuṇa* and so on as His different names. They prefer to offer prayers to their *ishta-devatās* (chosen gods), and are generally not averse to praying to other gods as well. They only feel satisfied if they worship the anthropomorphic form of gods as depicted in the *Purāṇas,* or idols or symbols or any other representation of their gods. In fact, some worship not only the gods of the *Vedas* and *Purāṇas,* but also trees, rivers, animals (cows, monkeys, snakes and so on), birds *(Garuḍa),* demons and departed ancestors. Even the various implements used in their professions are worshipped *(āyudhapūjā).*

Mystics have always tried to wean people away from this kind of outward worship, towards the worship of the one God. Thus, Kṛishṇa says in the *Bhagavad Gītā:*

> They who worship the deities *(devas)* will go to them;
> Those who worship the ancestors will go to them;
> Those who worship ghosts will go to them;
> And those who worship me will come to me.
>
> *Bhagavad Gītā 9:25*

Indian mystics have also tried to point out the place of the *devas* in the scheme of things. The *Ādi Granth* says bluntly that the thirty-three crores of Hindu *devas* are all in search of *Brahman;*[5] they beg for the generosity of the Lord;[6] and all of them are prone to death and dissolution.[7] Like all other beings, their existence is sustained by the mystic "Name":

> The thirty-one millions of gods *(dev),*
> strivers, adepts *(siddhs)* and men remember the Name,
> and the Name upholds the worlds and universes.
>
> *Guru Amardās, Ādi Granth 1393, MMS*

Kabīr says that neither the *devas* nor their representation as stone idols are suitable objects for human worship:

> Thou tearest off the leaves, O lady-gardener,
> but in every leaf there is life.
> The stone (idol) for which thou pluckest the leaves,
> that stone is lifeless.
> In this, thou art mistaken, O lady-gardener:
> the true *Guru* is the living Lord *(Deo).*
> *Brahmā* is in the leaves, *Vishṇu (Bishan)* in the boughs
> and god *Shiva (Shankardeo)* in the flowers.
> The three gods thou obviously breakest,
> then whose service performest thou?
>
> *Kabīr, Ādi Granth 479, MMS*

Guru Nānak observes that since the *devas* are a part of the heavenly worlds, they are caught in the illusion of *māyā:*

> *Māyā* has deluded all gods *(devas)* and goddesses *(devīs):*
> Death *(Kāl)* spares none without *Guru*'s service.
>
> *Guru Nānak, Ādi Granth 227, MMS*

Tukārām says that the gods and goddesses long for a human form:

> The body that we possess in this world
> is coveted by the gods *(devas).*
>
> *Tukārām, Gāthā 254, STG p.43*

Sardār Bahādur Jagat Singh, quoting Kabīr, says the same, explaining that this is because it is only in human form that the *devas* can begin the ascent to God. In a culture that traditionally worships deities, this is a significant point:

> Kabīr says: "The gods *(devas)* yearn for a human incarnation, for the Lord is realized in this body alone." The gods yearn for the human form because devotion to the Lord cannot be practised in any other form, whether physical or astral. People imagine that gods are superior to human beings. The fact is that they are souls who performed meritorious deeds, such as charities, sacrifices, etc. in their human

lives (but did not devote themselves to the practice of *Nām* (Name) or Sound Current), and are consequently in paradise, *svarg,* etc., enjoying the fruits of their good actions. At the end of the prescribed period of reward, these *devas,* gods or angels will again be pushed down into this world. All the Saints and scriptures support this view.

Sardār Bahādur Jagat Singh, Science of the Soul I:1, SOS p.6

1. *Nirukta* 7:6–7.
2. *Ṛig Veda* 1:139.11, 8:59.2.
3. *Shatapatha Brāhmaṇa* 4:5.7.2.
4. *Bṛihadāraṇyaka Upanishad* 3:9.1–9.
5. Guru Amardās, *Ādi Granth* 130.
6. Guru Nānak, *Ādi Granth* 504.
7. Guru Amardās, *Ādi Granth* 1100.

Devī (S/H) *Lit.* shining one; thus, a goddess; a female deity; the 'consort' or 'wife' of a *deva;* hence, a queen; a title of respect for a high-ranking society lady; also, specifically, the Great Goddess *(Mahādevī)* or just the Goddess *(Devī).*

A number of Hindu goddesses are commonly regarded as manifestations of the Great Goddess. In Vedic times, *devīs* were the feminine counterpart of the *devas* (gods), and were manifestations of the power of natural phenomena, such as the dawn *(Ushas),* night *(Rātri),* the river Ganges *(Gangā)* and so on. The idea of a Great Goddess who is identified with the Absolute, of whom other goddesses are manifestations, develops only in the fifth to seventh centuries CE. In the *Devī Upanishad* (a late text), *Mahādevī* is asked by the gods:

"Who are you, O Great Goddess *(Mahādevī)?*"
She replied: "I am the manifestation of *Brahman;*
From me the world arises
as nature *(prakṛiti)* and the self *(purusha).*"

Devī Upanishad 1, HTU p.470; cf. HEU p.484

The most important manifestation of the Goddess is *Durgā,* the warrior goddess who destroys *Mahisha,* the buffalo demon, and so restores harmony to the cosmos. The myth is told in the *Devībhāgavata Purāṇa* and the *Devīmāhātmya.* Apart from *Durgā,* the Goddess' other representations are in her terrible manifestation, as *Kālī,* and as the consorts or energies *(shaktis)* of the gods, particularly *Sarasvatī, Pārvatī* and *Lakshmī,* the consorts (respectively) of *Brahmā, Shiva* and *Vishṇu.* Sītā and Rādhā, the consorts of Rāmachandra and Kṛishṇa, incarnations *(avatārs)* of *Vishṇu,* are also well known.

Other manifestations of the Goddess include a group of generally ferocious seven mothers *(saptamātṛikā),* whose natures are ambiguous, preying on children yet also destroying demons. They are identified in esoteric tantric literature with the sounds of the Sanskrit alphabet and, indeed, the alphabet itself is known as *Mātṛikā* (Mother). The Goddess is also manifested in countless local village icons; in temples and household shrines; in forms neither human nor animal such as stones, poles, weapons, magical diagrams *(yantra)* and stylized female genitals *(yoni);* in natural phenomena such as rivers and mountains; and in 'mediums' possessed by the Goddess during religious festivals.

See also: **deva**.

dikpāl(a) (S/H) *Lit.* direction *(dik, disha)* guardians *(pāl);* the guardian deities of the ten directions in Indian mythology, according to the *Purāṇas.* Every action or movement in the creation takes place according to the divine law or divine will. According to traditional Hindu belief, therefore, all aspects of nature are controlled by a deity such as a sea deity, a river deity, a moon deity, a sun deity and so on. Similarly, there are said to be deities for each of the ten directions. The ten directions are the eight points of the compass, plus up and down, the deities being *Indra* (east), *Agni* (southeast), *Yama* (south), *Nairṛita* (southwest), *Varuṇa* (west), *Marut* (northwest), *Kuvera* (north), *Īshāna* (northeast), *Brahmā* (up) and *Ananta* (down).

Durgā (S/H) *Lit.* difficult of access or approach, impassable, unattainable; a narrow passage through a wood, over a river, stream, mountain and so on; as a name, the inaccessible or terrific goddess; an epithet of *Pārvatī,* wife of *Shiva.* According to Hindu mythology, she slew the demon *Durga,* thereafter assuming the demon's name. According to one legend, *Durgā* was created out of the flames issuing from the mouths of *Brahmā, Vishṇu, Shiva* and other gods, with the specific purpose of killing demons.

Durgā is portrayed in the *Purāṇas* and the *Mahābhārata* as a formidable female warrior, the bloodthirsty destroyer of giant *asuras* (demons). She is a fierce form of *Devī,* the consort of *Shiva,* the mild ones being *Sātī, Pārvatī* and *Umā. Durgā* assumes ten forms, the most notable being *Kālī* or *Kālī Mā.* Her beneficent aspect is indicated in Yudhishṭhira's hymn to her in the *Mahābhārata:*

> You are called *Durgā* by all
> because you save men from difficulty....
> You are the sole refuge of men.
>
> *Mahābhārata 6, Virāṭaparvan; cf. HG p.71*

Durgā's primitive and gruesome aspect can be seen in the human and animal sacrifices offered to her, the use of intoxicants and her epithet *Chhinnamastakā* (the Headless). She is portrayed as mounted on a tiger, holding weapons suitable for slaying demons in each of her eight arms. She is worshipped with great devotion and pageantry, especially in Bengal, during *Dashahrā. Durgā* is variously described as the mother, consort and creation of *Shiva,* something which serves to demonstrate how inconsistent Hindu mythology can sometimes be.

Durgā, also known as *Ashṭāngī,* the goddess with eight arms, is the presiding deity of the *kaṇṭha chakra* or throat centre. She is the mother of the three lower gods – *Brahmā, Vishṇu* and *Shiva,* who derive their power from her. She is also known as *Shakti,* who symbolizes *māyā,* the power of illusion. Mystics of a higher order have termed this goddess *Avidyā* (ignorance), because compared with the supreme consciousness and absolute knowledge of the higher planes, the consciousness of *Shakti* is ignorance and delusion. It is to emphasize this that Kabīr writes:

> Such is He, whose feet millions of goddesses *(Durgās)* shampoo,
> and for whom millions of *Brahmās* utter the *Vedas.*
> When I beg, then beg I only the Lord's Name:
> I have nothing to do with any other god.
>
> *Kabīr, Ādi Granth 1162, MMS*

See also: **Kālī**.

dūt(a) (S/H/Pu) (pl. *dūtān*) *Lit.* messenger, ambassador, envoy, courier; used in a variety of contexts in Indian mystic literature, often as a shortened form of *yamdūt* (angel or messenger of death). Dharamdās writes:

> In all the four ages,
> the swans (*haṃsas,* pure souls) go to the true region *(sat lok),*
> while the crows (sinners) keep wandering about,
> watched over by the *dūt (i.e. yamdūts).*
>
> *Dharamdās, Shabdāvalī, Nām Līlā 15, DDS p.71*

Similarly, Guru Nānak speaks of the death of those who have lived lives of absorption in the world:

> Both wealth and youthful beauty, which afforded them pleasure,
> have now become their enemies.
> The order was given to the *dūtān,*
> who having dishonoured them, took them away.
>
> *Guru Nānak, Ādi Granth 417, MMS*

From *yamdūt,* the term has come to mean 'demon' in a more general sense. Hence, human imperfections have been described as "demons":

> All the demons *(dūt)* and adversaries
> are warded off by Thee, O Lord,
> and manifest is Thy glory.
>
> *Guru Arjun, Ādi Granth 681, MMS*

See also: **yamadūta**.

elohim (He) *Lit.* gods; a biblical and rabbinic term for angels and other supernatural beings; also, at a human level, judges. One of the biblical psalms says that God has made angels *(elohim)* only a little above man, meaning – presumably – that the angels dwell in heavenly realms only a little above the physical universe:

> What is man, that You are mindful of him?
> And the son of man, that You visit him?
> For You have made him a little lower than the angels *(elohim),*
> and have crowned him with glory and honour.
>
> *Psalm 8:5–6, JCL*

See also: **angels**, **benei elohim**, **deva**, **mal'akh**, **nefillim**.

firishtah (P) (pl. *firishtagān*) *Lit.* angel; messenger; also, a good human being; equivalent to the Arabic term, *malak.*

See also: **angels**, **mal'ak**.

fravashi (Av) A class of supernatural beings who act as the guardian spirits of the world and of mankind. They are also the celestial prototypes or patterns of things in the material world. Although they are not mentioned in Zarathushtra's *Gāthās,* they have a prominent position in the Zoroastrian pantheon with special rites devoted to them. Zoroastrian scholar, M.N. Dhalla, says:

> The *fravashis* constitute a world of patterns of the earthly creations, and they have lived as conscious beings in the empyrean with *Ahurā Mazdā* from all eternity. The multifarious objects of this world are so many terrestrial duplicates of these celestial originals. The *fravashis* constitute the internal essence of things, as opposed to the contingent

> and accidental. Earthly creations are so many imperfect copies of these types. They are the manifestations of the energy of *Ahurā Mazdā.* When nothing existed and *Ahurā Mazdā* lived in His sublime singleness, He had the ideas, concepts of the material and spiritual creation which He contemplated creating in time. We have recognized the projection and manifestation of His Will and Thought, and the emanation of His creative Mind as *Spentā Mainyu* (Holy Spirit).
>
> Origen, the Alexandrian philosopher, is right when he says that the *Logos* represents the sum total of the world-thoughts of God. *Spentā Mainyu* is the embodiment of *Ahurā Mazdā*'s prototypal ideas, which are called *fravashis* in the Avestan texts. Creation is the materialization of these idealized contents of his (*Spentā Mainyu*'s) Mind, and through him of *Ahurā Mazdā*'s Mind. These idealized contents of the divine Mind are the *fravashis,* and creatures are their feeble replicas. The *fravashis* are not mere abstractions of thought, but have objective existence, and work as spiritual entities in heaven, like the angels and archangels.
>
> *M.N. Dhalla, History of Zoroastrianism, HZ pp.235–36*

M.N. Dhalla goes on to speak of the duties and activities of the *fravashis.* According to Zoroastrian belief, every object and every being has its own *fravashi.* When a child takes birth, his soul's eternal *fravashi* accompanies him, and acts as his guardian angel throughout his life. At death, however, the soul is responsible for its own actions, and its *fravashi* now lives an individualized life in the heavenly regions as the *fravashi* of that particular person.

Fravashis are of good and noble character. They are the means by which *Ahurā Mazdā* orders and runs His creation. The earth, the sky and all creatures are under their influence. They are involved in all aspects of existence, and interested in the welfare of all. They also like to receive sacrifices from the living, and do not like to be forgotten by the relatives of those among whom they once lived. They can grant abundant blessings, but may also curse those who offend them.[1]

See also: **guardian angels**, **ḥāfiẓ**.

1. M.N. Dhalla, *History of Zoroastrianism, HZ* pp.232–43.

Gabriel (He), **Jabra'īl** (A/P) *Lit.* man (He. *gabri*) + God (He. *El*); man of God; an angel, first appearing in the second-century (BCE) *Book of Daniel,* where he is a messenger of the doom about to befall the Israelites due to their iniquitous lives; generally anglicized as Gabriel. In Jewish legend, he commonly appears in company with the more important angel, Michael, guardian of Israel.

The second part of *Daniel* consists of four visions foretelling the end of the world, the second and third of which are interpreted by Gabriel. Meaning 'man of God', Gabriel is sometimes referred to by name, and sometimes as a man or "one in the likeness of a man". Here, Gabriel interprets Daniel's third vision:

> And while I was speaking, and praying, and confessing my sin and the sin of my people Israel, and presenting my supplication before the Lord my God for the holy mountain of my God; and while I was speaking in prayer, the man Gabriel, whom I had seen in the vision at the beginning, came to me in swift flight at the time of the evening sacrifice.
>
> And he made me understand, and talked with me, and said, "O Daniel, I have not come out to give you wisdom and understanding. At the beginning of your supplications the command came out, and I have come to tell it to you; for you are greatly beloved; therefore consider the word, and understand the vision.
>
> "Seventy weeks are decreed upon your people and upon your holy city, to finish the transgression, and to put an end to sin, and to atone for iniquity, and to bring in everlasting righteousness, and to seal up the vision and prophecy, and to anoint the most holy place."
>
> *Daniel 9:20–24, JCL*

Gabriel then goes on to describe the end of the world in greater detail.

Daniel's fourth vision is explained by a "man clothed in linen", generally presumed to be Gabriel, though the text does not say so. Daniel first explains that he had been undergoing penance ("mourning") for three weeks prior to his vision:

> In those days I, Daniel, was mourning for three full weeks. I ate no pleasant bread, nor did meat nor wine come into my mouth, nor did I anoint myself at all, till three whole weeks were fulfilled.
>
> And in the twenty-fourth day of the first month, as I was by the side of the great river, which is Hiddekel, I lifted up my eyes, and looked, and behold a certain man clothed in linen, whose loins were girded with fine gold of Uphaz; his body also was like the beryl, and his face like the appearance of lightning, and his eyes like lamps of fire, and his arms and his feet in colour like polished bronze, and the sound of his words like the voice of a multitude.
>
> *Daniel 10:2–6, JCL*

Daniel then describes how only he can see the vision, his companions fleeing in terror. On hearing the voice of the "man clothed in linen", he falls face down on the ground, fast asleep. The angel touches and awakens him, telling him that he has come to foretell the fate of Israel. This the "man" does, describing various historical events that have yet to take place. In modern times, it is generally understood that the 'revelation' is being written after the events so 'prophesied', a common feature of ancient revelational texts, both Jewish and Christian.

Gabriel's only other biblical appearance is in Luke's gospel, to Mary the mother of Jesus and to Zacharias, the father of John the Baptist, foretelling the birth of their respective children.[1] These stories are only related by Luke. Here, he is is the bearer of good news, and it is in this way that he is remembered in the Christian tradition. In the oft-repeated words of Luke:

> And in the sixth month the angel Gabriel was sent from God unto a city of Galilee, named Nazareth, to a virgin espoused to a man whose name was Joseph, of the house of David; and the virgin's name was Mary. And the angel came in unto her, and said, "Hail, thou that art highly favoured, the Lord is with thee: blessed art thou among women." And when she saw him, she was troubled at his saying, and cast in her mind what manner of salutation this should be.
>
> And the angel said unto her, "Fear not, Mary: for thou hast found favour with God. And, behold, thou shalt conceive in thy womb, and bring forth a son, and shalt call his name Jesus. He shall be great, and shall be called the Son of the Highest; and the Lord God shall give unto him the throne of his father David; and he shall reign over the house of Jacob for ever; and of his kingdom there shall be no end."
>
> Then said Mary unto the angel, "How shall this be, seeing I know not a man?"
>
> And the angel answered and said unto her, "The Holy Ghost shall come upon thee, and the power of the Highest shall overshadow thee: therefore also that holy thing which shall be born of thee shall be called the Son of God. And, behold, thy cousin Elisabeth, she hath also conceived a son in her old age: and this is the sixth month with her, who was called barren. For with God nothing shall be impossible."
>
> And Mary said, "Behold the handmaid of the Lord; be it unto me according to thy word." And the angel departed from her.
>
> *Luke 1:26–38, KJV*

Although these are the only two biblical appearances of Gabriel, Gabriel and Michael are identified in Jewish and Islamic legend as the unnamed angels who appear in the Bible to many of the prophets and patriarchs, bringing messages from God or interceding in history. In the *Aggadah* (rabbinic stories), Gabriel and Michael are among the four angels who surround the throne of the Almighty.[2] They are two of the three angels who visit Abraham after his circumcision,[3] Gabriel's task being to destroy Sodom, and Michael's to announce the future birth of Isaac.[4] There is also a tradition that it was either Gabriel or Michael who wrestled with Jacob,[5] and appeared to Moses at Ḥoreb.[6] They were also among the angels who accompanied God when He descended on Mount Sinai.[7]

It is also believed that both Gabriel and Michael will accompany the Messiah, and fight the wicked.[8] Over time, the characters of Gabriel and Michael have also evolved, becoming associated, respectively, with the opposing qualities of judgment and mercy. Hence, it is said that Gabriel is made of fire and Michael of snow. They cause no harm to each other, however, though standing close, indicating the power of God to "make peace in His high places".[9]

Gabriel is one of the four archangels, the others being Michael, *Uri'el* and *Phenu'el*. In post-biblical gnostic literature, such as the *Testament of Abraham,* Gabriel is one of seven archangels, his role being that of the ruler of paradise. In the *Book of Enoch,* he is one of the angels of the (divine) Presence.[10]

In Islam, Gabriel becomes the Arabic *Jabra'īl,* and the legends associated with him assume a different character. According to Islamic tradition, *Jabra'īl* appeared to Adam after the 'fall', consoling him and teaching him the alphabet, as well as advising him how to live in the material world. *Jabra'īl* is also one of the four archangels of Islam, the other three being *Mīkhā'īl* (Michael), *Isrāfīl (Seraphi'el)* and *'Izrā'īl* (Azrael, the angel of death).

Most significantly, however, *Jabra'īl* is the one who brings the divine revelation to Muḥammad. According to a brief account in the *Qur'ān,* elaborated by tradition, *Jabra'īl* accompanies Muḥammad on his ascent to the presence of God. But he is only able to guide Muḥammad a certain distance. As they approach the *Sidrat al-muntahá* (the Lote Tree of the uttermost limit) on the upper boundary of the seventh heaven, *Jabra'īl* falls back. Legend relates that when Muḥammad asks his guide why he has fallen behind him, *Jabra'īl* replies that if he were to go a fingertip closer he would be burned. The Prophet therefore goes on alone to within "two bow lengths" from the presence of God, "or nearer",[11] though it is unclear from the narrative in the *Qur'ān* whether Muḥammad advances to God or God to Muḥammad.

Jabra'īl's inability to reach God indicates Muḥammad's spiritual ascendence over even the highest of divine powers or angels. In fact, in retelling the story, Rūmī depicts *Jabra'īl* as the power of intellect and discursive reason *('aql)*. However, "noble and revered" it may be, it is no lover like the moth who willingly merges itself into the candle, sacrificing its own individuality, like the soul in God. The intellect divides and is fond of its own identity, just as *Jabra'īl* holds back from being consumed in the divine fire:

When Muḥammad passed beyond the Lote Tree
and *Jabra'īl*'s observation post and station and farthest limit,
he said to *Jabra'īl,* "Come, fly after me!"
He replied, "Go! Go! I am your companion no further!"
Again, he said, "Come, O burner of veils!
I have still not reached my zenith."
He replied, "O my illustrious friend!
If I fly beyond this limit, my wings will burn." …
O *Jabra'īl!* Although you are noble and revered,
you are neither moth nor candle.
When the flaming candle sends its invitation,
the moth's spirit does not hold back from being consumed!

Rūmī, Maśnavī IV:3801–4, 3807–8; cf. MJR4 pp.480–81, in SPL pp.222–23

Elsewhere, Rūmī is even more specific:

Intellect *('aql)* says, like *Jabra'īl,* "O Muḥammad,
if I take one more step, it will burn me;
You must leave me, henceforth advance alone:
this is my limit, O sultan of the soul!"

Rūmī, Maśnavī I:1066–67; cf. MJR2 p.60

Because of his role as guide to Muḥammad, *Jabra'īl* nevertheless becomes a symbol of high spiritual station in many Sufi writings, a guide and companion on the spiritual quest. *Jabra'īl* has also been given the epithet, *al-Rūḥ al-Amīn,* the Trusted Spirit (being trustworthy in bringing the divine message), as well as *Rūḥ al-Ilqā',* the Spirit of Casting into (since he 'casts' the divine inspiration into the prophets). *Jabra'īl* is also associated with *al-Rūḥ,* the angel who is so much larger than the other angels that when the angels stand in ranks he is said to take up a whole row by himself. In some Sufi orders, *Jabra'īl* is also the name of the *laṭīfah* (subtle bodily energy centre) located at the heart.

See also: **Surūsh**.

1. *Luke* 1:11–20, 26–38.
2. *Midrash Rabbah, Numbers* 2:10; *cf. Enoch* 9:1.
3. *Midrash Rabbah, Genesis* 48:9.
4. *Midrash Rabbah, Genesis* 50:2.
5. *Midrash Rabbah, Genesis* 78:1.
6. *Midrash Rabbah, Exodus* 2:5.
7. *Midrash Rabbah, Deuteronomy* 2:34.
8. *The Alphabet of Rabbi Akiva 2,* in *BMJ3* p.12*ff.*

9. *Job* 25:2; *Midrash Rabbah, Deuteronomy* 5:12.
10. Gabriel in Jewish tradition derived from "Michael and Gabriel", in *Encyclopedia Judaica, EJCD.*
11. *Qur'ān* 53:9.

galgal (He) (pl. *galgalim*) *Lit.* wheel; also, a group of wheels turning together; a category of angel or supernatural being first mentioned in the vision of the biblical prophet Ezekiel, and later in the Jewish *Hekhalot* and *Merkavah* literature; also called the *ofanim* (wheels).

See also: **ofanim**.

Gaṇapati (S/H) *Lit.* lord *(pati)* of gatherings *(gaṇas);* an alternative name for either *Shiva* or *Gaṇesh. Gaṇas* are gatherings of lesser deities or demigods, specifically, *Shiva*'s attendants.

See also: **Gaṇesh**, **Shiva**.

Gaṇesh(a) (S/H) *Lit.* lord *(īsh)* of gatherings *(gaṇas), gaṇas* being gatherings of lesser deities or demigods, specifically, *Shiva*'s attendants; hence, the lord of a gathering of demigods; a Hindu deity portrayed as a short fat man with a protuberant belly and an elephant's head with only one tusk, considered to be the god of wisdom and the remover of obstacles; hence, among Hindus, he is invoked at the start of all undertakings; also called *Gaṇapati.*

Various legends exist to explain how *Gaṇesh* came to possess the head of an elephant with one tusk. The *Shiva Purāṇa* says that *Pārvatī,* consort of *Shiva,* fashioned *Gaṇesh* from the mud taken from a pond. According to another account, she made him from the scurf and impurities of her body, and posted him at the door to keep watch when she was bathing. When *Shiva* arrived, the child stopped him from entering, whereupon *Shiva* cut off his head. *Pārvatī,* naturally enough, began to cry. To soothe her, the child's head was replaced with the first head that could be found, which happened to be the head of an elephant with one tusk. According to another version, *Gaṇesh* lost one of his tusks in a conflict with a *ṛishi* who was denied access to *Shiva* while the latter was meditating.

It is said that *Gaṇesh* was the scribe who wrote down the *Mahābhārata* at the dictation of Ṛishi Vyāsa who had secured his services from the god *Brahmā.* The only condition *Gaṇesh* imposed was that the *ṛishi* should not cease dictating until the work was done.

Gaṇesh is also identified in tantric texts as the deity or ruling power of the *mūlādhāra* or rectal *chakra,* the lowest *chakra* of *piṇḍa.* The *tattva* administered at this centre is that of *pṛithvī* or earth. *Gaṇesh*'s elephant head perhaps symbolizes the firm foundation of earth, the *mūlādhāra chakra* being the base upon which the other *chakras* rest.

ghost The disembodied soul or spirit of a dead person, believed to manifest to the living either as a nebulous image or in a spectral likeness of the deceased; also, an archaic word for the soul or spirit, persisting in the 'Holy Ghost' (Holy Spirit); from the Old English *gast* (spirit, soul), of Germanic origin, related to the German *geist,* the Dutch *geest,* and the Flemish *gheest;* also, the mind or spirit, as in the expression, "the ghost in the machine", referring to the mind or spirit within that makes the body function.

Ghosts are generally understood to be trapped in the material world because of a strong emotional association with a particular place or the traumatic events of their previous bodily existence, especially their death. Haunted individuals are sometimes associated with the ghost's unhappy past. As well as visible appearances of the ghost, hauntings are said to include the movement of objects, the manifestation of peculiar lights, sounds such as screams and laughter, eerie footsteps, the ringing of bells, and the spontaneous playing of musical instruments. The funeral rites of many cultures are intended to prevent the ghost of the deceased from haunting the living.

See also: **bhūta**, **preta**.

god(s) Supernatural beings credited with being the controllers of some parts of the creation or some aspects of life, or the personifications of some force. The term is used variously throughout the literature of the world, its meaning dependent upon the particular religious or mythological context, and so on. Mystically, the gods are the many rulers or centres of power in the hierarchy of creation. In many instances, particularly in the polytheistic religions of the past and present, such as the ancient Mesopotamian religions, Greek religion and Hinduism, religious practice has entailed the worship of the lesser gods by means of sacrifice, idols, prayer, rituals and the like. Polytheism, however, has commonly existed alongside monotheism, for the mystics within these cultures have pointed out that all the gods derive their existence from the one supreme God. Some gods – perhaps many – are mythological and fictitious imaginations of the human mind, though others may be representative of certain powers within.

At the time of Jesus, Judaism was the only truly monotheistic religion in the Middle East. Hence, Paul, writing to his Greek converts in Corinth, speaks of the many gods, all originating from the "one God":

> There is none other God but one. For though there be (them) that are called gods, whether in heaven or in earth – as there be gods many, and lords many – but to us there is but one God, the Father, of whom are all things (created).
>
> *1 Corinthians 8:4–6, KJV*

Similarly, speaking of the projection of the many powers and deities of creation, one of the Nag Hammadi gnostic texts reads:

> He (a great power) was given great authority,
> and he ruled over all creation.
> He created gods and angels and archangels,
> myriads without number for retinue from that Light.
>
> *Eugnostos the Blessed 77; cf. NHS27 p.90*

In another gnostic text, the writer points out that, on its inward ascent, the soul goes higher than the lesser gods:

> But when you reach the six *aeons* (powers), they will restrain you until you receive the mystery of the forgiveness of sins, because it is the great mystery which is in the treasury of the innermost of the innermost. And it is the whole salvation of the soul. And all those who will receive that mystery will surpass all gods and all rulerships of all these *aeons* … for this is the great mystery of the unapproachable One which is in the treasury of the innermost of the innermost.
>
> *Second Book of Jeu 117:49, BC pp.162–63*

It is because the soul in human form has the potential to rise higher than all lesser gods that mystics advise against the practice of worshipping or venerating them.

See also: **deva**.

gods (Greek) Gods such as *Zeus, Aphroditē, Hermēs* and so on are infamous in Greek mythology for their exploits and immorality. A number of ancient writers of the Greek world have indicated that they considered the Greek myths to have originally been meant as allegories. In the *Republic,* Plato has Socratēs suggest that the legends of Greek gods and heroes should not be told to children, for even though these myths may be allegorical, children could not be expected to understand them and, taking them literally, would be given poor guidance on how to behave. Socratēs is speaking of his ideal "State":

> These tales must not be admitted into our State, whether they are supposed to have an allegorical meaning or not. For a young person cannot judge what is allegorical and what is literal; anything that he receives into his mind at that age is likely to become indelible and unalterable; and therefore it is most important that the tales which the young first hear should be models of virtuous thoughts.
>
> *Plato, Republic 2:378d–e, DP2 p.223*

In the early Christian *Clementine Homilies,* Appion, one of the characters in the narrative, is speaking to a Christian friend in defence of the Greek gods, giving an account of their esoteric and symbolic meaning. Referring to the many lurid tales told of their supposed exploits, he prefaces his account with the words:

> Our gods are neither adulterers, nor murderers, nor corrupters of children, nor guilty of incest with sisters or daughters. But the ancients, wishing that only lovers of learning (*i.e. gnosis,* mystical knowledge) should know the mysteries, veiled them with those fables of which you have spoken.
>
> *Clementine Homilies IV:24, CH p.100*

The twelfth-century Archbishop Eustathius of Thessalonica took the idea further. He wrote an allegorical commentary on Homer's *Odyssey,* the famous Greek adventure story that relates the trials and tribulations that Odysseus (Ulysses) – famed for his courage, resourcefulness, ingenuity and strength – encountered during the return journey to his native Ithaca, after the siege of Troy (as related in Homer's *Iliad*). The journey takes the hero ten years, during the course of which he loses all his companions, and is only recognized by his wife Penelope after killing all her suitors, who had presumed Odysseus to be dead.

When the narrative opens, Odysseus, longing for his wife and home, is being detained on the island of Ogygia by the seductive sea nymph, Calypso, who has held him as her captive lover for seven years. Odysseus is only permitted to escape and return home through the mediation of *Hermēs,* the messenger of the gods, whom Eustathius interprets as symbolic of the *Logos:*

> The allegory presents, in Calypso, our body, which conceals and encloses, like a shell, the pearl of the soul: that nymph, indeed, imprisoned the wise Ulysses, even as man is a prisoner in the flesh.… Thus Ulysses had difficulty in leaving Calypso, inasmuch as he was naturally attached to life.
>
> But by the mediation of *Hermēs* … that is to say, of the *Logos,* Ulysses regained the philosophic homeland he had so longed for; that

> is the spiritual world. Similarly, he regained Penelope – the (divine) Philosophy (Wisdom) – after being released and disencumbered from that Calypso.
>
> *Eustathius, Commentary on Homer's Odyssey, CHO1 1389:42–46 p.17, SBEG p.191; cf. MHG p.461*

By means of the *Logos,* the soul returns to its true spiritual home, the "philosophic homeland" or "spiritual world", the true fatherland of the soul in the eyes of the Platonists.

governor(s) See **archon**, **rulers**.

guardian angels Originally, a category of angels common in the religious lore of the ancient Middle Eastern Semitic world; identified with the Hebrew *ẓofei shamayyim* (*lit.* watchers or guardians of the heavens); a generic term used in ancient Judaic apocryphal literature for the various types of angels and their duties. The guardian angels have also been identified specifically with the Judaic *irin* (watchers). In later Judaic and Christian lore, the term evolved to describe the concept of an angel assigned to protect a particular person or people. In this sense, Michael was considered the guardian angel of ancient Israel.

See also: **ḥāfiẓ**, **watchers**.

ḥāfiẓ (A/P) (pl. A. *ḥāfiẓīn, huffāẓ;* P. *ḥāfiẓān*) *Lit.* keeper, guardian, protector; also, one who has memorized the *Qur'ān* (from *ḥāfiẓah,* memory).

A verse in the *Qur'ān,* "There is no soul, but has a protector *(ḥāfiẓ)* over it,"[1] has been interpreted by Sufis to refer not to God, but to the keeper of the soul in this world. Particularly in the plural, the keepers *(ḥāfiẓīn)* refer to unseen powers working for good or evil in the government of the world and in the individual soul. A *ḥadīth* (traditional saying) says, "There is none of you but there have been set over him two familiar spirits *(qarīn),* a satan and an angel." These keepers *(ḥāfiẓīn)* or familiar spirits are understood either as two of the *jinn,* or as a devil and an angel or, metaphorically, as the *nafs* (human mind) pulling towards sense enjoyments and the *rūḥ* (spirit) pulling towards God.

Sufis have said that the *ḥāfiẓīn* keep every individual under vigilant surveillance. They are unseen powers, keeping a person from "quitting his appointed station and controlling all his movements".[2] Interpreting the "keepers" as the habits and aspects of the human mind or "fleshly soul *(nafs)*", Rūmī describes the human condition:

In this world of search and seeking,
all the various kinds of people have been tied
in stables peculiar to them;
And over each stable,
a trainer has been appointed;
Save by his permission,
no recalcitrant enters another place.
If, from vain desire, he should break away
from the stable and intrude into the stable of others,
at once the nimble and goodly stablemen
seize the corner of his halter and drag him back.

O cunning one, if you behold not your keepers *(ḥāfiẓān),*
at least know your choice to be involuntary.
You are making a choice,
and your hands and feet are loosed:
Why then are you imprisoned? Why?
You have betaken yourself to denying
the action of the keeper *(ḥāfiẓ):*
You have called it the 'threats of the fleshly soul *(nafs)*'.

Rūmī, Maśnavī III:2077–83; cf. MJR4 p.116

1. *Qur'ān* 86:4, *AYA.*
2. R.A. Nicholson, *Commentary on Maśnavī* III:2077, *MJR8* p.58.

ḥawrā', ḥūrīyah (A/P), **ḥūr** (P) (pl. A. *ḥūr, ḥūrīyāt;* P. *ḥūrān*) *Lit.* one whose eyes are characterized by a marked contrast between black and white; houri (an anglicized form of *ḥawrā'*), nymph, virgin of paradise. The masculine form of *ḥawrā'* is *aḥwar,* having the same meaning, but also implying a pure, clear intellect. In Persian, *ḥūr* has become singular, the plural being *ḥūrān.*[1]

According to the *Qur'ān,* the *ḥūr* are female companions of the saved in paradise. The male counterparts are *wildān mukhalladūn,* eternal youths of paradise, whom the *Qur'ān* describes as waiting on the saved.[2] Both are regarded as beings of great purity, not enticements to seduce believers, though they have come to mean that in the popular mind. The *Qur'ān* describes these beings as "companions pure and holy".[3]

Although the *ḥūr* or houris are commonly portrayed as beautiful nymphs of paradise who offer sensual delights, Mawlānā Muḥammad 'Alī, in *The Religion of Islam,* offers two quite different interpretations. He says that the *ḥūr* may be understood as the women of paradise, meaning women who, having lived rightly here, have earned paradise. In support of this, he cites an incident in which the Prophet is said to have told an old woman that she would be made young again, made into a pure one *(ḥūrīyah),* when she entered paradise. Alternatively, 'Alī says that the *ḥūr* may be understood as a blessing of paradise:

> Just as the gardens, rivers, milk, honey, fruits and numerous other things of paradise are both for men and women, even so are *ḥūr.* What these blessings actually are, no one knows, but the whole picture of paradise drawn in the *Qur'ān* strongly condemns the association of any sensual idea therewith.
>
> *Muḥammad 'Alī, Religion of Islam, RI p.223*

However, both the *Qur'ān* and traditional sayings *(ḥadīth)* contain numerous disparaging remarks concerning women and the superiority of men over woman. The delights of paradise are also portrayed in sensual terms. So maybe the *ḥūr* have no true metaphorical interpretation.

In order to deflect people from acting out of the fear of hell or the hope of heaven, many Sufis have declared that they do not long for the delights of heaven, nor do they fear the horrors of hell. Their desire is only for the Lord who lies above and beyond all aspects of His creation. Ḥāfiẓ says:

> Ease is not his who –
> for the pleasure of paradise and the lip of the *ḥūr* –
> lets slip his hand from the skirt of my heart possessor (God).
> O Ḥāfiẓ! If the favour of God's grace be shown to you,
> be free from the grief of hell,
> and the comfort of paradise.
>
> *Ḥāfiẓ, Dīvān, DHM (93:6–7) pp.114–15, DIH p.60; cf. DHWC (61:6–7) p.152*

1. Hans Wehr, *Dictionary of Modern Written Arabic, DMWA* p.247.
2. *Qur'ān* 56:17, 76:19.
3. *Qur'ān* 2:25, 4:57, *AYA.*

ḥayyot (He) *Lit.* living creatures, living beasts; a high class of angel, subordinate only to God. The prophet Ezekiel, in a vision, describes four of these beings supporting the throne on which the divine Presence is seated. He later identifies them with the cherubim, a more commonly used term. The gnostic *Apocryphon of John* represents God as transcendent, emanating His essence as light, the four *ḥayyot* or cherubim being the bearers of His light in the process of emanation.[1]

See also: **cherubim**.

1. *Apocryphon of John* 9, 20, 22–23.

Indra (S/H), **Indar** (Pu) Hindu god of the air and the sky; the god of rain, storm, thunder and lightning; the principal deity of Vedic times, adopted from earlier pre-Vedic religion; commonly portrayed mounted on the white elephant *Airāvata,* though he also possessed the fabulous horse *Ucchaiḥshravas,* both of which rose from the mythological ocean of milk. *Indra* is portrayed as drinking large quantities of *soma,* an intoxicant much used in Vedic ritual and made from the *soma* plant, which he is said to have brought to earth from heaven. Traditionally, *Indra* is depicted as a divine and mighty warrior with four arms. His main weapon is his mighty thunderbolt *(vajra),* but he also wields a huge two-handed lance *(paranja),* carries a net, and shoots arrows, using the rainbow *(shakradhanus)* as his bow. He was also the possessor of *Pārijātaka,* one of the five great trees of paradise. In later mythology, he is called the lord of *svarga* (paradise) and the king of all the *devas* (gods).

Indra is the subject of considerable mythology. According to the *Purusha Sūkta* of the *Ṛig Veda,*[1] the entire universe, including gods and men, are born from the *Purusha* (cosmic Being, cosmic Man). The first-born gods inwardly worship this cosmic Man, their worship being metaphorically described as a sacrifice in which *Purusha* participates. As a consequence, the various parts of the universe, animate and inanimate, emerge from his different 'bodily' parts, *Indra* and *Agni* (the fire god) being born from his mouth.[2] The *Ṛig Veda* also describes how Aditi carried the mighty *Indra* within herself for many years in an imperceptible way, knowing him to be majestic and forceful, reluctant to permit him to be born because of her desire to protect him. Finally, he was born from her side.

Like of all mythological heroes, *Indra* is the performer of great deeds. In one of his most frequently mentioned exploits, using his great weapon, the thunderbolt *(vajra), Indra* frees the world by slaying the dragon *Vṛitra,* who had swallowed it.[3]

In early Vedic mythology, *Indra* is portrayed as warring constantly against the *asuras* (demons). His deeds – and generosity – being considered of great benefit to mankind, he is addressed in more Vedic prayers and hymns than any other deity except *Agni.* He is described in a hymn of praise that goes on to recount many of his heroic acts:

> He of lofty spirit, who, from the moment he was born,
> was first among gods;
> He who, by his power and might, became protector of the gods,
> He, before whose breath and greatness of valour,
> the two worlds tremble –
> He, O men, is *Indra.*
>
> *Ṛig Veda 2:12.1*

He is considered all-powerful:

The extent of his powers cannot be fathomed:
neither by the gods, though divine,
nor by mortals, nor yet by the (primeval) waters.
Ṛig Veda 1:100.15

As a divine hero and valiant warrior, he is invoked as an ally in times of trouble:

May *Indra* help us when our flags are flying,
may our weapons be victorious.
May our brave warriors return with flying colours:
O lord, protect us in the turmoil of battle.
Ṛig Veda 10:103.11

O *Indra,* defeat the speech of him
who opposes us out of malice;
Strengthen us with your power and might:
make me superior in debate!
Atharva Veda 2:27.7

He is also a fountain of generosity:

O *Indra,* there is no one, god or mortal,
who can prevent your generosity,
when you are praised,
and wish to give rich gifts....
O *Indra,* we ask your help,
you who have become illustrious,
and have won all treasures.
Ṛig Veda 8:14.4, 6

He is the hidden archetype behind every outward form. Through *māyā* (illusion), he makes every form and is present in them:

Of every form, he is the pattern:
his is the only form to be regarded.
Indra, through *māyā,* assumes many forms.
Ṛig Veda 6:47.18

Ultimately, because of these characteristics, he superseded the more lofty and spiritual *Varuṇa,* and came to be regarded as the lord of all the gods *(devas)* and the lord of *svarga* (paradise).

By the time of the *Upanishads* (*c.*900–600 BCE), long after the writing of the *Vedas, Indra* has taken on a variety of less mythological guises. In the *Aitareya Upanishad,* he is identified with the supreme Self, *Ātman,* which incarnates as the *jīva,* the isolated soul, and later realizes the eternal.[4] In the *Taittirīya Upanishad,* he is the bestower of wisdom.[5] The *Kena Upanishad* depicts him as the greatest of the gods. But, being limited by time and space, he does not know the eternal *Brahman.*[6] In the *Chhāndogya Upanishad,* he is a student of *Prajāpati* (lord of creatures) who teaches him the doctrine of *Brahman.*[7]

In later mythology, *Indra*'s prestige declines: his human characteristics and foibles are portrayed, and he is subordinated to the triad of *Brahmā, Vishṇu* and *Shiva. Ṛishis* like Durvāsā, Agastya and Vishvāmitra contemptuously threaten to usurp his heavenly throne by their practice of austerities. Alarmed, he tries to distract them from their meditation by dispatching *apsarās,* heavenly nymphs, not always successfully. In fact, he himself is not immune to temptation, and several accounts are given of his escapades with mortal women.

As *Indra*'s power declines, he is overpowered and captured by Meghanāda, son of Rāvaṇa, through the use of magical powers, especially invisibility, as related in the *Rāmāyaṇa.* He is also overcome by Kṛishṇa who carries off the famed *Pārijātaka* tree from *Indra*'s heaven. He is even cursed by Ṛishi Durvāsā, master curser of the *Purāṇas,* for giving a garland – which Durvāsā had given to him – to a pet elephant, the *ṛishi* taking it as a slight.

In Indian mythology, *Indra* is the father of Arjuna, whose mother is Kuntī, wife of Pāṇḍu. Pāṇḍu and Kuntī were the parents of the Pāṇḍavas, famous from the epic legend of the *Mahābhārata.* Arjuna is Kṛishṇa's faithful disciple and the one with whom Kṛishṇa holds his battlefield dialogue in the *Bhagavad Gītā.*

Because of the prevalent worship of these lesser deities in Hinduism, Indian mystics have frequently pointed out that *Indra* and the other gods themselves owe their origins to the supreme Lord, as do man and all other souls. It is God alone, therefore, who is worthy of worship:

> *Shiva (Īshar), Brahmā,* goddesses, gods,
> *Indra (Indar),* penitents, and silent sages long for Thy service.
> Celibates, the men of piety and the good many forest dwellers
> obtain not the Lord's limit.
>
> *Guru Nānak, Ādi Granth 1034, MMS*

Mystics also point out that the positions of *Indra* and other gods are not permanent. They are earned as a reward for ascetic and other practices, but at length even those souls fall back into birth and death:

Indras seated on their thrones are in the fear of death:
they do many deeds, but *Jam* (the lord of death) spares them not.

Guru Amardās, Ādi Granth 1049, MMS

See also: **Indraloka** (4.1).

1. *Ṛig Veda* 10:90.
2. *Ṛig Veda* 10:90.13.
3. *Ṛig Veda* 1:32.1–15.
4. *Aitareya Upanishad* 1:3.14, 3:1.3.
5. *Taittirīya Upanishad* 1:4.1.
6. *Kena Upanishad* 3–4.
7. *Chhāndogya Upanishad* 8:7–12.

irin (Am) *Lit.* watchers; a type of angelic being mentioned in the biblical *Book of Daniel*[1] and the apocryphal *Genesis Apocryphon.*

See **watchers**.

1. *Daniel* 4:13, 17, 23.

Īshvar(a) (S/H/Pu), **Īsar** (Pu) *Lit.* lord; used throughout Indian mystic and religious literature, sometimes with a general meaning and sometimes specifically, often for *Shiva.* In *Advaita Vedānta, Īshvara* is specifically associated with *saguṇa Brahman* (*Brahman* with attributes), the first step downward in the process by which *Brahman* is expressed in the creation. Swāmī Nikhilānanda explains:

> *Brahman* associated with the *upādhi* (limitation) of collective ignorance is designated by Vedantists as *Īshvara* or *saguṇa Brahman,* who corresponds roughly to the personal God of various religions. According to non-dualistic *(Advaita) Vedānta,* the personal God is one step lower than *Brahman,* though he is the highest symbol of manifestation of *Brahman* in the relative world. *Īshvara* is endowed (in his own realm) with such qualities as omniscience, omnipresence, universal lordship and unlimited power. *Brahman* cannot be described by any specific attribute. It is *Īshvara,* and not pure *Brahman* who, in his different aspects, is called the creator, preserver and destroyer of the universe. *Īshvara,* or *saguṇa Brahman,* with the help of *sattva,* creates; with the help of *rajas,* preserves; and with the help of *tamas,*

destroys. He is the inner controller of the universe. The light of *Īshvara* that illumines the cosmic ignorance is the light of *Brahman.* From the standpoint of pure *Brahman,* there is no creation; hence none of the attributes ascribed to *Īshvara* apply to *Brahman.* As gold without dross cannot be used for ornaments, so pure *Brahman,* without the dross of *māyā,* cannot create the universe. *Īshvara* is, as it were, a corruption or deterioration of *Brahman.*

Swāmī Nikhilānanda, Introduction to Ātmabodha, SKS p.59

Isrāfīl (A/P) The angel of resurrection; one of the four main archangels of Islam: *Mīkhā'īl, Isrāfīl, Jabra'īl* and *'Izrā'īl. Isrāfīl* is the archangel who is to blow a trumpet on the Day of Resurrection, calling the dead to arise. 'Ināyat Khān says that, for the Sufis, *Isrāfīl* is the angel who explains revelations.[1]

Isrāfīl is also called the sustainer of life. According to some Sufi orders, *Isrāfīl* is the deity associated with the *laṭīfah* (subtle centre) located at the navel.

See also: **Gabriel**, **'Izrā'īl**, **Mīkhā'īl**.

1. 'Ināyat Khān, *Sufi Message, SMIK5* p.104.

'Izrā'īl (A/P) The angel of death; one of the four main archangels of Islam; also called *'Azrā'īl* and *Qudrah* (Power); anglicized as Azrael. Death being an ever present possibility and, in the end, inevitable, many stories, often allegorical, have been told concerning *'Izrā'īl* and his relationship to man.

In the *Maśnavī,* Rūmī relates a story concerning the four archangels, *Mīkhā'īl, Isrāfīl, Jabra'īl* and *'Izrā'īl,* and the creation of man. God decides to create a man, Adam, and sends *Mīkhā'īl* to earth to collect a handful of clay. Earth complains, not wanting to be drawn into the strife and responsibility of being human, and *Mīkhā'īl* fails to get the required handful.

God then sends *Isrāfīl* and *Jabra'īl,* both of whom are likewise unable to overcome earth's resistance to becoming human. Finally, God calls on *'Izrā'īl,* 'Captain of the divine Decree', to fetch the necessary handful of clay. *'Izrā'īl* turns a deaf ear to earth's laments, and takes the clay.

God then appoints *'Izrā'īl* as the angel of death, the "executioner" whose function (metaphorically) is to "strangle them at death". Rūmī writes of an imagined conversation between God and *'Izrā'īl* in which the angel of death complains that his role will make him hated among men. But God says that he will so arrange it that men will see secondary causes such as "disease", "spear wounds" and so on as the apparent causes of death:

He *('Izrā'īl)* brought the inconsiderate clay to God:
the runaway back to school.
God said: "By my resplendent knowledge,
I will make you executioner of these creatures."

He replied, "O Lord, Your creatures will regard me
as their enemy when I strangle them at death.
Do You deem it right, O exalted Lord,
to make me hated and like a foe in appearance?"

He (God) said, "I will bring into clear view certain causes,
such as fever and dysentery and phrenitis and spear wounds;
Thus will I turn their attention from you
to disease and the threefold causes of death."

Rūmī, Maśnavī V:1693–98; cf. MJR6 pp.102–3

On hearing this, *'Izrā'īl* points out that there are some souls, the mystics, whose job it is to rend the veil of illusory causes:

He *('Izrā'īl)* replied, "O Lord, there are also servants
of Yours who shatter the illusion of causes, O Almighty."

Rūmī, Maśnavī V:1699; cf. MJR6 p.103

To which Rūmī adds:

How should the perception of the mystic
be veiled by these secondary causes,
which are a veil to catch the dolt?

Rūmī, Maśnavī V:1708; cf. MJR6 p.103

But God responds that such souls will not be concerned about death, whatever the apparent cause, for even *'Izrā'īl* is a secondary cause, though "more concealed than those (other) causes":

"One who does not
regard causes and diseases and sword wounds
will likewise pay no regard to your action, O *'Izrā'īl,*
for you too are a secondary cause,
although you are more concealed than those causes."

Rūmī, Maśnavī V:1710 (heading); cf. MJR6 p.103

The mystics, Rūmī continues, are happy to face death, "since they go from a dungeon and prison into a garden":

And those to whom death is as sugar –
how should their sight be dazzled
with the fortunes of this world?
Bodily death is not bitter to them,
since they go from a dungeon and prison into a garden.

Rūmī, Maśnavī V:1712–13, MJR6 pp.103–4

In another traditional anecdote, Rūmī humorously points out the futility of trying to avoid an appointment with the angel of death:

> One forenoon, a freeborn noble man arrived and ran into Solomon's hall of justice, his countenance pale with anguish and both lips blue. Then Solomon said, "Good sir, what is the matter?"
>
> He replied, "*'Izrā'īl* cast on me such a look, so full of wrath and hate." "Come," said the king, "what do you desire now? Ask!"
>
> "O protector of my life," said he, "command the wind to bear me from here to India. Maybe, when your slave has gone there, his life will be saved." … He (Solomon) commanded the wind to bear him quickly over the water to the uttermost part of India.
>
> Next day, at the time of conference and meeting, Solomon said to *'Izrā'īl:* "Did you look with anger on that Muslim in order that he might wander (as an exile) far from his home?"
>
> *'Izrā'īl* said, "When did I look angrily at him? I saw him as I passed by, in astonishment, for God had commanded me, saying, 'Hark, today do you take his spirit in India.' From wonder, I said to myself, 'If he has a hundred wings, 'tis a far journey for him to be in India today.'"
>
> In like manner, judge all the affairs of this world, and open your eye and see! From whom shall we flee? From ourselves? O absurdity! From whom shall we take ourselves away? From God? O crime!
>
> *Rūmī, Maśnavī I:956–60, 963–70; cf. MJR2 p.54*

See also: **Ādam** (5.1), **Yama**.

jamdūt (H/Pu) See **yamadūta**.

jewel(s) A precious or semiprecious stone, often sparkling; hence, something precious or sparkling; a metaphor found particularly in Manichaean texts where it refers to the inner powers, gods or celestial beings in creation:

Many gods, deities and jewels have been created,
called forth and set up as attendants of the Lord of paradise.

Manichaean Hymns, MDT p.553ff., RMP ab, GSR p.31:3.2

The heavenly creation is also described as the "house of jewels":

The house of jewels is a place full of blossoms,
with countless lands, houses and thrones.

Manichaean Hymns, PP p.645, RMP aka; cf. GSR p.33:6.1

These "deities, jewels" and heavenly realms are said to "rejoice" constantly in God:

The land of light (eternal realm) …
is fragrant with sweet breezes;
It shines in all regions.…
Powers, gods and deities, jewels and joyful *aeons* (realms),
trees, springs and plants rejoice in Him daily.

Manichaean Hymns, PAH p.443ff., RMP al; cf. ML p.118

In one hymn, the Saviour promises great gifts to his disciple. He will take him to his eternal home, the "blessed abode", where he will dwell joyfully among the "jewels and the venerable gods":

I shall … lead you to your home, the blessed abode.
Forever shall I show to you the noble Father:
I shall lead you in, into His presence, in pure raiment.
I shall show to you the Mother of the beings of light:
forever shall you rejoice in lauded happiness.
I shall reveal to you the holy Brethren:
the noble and the pure, who are filled with happiness.
Forever shall you dwell joyful among them all,
beside all the jewels and the venerable gods.
Fear and death shall never overtake you more,
nor ravage, distress and wretchedness.
Rest shall be yours in the place of salvation,
in the company of all the gods
and those who dwell in quietness.

Manichaean Hymns, Angad Rōshnān VI:67–73; cf. MHCP pp.150–53

In some contexts, the jewel is a metaphor for the supreme power of the Creative Word.

See also: **jewels** (3.1).

jinn (A/P) (sg. *jinnī*) Certain inhabitants of the subtle material world, the etheric world; also, a term for strangers or evil men; derived from *janna* (to hide, to conceal, to cover, to veil). *Jinnī* is anglicized as 'genie'.

In the language of the *Qur'ān,* angels were created out of light *(nūr),* man out of clay (earth), and the *jinn* out of subtle or "essential fire":

> The *jinn* did We create aforetime of essential fire.
>
> *Qur'ān 15:27, MGK*

> And the *jinn* did He create of smokeless fire.
>
> *Qur'ān 55:15, MGK*

'Ināyat Khān explains his understanding of the *jinn* as angelic beings:

> The soul which has passed through the angelic heavens in its descent to earth comes next into the sphere of the *jinn*.... This is the sphere of mind.... The souls who halt in this sphere, being attracted by its beauty, settle there; also the souls who have no power to go further into outer manifestation become the inhabitants of this sphere....
>
> The *jinn* is an entity with a mind; but not a mind like that of man; a mind more pure, more clear, and illuminated by the light of intelligence. The mind of the *jinn* is deeper in perception and in conception, because it is empty, not filled with thoughts and imaginations as is that of man....
>
> The *jinn* comes closer to man than the angel; for in the *jinn* there is something like the mind which is completed in man. All the intuitive and inspirational properties are possessed by the *jinn,* because that is the only source that the *jinn* has of receiving its knowledge. Subjects such as poetry, music, art, inventive science, philosophy, and morals are akin to the nature of the *jinn.* The artist, the poet, the musician, and the philosopher show in their gifts throughout their lives the heritage of the *jinn.*
>
> *'Ināyat Khān, Sufi Message, SMIK1 pp.124–25*

Here, the *jinn* are regarded as beings higher than man. On the other hand, various *ḥadīth* (traditions) show the *jinn* in a baser role, indicating that "every man has with him an associate from among the angels who inspires him with good and noble ideas, and an associate from among the *jinn* who excites his baser passions."[1] However, the example of Muḥammad illustrates that through spiritual uplift the ignoble *jinn* can be transformed from an enemy to a friend:

> (Muḥammad) was asked if he too had an associate *jinn.* "Yes," he said, "but *Allāh* has helped me to overcome him, so he has submitted and does not command me aught but good." His devil is said to have submitted to him *(aslama)* and, instead of making evil suggestions, commanded him naught but good, that is to say, became a help to him in the development of his higher life.
>
> *Muḥammad 'Alī, Religion of Islam, RI p.144*

In this context, man's attendant *jinn* serve as an explanation of human instincts – higher or lower. This understanding of the *jinn* is consistent with the ancient Middle Eastern perception of human imperfections as demons or devils.

See also: **ḥāfiẓ**, **parī**, **Shayṭān** (6.1).

1. Muḥammad 'Alī, *Religion of Islam, RI* p.143.

jyoti-svarūp Bhagvān (H), **jyotiḥ-svarūpa Bhagavān** (S) *Lit.* Lord *(Bhagavān)* in the form *(svarūp)* of a flame *(jyoti)* (of light); the flame-shaped god; the lord of *sahans dal kanwal,* the first spiritual region.

Jyot Nirañjan, **Jyoti Nirañjan** (H) *Lit.* light *(jyot, jyoti)* without *(nir)* stain *(añjan);* pure flame, pure light; a name given to the ruler of *sahans dal kanwal,* the first spiritual region:

> Fix your attention on the third eye *(til),*
> and the thousand-petalled (lotus) will open.
> There you will find *Jyoti Nirañjan,*
> and hear the unending *Shabd.*
>
> *Swāmī Shiv Dayāl Singh, Sār Bachan Poetry 20:24.7–8, SBP p.167*

See also: **Nirañjan** (2.1, 4.2), **Nirañjan desh** (4.1).

Kālī (S/H) *Lit.* black, blackness; the Hindu goddess of war, death and destruction; the consort of *Shiva;* also known as *Durgā* (the Inaccessible), renowned as the slayer of demons *(asuras),* as well as *Bhairavī* (the Terrible) and *Chaṇḍi* (the Violent); a personification of the terrifying and terrible aspects of *Shakti* or divine energy.

Kālī is a ferocious form of the Goddess *(Devī* or *Mahādevī),* in contrast to the benign aspects of the Goddess such as *Lakshmī* and *Pārvatī.* She is portrayed as terrifying: a hideous, black, naked, four-armed woman with rolling eyes, a lolling tongue, and with fangs as teeth, who devours all beings, dancing in the cremation ground, girdled by severed arms, garlanded with heads. In her four hands, she holds a noose *(pāsha),* a club or staff topped with a skull *(khaṭvānga),* a sword *(khadga)* and a severed head. Her weapons symbolize her power to destroy; the severed head signifies that time cannot be escaped – that all, in time, will fall prey to death and rebirth.

Though terrible, *Kālī* is regarded by her devotees as the destroyer of evil. She demands appeasement and blood offerings, and goats are generally sacrificed to her (at the famous Kālīghāṭ temple in Calcutta, for example). She is often associated with plague and disease, in the form, for example, of *Shītalā* or *Mariamman,* goddess of pustular diseases such as smallpox. She represents time and death, aspects of life that all who desire spiritual progress must face; she can thus become a symbol of liberation as the destroyer of time. Although referred to in earlier texts, she first appears fully in the *Devīmāhātmya* where she is born from the anger of *Durgā,* and destroys demons.

In Tantrism, *Kālī* is *Shiva*'s energy *(shakti),* depicted as dancing upon his phallus-like corpse, a form expressing his passive consciousness *(purusha)* and her active energy *(prakṛiti)* that, together, comprise the universe. Followers of the left-hand *(vāmāchāra)* tantric path worship *Kālī* in cremation grounds, and offer food to jackals who are regarded as her manifestation.

Illustrating the diversity and frequent inconsistency of Indian mythology, there is also a group of texts devoted to *Kālī* in the esoteric traditions of Kashmir Shaivism, where she is identified with Absolute Consciousness. From this supreme state, there emanate twelve *Kālīs,* representing successive stages in the projection and reabsorption of consciousness. In the eighteenth and nineteenth centuries, the Bengali poet Rāmprasād and the mystic Rāmakṛishṇa were her devotees. Rāmakṛishṇa writes of her:

> O *Kālī,* my mother full of bliss,
> enchantress of the almighty *Shiva* –
> In thy delirious joy thou dancest,
> clapping thy hands together.
> Eternal one! Thou great First Cause,
> clothed in the form of the void....
> Thou art the Mover of all that move,
> and we are but thy helpless toys.
> We move along as thou movest us,
> and speak as through us thou speakest.
>
> *Rāmakṛishṇa, in Gospel of Sri Ramakrishna, GOSR p.159*

See also: **Durgā**, **Kāl** (6.1).

kedoshim (He), **kadishin** (Ar) *Lit.* holy ones; holy beings, angels, supernatural beings; a biblical term, as in:

> God is greatly feared in the assembly of the holy ones *(kedoshim),*
> and held in reverence by all those who are around Him.
>
> *Psalm 89:8, JCL*

The most common biblical term used for angels is *mal'akh.*

See also: **angels**, **benei elohim**, **mal'akh**.

Kṛishṇa (S/H), **Krishan** (Pu) *Lit.* black, dark, dark blue; the eighth incarnation of *Vishṇu;* the most celebrated hero of Indian mythology and the most popular of all the deities in the Hindu pantheon, often represented as an attractive young man with flowing hair and a flute in his hand. According to legend, he was born with very dark skin and a peculiar mark on his chest. Although the son of Vasudeva and Devakī, for security reasons he was raised by Nanda and Yashodā, spending his childhood with them. It was here that his divine character was gradually revealed.

His childhood escapades are the subject of many songs sung by the Vaishnavites (devotees of *Vishṇu*), who worship Kṛishṇa as *Vishṇu,* seeing mystic symbolism in the legends surrounding him. The sound of his flute had an irresistible fascination for all the cowgirls *(gopīs)* with whom he played as a child, their love for him being interpreted as symbolic of the love of the soul for God. The sound of his flute is also interpreted as the Voice of God, the unstruck Sound *(anāhata Shabda),* calling souls back to God from the material world.

When his flute beckons, the call is compelling and the cowgirls (souls) forget everything, even their own bodies, and run to him. But Kṛishṇa plays the game of love with them, telling them that they do not need to come running to him:

> "O pure ones, your first duties are to your husbands and children.... You do not need to come to me for, if you will only meditate on me, you will attain salvation. Hence, return to your homes." ...
>
> But the cowgirls replied, "O cruel lover, we only want to serve you. You know the scriptural injunctions, and you advise us to serve our husbands and children. Yes, we will follow what you say. But you are all in all, and are all. By serving you, we serve all."
>
> *Bhāgavata Purāṇa 10:29.24, 27, 32, SBPS pp.492–93*

The longing *(viraha)* of his favourite *gopī,* Rādhā, is seen especially to represent the longing of the devotee or the soul for the Lord, *Hari.* There is much lush poetry written in Sanskrit and the Indian vernaculars on this theme, as in Jayadeva's *Gītagovinda,* which speaks of Rādhā's longing for Kṛishṇa when she hears his flute:

> Sweet notes from his alluring flute
> echo nectar from his lips.
> His restless eyes glance, his head sways,
> earrings play upon his cheeks.
> My heart recalls *Hari* here, in his love dance,
> playing seductively, laughing, mocking me.
>
> *Jayadeva, Gītagovinda 5:2, GGJ p.78*

Kṛishṇa was a close friend as well as the *Guru* of Arjuna, to whom he acted as charioteer in the war of the *Mahābhārata,* and it was his support of the Pāṇḍavas that resulted in their victory over the Kauravas. He was killed unintentionally by a hunter, Jaras, who shot him with an arrow mistaking him from afar for a deer. It is said that Jaras had been the celebrated monkey king, Bali, in his previous life, who had been killed by Rāmachandra, the seventh incarnation of *Vishṇu,* while hiding behind a tree. This event is commonly quoted as a good example of the karmic principle that whatever a person does will ultimately be done to them.

Stories concerning Kṛishṇa are related in the *Mahābhārata,* the *Bhāgavata Purāṇa* and the *Harivaṃsha.* Some of these acclaim his miraculous powers. Others are seemingly amorous, but are interpreted as symbolic of mystic love, longing and union with God. The dialogue between Kṛishṇa and Arjuna on the battlefield, on the eve of the battle in the *Mahābhārata,* forms the subject matter of the most popular and influential work in Hindu religious literature, the *Bhagavad Gītā.* Taking the battle as an allegory of life, the dialogue concerns the best way to live, while seeking spiritual realization through *yoga.* Here, Kṛishṇa also reveals that his role is to "re-establish righteousness" in the world:

> Although birthless and deathless
> and the lord of all creatures *(Prajāpati)* –
> Yet, making use of my own natural processes *(prakṛiti),*
> I take birth by my own inherent power.
> For whenever righteousness *(dharma)* languishes, O Bhārata,
> and unrighteousness *(adharma)* flourishes –
> Then I manifest myself for the protection of good,
> and the destruction of evil.

To re-establish righteousness *(dharma),*
am I born from age to age.

Bhagavad Gītā 4:6–8; cf. BGT

In the *Bhagavad Gītā,* Kṛishṇa, as the *Guru* of Arjuna, teaches him that liberation is attained through meditation, which brings about attachment to God and detachment from the world. "Gazing at the tip of the nose", in this passage, is usually understood to mean concentration "between the eyebrows *(bhrūvor madhye)*":

Dwelling alone in a solitary place,
disciplined in mind and body,
without hopes or expectations, without possessions –
Let the *yogī* steadfastly practise spiritual communion.

In a clean place, neither too high nor too low,
prepare a seat *(āsana)* out of grass,
covered with a skin and a cloth.
Firmly seated thereon, to purify the self *(ātman),*
practise *yoga* with a concentrated mind,
with the activity of the mind and senses under control.

Holding the body, head and neck
straight, motionless and firm;
Gazing at the tip of the nose and not all round;
Being without fear, serene, controlled in mind,
and established in a vow of celibacy;
Meditating upon me as the highest goal,
he should sit in communion with me.

With a mind restrained from going out to external things,
always united with the supreme Spirit *(Ātman)*
in spiritual communion,
the *yogī* attains supreme beatitude, peace,
and enduring establishment in me.

Bhagavad Gītā 6:10–15; cf. BGT

And again:

He who meditates continuously on me,
with a mind trained in the practice of spiritual communion,
freed from the tendency to wander onto other things,
he will go to the refulgent, Supreme Being *(Paramapurusha).*

He who with a steady mind and with devotion,
and with strength born of *yoga,*
correctly focuses his entire life force
between the eyebrows *(bhrūvor madhye)* –
At the time of death,
he will remember that Being who is all-knowing,
primeval, subtler even than an atom,
the sustainer of all, of incomprehensible form,
is as glorious as the sun,
and is beyond the darkness (of ignorance and inertia) –
Truly, he will attain the Supreme.

I shall now briefly describe to you that state
that Vedic scholars call the Imperishable *(Akshara),*
that renunciates, devoid of attachment, enter,
and, desiring which, lead a life of self-control.

He who closes all the doors of the body,
confining the mind to its centre (*hṛid, lit.* heart),
drawing all the vital energy of the soul *(ātman)* into the head,
establishes himself in yogic concentration *(yoga-dhāraṇā),*
repeating the single syllable *Om,* denoting *Brahman,*
remembering me, and abandoning the body,
leaves (the body) and reaches the highest state.

Bhagavad Gītā 8:8–13; cf. BGT

That Kṛishṇa is depicted here as a *Guru,* rather than a deity or incarnation of *Vishṇu,* is significant. The same role is apparent in the *Bhāgavata Purāṇa* in relation to his disciple Uddhava.

Kṛishṇa is seldom mentioned by name in the writings of the Saints, but the Supreme Being is often referred to by his epithets such as *Gopāl, Govind, Dāmodar, Mohan, Keshav* and *Madhusādan.*

See also: **Goswāmī** (2.1), **Govinda** (2.1), **Keshava** (2.1), **Vishṇu**.

kuǐ (guǐ) (C) *Lit.* ghost. According to Chinese belief, a *kuǐ* is a disembodied soul or earthbound spirit who lingers around the dead body or in the vicinity where the individual died. It is believed that when a person dies a sudden, violent death, the disoriented soul may become a ghost. *Kuǐ* represents the *yīn* or earthly quality of the soul, called *p'ò*. The *yáng* or heavenly aspect of the soul, known as *hún,* immediately rises to heaven at the time of death.

See also: **bhūta**, **hún** (5.1), **líng hún** (5.1), **p'ò** (5.1), **preta**.

Lakshmī (S/H/Pu), **Lacchmī**, **Lakhmī** (Pu) *Lit.* fortune, wealth, prosperity; also, beauty; the Hindu goddess of wealth; worshipped as the goddess of fortune and as the embodiment of loveliness, grace, charm, beauty, splendour and lustre; traditionally, the consort of *Vishṇu,* said to be coexistent with him, accompanying him in each of his *avatārs* (incarnations); identified, for example, as Sītā, wife of *Vishṇu*'s incarnation, Rāmachandra.

Lakshmī is generally regarded as having first existed as the daughter of the sage Bhṛigu. But during a time when the gods were exiled from their kingdom as a result of a *ṛishi*'s curse, she took refuge in the mythological ocean of milk. Later, during the churning of this ocean, *Lakshmī* is reborn as one of the fourteen precious things. She is fully grown, radiant and bears a lotus in her hand.

Worship of *Lakshmī* is usually in conjunction with that of *Vishṇu.* She represents the Lord's quality of mercy, which tempers His justice. When worshipped alone, she personifies the female energy of the Supreme Being.

lhā (T) *Lit.* a god; a Tibetan deity comparable with the *devas* of Indian mythology; the origin of *'Lhā-sā'* (land of the gods), the capital city of Tibet.

See also: **deva**.

Lilith (He) The foremost female demon in Jewish folklore and esoteric literature, originating in Babylonian or Sumerian demonology, where she is called *Lilu* and *Lilitu;* commonly derived incorrectly from the Hebrew *laylah* (night).

Like many mythological deities and demons, *Lilith*'s role and the nature of her evil activities evolved over the centuries. She was believed to be the mother of many demons; she creates problems for human mothers in childbirth and harms children. She was believed to be active at night, and caution was advised to those venturing out at night or sleeping alone. The *Talmud* records:

> Rabbi Ḥanina said: "It is forbidden to sleep in a house alone, for he who sleeps in a house alone is seized by *Lilith.*"
>
> *Babylonian Talmud, Shabbat 151b*

In some of the Jewish legends transmitted in the *midrashim* of the geonic period (after C7th CE), *Lilith* is the original wife of Adam before he was expelled from the garden of Eden, but is replaced by Eve for refusing to obey Adam's orders. After the expulsion of Adam and Eve from the garden, *Lilith* again sleeps with Adam, subsequently giving birth to evil spirits. In another legend, the evil spirits are born of her union with the devil.

By the time of the Kabbalah in the fourteenth century, *Lilith* had become the strangler of children and the seducer of men. She was regarded as the female partner of the form of the devil known as *Sama'el,* and so was queen of the forces of evil, the *sitra aḥra* (other side). Her negative role paralleled the positive, divine role of the *Shekhinah,* the personification of the divine presence in creation. It was common for many Jews to wear amulets to protect them from *Lilith.* In Islam, she was called *Karina.*

Mahādev(a) (S/H) *Lit.* great *(mahā)* god *(deva);* usually an epithet of *Shiva.*

See also: **Shiva**.

Mahā Kāl (H/Pu) *Lit.* Great *(Mahā)* Time *(Kāl);* by extension, Great Death, *Kāl* being the lord of death; in mythology, a name of *Shiva* in his destructive aspect, as the destroyer of the world; also, one of *Shiva*'s sons; also, the chief of *Shiva*'s attendants; to those who believe in *Kāl* as the primal Doer, *Mahā Kāl* is infinite *Kāl.*

Taking the name from mythology, Indian mystics have used the term in various ways. A poem attributed to Kabīr, for instance, speaks of a reflection in *aṇḍa* of all the highest regions of the soul. One such realm, a reflection of *Agam Purush* (the inaccessible Lord, a phase of the Godhead), he says is ruled by *Mahā Kāl:*

> The seventh *sunn* in *aṇḍ,* he has made
> as an imitation of the resplendent region.
> *Mahā Kāl* dwells there,
> but it is called *Agam Purush.*
>
> *Kabīr, Shabdāvalī 1, Bhed Bānī 23:4, KSS1 p.68*

In the *Ādi Granth,* though the context does not make the meaning clear, *Mahā Kāl* seems to be an alternative name for *Kāl,* the lord of death:

> O man, meditate thou on thy beloved Lord-Master:
> Contemplating the Lord's Name, thou shalt remain alive,
> and the great Death *(Mahā Kāl)* shall not again devour thee.
>
> *Guru Arjun, Ādi Granth 885, MMS*

Swāmī Shiv Dayāl Singh used the term as a name for the ruler of the realms of creation up to the threshold of eternity, *sat lok* (true region):

> *Mahā Kāl* reaches up to the gate of *sat lok:*
> beyond this he cannot go, and there he remains.
> *Swāmī Shiv Dayāl Singh, Sār Bachan Poetry 23:1.60, SBP p.199*

See also: **Kāl** (6.1).

Maheshvar(a) (S/H/Pu), **Mahesh** (S/H/Pu) *Lit.* great *(mahā)* lord *(īshvara);* lord of all *Īshvaras;* an epithet of *Vishṇu* (the preserver) and *Shiva* (the destroyer), in the Hindu triad; commonly used in contracted form, as *Mahesh.*

See also: **Shiva**, **Vishṇu**.

malā'ikat al-'adhāb (A), **malā'ik-i 'aźāb** (P) *Lit.* angels *(malā'ikat)* of torment *('adhāb);* the guardians of hell; sometimes called the *zubāniyah,* the tormentors.

See also: **yamadūta**.

mal'ak (A), **malak** (A/P) (pl. A. *malā'ikat, malā'ikah;* P. *malā'ikah, malā'ik*) *Lit.* emissary, angel; sometimes, specifically a male angel. According to the *Qur'ān,* the *malā'ikah* guard the gates of heaven and hell, including the protection of heaven from the onslaughts of Satan.[1] The four main archangels are also responsible for carrying the throne of heaven. 'Ināyat Khān describes angels in more general terms:

> There are two sorts of angels, those who have never manifested as man, and those spirits who upon their way back to the infinite have reached the world of the angels. Love, light and lyric are the attributes of the latter, and from them the soul receives these impressions. Devotion, service and worship are the attributes of the former. The angels are masculine and feminine; the former are called *malak,* the latter *ḥūr* (houris).
>
> *'Ināyat Khān, Sufi Message, SMIK5 p.113*

See also: **angels**.

1. *Qur'ān* 74:31.

mal'akh (He) (pl. *mal'akhim*) *Lit.* messenger, emissary; described in the Bible as appearing to various patriarchs and prophets as divine emissaries, although the distinction is not usually made whether the *mal'akh* (messenger) is human or supernatural. Many of the later Jewish philosophers and biblical interpreters, such as Maimonides (1135–1204), understood the *mal'akhim* as non-corporeal embodiments of the divine will.

See also: **angels**, **mal'ak**.

Metatron (He) An important angel in Judaism; a senior archangel, often called the prince of the divine Countenance (or Presence) and prince of the world. Not mentioned in the Bible, *Metatron* first appears in the *Talmud* as the heavenly scribe who records the good deeds of Israel. He plays an important role in Jewish mystical literature – both in the *Merkavah* and *Hekhalot* texts of antiquity, as well as the medieval Kabbalah. The derivation of the name is uncertain and may have been an invention.

In some of the earlier *Merkavah* texts, *Metatron* takes on the role of the Demiurge, a term used by the gnostics for a power secondary to God, identified by them as the biblical creator-god. As the Demiurge, *Metatron* governs the lower realms of creation, while the Supreme Being governs everything. God's power thus includes the power of *Metatron.* According to both orthodox Judaism and Christianity, however, the belief in a secondary god was heretical, and the *Talmud* saw fit to warn people not to confuse *Metatron* with the supreme Lord.[1] It relates the story of Elisha ben Abuyah who saw *Metatron* on his throne during his inner ascent, and thought there were two equal powers in heaven. Filled with doubt and confusion, he subsequently became an apostate.

A number of different Judaic legends and myths merge in the figure of *Metatron.* An early tradition teaches that the 'primordial *Metatron'* was created at the time of creation, and given the exalted tasks of scribe and gatekeeper to the heavenly realms. As prince of the world, he performs many of the duties generally ascribed to the archangel Michael, serving the heavenly throne (a metaphor for God). Most significantly, *Metatron* was the keeper of the inner wisdom – the esoteric secrets of the *Torah* and *Merkavah.* In the *Merkavah* and Kabbalist texts, he is viewed as a guide and protector of the soul on its inner ascent, deciding who was ready to receive knowledge of the inner mysteries.

The figure of the primordial *Metatron* was later merged with legends of the angel *Yaho'el.* Because the name *Yaho'el* contains several of the letters of the name of God *Yahweh, Yaho'el* was regarded as having God's name in him, and was considered a 'lesser *Yahweh*'. His name, like *Yahweh,* was deemed too holy to be spoken under normal circumstances, though it was used in incantations, and the name *Metatron* was used in its place. As

Metatron became identified with *Yaho'el,* eventually taking his place in the literature, he too became known as the 'lesser *Yahweh*'.

Another tradition merges the figure of *Metatron* with the biblical Enoch, who lived – according to *Genesis* – in the seventh generation of the human race.[2] Enoch, it is said, "walked with God; then he was no more for God took him".[3] This brief statement gave rise to many legends concerning his physical ascent to heaven while still living, the mission given him by God, his transformation into *Metatron,* his duties as archangel, and so on.

Both these traditions – the primordial *Metatron* who assumes the role of *Yaho'el* as the 'lesser *Yahweh*' and the transformed Enoch – become interwoven in the medieval *Zohar,* where Enoch-*Metatron* plays an important part. He is identified with the primal divine light that was God's first creation, when He said, "Let there be light!"[4] He is constituted of this celestial light, and one of his most important daily responsibilities is to dispense light to the souls who live on earth.

The description in *3 Enoch* of Enoch's divine transformation into *Metatron* is fiery and fantastic. His body grows to gigantic proportions and is transmuted into light:

> As soon as the Holy One, blessed be He, took me in (His) service to attend the throne of glory and the wheels *(galgalim)* of the *merkavah* (chariot) and the needs of the *Shekhinah* (divine presence), forthwith my flesh was changed into flames, my sinews into flaming fire, my bones into coals of burning juniper, the light of my eyelids into splendour of lightnings, my eyeballs into firebrands, the hair of my head into hot flames, all my limbs into wings of burning fire, and the whole of my body into glowing fire.
>
> *3 Enoch 15:1, HBE p.39*

The *Zohar* describes how Enoch received the divine knowledge from the angels in the garden of Eden, and how the divine light began to shine in him:

> He was beautified with the beauty of holiness, and the sparkling light rested upon him. He entered the garden of Eden and found the Tree of Life there, the boughs and the fruit of the Tree. He inhaled their scent and was refreshed with the spirit of the light of life. Messengers, heavenly angels, came and taught him supernal wisdom. They gave him a book that was concealed within the Tree of Life, and he studied it and got to know the paths of the Holy One, blessed be He, and he tried to follow them … until the light became perfect within him. When this light had become perfect below, it sought to ascend to its place and to demonstrate this perfection through the mystery of Enoch.
>
> *Zohar Ḥadash (Terumah) 42d, WZ2 p.627*

In the Kabbalah, *Metatron* is described as the keeper of the keys to the treasuries of secret wisdom, including the 'light of discernment', which allows the heart to understand even the subtlest of mysteries. He also conveys the prayers of Israel to God, assembling their souls every night and taking them up to sing to the Creator. Even after the souls of the righteous have left this world, he continues to be responsible for them, restoring them to their bodies at the time of resurrection.

Metatron's spiritual significance is that he symbolizes the human potential for divinity. Through Enoch's transformation into the luminous *Metatron,* Enoch embodies the supernal radiance that was originally represented by Adam's soul – a radiance that Adam lost when he sinned. This is a way of explaining that Enoch, in his earthly life, embodied the divine purity, "that supernal perfection for which man was destined from the very beginning of his creation".[5] Thus, just as Adam symbolizes man's fall, Enoch – through his transformation into *Metatron* and light – symbolizes his ascent, his ability to overcome the constraints and the impurity of existence in the physical world.

See also: **Demiurge** (6.1).

1. *Babylonian Talmud, Ḥagigah* 15a.
2. *Genesis* 5:18–24.
3. *Genesis* 5:23.
4. *Genesis* 1:3, *KJV.*
5. Isaiah Tishby, *The Wisdom of the Zohar, WZ2* p.627.

Michael (He), **Mīkhā'īl** (A/P) *Lit.* who *(mi)* is like *(kha)* + God *(El).* An angel who first appears in the biblical *Book of Daniel;*[1] in Jewish esoteric literature, the guardian angel of Israel, often accompanied by his counterpart, Gabriel. These two are the only angels mentioned by name in the Bible. However, according to the *Aggadah* (elaborations of biblical and rabbinic stories), Michael and Gabriel were the unnamed angels who appeared to the patriarchs and other biblical characters at important junctures. For example, it was believed that two of the three angels who appeared to Abraham after his circumcision[2] were Michael and Gabriel. Likewise, the *Aggadah* says that Michael was the angel who wrestled with Jacob in his dream,[3] appeared to Moses on Mount Ḥoreb,[4] and so on.

In the apocalyptic literature and later Jewish gnostic texts, Michael is one of the seven archangels; he is also counted as one of the four archangels who are called the 'angels of the Presence', standing on the four sides of the throne of God – sometimes depicted as its protectors, sometimes as those who carry the throne. They are often identified with the cherubim. In the later *Hekhalot* literature, the writings of the German *Ḥasidim* of the Middle Ages, and in the Kabbalah, the role and duties ascribed to Michael were taken over by the angel *Metatron,* who became the most important supernatural being in later esoteric Jewish literature.

An interplay between Michael and Gabriel was used by the later Kabbalists to illustrate the principle of the *sefirot* – the differentiation of the one divine power or Source into a series of emanations or qualities. At the source, the level of the Godhead, the divine power is described as one primal divine Light. As It emanates its essence or being outward, It becomes differentiated into positive and negative principles that become increasingly polarized the farther they are from their divine origin.

Accordingly, the Kabbalists portrayed Michael as 'Grace' – the *sefirah* (emanation) of *Ḥesed* (Love, Grace, Mercy) – who stands on the right side of the divine throne. Gabriel, on the other hand, represents the quality of judgment – symbolized as the *sefirah* of *Din* (Judgment) – and stands on the left side. In this way the personalities of Michael and Gabriel came to be represented as opposing forces, working in harmony. Thus, in *Daniel,* the *Hekhalot* and other esoteric literature, they work together, delivering God's messages, attending to His Presence, accompanying the Messiah, and so on. According to a legend in one of the early post-biblical esoteric texts, Michael is made of snow and Gabriel of fire. However, they both stand before God, without harm to each other, thus proving "the power of God to make peace in His high places".[5]

In Islam, *Mīkhā'īl* is one of the four main archangels adopted from Judaism. His Islamic role, however, is less important than that of *Jabra'īl* (Gabriel) who brings the revelation to Muḥammad, guiding him on his ascent into the presence of God.

Esoterically, *Mīkhā'īl* is also the name given to the *laṭīfah* (subtle bodily energy centre) located at the procreative centre.

See also: **Gabriel**, **Metatron**.

1. *Daniel* 10:13,21, 12:1.
2. *Genesis* 17:23–27.
3. *Genesis* 32:24–32.
4. *Exodus* 3:1–2.
5. *Job* 25:2; *Midrash Rabbah, Deuteronomy* 5:12.

Mithras, **Mithra** (Av/P), **Mitra** (S) An early Iranian deity known as *Mithra* in the early religious poetry of Persia or Iran, and *Mitra* in the *Vedas;* probably derived from a word meaning 'friend' or 'friendship' in Sanskrit and 'compact' in Avestan.

Although the character ascribed to *Mithra* changed with the passage of time, *Mithra* or *Mitra* was always perceived as a friend to man, appearing in many Vedic hymns as the ally and companion of the deity *Varuṇa. Mitra* is protector of the day, *Varuṇa* of the night; together they protect the universe, and are often invoked together. Their essential function is the maintenance of universal order *(ṛita)* – sacred, cosmic and moral:

I invoke those lords of order *(ṛita)* and of light,
  Mitra and *Varuṇa,*
  who uphold order *(ṛita)* by means of order *(ṛita).*

Ṛig Veda 1:23.5

The *Ṛig Veda* also contains a hymn addressed exclusively to *Mitra.* He "looks upon man with unwinking eye", suggesting a solar deity, as *Mithra* was later depicted in the Roman religion centred on this deity. *Mitra* is "adorable" and "benign", the sustainer of "earth and heaven" and the giver of good health, "abundant food", "wealth", "wisdom", "fame" and so on:

Mitra, when worshipped, inspires men to action.
Mitra sustains both earth and heaven,
Mitra looks upon man with unwinking eye.
With holy oil, offer to *Mitra* your devotion.

O *Mitra,* eternally infinite,
  may he enjoy abundance who abides by your sacred law.
He whom you protect is neither conquered nor dies;
From far or near, no affliction overcomes him.

Free from disease and enjoying abundant food,
  wandering at ease upon the earth's broad face,
  following in the sacred law of the eternal infinite.
  may we remain in *Mitra*'s gracious favour.

Adorable, benign, *Mitra* – king and controller –
  has come with dominion over all:
May we enjoy the grace of him, the holy,
  resting in his propitious, lovingkindness.

The great, eternal and infinite one,
  to be served, worshipfully,
  the inspirer of men to action –
He is the giver of happiness.
To *Mitra,* upon whom be the highest praise,
  offer homage with ardour and reverence.

Great wealth, wisdom and glorious fame
  are the gifts of the divine *Mitra,*
  the sustainer of mankind.

The glory of *Mitra* spreads afar,
His might surpasses heaven;
His renown surpasses the whole earth.

All the five races of man pray for *Mitra*'s favour,
  for he sustains the gods.
To gods, to living men, to those who practise piety,
  Mitra grants the sustenance of his sacred law.

Ṛig Veda 3:59

In Iran, from inscriptions found in 1907 at Boghazköy by H. Winckler, particularly a treaty between the Hittite king and the king of Mitanni in northern Mesopotamia dating from the fourteenth century BCE, it is clear that *Mithra, Varuṇa, Indra* and the *Nāsatya* (the Twins) were worshipped in Mitanni at that time. Later inscriptions provide evidence of a prominent position accorded to *Mithra* in the Persian pantheon. The character ascribed to *Mithra* at different times and places, however, seems to have varied due to the influence of local beliefs as well as the rise of Zoroastrianism.

Mithra is never mentioned in the surviving fragment of Zarathushtra's original *Gāthās.* Some of the texts of later Zoroastrianism, however, extol the virtues of *Mithra,* as in the long Avestan hymn addressed to "*Mithra,* lord of wide pastures" or "grassland magnate *Mithra*", as one translator has it:[1]

Thus spake *Ahurā Mazdā* to the holy Zarathushtra:
When I created *Mithra,* lord of wide pastures,
  then, O holy one, I created him worthy of worship,
  as worthy of prayer as myself, *Ahurā Mazdā.*

Yasht 10:1.1; cf. AHM pp.74–75, ABP1 p.57

The *Yasht* then continues in a more specific vein, extolling the particular virtues of *Mithra:*

Mithra, lord of wide pastures, we worship –
  who speaks the truth, who purifies,
  the thousand-eared, the comely, the ten-thousand-eyed,
  the exalted, lord of broad horizons,
  the strong, the sleepless, the vigilant.

Yasht 10:2.7; cf. AHM pp.76–77, ABP1 p.58

Mithra is also the sun god who rises on the mountain tops:

> The first of the heavenly *Yazatas* (deities),
> who rises over the mountain before the immortal sun,
> driver of swift horses;
> Who is the first to reach the fair and gold-decked summits,
> whence he, the most mighty,
> surveys the entire land of the Iranians.
>
> *Yasht 10:4.13; cf. AHM pp.78–79, ABP1 p.58*

In the Zoroastrian worship of *Mithra* can be seen the influence of pre-Zoroastrian Iranian religion, as Zarathushtra's teachings became synthesized with existing religious beliefs. In the later Sassanian period, however, beginning in the mid-third century CE, Zoroastrian texts such as the *Bundahishn* speak of the soul as a spark of the divine light, descended from the eternal heaven to this world, acquiring an earthly body in the process. Here, it is *Mithra* who is portrayed as the Redeemer and commander of the faithful followers who fight against the dark forces of the prince of darkness, *Ahriman.* This is a story familiar from more universal spiritual teachings. In fact, *Mithra* also appears as a Redeemer in Manichaean literature, Mānī having been a third-century Iranian mystic who taught from the teachings of Zarathushtra, Jesus and Buddha, according to the religious background of his audience.

Becoming a religion in its own right, Mithraism spread to the West, especially during the first three centuries of Christianity, becoming particularly popular in the Roman Empire, especially among the soldiers. Mithraic temples built by the Romans have been found throughout Europe, North Africa and the Middle East.

Mithra was worshipped as the sun god, and an annual festival in honour of the 'birthday of the invincible sun' was held on the winter solstice, the twenty-fifth of December in the Julian calendar, the shortest day of the year. It was an event of great significance in the Roman world, marked by general festivities, including the Great Games. Naturally, it was a public holiday, making it a convenient day on which to celebrate the birth of Jesus in the competing – but at that time minority – religion of Christianity. As Christianity took over from Mithraism, especially after the acceptance of Christianity by the Emperor Constantine in the early fourth century, the festivities were reascribed to Jesus.

1. See *AHM* p.75*ff.*

Nāmūs (A/P) *Lit.* law; from the Greek, *nomos,* a term borrowed from Christianity, also referring to the Judaic *Torah* or Law, personified as an angel, particularly *Jabra'īl* (Gabriel), who – according to the *Qur'ān* – brought revelation to Muḥammad.

According to Islamic tradition, when Muḥammad told Waraqah the Jew, a cousin of the Prophet's wife, Khadījah, what he had experienced on Mount Ḥirā', Waraqah said, "This is the same *Nāmūs* whom *Allāh* had sent to Moses."[1]

1. *Ḥadīth Ṣaḥīḥ al-Bukhārī* 9:87.111, *HSB.*

Nārāyaṇ(a) (S/H), **Narāiṇ**, **Nārāiṇ** (Pu) *Lit.* Lord, God; the mythological Hindu deity from whom all creation has emerged; a synonym of *Vishṇu,* the supreme Lord of the Vaishnavites (devotees of *Vishṇu*); also identified in some texts with *Brahmā* (the creator-deity) and, by implication, *Brahman* (supreme Reality); of uncertain derivation, possibly from *nārāh* (the primeval waters) and *ayana* (dwelling or moving), hence, one whose dwelling is water or one who moves upon the waters, waters being the first dwelling of the supreme Personality, *Nārāyaṇa,* according to the Hindu creation myth; alternatively, from *nar* (mankind) and *ayana* (place), hence, one who is present in all men; or, the shelter *(ayana)* of mankind *(nar).*

Retelling the ancient myth, the *Mahā Upanishad* says that before the beginning of the creation, there was only the self-existent *Nārāyaṇa.* There was no *Brahmā,* no *Shiva,* no fire, no moon, no stars in the sky and no sun.[1] *Nārāyaṇa,* as *Vishṇu,* rests on a couch formed by the coils of the serpent *Ananta* (also known as *Shesha Nāga*), which floats on the primeval waters. At the start of every age, *Nārāyaṇa* awakens, bringing the creation into being, dissolving it again into an undifferentiated state at the end of the cycle. All of creation, including the creator-deity, *Brahmā,* emerges from *Nārāyaṇa:*

> As he *(Nārāyaṇa)* stood, absorbed in meditation, sweat came forth from his forehead, and expanded into the primeval waters. In them was born the *Tejas,* as a golden egg, within which was born the god *Brahmā,* with four faces.
>
> *Mahā Upanishad 3; cf. SUV p.800*

When, after a period of rest, the next age is due to begin, *Nārāyaṇa* again awakens and recreates the world out of himself. This creation myth has been interpreted in a number of ways, often to substantiate particular beliefs. According to Vaishnavite texts, *Nārāyaṇa* is *Vishṇu,* the deity who precedes the creation. The creator-deity *Brahmā* is born in a lotus that emerges from *Vishṇu*'s navel. In some texts, *Nārāyaṇa,* as *Vishṇu,* is also identified with *Brahman.*[2] *Vishṇu* is also worshipped as the personification of *Brahman* – as *saguṇa Brahman (Brahman* with attributes, *Īshvara).*

Other texts identify *Nārāyaṇa* with *Brahmā* who emerges from the golden egg *(hiraṇyāṇḍa)* formed in the primeval waters, both creations of the self-existent One. The *Manu Smṛiti* relates:

He (the Self-Existent),
desiring to produce beings of various kinds from His own body,
first created the waters with a thought,
and placed His seed in them.

That seed became a golden egg *(hiraṇyāṇḍa),*
in brilliancy equal to the sun;
In that egg, he himself was born as *Brahmā,*
the progenitor of the whole world.

The waters are called *nārāh,*
for the waters are, indeed, the offspring of *Nāra;*
And because they were his first residence *(ayana),*
he *(Brahmā)* is therefore named *Nārāyaṇa.*

Manu Smṛiti 1:8–10; cf. LM p.5

This creation story is also linked to the spiritual awakening of the devotee who meditates on *Nārāyaṇa.*

See also: **Nārāyaṇa** (2.1).

1. *Mahā Upanishad* 1.
2. *Vishṇu Sahasranāma* 664, *TVS* pp.169, 261.

nefillim (He) *Lit.* fallen ones; fallen angels. The notion of fallen angels arises from an ancient belief that, in times past, certain gods or supernatural beings were banished from heaven for their rebellious nature, or fell to earth from the spiritual realms, where they exist in an accursed state. The *nefillim* first appear in *Genesis:*

When men had begun to be plentiful on the earth, and daughters had been born to them, the sons of God *(benei Elohim),* looking at the daughters of men, saw they were pleasing, so they married as many as they chose. *Yahweh* said, "My spirit must not for ever be disgraced in man, for he is but flesh; his life shall last no more than a hundred and twenty years." The *nefillim* were on the earth at that time (and even afterwards) when the sons of God *(benei Elohim)* resorted to the daughters of man, and had children by them. These are the heroes of days gone by, the famous men.

Genesis 6:1–4, JB

In the *Genesis* story, it is the "sons of God *(benei Elohim)*" who consort with the "daughters of men", their issue becoming the "heroes of days gone by". In Jewish legend, however, the story is altered, and it is the *nefillim,* as rebellious supernatural beings, who take the "daughters of men" as wives. Moreover, in *Genesis,* the *nefillim* are not portrayed as being rebellious. Even if the story is read as the *nefillim* being synonymous with the "sons of God", then again they are not portrayed as behaving badly; rather they are praised as heroes of the past, the fathers of the illustrious ones.

Contemporary scholars therefore suggest that the biblical account was applied to the belief in vanquished gods or angels in order to provide scriptural and official religious authority for what had by then become a commonplace element of the folk religion. Mystically, the story of the fallen angels or rebellious supernatural beings who fall to earth is perhaps a mythic and dramatic way of explaining the philosophically and theologically difficult subject of how evil entered the creation.

There are several variations to the folk beliefs concerning the demonic nature of the *nefillim.* The third-century (BCE) *Book of Enoch* recounts that some of the angels in heaven lusted after human women. The angels therefore came to earth and united with the women, their issue being giants who were bent on destroying human life, teaching all forms of depraved behaviour, including the use of weapons. Each angel taught a particular perversion. This was called the demonic wisdom, and led to the corruption of mankind. The *nefillim* are associated in these legends with the wrong use of spiritual powers in magic and the control of supernatural forces. The angel *Metatron,* by contrast, is associated with teaching man the inner mysteries, the spiritual teaching, to glorify God – for good purposes.

In the apocryphal *Book of Jubilees,* the angels are portrayed as having originally been good. They had descended to earth to teach mankind the higher wisdom, but – so the story goes – they were seduced by human women. Talmudic sources relate a different version of the legend. Seeing how corrupt man had become after the great flood (as described in the Bible), the angels complained to God that man was not fit for His goodness. God therefore challenged them by saying that they too would be unable to maintain their virtue if they lived on earth. They insisted they would only glorify His name and not fall into sin, offering to prove this by descending to earth. But having arrived, they immediately fell into sin, unable to control their sexual desire, and entered into union with the "daughters of men". According to the story, they even revealed the Name of God to a woman who, by its use, was able to ascend to heaven. There are many other versions, but in all the Talmudic stories, the angels only sin after coming to earth.

In some Talmudic sources, and according to Maimonides, the term 'sons of the gods' is interpreted to mean the sons of judges and rulers, since the term *elohim* is used in both physical and supernatural contexts, and the entire story is removed from the realm of the supernatural. In the *Midrash ha-Ne'elam* (part of the *Zohar*), the *nefillim* are interpreted as Adam and Eve, who descended to earth after their banishment from the garden of Eden, and who were "born" without having a father and mother.

Other sources associate the fallen angels with another legend of seventy rebellious angels who were assigned by God to protect Israel, but who instead persecuted her. The character of Satan also originates in part from legends of fallen angels.

See also: **benei elohim**.

Nirañjan(a) (S/H/Pu) *Lit.* without *(nir)* stain *(añjan);* without taint, spot, mark, blemish; *añjan* literally means lampblack or soot, hence stain, spot or mark; in Sanskrit, *nirañjana* is used as an adjective in descriptions of the Supreme Being. In later Indian literature, *Nirañjan* is a name for the supreme Lord, also being used as an appellation of the ruler of the first spiritual region, particularly as *Jyoti Nirañjan.* Regarding the existence and role of *Nirañjan* as a ruler in the inner regions, Mahārāj Charan Singh writes in a letter to a disciple:

> *Nirañjan* is not a set of laws or principles. It is a real being that rules this world. Intellectual discussions about such matters take one nowhere. These entities are to be seen by the eye of the soul, and experienced inside.
>
> *Mahārāj Charan Singh, Divine Light 366, DL p.335*

See also: **Jyot Nirañjan, Nirañjan** (2.1).

ofanim (He) *Lit.* wheels; a category of angel or supernatural being first mentioned in the vision of the biblical prophet Ezekiel, and later in the Jewish *Hekhalot* and *Merkavah* literature; also called the *galgalim* (wheels). Ezekiel describes his vision:

> And when I looked, behold there were four wheels *(ofanim)* beside the *keruvim* (cherubim), one wheel beside one *keruv,* and another wheel beside another *keruv;* and the appearance of the wheels was like the colour of an emerald stone. And as for their appearances, the four had one likeness, as if a wheel had been in the midst of a wheel. When they moved, they moved from any of their four sides; without turning as they moved, but to the place where the head turned they followed it; without turning as they moved. And their whole body, and their backs, and their hands, and their wings, and their wheels,

> were full of eyes around, even the wheels that the four had. As for the wheels *(ofanim),* they were called in my hearing, the Wheelwork *(galgal).*
>
> *Ezekiel 10:9–13, JCL*

The comparison of the *ofanim* to wheels is perhaps an attempt to depict the whirling of energies at some particular centre or station in the heavenly realms. Centres of subtle or higher energy are also called wheels *(chakras)* in yogic teachings.

The *ofanim* and *galgalim* are often mentioned in the Jewish *Hekhalot* literature and later mystical tracts. *Sandalfon,* one of the most important angels in Judaic angelology, is regarded as one of the *ofanim.* He creates a crown out of Israel's prayers to place on the head of God – a symbolic way of describing his role as intercessor between man and the Divine.

See also: **cherubim**, **galgal**.

Onkār(a) (S/H/Pu) *Lit.* the syllable *Om;* a symbol or external sound synonymous with *Om,* used in the *Upanishads* and by various yogic paths to represent *Brahman,* the absolute Reality; also, the creative Sound *(Om)* that emanates from *Brahman;* also, a name given by a number of Indian Saints to the ruler of the second spiritual realm, which they have equated with *Brahman;* regarded as the most sacred word of the *Vedas,* and hence commonly used by yogis as a *mantra.*

See also: **Onkār** (2.1, 3.1).

parī (P) *Lit.* winged one; a beautiful, supernatural being in Persian folklore; a fairy; a female being from the *jinn* world; from the Avestan *pairika* (a witch); anglicized as peri.

Rūmī says that the "prophets" or mystics know of music or "notes" within themselves that neither man nor the *parī* can hear, for both are captive in this world, the "prison of ignorance":

> The prophets also have (spiritual) notes within,
> whence there comes life beyond price to them that seek.
> The sensual ear does not hear those notes,
> for the sensual ear is defiled by iniquities.
> The note of the *parī* is not heard by man,
> for he is unable to apprehend the mysteries of the *parīs,*
> although the note of the *parī* too belongs to this world.

The note of the heart is higher than both breaths (notes),
for *parī* and man are prisoners:
Both are in the prison of ignorance.

Rūmī, Maśnavī I:1919–23, MJR2 p.104

See also: **jinn**.

Pārvatī (S/H/Pu), **Pārbatī** (H/Pu) *Lit.* mountainous, hilly; the one from the mountain; the daughter of the mountain; from *parvata* (mountain); one of the many names for the Hindu goddess depicted as the consort of *Shiva*. *Pārvatī* is *Shiva*'s consort in her mild and beautiful form; also known as *Umā* and *Gaurī*. As with all Hindu goddesses, *Pārvatī* also has a dark side to her nature, the same goddess appearing in terrible and horrific form as *Durgā* or *Kālī*.

The story of the beautiful, benign goddess *Pārvatī* appears in the *Mahābhārata* and in the *Purāṇas*. *Shiva* is meditating in his solitary abode on Mount *Kailāsh*, having gone there grieving for the death by immolation of his wife *Sātī*. In the meantime, a demon *Tāraka* threatens the stability of the cosmos. The gods therefore send *Kāma*, the god of love, to awaken *Shiva* from his meditation in order that he may fall for *Pārvatī*, with the intention that they should beget a son who would destroy the demon *Tāraka*. *Shiva*, however, destroys *Kāma* with a ray from his third eye, and is not interested in *Pārvatī*. *Pārvatī* therefore performs austerity *(tapas)*; *Shiva* is eventually impressed, and she becomes his consort. Subsequently, they have a son, *Skanda*, who destroys the demon *Tāraka*; later, a second son, *Gaṇesh*, is born to them.

Pārvatī is often portrayed as a model of female docility and service to her husband. She is also depicted as an example of service and surrender to God. Family tensions are also seen in the relationship of *Pārvatī* to *Shiva*. In Bengali sources, *Shiva* is portrayed as rather irresponsible, smoking marijuana and neglecting his duties, and *Pārvatī* complains to her mother about his behaviour.

See also: **Durgā**, **Kālī**.

powers Persons or groups exercising influence, control or authority over others; mystically, the various rulers or centres of energy and consciousness within the hierarchy of creation. As St Paul writes:

By him (the Son, the Word) were all things created
that are in heaven, and that are in earth,
visible and invisible;

Whether they be thrones, or dominions,
or principalities, or powers:
All things were created by him, and for him.

Colossians 1:16, KJV

As the writer of the *Teachings of Silvanus* observes, all lesser powers are derived from the one creative Power:

For he (Christ) is an incomprehensible Word, and he is Wisdom and Life. He gives life to and nourishes all living things and powers.

Teachings of Silvanus 113, NHS30 pp.354–55

These powers, therefore, are by no means supreme. In fact, in the gnostic tractate, the *Trimorphic Protennoia,* the writer says that these powers themselves do not know their own source:

And none of them (the powers) knew me (the Word),
although it is I who work in them.
Rather they thought that the All was created by them
since they are ignorant, not knowing their Root,
the place in which they grew.

Trimorphic Protennoia 47:24–28, NHS28 pp.426–27

From an altogether different time and place, the same idea is expressed by the Native North American Lakota holy man, Frank Fools Crow (1891–1989). He is speaking of the various "powers" that he sees during his mystic experiences:

"When I am surrounded by the higher powers, I call their powers in to me. But when I am enclosed with the higher powers, I can go to where they are, and visit with them."

"How do you go to visit them?"

"*Wakan-Tanka* (Great Spirit) has given me the power to travel in the spirit to where they are, and I go and talk with them." …

"What do they look like?"

"Lights."

"Are all of the lights the same colour?"

"No. *Wakan-Tanka* is a huge white light. *Tunkashila* is a huge blue light. Grandmother Earth is a big green light. Each of the Persons is the colour of his direction." …

"Is anyone there with the powers when you visit them?"

"No. All I see is the lights."

Fools Crow, in FCWP pp.104–9

Thomas Mails, author of *Fools Crow: Wisdom and Power,* explains something of Fools Crow's manner of understanding things:

> Unlike most other Lakota holy and medicine men, Fools Crow did not think of *Wakan-Tanka* and *Tunkashila,* as one and the same. They were one in mind and spirit, but individual Persons. When he defined their roles, he saw *Wakan-Tanka* as akin to the Father figure of the Bible, and *Tunkashila* as akin to the Son, Jesus Christ. "Why," he asked, "would we have two names for the same person, and why is it that our stories of our beginnings talk about a person like *Tunkashila* coming to our land long ago and walking about among us? No one ever says that this person was *Wakan-Tanka.*"
>
> *Thomas Mails, FCWP p.37*

See also: **archon**, **dominions** (4.1), **rulers**, **sovereignty** (4.1).

pret(a) (S/H/Pu) *Lit.* gone *(ita)* before *(pra);* departed; related to *pretya* (having departed, after death); the deceased, the dead; a spirit, a spectre, a phantom; the departed spirit, especially before funeral rites are performed; a disembodied spirit who hovers for some time around the places to which it is attached; a ghost, an evil being. The *Īshāvāsya Upanishad* describes the worlds inhabited after death by those who "destroy their own souls" by becoming engrossed in materiality:

> Sunless and enveloped in blind gloom are those worlds
> to which all those who destroy their own souls
> go after death *(pretya).*
>
> *Īshāvāsya Upanishad 3*

According to mystical understanding, when a soul departs from physical life, it does not disappear, but passes into some other state of consciousness. If, in life, the soul is steeped in gross forms of ignorance, then the after-death state is one of darkness and gloom, rather than light and bliss.

In traditional Hindu belief, after the physical body has been disposed of, the subtle body, having nothing to sustain it, exists as a *pret* until judged in *pretaloka* (world of the *pret*). If no help is given to it by rites, it becomes a *bhūt* (ghost or demon), wandering about restlessly. Some believe that the dead remain as *pretas* for one year or until the *shrāddha* ceremonies (food offerings) are completed.

Guru Arjun speaks of ghosts and spirits as some of the many forms the soul can inhabit:

In many ways, the false person wanders in the existences
of animals, birds, hobgoblins and phantoms *(pret).*
Wherever he goes, there he is not allowed to stay:
this placeless (homeless) one arises, and runs again and again.
Guru Arjun, Ādi Granth 1005, MMS

See also: **ghost**, **bhūta**.

Rapha'el (He) *Lit.* God *(El)* + heals *(rapha);* a chief angel in Judaism; generally included along with Michael, Gabriel, *Uri'el* and others, as one of the four – or seven – archangels; sometimes interchanged with *Phenu'el.* In the *Talmud, Rapha'el* is identified as one of the three angels who, according to *Genesis,* visited Abraham after his circumcision.[1] As an archangel, he is one of the four angels (the cherubim) who carry the throne of God. In the apocryphal and later Judaic *Merkavah* and *Hekhalot* literature, *Rapha'el* is given certain important roles and high rank among the angels. He governs primordial matter and the four rivers flowing from Eden.[2] In the Kabbalah, he is credited as healer of the sick.

1. *Genesis* 17:23–27.
2. *Genesis* 2:10–14.

Rārankār (H) *Lit.* light *(rārā)* -maker *(kār);* of uncertain derivation, *rārā* being an uncommon Sanskrit word meaning beauty, light, splendour, brightness;[1] the lord of the spiritual realm situated above that of the universal mind *(trikuṭī),* called *daswān dwār* (tenth door) and other names by some Indian Saints.

The name is used by Kabīr and Swāmī Shiv Dayāl Singh in poems that describe the hierarchy of creation. Kabīr, for instance, speaks of the light and sound of *daswān dwār,* also called *sunn* (void) or *set sunn* (white void):

With a four-petalled lotus is *trikuṭī* decorated,
Onkār is the deity seen there.
(Next is) the stage of *Rārankār,*
lying in the midst of *set sunn,*
described as a six-petalled lotus.
Kabīr, Shabdāvalī 2, Shabd 17:5–6, KSS2 p.52

Swāmī Shiv Dayāl Singh also locates the sound of *rārankār* in *sunn* (void), going on to speak of the soul's ascent through *bhanwar guphā* (rotating cave) to *sat lok* (true region, eternity):

Draw your soul inwards, and see the door (eye centre):
On the right side is the Sound Current,
  on the left, the snare of *Kāl*.
Pass it by, holding the soul attentively.
Listen with love to the bell and conch,
  and beyond that to the melody of *Onkār*.
Hear *rārankār* in *sunn*,
  and the melodious strains of the flute in *bhanwar guphā*.
In *sat lok* listen to the melody of the *bīn (vīṇā)*.

Swāmī Shiv Dayāl Singh, Sār Bachan Poetry 9:4.17–21, SBP pp.90–91

1. See "rārā", *Hindi Vishvakosh, HV19* p.541.

Razi'el (He) *Lit.* God *(El)* + mystery, secret *(razi);* an important angel in Judaism. Esoteric legends of the Talmudic period (100–500 CE) depict *Razi'el* as the preserver of spiritual wisdom or light when in danger of being lost, ensuring its passage through the generations. Over time, he became associated with esoteric and magical teachings. Manuals of incantations bearing the name of *Razi'el* were used by Jewish mystical seekers from the rabbinic period (200 BCE – 400 CE) onwards.

According to a fifth-century legend, when Adam and Eve were banished from the garden of Eden, they lost the primordial celestial light that was God's first creation. This miraculous light had allowed Adam "to see from one end of the world to the other". It was *Razi'el* who brought Adam some comfort in the form of a jewel, the *Tzohar,* which "sometimes glowed and sometimes hid its light".[1]

At his death, Adam entrusted the stone to his son Seth who used it to help him gain spiritual insight. The story says that Seth peered into the stone and became a great prophet. From there, it was passed down to Enoch, and thence through the early generations of man, the patriarchs and prophets, revealing how each one – Methusalah, Noah, Abraham, Isaac, Jacob, Joseph and Moses – used the stone to come closer to God and gain spiritual insight.

The jewel seems to symbolize the primal divine wisdom, the spiritual knowledge, the inner light that is the heritage of humanity. It is the link between man and God. The legend says God had originally bestowed this divine light or wisdom upon Adam. Adam lost touch with it when he was disobedient to God and listened to the voice of his ego. Its preservation as a stone that *Razi'el* then gave to Abraham is a poetic way of saying that this wisdom, this light, still remains within the realm of human realization. This is demonstrated by the lineage of spiritually realized souls through whom it was passed down.

In another legend from the Kabbalah, Rabbi Yosse was searching for a treasure his father had predicted he would find at a particular place. He searches between some rocks and finds a hidden book. On opening it, he finds the seventy-two-letter name of God – a secret name that the angel *Razi'el* had confided to Adam.

> And it was known that whoever knew that secret Holy Name would have the portals on high opened to him.
>
> *Book of Adam, in GPJ pp.74–75; cf. Zohar 1:117b–118a*

Mystically, the true "secret Holy Name" is identified with the divine Wisdom or creative Power. Eventually, contact with the hidden spiritual wisdom was symbolized by knowledge of 'hidden' or 'secret', yet external, names of God. The letters of these names and permutations of these letters were used in meditational and magical practices often attributed, once again, to *Razi'el.*

Rabbi Abraham Abulafia, who used the pseudonym *Razi'el,* taught these types of name practices in the thirteenth century. In the *Zohar, Razi'el* is also identified with the archangel *Uri'el,* who brings the deeper meanings of the *Torah* to man.

See also: **Ādam** (5.1), **jewels** (3.1), **pearl** (3.1).

1. "The *Tzohar*", in *GPJ* pp.59–62; based on the *Babylonian Talmud, Ḥagigah* 12a; *Midrash Rabbah, Genesis* 31:11, and other sources.

Rūḥ, al- (A/P) *Lit.* the Spirit. *Al-Rūḥ* is an epithet of *Jabra'īl* (Gabriel), the angel said to have brought the revelation to Muḥammad and other prophets. According to Islamic tradition, the Prophet records that sometimes this Spirit spoke to him like a man and sometimes like the ringing of bells. Another name for *Jabra'īl* in Islamic writings is *al-Rūḥ al-Ilqā'* (the Spirit of Casting into) because he is the angel appointed to 'cast' revelations into the *Rusul* (Prophets, Messengers of God). He is also called *al-Rūḥ al-Amīn* (the Trusted Spirit).

Al-Rūḥ is portrayed in the *Qur'ān* as a divine messenger and bringer of inspiration:

> Raised high above ranks (or degrees),
> (He is) the Lord of the throne (of authority):
> By His Command does He send the Spirit *(al-Rūḥ)* (of inspiration)
> to any of His servants He pleases,
> that it may warn (men) of the day of mutual meeting.
>
> *Qur'ān 40:15; cf. AYA*

Therein come down the angels and the Spirit *(al-Rūḥ),*
by *Allāh's* permission, on every errand.

Qur'ān 97:4, AYA

The primary source of mystic inspiration, however, is the divine creative power. Hence, *Jabra'īl* or *al-Rūḥ* is generally taken by Sufis to be symbolic of *al-'Aql al-Awwal,* the Primal Intelligence or creative Power, the true divine Spirit.

See also: **rūḥ** (5.1), **Gabriel**.

rulers Those who rule or command; mystically, those powers who rule or administer particular areas of the inner creation, especially within the realm of the negative power; commonly used to translate the Greek word *archon,* a favourite term with gnostic writers. Even St Paul writes that the spiritual struggle is essentially against these higher powers or "rulers":

We wrestle not against flesh and blood,
but against principalities, against powers,
against the rulers of the darkness of this world,
against spiritual wickedness in high places.

Ephesians 6:12, KJV

As the soul ascends, it has to pass through the regions administered by these rulers. Thus, in the *Acts of Thomas,* Judas Thomas praises Jesus as the

Voice that came forth from the Height,
Comforter dwelling within the hearts of your believers,
port and harbour of them
that pass through the regions of the rulers.

Acts of Thomas 156; cf. AAA p.288, ANT p.432

The Power that draws the soul through these regions is the divine "Voice", the creative "Power" that comes from God and is able to lead souls past the "rulers":

Jesus Christ, Son of compassion and perfect Saviour,
Christ, Son of the living God,
the undaunted Power that has overthrown the Enemy;
And the Voice that was heard of the rulers,
and made all their powers to quake,

Acts of Thomas 10; cf. ANT p.369

See also: **archon**, **dominions** (4.1), **powers**, **sovereignty** (4.1).

Sandalfon (He) One of the *ofanim* (angels, *lit.* wheels); one of the most important angels in Judaic angelology during the rabbinic period (200 BCE – 400 CE), especially in the *Merkavah* and later literature. Of uncertain origin, the name may be from the Greek *synadelphos* (colleague), *Sandalfon* being considered the colleague of *Metatron. Sandalfon* is described as forming the ascending prayers of Israel into two crowns for the head of God, symbolizing his role as an intermediary between man and God.

See also: **ofanim**.

Sarasvatī (S/H/Pu) The Hindu goddess of the creative arts, especially poetry, music, wisdom, learning, knowledge and science; credited with having invented the *devanāgarī* alphabet and the Sanskrit language; described as the mother of the *Vedas;* may originally have been a goddess of the waters, identified with the legendary river, *Sarasvatī.* Fanciful derivations of the name include lady *(vatī)* of the lake *(saras),* and she who possesses *(vatī)* eloquence or speech *(saras).*

Originally a Vedic water deity, *Sarasvatī* was later identified with *Vāch,* the goddess of speech. *Vāch* was credited with extensive powers, pervading heaven and earth, the power behind all phenomena, and the mistress of all. *Vāch* is also said to have discovered *Amṛit*a (Nectar of Immortality). In later myths, *Sarasvatī* is represented as the female half created from *Purusha* or *Prajāpati* (lord of creatures), and is thus the instrument of creation.

The *Ṛig Veda* invokes *Sarasvatī* as the brightness of intellect:

> *Sarasvatī,* the mighty ocean (of light)
> illumines with her light:
> She brightens all intellects.
>
> *Ṛig Veda 1:3.12, CV p.197*

> May the divine *Sarasvatī,*
> rich in her wealth, preserver of intellectual powers,
> protect us well.
>
> *Ṛig Veda 6:61.4, CV p.198*

Various stories concerning *Sarasvatī*'s birth and life are related in Indian mythology. In later accounts, she is generally regarded as the creation and consort of *Brahmā.* It is said that *Brahmā* first formed a woman from his own immaculate substance. She was known as *Satyarūpa, Sarasvatī, Sāvitrī,*

Gāyatrī or *Brahmāṇī*. *Brahmā* fell in love with her, and could not keep his eyes off her. When she moved to the right to avoid his gaze, a new head sprang up from *Brahmā*'s shoulders so that he could keep on looking at her. Likewise, when she moved to his left, then behind and finally above him, three new heads immediately grew from *Brahmā*'s shoulders. This is how *Brahmā* came to possess five heads. *Brahmā* suggested to her that they beget all living things: men, *suras* (angelic beings) and *asuras* (demons). She thereupon returned to the earth, *Brahmā* married her, and thus she became the instrument of creation. *Sarasvatī* provides the power to execute what *Brahmā* conceives with his intelligence.

Esoterically, *Brahmā* and *Sarasvatī* are said to originate in the heavenly realms. According to various tantric texts, they are then reflected as the two deities 'presiding' over the *svādhishṭhāna chakra* (the genital *chakra*).

Savitṛi (S/H) *Lit.* the generator; from the Sanskrit root *su* (to bring forth); sometimes distinguished from and sometimes identified with *Sūrya* (the deity of the Sun), regarded as the source of light and the antithesis of darkness; hence, metaphorically, the dispeller of ignorance; depicted in the *Ṛig Veda* (where eleven hymns and parts of others are devoted to him) with golden hair, eyes and hands, riding in a chariot drawn by glittering steeds.

Sāvitrī is the name of a well-known verse in the *Ṛig Veda,* so called because it is addressed to *Savitṛi.* The verse is also called *Gāyatrī,* because of its metre:

> Let us meditate on the adorable splendour of *Savitṛi:*
> may he inspire our mind.
>
> *Ṛig Veda 3:62.10*

The *Gāyatrī* is used as a *mantra* that devout Hindus of the three upper classes are supposed to repeat every day, to promote mental development, leading to enlightenment.

See also: **Gāyatrī mantra** (▸2).

Sāvitrī (S/H) The name of a number of characters in Hindu mythology, especially, the consort or female companion of *Brahmā;* also, the heroine of the legend of conjugal love and devotion between *Sāvitrī* and *Satyavān;* also, the name of a well-known verse in the *Ṛig Veda,* addressed to the deity *Savitṛi.*

See **Sarasvatī**.

Shakti (S/H/Pu) *Lit.* power, strength; primal force; also, the Hindu goddess, power or female energy known as the mother of the universe; also, the highest form of *māyā* (illusion), the three forms being *māyā, mahāmāyā* and *Shakti* – relating to *māyā* as it is experienced in the physical, astral and causal realms. The term has a wide spread of meaning and usage in Hindu thought.

Being the power of *māyā, Shakti* is also depicted as the consort or female energy associated with any Hindu deity, particularly *Shiva.* In general, *Shakti* represents the creative power of illusion that beguiles the mind, and surrounds the soul while it is in the regions of the mind. At every level, whether in the finest subtlety of the causal realm or in the grossness of the physical universe, the primary power of illusion is known as *Shakti.*

Shakti is also known as *Mahāmāī,* the great Mother of *Brahmā, Vishṇu* and *Shiva,* as *Durgā* or *Kālī* (the goddess of destruction), and as *prakṛiti* (nature). In reflected form, *Shakti* is also the name given to the deity of the throat or *kaṇṭha chakra,* where she is called *Devī, Ashṭāngī* or *Avidyā,* and described as the highest form of *piṇḍī māyā,* the illusion and spiritual ignorance *(avidyā)* of this world.

Like a number of Hindu deities, *Shakti* refers to a focus of power, being or energy in the hierarchical and dynamic structure of creation that has been described by mystics and yogis. Because of the manner in which the creation process is ordered, manifestations of the same power are found at different levels. It is for this reason that *Shakti* is both the presiding power at the throat centre, relating to the formative energy of the physical *ākāsha,* as well as being synonymous with, or a reflection of, the higher energy and illusory power of *prakṛiti,* the primal seed form of all the diversity of nature below.

Many Hindus recognize intellectually that *Shakti* refers to a focus of power in the dynamic structure of creation, but nevertheless worship her in temples and at home, as they feel the need to pray to an embodiment, however symbolic and inanimate, of that power.

See also: **māyā** (6.2).

Shankar(a) (S/H) *Lit.* happiness *(sham)* causing *(kara);* bringer of happiness or good fortune; one who brings happiness or confers good fortune; hence, auspicious, propitious; an epithet of the Hindu deity, *Shiva.*

Shesh(a) Nāg(a) (S/H), **Sekh Nāg**, **Ses Nāg** (Pu) The thousand-headed, cosmic serpent *(nāg)* of Hindu mythology; a symbol of eternity; also called *Ananta* (Endless); the king of the race of serpents who inhabit the realms 'below' the earth *(pātālaloka).* According to the *Vishṇu Purāṇa,* the head of *Shesha Nāga* sustains the earth.[1] It is also the fiery breath of *Shesha Nāga* that destroys the universe at the end of every age. The remaining ashes of the universe sink into the 'primordial waters', which represent the undifferentiated state of the cosmos. Only *Vishṇu* and *Shesha Nāga* remain. *Vishṇu* and his consort *Lakshmī* recline on the coils of *Shesha Nāga* whose thousand heads serve as their canopy, his coils signifying the cycles of time. *Shesha Nāga* is perhaps so-called because *shesha* means 'remainder', signifying that *Shesha Nāga* remains after dissolution.

The myth or legend possibly symbolizes *sahans dal kanwal,* the energy confluence in the astral plane comprising one thousand spiritual rays, flames, petals or currents of energy. Since *sahans dal kanwal* is the energy dynamo supporting and administering all creation below it, so can the world be said to rest, metaphorically, upon the head of a thousand-headed serpent.

1. *Vishṇu Purāṇa* 2:5.

Shiv(a) (S/H/Pu) *Lit.* auspicious, propitious, gracious, benevolent, benign; one of the three deities of the Hindu trinity, the other two being *Vishṇu* and *Brahmā. Shiva* occurs frequently in the *Ṛig Veda* as an appeasing epithet applied to the storm god *Rudra* (*lit.* Howler) who is implored to look upon his supplicants with compassion. *Rudra* was regarded as a fierce divinity, the bringer of plague and disaster, indiscriminately laying waste the countryside. Nevertheless, he brought the rain without which crops failed and people starved; he was also the guardian deity of healing herbs. Not unnaturally, he was addressed by appeasing epithets such as *Shiva* (Auspicious) in the hope of averting his violence, and attracting good health.

By the second century BCE, the epithet *Shiva* had acquired a separate identity, and was represented by images as an object of worship. The disassociation of *Shiva* and *Rudra* is suggested by the synonym *Shankara* (causer of happiness), often used for *Shiva* in the *Mahābhārata* and *Purāṇas.*[1]

Shiva is depicted with a third eye (the *Shivanetra*) open in the middle of his forehead. According to the myth, the eye burst forth in order to save the world from darkness when *Shiva*'s consort *Pārvatī* playfully covered his two eyes with her hands. This eye is also famous as an organ of destruction. *Kāmadeva,* the Hindu god of love, was reduced to ashes by the fire from *Shiva*'s third eye, for trying (unsuccessfully) to arouse desire in *Shiva* for *Pārvatī,* while *Shiva* was meditating. The gods wanted *Shiva* to fall for *Pārvatī,* and thus to father a son who would be able to destroy the powerful demon, *Tāraka,* who had swallowed the world. They therefore sent *Pārvatī* to *Shiva,* together with *Kāmadeva.* But, in the end, it was *Pārvatī*'s practice of austerities that aroused *Shiva*'s interest.

Traditionally, *Shiva* is depicted with one head, a blue neck adorned with a garland of skulls, snake earrings, matted hair and ash-smeared body, sitting on a tiger skin under a tree, and engaged in deep meditation. But there are other representations. Another popular image has *Shiva* with a blue neck, a crescent moon on his forehead and snakes as ornaments, wearing a tiger skin, and receiving the (holy) river Ganges on his matted hair.

The forms of deities are generally symbolic. Thus, the garland of skulls represent the forces of destruction, while the matted hair, ash-smeared body, tiger skin and posture of meditation show him as a yogi – a god, not of rites and sacrifices, but of austerities and meditation, and therefore of superior spiritual power to other gods. *Shiva*'s dwelling is said to be Mount *Kailāsh.* His weapons are the trident *(trishūla),* the staff *(pināka),* the bow *(ajagava)* and the noose *(pāsha).*

Shiva's characteristic blue neck originates in a story that illustrates his role of beneficent service to the other gods and to the entire universe. The gods were churning the primeval ocean of milk in order to produce *Amṛita* (the Nectar of Immortality), to strengthen them in their fight against the *asuras* (giant demons), using the serpent *Vāsuki,* king of cobras, as a churning rod. The serpent, not unnaturally, became nauseous, and vomited poison. The poison was about to fall into the ocean of milk, contaminating the *Amṛita,* as well as destroying all the gods, men, animals and plants, when *Shiva* came to the rescue by catching the poison in his mouth. He himself was saved from swallowing it by his wife *Pārvatī,* who caught him tightly by the throat and, by almost strangling him, prevented him from swallowing the poison. As a result, his throat became blue, and thus *Shiva* is also called *Nīlakaṇṭha* (the blue-throated).

Many other myths are recounted concerning *Shiva.* The *Shiva Purāṇa* relates that *Menā,* mother of *Pārvatī,* fainted when *Shiva* came to marry her daughter, for he arrived with five heads, three eyes, ten arms, an ash-smeared body, wearing a tiger skin and a garland of skulls, and riding on the bull, *Nandīn* (representing fertility). When *Menā* threatened to cancel the marriage, and to kill both herself and *Pārvatī, Shiva* showed his real form, at the request of Ṛishi Nārada. *Menā* and the others present were delighted to then see him in a form resplendent as a thousand suns. A crown sparkled on his head, his clothes glittered, and the lustre of his jewels was so bright that it put the stars to shame.

The devotees of *Shiva* are known as Shaivites. The worship of *Shiva* is centred on fear and uncertainty of the unknown, the powerful and unbridled forces of nature, and the dread of death and destruction. His person is imbued with the attributes of the forces of nature, in both their mysterious and hostile aspects. In an ultimate expression of this, he became *Mahādeva* (*lit.* great god) and *Bhava* (*lit.* existence), personifying fatality and destruction in the cycle of the universe. *Shiva* is also *Naṭarāja* (*lit.* lord of the dance) who executes the cosmic dance that typifies the ordered movement of the universe.

Shaivites sometimes treat *Shiva* as being pre-eminent, higher than *Vishṇu* and *Brahmā.* In *Shakti* and tantric cults, *Shiva* becomes another name for God Himself. Vaishnavites view *Vishṇu* in a similar manner.

According to legend, *Shiva* was obliged to practise perpetual asceticism for cutting off the fifth head of *Brahmā,* when he was angry at *Brahmā*'s disrespect. For this reason, he is regarded as the god of asceticism, and the first yogi or the first ascetic, the one who first worked out the various practices of *yoga,* and gave them to humanity. He is thus known as *Mahāyogī* (great *yogī*). In fact, *Shiva* is said to have 1008 names or epithets.

As the third deity of the Hindu triad who personify the three *guṇas* (attributes), *Shiva* is the destroyer, the other two being *Brahmā* (the creator) and *Vishṇu* (the preserver). *Shiva* is associated with *tamas,* the *guṇa* responsible for breaking things down or taking them into quiescent or seed form, as in death, decay, catabolism, winter and so forth. *Shiva* thus personifies the forces of dissolution and destruction. The *guṇas* first manifest in the higher reaches of the mind, in *trikuṭī,* and are present in every aspect of creation within the mind worlds. They also are present in a focused, 'administrative' form in various reflected centres. Hence, *Shiva* is also described in tantric texts as the deity or power of the *hṛidaya chakra,* the heart centre in the physical body.

Shiva, however, is not only a destructive deity, as is often depicted. He is both the god of destruction and the god of regeneration. In representations of *Shiva,* one of his hands is poised in the *mudrā* (gesture) of protection. His character, in fact, portrayed in different legends, seems full of contrasts. He is the principle of destruction, yet is merciful. He is indifferent to pleasures, yet there are many stories concerning him and his consort, and he is worshipped as the principle of generation. This dichotomy of personality is rationalized as an indication that good and evil are underlain by the same principle.

To Shaivites, Shaivism points to the destruction of illusion, without pessimism or inertia. It indicates harmonious participation in the *līlā* (game) of life. *Shiva* is the king of dancing, *Naṭarāja.* In that form, his surrounding nimbus fringed with fire symbolizes the entire creation. His dance signifies divine activity as the source of movement in the universe, of the cosmic functions of creation and destruction, incarnation and liberation. The object of the dance is to rid human beings of illusion. The cremation ground, where *Shiva* was 'condemned' to wander, also symbolizes the devotee's heart, where the ego and its deeds are consumed, where everything has to disappear except the divine Dancer himself with whom the soul is finally identified.[2]

'Ināyat Khān explains some of the symbolism in representations of *Shiva:*

> The Hindus were the earliest to form the conception of three aspects of the Divinity, which they call *trimūrti: Brahmā* the creator, *Vishṇu* the sustainer, and *Shiva* the destroyer. These three powers keep the whole universe in balance, and they are active in everything in the world.... The picture of *Shiva* is that of an ascetic, from whose head spring rivers, round whose neck is a cobra, ashes on his body, a bull his vehicle. In this picture the cobra signifies destruction which has been accepted: all that man fears is wrapped round his neck, while ashes are significant of annihilation: everything that has gone through a perfect destruction turns into ashes. Rivers springing from the head show a constant spring of inspiration, as the inspiration of the mystic is limitless; and the bull signifies one with simple faith, who without reasoning, accepts the truth, which one cannot readily accept intellectually.
>
> *'Ināyat Khān, Sufi Message, SMIK9 p.206*

It is also mentioned in the *Ādi Granth* that *Shiva* and *Shakti* dwell within the body.[3] Here, *Shiva* symbolizes the soul and *Shakti* represents *māyā.*

See also: **Brahmā**, **guṇa** (5.2), **Shivaloka** (4.1), **Vishṇu**.

1. Some details drawn from "Śiva" in *A Dictionary of Hinduism, DH* p.279.
2. See "Indian Mythology: The Religion of Siva", in *New Larousse Encyclopedia of Mythology, NLEM* pp.374–75; Veronica Ions, *Indian Mythology, IM* pp.42–45.
3. Guru Rāmdās, *Ādi Granth* 1056.

sur(a) (S/H/Pu) *Lit.* a god, a deity; a sage, a learned man; specifically, angelic or pure beings, according to Vedic lore, as opposed to the *asuras,* the demons with whom they were in conflict; of uncertain derivation, probably originating as the converse of *asura,* or perhaps derived from *svar* (light, heaven). Portraying the constant struggle between good and evil, Hindu mythology contains many legends concerning the ceaseless struggles between the *suras* and the *asuras.*

See also: **asura**.

Surūsh (P) *Lit.* voice (from heaven); messenger, angel; a Zoroastrian term, used in Islam for the angel *Jabra'īl* (Gabriel), the divine messenger. Ḥāfiẓ says that *Surūsh* is the herald of "divine pardon" and "mercy":

Divine pardon does its own work:
Surūsh caused the glad tidings of mercy to arrive.
God's grace is greater than our sin:
this is a subtlety hard to understand.
You have something to say (about it)? Silence!

Ḥāfiẓ, Dīvān, DHA p.153, DHM (329:2, 4) p.314, DIH p.263;
cf. DHWC (333:2–3) p.574, SROH p.12

And again:

Last night, *Surūsh* of the invisible world *('ālam-i Ghayb)*
brought me this good news:
"No one will be rejected at the door of His munificence!"

Ḥāfiẓ, Dīvān, DHA p.82, DHM (195:6) p.201, DIH p.166; cf. DHWC (471:4) p.780

In another poem, Ḥāfiẓ gives spiritual counsel to his reader as if it were coming from "*Surūsh* of the invisible world *('ālam-i Ghayb)*". He means that he has received inspiration from the divine messenger, the "wine tavern" here referring to the spiritual intoxication of contact with this sublime source of inspiration:

Last night, completely intoxicated in the wine tavern,
Surūsh of the invisible world *('ālam-i Ghayb)*
brought me such glad tidings!
Said he: "O falcon of lofty vision,
perched high on the *Sidrah* tree (of the highest heaven),
build no nest in this trouble-filled corner (the world).
From the pinnacle of the highest heaven *('arsh),*
they call out to you;
In this place of snares,
I know not what has happened to you.
I offer you counsel:
take it to heart, put it into action;
For I recall this matter
from the Master *(Pīr)* of the path *(ṭarīqat):*

"From this world of unstable nature,
seek no firm commitment.
For this old woman is the bride of a thousand lovers.
Suffer no grief for the world:
let not my counsel slip from your mind."

Ḥāfiẓ, Dīvān; cf. DHA p.19; DHM (23:3–8) pp.53–54,
DIH p.54; cf. DHWC (32:3–8) p.89

The name *Surūsh* is probably derived from the Avestan, *Sraosha,* meaning Sound, a Zoroastrian term for the creative Power. In this sense, the divine Sound is indeed the messenger of God – the role ascribed to the angel Gabriel in Judaism, and later in Christianity and Islam.

Using another Zoroastrian term, *Ahriman,* for the devil, Ḥāfiẓ counsels avoiding temptation by listening with the "ear of the heart", the inner ear, to the "message of *Surūsh*":

In the path of love,
  the temptations of *Ahriman* are many;
Keep your head: put close the ear of the heart
  to the message of *Surūsh.*

Ḥāfiẓ, Dīvān, DHA p.208, DHM (446:6) p.404, DIH p.336; cf. DHWC (444:6) p.744

Likewise, he writes that the ear of the King's heart receives secrets from *Surūsh.* By "King", he means the spiritual Master:

Exercise the mind in nothing else
  but the praise of his (the King's) grandeur.
For the ear of his heart is the confidant of *Surūsh.*

Ḥāfiẓ, Dīvān, DHM (321:8) p.308, DIH p.258; cf. DHWC (327:8) p.567

Surūsh or *Jabra'īl* is also known in Islam as *al-Rūḥ* (the Spirit), the divine messenger who brings revelations to the seers.

See also: **Gabriel**, **al-Rūḥ**, **Sraosha** (3.1).

Surya (He) One of the important angels of Judaic angelology; possibly derived from *sar* (prince), hence the name *Sarah* (princess); the angel of the Presence (of God), whose protection was invoked by the devotee when attempting the 'ascent in the *merkavah* (chariot)' – a metaphor for the journey through the heavenly realms. During the spiritual journey, a seal from *Surya* is shown to one of the guards of the left-hand side. This is a necessary password, so to speak, and the guards cause radiance to descend on the soul, before sending it on its way to the next gate.

tì (dì) (C) *Lit.* lord, ruler; used for rulers both heavenly (*Shàng Tì,* Lord on High) and earthly (*tì wáng,* lord-ruler). It was thought that in the mythology of prehistoric tribal China some outstanding *tì wáng* were elevated to the position of *Shàng Tì,* or rulers on high with divine attributes.

See also: **archon**, **rulers**, **Shàng Tì** (2.1).

Trilochan(a) (S/H/Pu) *Lit.* three-eyed *(tri-lochan);* an epithet of the Hindu deity *Shiva,* who is characteristically portrayed with a third eye open vertically upon his forehead, symbolizing the all-seeing gaze of the deity. According to the legend, his third eye is supposed to have spontaneously burst from his forehead when his consort, *Pārvatī,* playfully covered both his eyes with her hands, plunging the world into darkness. The eye of *Shiva (Shivanetra)* is used by mystics as a term for the inner eye of the soul.

See also: **Shiva**, **Shivanetra** (▸2).

trimūrti (S/H) *Lit.* three *(tri)* -formed *(mūrti);* one possessing three forms or modes of being; the Hindu triad of deities, *Brahmā, Vishṇu* and *Shiva,* representing, respectively, the three primary cosmic functions of creation, preservation and destruction. *Trimūrti* is depicted as a body with three heads: *Brahmā*'s in the middle, *Vishṇu*'s to the left and *Shiva*'s to the right. The *Purāṇas* say that they are three aspects of one supreme God:

> Though *Brahmā, Vishṇu* and *Shiva* are three, they are one entity. The only differences between the three are with respect to their attributes.
>
> *Padma Purāṇa 2:71.18b–26; cf. PP3 p.1174*

And:

> The Lord God, though one without a second, assumes the three forms, respectively, of *Brahmā, Vishṇu* and *Shiva* for creation, preservation and dissolution of the world.
>
> *Vishṇu Purāṇa 2:66, in SHI p.136*

In some of the *Upanishads* these three deities are identified with the three *guṇas* (attributes or characteristics of nature). This is a metaphysical way of describing the same cosmic reality. 'Ināyat Khān observes:

> Deep thinkers have in all ages recognized the threefold aspect of nature. Teachers have called these three aspects by different names according to their religious terminology, and they gave them an interpretation which suited the time and the place. Tracing back this idea, we find that it already existed among the Hindus in very ancient times; they called it *trimūrti,* and they personified these aspects by giving them characters such as *Brahmā* the creator, *Vishṇu* the sustainer, and *Mahesh* or *Shiva* the destroyer or assimilator....
>
> Everything in nature shows these three aspects. For instance, there is fire; there is fuel which is sustenance; and there is the air that can come and blow out the flame.

In all things and beings, in their actions and in their effects, these three aspects can be seen every moment of the day. Every object shows them, though perhaps one aspect is more significant than another in a certain thing, and also every individual; in everything we do, we can see these three aspects. Thinking is the creative action, remembering is the action of sustaining, and forgetting is the third action, assimilating. The assimilation of something is in a way its complete destruction; although it is turned into something, its name is different, and it is not the same thing any more.

'Ināyat Khān, Sufi Message, SMIK11 p.49

Echoing the *Purāṇas,* 'Ināyat Khān also describes the Hindu triad as three aspects of the supreme Lord as well as the three aspects of nature:

There are three aspects (of God and nature which) the Hindus have personified as *Brahmā, Vishṇu* and *Mahesh* – the creator-god, the sustainer-god and the destroyer-god.

'Ināyat Khān, Sufi Message, SMIK1 p.193

Although God is undoubtedly within everything, some mystics have pointed out that the three *guṇas* are an aspect of *māyā* (illusion). The supreme Lord is beyond all attributes. He does not, in Himself, display a trinity of attributes. Kabīr, for instance, writes that *māyā* (illusion) – personified here as a wife who is faithful to her duty *(sohāgan)* – holds *Brahmā, Vishṇu* and *Shiva* in captivity:

Mammon *(sohāgan, i.e. māyā)* has conquered three worlds;
The eighteen *Purāṇas* and the places of pilgrimage love her as well;
She has pierced the hearts
 of *Brahmā, Vishṇu (Bishan)* and *Shiva (Maheshar);*
She has destroyed the great lords of earth and kings;
Mammon *(sohāgan)* has no this or that shore:
 she is in collusion with the five evil passions.

Kabīr, Ādi Granth 872, MMS

See also: **guṇa** (5.2).

Uri'el (He) *Lit.* light *(ur)* + God *(El);* described in the *Midrash* as one of the four archangels or angels of the Presence, whom God has placed around His throne; sometimes called the cherubim or *ḥayyot.*

> As the Holy One, blessed be He, created the four cardinal directions and four standards corresponding to them, so also did He set about His throne four angels – Michael, Gabriel, *Uri'el* and *Rapha'el.* Michael at His right, corresponded to (the tribe of) Reuben.... *Uri'el* at His left, corresponding to (the tribe of) Dan, who was on the north side. Why was his name called *Uri'el?* On account of the *Torah,* the *Prophets* and the *Hagiographa,* by means of which the Holy One, blessed be He ... gives light *(aur)* unto Israel, as it is said, "Arise, shine, for thy light *(aur)* is come."[1] David also said, "The Lord is God, and hath given us light."[2] This explains the name *Uri'el.* Scripture also states, "Though I sit in darkness, the Lord is a light *(aur)* unto me."[3]
>
> *Midrash Rabbah, Numbers 2:10, JCL*

Uri'el first appears in *1 Enoch,* along with the other archangels, as a guide to Enoch in the upper heavens, where his main role was to govern the armies of angels and the inhabitants of *Sheol,* the nether world.

1. *Isaiah* 60:1.
2. *Psalm* 118:27.
3. *Micah* 7:8.

'uthra(s) (Md) *Lit.* spirit(s); pure souls; pure spiritual beings in Mandaean mythology who inhabit the inner realms *(shkinata),* appearing as guardians, messengers and rulers of the inner realms. Their coming into being at the time of creation is described in a Mandaean poem, where the "Cry" is the Creative Word:

> Then He, the great mighty *Mānā* (Intelligence) pondered, ...
> and created companionship for Himself.
>
> In the beginning, He uttered a first Cry
> and created companionship for Himself.
> In the beginning, He uttered a first Cry
> and created four hundred and forty-four thousand *'uthras,*
> and set them upon His right.
> With His second Cry,
> He created three hundred and sixty-six thousand *'uthras,*
> and set them at His left.
> And at His third Cry,
> He called into being twenty-four thousand *'uthras,*
> and set them before Himself.

And He clothed them in His radiance
and covered them with His light;
And placed upon their heads outflowings of radiance and light,
and created for them wreaths in the likeness of His own wreath,
the great mighty *Mānā*'s.
He placed in their hands a staff of Living Water,
and established in their right hand the holy handclasp of Truth.
He spoke with His pure mouth,
and blessed them with His honest tongue,
and with faithful lips of radiance, light and glory.

He created habitations *(shkinata)* for them,
and drew down jordans (rivers) of Living Water for them,
and said to them:
"You shall rejoice and be glad in your habitations *(shkinata),*
like a jordan of Living Water.
Your consort will resemble the Cloud (divine Spouse)
from which you came into existence,
And the fragrance of *'uthras,*
(will be known) for its perfume and sweet odour."

Mandaean Prayer Book 379; cf. CPM pp.292–93

Then, in a continuation of the same creation story:

And a dwelling *(shkinta)* was created:
it was founded, it was, it appeared of itself.
It was a great pavilion for the great unique Holy One,
a pavilion of radiance, light and glory....
And it stretched out before Him,
so that it concealed His appearance from the *'uthras.*

Then the great mighty *Mānā* (Intelligence) planned,
and created vast and pure worlds of light.
Jordans He deployed, He made dwellings *(shkinata),*
installed *'uthras* and appointed *Ashgandia* (Messengers, Envoys).
And chief of these Envoys *(Ashgandia)* before Him was *Adakas:*
'the Great Word' is his name;
For he is a go-between, bestowing the gifts
of praise, blessing, prayer, heedfulness and enlightenment....
And the envoy *(ashganda)* receives the praise of the *'uthras,*
and conveys it into the presence of the great mighty *Mānā,*
and stores it in His treasure house.

Mandaean Prayer Book 379; cf. CPM p.293

See also: **angels**.

Vāgdevī (S/H) *Lit.* the goddess *(devī)* of speech *(vāc);* an alternative name for *Sarasvatī,* the Hindu goddess of learning; also called *Vāk.*

See also: **Vāk** (3.1), **Sarasvatī**.

Vishṇu (S/H), **Vishnū**, **Bishan**, **Bisan**, **Bisnu** (Pu) *Lit.* one who pervades, from the root *vish* (to enter); that which has the nature of pervasiveness; a major Hindu deity; in the *Vedas,* a personification of the sun; as one of the Hindu trinity *(trimūrti),* the sustainer of the universe. *Vishṇu* is the one who pervades all, but nothing other ever pervades him; he is considered to be the all-in-all; the entire world of things and beings are pervaded by him; his consort is *Lakshmī* (goddess of wealth and beauty).

Vishṇu is regarded by his devotees (Vaishnavites) as the transcendent Lord who sustains and pervades all, dwelling in the highest heaven *(vaikuṇṭh),* at the top of the cosmic egg of creation. Through devotion *(bhakti),* and with *Vishṇu*'s grace, devotees go to this or another of *Vishṇu*'s heavens upon their liberation *(moksha).* Vaishnavites believe that *Vishṇu* not only dwells in far-off *vaikuṇṭh,* but enters the world in the form of ten incarnations *(avatārs),* through his various idols and icons *(mūrti, arcā)* in temples and household shrines, and in the hearts of all beings as their inner controller *(antaryāmī).*

According to *Vishishṭa Advaita,* which sought to provide an Upanishadic basis for Vaishnavism, *Vishṇu* is the sole Reality, one without a second, perceived as *Brahman* the Absolute in a form that may be approached or related to by *jīvas* (souls incarnate in this world). His influence is felt in their minds and hearts as the love for and enjoyment of life, the instinct of self-preservation, and the longing for perfection or fulfilment of life's spiritual purpose. He is the means to liberation and the goal to be attained. He is worshipped under a thousand names, enumerated in the *Vishṇu Sahasranāma.* It is believed that repetition of his names brings merit, both spiritual and temporal, to the devotees.

In Hindu mythology, *Vishṇu* is the guardian of righteousness *(dharma),* having incarnated on earth a number of times to save mankind from suffering and wickedness. These *avatārs* (descents or incarnations) symbolize his role as preserver and sustainer of the world. They form a sequence rising from animal to human: the fish *(Matsya),* tortoise *(Kūrma),* boar *(Vārāha),* the man-lion (Narasiṃha), the dwarf (Vāmana), Rāma with the axe (Parashurāma), Rāmachandra, Kṛishṇa, the Buddha, and the future incarnation, Kalki, who is to come at the end of the present cosmic cycle. It is because of the mythology and doctrine of these ten *avatārs* that *Vishṇu* has become such a major deity. During times of darkness, as Kṛishṇa says in the *Bhagavad Gītā,* he incarnates in the world to restore righteousness *(dharma).*[1]

Like all Hindu deities, the role and character ascribed to *Vishṇu* have evolved over time. In the *Vedas, Vishṇu* is a minor deity personifying the energy of the sun, described as striding through the seven regions of the universe in three steps. In the later adjuncts to the *Vedas,* the *Brāhmaṇas* (*c.*900 – 700 BCE), *Vishṇu* acquires new attributes, and is found in a number of legends unknown to the *Ṛig Veda.*

Later still, in the *Purāṇas* (*c.*400 BCE – 500 CE), *Vishṇu* is frequently referred to as *Nārāyaṇa,* the ever present and all-pervading Spirit. Here, he is depicted in two ways. Either he is a handsome, dark blue youth with four arms, holding a conch shell *(shankha),* a discus *(chakra),* a mace *(gadā)* and a lotus *(padma),* and wearing a necklace known as *kaustubha* around his neck. Or he is reclining on a lotus or among the coils of the great snake, *Shesha Nāga,* floating on the primeval waters (symbolizing the spiritual essence of all things). On waking, a lotus arises out of *Vishṇu*'s navel, upon which the god *Brahmā* appears and creates the cosmos. *Vishṇu* then sustains it and finally, as *Vishṇu* falls asleep once more at the end of the cosmic cycle, *Shiva* destroys it. All is then reabsorbed back into *Vishṇu* until he wakes again, a cyclic process that has no beginning or end. It is in the late *Upanishads* and in the *Purāṇas,* that these three deities achieve something of an equal status,[2] and *Vishṇu* becomes the preserver of the universe and the embodiment of goodness and mercy.

As the incarnation Kṛishṇa, *Vishṇu* is worshipped in a majestic form *(aishvarya),* as when he reveals his awesome universal form *(vishvarūpa)* to Arjuna in the *Bhagavad Gītā,*[3] and as a young lover, playing the flute and making love to the cowgirls *(gopīs)* in Vṛindāvan, as portrayed in the *Bhāgavata Purāṇa.* Here, the relationship of the cowgirls to Kṛishṇa is interpreted symbolically, as the love of the soul for God.

In some *Upanishads* and in later Hindu thought, *Vishṇu* came to be seen as a personification of the *sattva guṇa* – the *guṇa* or attribute of preservation and harmony, with *Brahmā* and *Shiva (Rudra)* as personifications of *rajas* and *tamas,* respectively.

Indian Saints have pointed out that all these controlling or administrative powers lie within the realms of *māyā.* As such, they should not be worshipped. In the *Ādi Granth,* there are numerous references to *Vishṇu,* the majority of which seek to place *Vishṇu* as a lesser deity in creation, a part of *māyā,* whose role is both to serve and to deceive man, rather than be worshipped. Guru Arjun says, "There are millions of incarnated *Vishṇus,*"[4] while Guru Amardās says that *Vishṇu* is forever engaged in reincarnating himself.[5] He also says:

I have thought about *Brahmā, Vishṇu (Bishan)* and *Shiva (Mahesh):*
They are bound down by the three dispositions (*guṇas,* attributes),
so, salvation (*mukat,* liberation) remains far from them.

Guru Amardās, Ādi Granth 1049, MMS

And Paltū, writing in the name of God, says that all such powers or deities are aspects of the Lord's creation:

I was in the beginning,
in the ages primeval, I was.
Even when the world comes to an end,
I shall still abide.
In every particle, I abide:
there is none other.

Brahmā, Vishṇu and *Shiva,*
all are but forms in which my Essence manifests;
I am the power that creates all,
and I am the power that annihilates.

Paltū, Bānī 1, Kuṇḍalī 178:1–4, PSB1 p.75

See also: **Brahmā**, **Shiva**, **Vishṇuloka**.

1. *Bhagavad Gītā* 4:6–8.
2. See *Maitrī Upanishad* 5:1; *Rāma Uttara Tāpinīya Upanishad* 4–5, 8; *Skanda Upanishad* 4, 8–9.
3. *Bhagavad Gītā* 11:1*ff.*
4. Guru Arjun, *Ādi Granth* 455.
5. Guru Amardās, *Ādi Granth* 559.

watchers (He. *irin,* Gk. *phylax*) Certain angels or 'administrators' of the inner realms, appearing particularly in Judaic and gnostic writings, as in the *Second Book of Jeu,* where Jesus is describing the inner ascent of his disciples:

Then the watchers of the gates of the treasury of the Light see the mystery of the forgiveness of sins which you have performed.… And they see the seal on your foreheads, and they see the cipher in your hands. Then the nine watchers open to you the gates of the treasury of the Light, and you go into the treasury of the Light. The watchers will not speak with you, but they will give you their seals and their mystery.

Second Book of Jeu 118–19:49, BC pp.164–67

The term seems to have originated in pre-Christian, Judaic angelology. It appears, for instance, in the *Book of the Watchers* (dating from around the third century BCE), a part-Judaic, quasi-mystical revelation with which the larger *1 Enoch* begins. The book opens with a vision of Enoch the scribe in which he is sent to reprimand and to intercede for the "heavenly watchers", also called the "children of heaven", who had left their heavenly home to consort shamelessly with the daughters of men, as described in *Genesis.*[1]

The term is also found in the mid-second-century BCE biblical text, the *Book of Daniel,* where the prophet claims his revelation or vision to have been heralded by a "watcher and an holy one":

> I saw in the visions of my head upon my bed and, behold, a watcher *(irin)* and an holy one *(kadishin)* came down from heaven.
>
> *Daniel 4:13, KJV; cf. Daniel 4:17, 23, KJV*

A much later text, *3 Enoch,* dating from the fifth or sixth century CE, written in the style of a revelation and attributed to a certain Rabbi Ishmael, contains a complex angelology in which countless myriad angels are grouped in various categories and hierarchies. Among them are *galgalim* (wheels), *ḥayyot* (living creatures), *keruvim* (cherubim), *ofanim* (wheels), *serafim* (seraphim), *irin* (watchers) and *kadishin* (holy ones), *ḥashmallim* (light angels) and *sin'anim, elim* (gods, angels), *er'elim* (angels, messengers), *tapsarim* (angels, appointees) and *elohim* (gods).

The *Merkavah* mystics, from whose milieu *3 Enoch* originated, were eager to know the names of these angels since, in a belief common to many occult and magical traditions, to know the name of an angel is to have power over it. According to the accepted tradition of revelational texts, Rabbi Ishmael is provided with an angelic guide, in this case, the angel *Metatron,* who describes to the rabbi the hierarchical arrangement of the heavenly host. At one point, the text places these "watchers and holy ones" next to God in the divine court:

> Rabbi Ishmael said: The angel *Metatron,* prince of the divine Presence, said to me: "Above all these are four great princes called watchers and holy ones, high, honoured, terrible, beloved, wonderful, noble and greater than all the celestials, and among all the ministers there is none equal to them, for each of them singly is a match for all the others together. Their abode is opposite the throne of glory, and their station is facing the Holy One, blessed be He, so that the splendour of their abode resembles the splendour of the throne of glory, and the brilliance of their image is as the brilliance of the *Shekhinah.* They receive glory from the glory of the Almighty, and are praised with the praise of the *Shekhinah.* Moreover the Holy One, blessed be He,

does nothing in His world without first taking counsel with them; then He acts, as it is written, 'Such is the sentence proclaimed by the watchers, the verdict announced by the holy ones.'"

3 Enoch 28:1–4, OTP1 pp.282–83

See also: **archon**, **rulers**.

1. *Genesis* 6:1–6.

wheels (He. *galgal, ofanim*) A category of angel mentioned in Judaic angelology.

See **galgal**, **ofanim**.

wildān mukhalladūn (A/P) *Lit.* eternal youths of paradise, the male counterpart to the houris (the *ḥūr*).

See also: **ḥawrā'**.

Yaho'el, **Yoel** (He) *Lit.* God *(Yah, Yaho)* God *(El);* an angel in Judaic angelology; *Yah* and *Yaho* are both abbreviated forms of *Yahweh.* In the *Hekhalot* literature, *Yaho'el* was known as the lesser *Yaho,* and his power stemmed from having the name of God in him. *Yahweh* was considered to be a powerful and awesome name, repeated mentally during the practice of meditation, but not spoken audibly.

Yaho'el appears to have been the original name of the angel *Metatron,* the latter gradually replacing it in the literature. *Metatron* assumes the role of prince of the divine Presence, the archangel, and is sometimes regarded as the gnostic Demiurge or lower creator-god, in contrast to the higher, transcendent level of the Godhead.

See also: **Metatron**.

yaksha (S/H), **yakka** (Pa), **jakkh** (Pu) A collective name for a class of elemental or supernatural beings, demigods or nature spirits said to live in trees, forests and mountains. Their favourite haunts are the sacred trees common in most villages. Their presence is encouraged since they are believed to ensure the prosperity of a village. Since *yakshas* can assume any form, their activities are often unpredictable. They may be either beneficent or malignant, and hence it is considered necessary to propitiate them with appropriate offerings.

According to Hindu mythology, *yakshas* are the attendants of *Kuvera,* the god of wealth, their role being to guard *Kuvera*'s gardens and treasures. These *yakshas* are not violent, and are called *puṇyajana* (good beings), and their master, *Kuvera,* bears the epithet *Puṇyajaneshvara* (lord of *puṇyajanas*). They are generally benevolent towards human beings, but can become hostile when the treasures they guard have to be protected.

In Buddhism, *yakshas* or *yakkas* are often hostile to those leading a spiritual life, disturbing the meditation of monks and nuns. In Jainism, *yakshas* are among the attendants of each of the twenty-four *Tīrthakaras* (Saints).

Yakshas are thought to have been a part of the folk culture of pre-Vedic times. Suppressed during the early Vedic period, the popular cult of the *yakshas* enjoyed a revival with the emergence of non-Vedic systems such as Buddhism and Jainism. According to a late myth from the *Brāhmaṇas,* when *Brahmā* began his work of creation, he was not omniscient. On his first attempt, he created *Avidyā* (Ignorance) and discarded her. She, however, survived, becoming Night, and from her issued beings of darkness – the bloodthirsty *rākshasas,* who became the enemies of the human race, and the grotesque *yakshas.*

Yam(a), **Yam(a) Rāj(a)** (S/H), **Jam**, **Jam Rāj** (H/Pu) *Lit.* restrainer *(yama)* king *(rāja),* from *yam* (to curb); a character from Hindu mythology who administers the fate of souls after their death; thus, the lord of death, the angel of death, the ruler and judge of the dead, lord of departed spirits; also known as *Dharam Rāi* (lord of justice) and *Kāl* (lord of death).

See also: **Dharma Rāj** (6.1), **Kāl** (6.1), **Yama** (6.1).

yamadūta (S), **yamdūt** (H), **jamdūt** (H/Pu) *Lit.* an agent *(dūt)* of *Yama,* the lord of death; a messenger of death; an angel or agent of death who meets and takes charge of souls at the time of death, unless an individual is under the protection of a Master; sometimes referred to as a *yam* or a *dūt,* where *yamdūt* is implied.

In this world, the natural order of things requires departments, subdepartments and law enforcement agencies for the administration of justice. The same is the case in other parts of the creation. Just as a baby needs a midwife to help in the process of birth, so too is it necessary for a soul to be met when entering the astral or subastral worlds. It is part of the natural process. Even souls who have had near-death experiences, in which they leave this world but return again, report that, after passing through a tunnel, they are met on the threshold of the inner worlds by other souls. Not all such experiences are pleasant, however, for when deprived of the physical body, experience is derived directly from the person's own mental impressions. These will normally be a mixture of both good and bad, happy and miserable, peaceful and agitated.

The kind of reality – heavenly, hellish or intermediate – that an individual experiences after death is therefore dependent upon his mental content, as indeed it is in physical life. A person's mental content relates precisely to the impression or record of his deeds, thoughts, desires and mental activities during life. The immediate after-death experience of those who have led worldly lives is described symbolically as the *yamdūts* leading the weary soul to *Yam* through a desert where there is neither shade nor water.

Following such traditional Hindu accounts, mystics have commonly painted a similar, grim picture of the soul's plight after death. However, in the case of those initiated by a perfect Master, the one who meets them is their Master in His radiant or astral form. He keeps their accounts and determines their future course, with a view to ensuring their final liberation. *Yamdūts* have to keep away, having no role to play. Hence, Guru Arjun writes:

> The pervading God is with me:
> so the *jamdūt* draws not near me.
> *Guru Arjun, Ādi Granth 630, MMS*

See also: **Yama** (6.1).

yazata (Av) *Lit.* worthy of reverence; the adorable ones; divine beings in the Zoroastrian pantheon; next in rank after *Ahurā Mazdā* and the *Ameshā Spentās,* and generally considered well-disposed towards humanity and to be the source of various blessings. The deity *Mithra,* prominent in pre-Zoroastrian Iranian religion, became a notable *yazata* in later Zoroastrian times. In the *Gāthās* of Zarathushtra, *yazatas* such as *Sraosha* (inner Sound) are aspects of the Divine, becoming personalized only later, as the religion developed, drawing on religious beliefs and mythology of the times.

Yǜ Huáng (Yù Huáng) (C) *Lit.* Jade *(Yǜ)* Emperor *(Huáng).* A well-known mythical figure of Chinese culture, regarded as the highest ruling deity of Heaven and Earth, having within his administration multitudes of lesser gods or deities who govern the minor aspects of heaven, hell and the physical world. According to legend, shortly after being appointed king of a part of China, Yǜ Huáng renounced his throne and went into seclusion to study the *Tào.* After attaining perfection, he left his seclusion to help suffering humanity. Upon his death, he became an Immortal *(Hsiēn)* and after many millions of aeons was appointed by the supreme Power, *Yüén Shĭh T'iēn Tsūn,* to be administrator of Heaven and Earth.

One of *Yǜ Huáng*'s main subordinates, regarded as the ruler of the physical world, is *T'ài Yüèh Tà Tì* whose principal duties are to determine the time of birth and death of individuals, and to keep a record of their lives and incarnations. He also dispenses social status, progeny and wealth. It is believed, however, that through purification and meditation practices, the Taoist can influence the Jade Emperor to remove his name from the registers of death and record it in the registers of life, thereby entitling the practitioner to immortality.

See also: **Chitragupta** (6.1), **T'ài Yüèh Tà Tì** (6.1), **Yüén Shĭh T'iēn Tsūn** (2.1).